MARJORIE ROSEN is a young film critic who grew up in the neighborhood Loew's and RKO, where, from the age of two, films have been her "secret garden." She holds a master's degree in film from New York University and has been editor of a number of film magazines. Her articles on film and filmmakers have appeared in *Saturday Review, New York,* and other magazines.

POPCORN VENUS

POPCORN VENUS

WOMEN, MOVIES & THE AMERICAN DREAM

MARJORIE ROSEN

Coward, McCann & Geoghegan

New York

PERMISSIONS

The author wishes to acknowledge the Bourne Music Publishers for permission to use excerpts from *Since Katy the Waitress Became an Aviatress*,
originally copyrighted in 1919 by Irving Bibo and Will Curtis; Copyright © by
Bourne, Inc., assigned 1961 to Bourne Co. Copyright renewed. Used by permission of the copyright owner; and Paul Killiam, proprietor of the Biograph
Collection and Griffith Estate, for permission to excerpt from David Wark
Griffith's 1928 Radio Speech.

for my mother
for my father
and for tibor
with love

ACKNOWLEDGMENTS

Special thanks to Paul Spehr at the Library of Congress, and to Eileen Bowser, Laurence Kardish, and Charles Silver of the Museum of Modern Art's Film Department for so generously opening up their files and facilities to me. Also, to Dorothy Arzner for her tireless correspondence, and Ida Lupino for her frankness in conversation.

For their various courtesies and cooperation, my appreciation is extended to Gale Glass, Joe Kane, Shirley Krauss, Susan Gilman, Merle Pollak, Carol Meszaros, and Beverly Linet.

I gratefully acknowledge the following companies for permission to reprint stills from their films: Paramount, MGM, Warner Brothers, Twentieth Century-Fox, Universal, RKO-National, United Artists, and Columbia. Also many thanks to William Kenley of Paramount Pictures, Dorothy Arzner, and Lou Valentino for their contributions.

But most especially I am deeply indebted to Jacqueline Goldenberg for her time and fine editorial insight when this project was but a fancy; to Patrick Merla for his time and fine critical judgment; to my researcher, Barbara Shear, for her discriminating intelligence and initiative. And finally, to my agent, Phoebe Larmore, and editor, Patricia B. Soliman, whose constant enthusiasm, encouragement, and guidance were my invaluable good fortune.

CONTENTS

POPCORN VENUS

PREFACE

When I was two, my mother took me to my first darkened theater, where, to her amazement and for the first time in my life, I sat quietly through Walt Disney's *Pinocchio*. Even then the screen world created for me a secret garden, a special haven.

Never was there a better incentive for learning to read either. Before I entered the first grade, I was the astonishment of the neighhood. Riding along the Grand Concourse in the Bronx, the adults were just not quick enough to call out the features at the Earl, the Luxor, or the Loew's Paradise. To keep up with (what for me was) the world, I had to get a grip on my ABC's fast.

At five I would take my twenty-two cents and trot around the corner to the Kent Theater, where I thrived on charlotte russes and the Saturday double bill. Children's movies were fine; adult ones, equally so. June Haver and Mark Stevens in *Oh, You Beautiful Doll* were as provocative as Margaret O'Brien in *The Unfinished Dance* or Br'er Rabbit in *Song of the South*. Movies were such a formative part of my life that for years I never questioned the visions of reality they presented.

My vocabulary and my visual associations, too, were marked by a Walter Mitty other life. To this day, my mother looks like a cross between Katharine Hepburn and Rita Hayworth; my funny uncle, whom I dearly love, *is* Red Skelton; my own Auntie Mame, always floating in and out on a cloud of Aphrodisia and ruby rings, can be none other than Lana with jet black hair. And my father—well, he's the spitting image of Randolph Scott and Roy Rogers.

When at eight I floundered around at camp, my bunkmates excused

11

my sloppy hospital corners only because I was the recipient of post-cards from Bob Hope and Margaret O'Brien (courtesy of my uncle on a business trip to the Coast). Margaret was my idol; and if my braids weren't as long or as neat or as beautiful, well, it was my mother's fault, not mine. And if those signatures weren't bona fide and sent with love, you'd have fooled us all.

Movies have been my landmarks. My first tragedy was James Dean's death. My first date, to see Danny Kaye in *Merry Andrew*, was an adolescent with well-oiled hair. Reruns of that film still fill my nose with hair tonic. *Green Mansions* meant escape the night before college boards. And *The 400 Blows*, at a tiny theater in Malverne, Long Island, was my introduction to the world of foreign films.

Jules et Jim couldn't have been anybody but me and my two dearest male friends at college in Ann Arbor. *The Umbrellas of Cherbourg* produced a near collapse when the then-love of my life turned to me and said with the honesty of a man about to doom a relationship, "That's us, isn't it?"

He needn't have asked. If "that" wasn't always "us" on screen, at least it was always me. Even today, when my consciousness has been raised and my fantasies exorcised, I have a soft spot for the Robert Redfords, Marlon Brandos, and Paul Newmans who make love to me in glorious Technicolor, breathtaking Cinemascope, and stereophonic sound.

I am all too painfully aware that so, so much is illusion, that much of my adult life has been spent in vain attempts to emulate Gina or Brigitte or Sophia or Ali. I wonder how many others, perhaps less involved with film but just as impressionable, have also been victims of the Hollywood whitewash? I remember a friend at college who, after her frizzy hair had been straightened right off her scalp, confided that with her new wig everyone mistook her for Elizabeth Taylor. Then I envied her, but now I laugh. She looked as much like Liz as I do. And that's not much. (Although one man a few years ago *did* mention that from my lower lip to my chin, I reminded *him* of her).

How profoundly Hollywood's values have influenced a gullible pub-lic—like myself. But why did the public—and especially its females —so passively embrace the industry's interpretations of life? After all, an image—even one created by so rare an animal as a movie mogul—is molded from prevailing audience attitudes; indeed, the public determines the life or death of a movie. Louise Brooks, an actress of the twenties, wrote: "Producers found the trick of curbing the stars and standardising their product according to their will and personal taste." But "it was never their will, but the public's which made them exploiters of the great personalities and builders of enduring stars."[1]

What, indeed, *was* the public's will? The industry's? Woman's? And what determined it? Abundant material is available about film technique and editing, about directors and Western heroes, about Hollywood myths, the star system, the studio system, about blacks in film, Indians in film, sex in film, even animals in film. Yet about women, there is virtually nothing—except elegies to tragic movie queens or homages to sex goddesses. In all the pedestal pushing and crumbling, nobody has thought to study woman's role in cinema. But in at least 90 percent of all films, women have occupied a pivotal psycho-sociological role.

Because of this and because of the bulk and complexity of the material on woman's role in society, I have chosen to explore parallel interrelated trends within each decade. Trends in film. And in the way women have opted, or been encouraged, to view themselves.

Does art reflect life? In movies, yes. Because more than any other art form, films have been a mirror held up to society's porous face. They therefore reflect the changing societal image of women—which, until recently, has not been taken seriously enough.

Does life reflect art? Again, yes. Because of the magnetism of movies—because their glamor and intensity and "entertainment" are so distracting and seemingly innocuous—women accept their morality or values. Sometimes too often. Too blindly. And tragically. For the Cinema Woman is a Popcorn Venus, a delectable but insubstantial hybrid of cultural distortions.

In this book we shall chart the course of women in films. And we shall see.

New York City
July, 1973

ONE

EMERGING FROM VICTORIANISM

The Family is the source of society;
the wife is the source of the family.
If the fountain is not pure, the stream
is sure to be foul and muddy.

—CARDINAL GIBBONS,
"Pure Womanhood,"
Cosmopolitan, 1905

1

A VICTORIAN PRIMER
their hearts were young and (not so) gay

1900: Our *fin de siècle* females had been properly, potently anesthe-tized. The nation had emerged from the 1800's with its Victorian prudishness intact, and women were defined chiefly by birth or marriage.

Those upper- and middle-class women who, through the benefits of industrialization, knew lives of increasing leisure occupied positions of social prestige. "It would be interesting to note if we could the stages by which, through the accumulation of property and through the man's aesthetic development and his snobbish impulses acting in harmony, he came to feel that it was more desirable to have an idle than a working wife," wrote Emily James Putnam, the first dean of Barnard College. "The idle wife ranked with the ornamentally wrought weapon and with the splendid offering to the gods as a measure of the man's power to waste, and therefore his superiority over other men."[1]

If women were restless about what was expected of them and what they were receiving in return, they had only to consult the ladies' magazines, which by 1900 had become their Bible. As if pampering princesses, Mrs. Sangster, in her *Ladies' Home Journal* column "Heart to Heart Talk with Girls," in 1904 preened: ". . . allow yourself the benefits to which, as young women you are entitled. Be waited upon, and receive kind attentions graciously."

Gloved, bustled, and yoked up to their necks and down to their wrists, young women of means were encouraged to exist as frivolous ap-pendages to men. They were hearth decorations; their heads useful only for soaking up trifles such as the price of bombyx taffeta (54 cents a

17

yard) or an hourglass figure ($1 and $1.50 for elaborate corsets). They were advised on how to grow lavender, how to make a good English breakfast, and how to view their lives. Occasionally the magazines would include an instructive article for that deprived mistress of the house who had no servants; but generally the literature read like pamphlets for the retarded: "It has been said that the average woman is incapable of accuracy, which may account for the taking of the careful measurements necessary being always entrusted to men who go about their work so carefully and with such precision. . . ."[2]

Running a smooth household was for middle-class women the greatest blessing and the greatest challenge, and any idle fantasies about going out into the world were discouraged. "To many women the business world looks like a great mysterious whirl, of which she can understand nothing," cautioned the *Woman's Home Companion* in 1900. "To almost any girl, the pleasure alone of working for those she loves is sufficient to make housework attractive." If a lady were forced to earn a living, the editors even supplied reassurance: "If you learn how to be a good homekeeper and homemaker, and then the time comes when you must go out into business to earn bread instead of bake it, you will know how."

Since ornamental women enhanced their men's masculinity, naturally independent ones detracted from it. Regarded as subtly emasculating, they were cautioned about the dangers of becoming masculine themselves. It is no surprise then that women's magazines glorified the passive housewife. A 1904 statistical poll by the *Ladies' Home Journal*, in which 100 men listed the most attractive qualities of their ideal woman, brought comforting results. According to author Carolyn Halstead, these influential males were overwhelmingly in favor of "domestic tendency" by a margin of two to one. Other qualities they preferred, in descending order, were: love, good disposition, sympathy, Christianity, common sense, intelligence, and taste in dress. If this listing reads like an ad for a private duty nurse or a housekeeper, it is no coincidence.

Nor is it coincidence that sexuality was omitted. Woman's sexual role in the early 1900's was as limited as her social one—it was the role of conjugal obligation. Pleasure or sensuality for her was of no consequence. Sexually ignorant ladies interred the female libido in the most private parts of their minds, heeding instead the church, the state, and the impassioned Cardinal Gibbons, who passed on his vision to *Cosmopolitan* readers by drawing a lesson to be learned from history's pagan wives: ". . . in many of the ancient empires of Asia, the wife was bought as a slave in the market place. Her life was one of abject misery and unrequited toil. . . . One day she ministered to the capricious passion of her husband. The next she was exposed to all the revulsions of feeling that follow the gratification of animal appetites."

Female appetites of any kind (save those satisfied via the pantry) were not kindly received. Even expressions of affection were sublimated within the permissible domestic routine. Charlotte Perkins Gilman, a feminist sociologist, wrote in 1898:

> Is it not time that the way to a man's heart through his stomach should be relinquished for some higher avenue? The stomach should be left to its natural uses, not made a thoroughfare for stranger passions and purposes; and the heart should be approached through higher channels. We need a new picture of our overworked blind god,—fat, greasy, pampered with sweetmeats by the poor worshippers long forced to pay their devotion through such degraded means.
>
> No, the human race is not well nourished by making the process of feeding it a sex-function. The selection and preparation of food should be in the hands of trained experts. And woman should stand beside man as the comrade of his soul, not the servant of his body.[3]

Womankind, however, was not represented only by the middle and upper class. There was also the labor force. In 1900 it consisted of 4,999,000 women; according to U.S. Department of Labor statistics, they accounted for 18.1 percent of the working population and 20 percent of the adult female population. Most of these women didn't know what lavender was and were lucky if they got *any* breakfast, let alone an English one. Largely from the urban lower class, they were imprisoned in factories and sweat shops, doing manual labor (forty-eight to sixty hours a week) at slave wages ($3 to $6 a week) under impossible conditions. Condemned by a society which resisted training them for meaningful work and had relegated them into submissive acceptance of menial tasks, these women were perfect targets for the exploitative early industrialists. Only after a number of tragedies like the 1911 Triangle fire, which incinerated 146 female operators in a New York shirtwaist factory loft, was protective legislation passed. The owners of the Triangle shop were acquitted of any blame, although one partner was significantly fined a token $20. Female lives were cheap then.

But their bodies were more expensive. And prostitution became big business. Unremitting misery drove servants, factory workers, sweatshop girls into the male-organized, male-patronized, and ultimately male-ostracized profession. Still, survival "in the trade," while not much more degrading than the sweatshop, provided an easier existence. R. E. L. Masters and Harry Benjamin report:

> In the Nineteenth Century, and early in the Twentieth, it was well established that a large proportion of all prostitutes then came from the ranks of the domestic servants. Prostitution and the domestic service . . . were almost the only careers open to an unmarried girl of the lower classes, and the near-starvation wages . . . long working hours, grueling toil, and, frequently, cruel treatment, would have made prostitution the obvious career choice for most of such women had prostitutes been less harshly condemned by society. As it was, many women preferred censure to a thankless and ill-paid servitude.[4]

Political feminist Emma Goldman wrote, "Thus it is merely a question of degree whether she sells herself to one man, in or out of marriage, or to many men. Whether our reformers admit it or not, the economic and social inferiority of women is responsible for prostitution."[5]

Ideally the Women's Movement should have appealed for better jobs, working conditions, and wages. It had gathered some impetus during the post-Civil War era, thanks to Susan B. Anthony and Elizabeth Cady Stanton's National Woman Suffrage Association and to Lucy Stone's National American Woman Suffrage Association. But by 1900 the resistance of a nation so opposed to the notion of working-women had exhausted the movement's leaders and forced them to redefine their goals. To appease the opposition and continue their fight for suffrage, they all but ignored the issue of female labor. Still, suffragettes were treading a precarious line with their single, small demand—that women be recognized (as the blacks had been years earlier) as full citizens.

The harsh urban climate presented a gruesome prospect for women without means. Nevertheless, its vitality fostered hope, and the lure of the city began to attract small-town lower-class girls. Their fantasies of joining the genteel bourgeoisie or of encountering a colorful but refined hero had been spawned by Gothic romances, just as films and their heroines and heroes would in future generations inflame feminine dreams. But in 1900 these courageous girls were rare optimists, daring conventions and taboos and city squalor in the faint hope of improving their lives. In 1900 Dreiser voiced a bleak admonition in *Sister Carrie*: "When a girl leaves her home at eighteen, she does one of two things. Either she falls into saving hands and becomes better, or she rapidly assumes the cosmopolitan standard of virtue and becomes worse. Of an intermediate balance under the circumstances, there is no possibility."[6]

Men all over the country were, so to speak, keeping the ladies down on the farm. Their superiority, their very masculinity depended on it. Besides, gardens needed tending, and if Eve refused to cultivate the fruits of domesticity, who *would?*

2

THE MOVING PITCHA SHOW BEGINS
hobbling out of the darkness

The birth of movies coincided with—and hastened—the genesis of modern woman. Even in its infancy, the medium proved itself a commercially rewarding and inexpensive entertainment for the masses. It was also potent escapism and a form of popular culture whose scope was so encompassing that it at once altered the way women looked at the world and reflected how men intended to keep it. Money, entertainment, and morality were inextricably intertwined, yet often they worked at cross-purposes.

First came Edison's Kinetoscope. On April 23, 1896, he projected onto a twenty-foot screen at Koster and Bial's Music Hall Broadway's first movie, a crude but electrifying series of images—dancing girls, huge waves curling up onto a beach; two comedians burlesquing a boxing match; a girl performing a hula. Moving picture shows, back then, were but the indulgent and harmless explorations of adult male children playing out fantasies of adventure and intrigue.

In 1902 the visionary Frenchman Georges Méliès boyishly contemplated space travel with *A Trip to the Moon* and later *The Impossible Voyage*. Edwin S. Porter played on every youth's fascination with *The Life of an American Fireman*. In 1903 his *The Great Train Robbery* made history as the first root-em-toot-em-shoot-em-up Western. Making "flickers" seemed an innocuous pastime. Then.

These same primitive themes intriguing the adult male children who made movies also intrigued the adult male audience, primarily workers and immigrants without the time or education to cultivate their personal fantasy lives in any other way. Early plots were simple: pioneers, Western heroes, thieves caught in the act, peasants magically delivered from their sad lot. In 1907 Edison ran a series of Civil War films and advertised "a catalogue containing over 1000 other subjects sent on request." The Kalem Company found gold with its Everglade Series, which included *A Florida Feud*, *The Seminole's Vengeance*, and *Hunted Through the Everglades*, among others.

As a business, moving pictures, each running about five minutes in length, were already becoming profitable. In 1905 *Variety* all but ignored them, but in 1906 the new industry's growth was begrudgingly acknowledged in a report that film producer Archie L. Shepard had leased twenty-two theaters in New York "which he supplies with a series for a complete entertainment." By 1908 there were 550 nickelodeons in New York City with a daily patronage estimated at 200,000—three-quarters of whom were women and children.

Clearly, females also were being drawn by screen glimpses of the male world—albeit, in fantasy. And plots began expanding and exploiting romance—or its masculine interpretation. One of the more popular Biograph films of 1908, *The Kentuckian*, is a classic. Word Fatherly (even his name is paternalistic), the son of a wealthy and indulgent Kentucky aristocrat, heads West where he marries a pretty Indian girl who has saved him from death. They have a son and, according to the Biograph blurb, "live in blissful peace." When Fatherly's father dies, the hero refuses the enormous fortune left him, realizing that Kentucky high society will never accept his "squaw." But because she does double duty in servility as a woman and an Indian, the maiden "at once realizes the situation. She must make the sacrifice, which she does by sending a bullet through her brain—a woman's devotion for the man she loves."

Plots like this may have been melodramatic and crude, pictures fuzzy, and the motion jerky, but the audience felt the emotional force of the medium. On November 8, 1906, *Variety* carried this humorous but foreboding item:

MOVING PICTURES MOVED BOYS

London,
November 8

The cinematograph is in for it now. There is a possibility that the authorities may take a hand in regulating the subjects to be thrown upon the white drop in London music halls. At Bond three youngsters of tender age were sent to the Reformatory on a charge of burglary. One of the small culprits said to the court during the trial of the case: "I had seen the cinematograph pictures at St. George's Hall and I was trying to copy them. When I grow up I'm going to be a burglar."

Were not women *circa* 1906 as impressionable and malleable as these children? For the first time in history youngsters could vividly envision experiences far removed from their own and be susceptible to misinterpreting them. Technically, women were "adults." But they were in urgent need of escape—and brought to early picture shows their empty lives waiting to be filled by any distraction.

The impact was staggering. In a shocking dispatch earlier that year, *Variety* revealed:

MOVED BY MOVING PICTURES
(special to *Variety*)

Denver, Colorado
February 22

It developed at the inquest on the body of the woman who committed suicide on the stage of the Crystal Theatre Monday that she was moved to the act by a motion picture subject which showed the suicide of a criminal at its climax. The woman had been in a bad mental state for some time, and was taken to the theatre in the hope that the entertainment would cheer her up. Instead, the showing of the pictures brought on acute suicidal mania and she stepped to the stage and shot herself.

If, only three years after *The Great Train Robbery*, movies could be the great escape, the bridge between life and death, think what their potent fantasy value would be when given shape by strong plots, sophisticated techniques, and hard-sell ideas and images.

Think too about the cross-pollination of life and art. Although to identify the films of 1906 as art is to be not merely generous but silly, the effect of this "art form" was striking even then when its shape and melodramatic content were being fused out of the crude and simplistic material of Victorian living. Yet moviegoing audiences were moved by pictures in a way they had never been by the stage; they were assaulted by images larger than life. Why, if art is so directly reflective and thus familiar, is it in this medium so powerful? Which

is strongest—the reality out of which the illusion is created, the celluloid illusion itself, or the need for illusion? Do we hold the mirror up
and dive in? And if we do, what are the consequences?

And what are the responsibilities of the illusion makers?

For the maverick producers gambling on this new entertainment,
money overshadowed responsibility. Profits were quickly aligning
themselves with images that were sensational. With sex. And sex with
moral outrage. Immediately, this pattern, which would weave through
the history of films, was established when in 1896 Edison filmed the
first screen kiss. It was enacted by John C. Rice and May Irwin,
costars in a current hit play, *The Widow Jones*. The scene, lasting but
seconds, met with violent reactions, including that of film critic
Herbert Stone, who observed: "Magnified to gargantuan proportions,
it is absolutely disgusting. Such things call for police intervention."[1]
And this despite the fact that both May and John were middle-aged
and homely.

Then, in 1906, the exotic belly dancer Fatima, who had made such a
sensation at the St. Louis Exposition two years earlier, performed her
dance of the veils in New York peep shows. Men, who'd made conjugal robots of their wives, found raw sexuality seductive, queuing for
hours for their moment at the machine. However, police action
abruptly terminated Fatima's run.

Only two years later this report was printed in *Variety*:

PICTURES FOR MEN ONLY

Paris, June 20 (1908)

The moving picture places here have what are known as "men's
days," when moving pictures are shown for the gaze of the male
gender only.

The subjects as might be expected are spicy, quite, and excite
the interest of the community to such an extent that women dress
in male attire to attend.

Pictures here commonly reported in other countries as "broad"
are shown at these exhibitions, and are not open to the general
public respective of sex and age as supposed.

Translation: Men, standard-bearers of feminine purity, watchdogs
of their virtue, had stumbled upon that delightful Xanadu, "moving"
pornography. Drawings and still photographs had already supplied a

secret source of it for collectors, but films were ever so much more explicit—and perilous.

On a more viable commercial level, production companies like Vitagraph, Biograph, Edison, and Pathé, competing for the nickelodeon crowd in 1906, the year that Harry Thaw "struck for the purity of the wives and homes of America" by killing elderly architect Stanford White, shrewdly ascertained that the more intriguing the movie titles, the more people would flock to see them. Although these plots rarely deviated from formula trifles, titles such as *In the Days of Witchcraft*, *In Her Boudoir*, and *An Old Man's Darling* were provocative and drew crowds.

That year the moving-picture industry was also made painfully aware of its potential "immoral" influence by the New York Society for the Prevention of Cruelty to Children. This organization, known as the Gerry Society, began pressing for strict adherence to the law forbidding children under sixteen to enter a movie house unless accompanied by a parent or guardian. The overriding fear of the impact of movies which this action betrays gave the industry new prestige and power.

By 1907 the Chicago *Tribune* was begging for the suppression of films as having an "influence wholly vicious." In 1908 New York City clergymen of all denominations, along with the Society for the Prevention of Crime, objected to Sunday showings of films which tended "to degrade the morals of the community."[2] The nation had a responsibility to its youthful and its "fair" citizens which it intended to enforce.

It is interesting that in the name of moral outrage women and children were always lumped together; rarely was the "community" wary of the influence of movies on men. Males kept females helpless and childlike, subject to their own views of what was proper, and had no intention of relinquishing that control. In 1908, when women began imitating the European vogue of smoking in public, the Sullivan Ordinance was passed making it illegal. Outrage wasn't sparked by the sordid nature of workingwomen's lives or by the despairing boredom of upper-class wives and daughters. But where woman's moral health was concerned, public opinion was an exacting guardian. So exacting, in fact, that the People's Institute of New York City in conjunction with the Motion Picture Patents Company formed the first National Board of Censorship in 1909. Production companies, in order to ensure the respectability of their efforts and steer clear of the board's wrath,

continued grinding out those innocent melodramas which had originally enchanted the working class. In addition, they often preached
their own virtuous censorship. This ad for the Kosmik Film Service, a
division of the Kleine Production Company, repeatedly appeared in
the trade papers:

ALL KOSMIK subjects are of the highest class morally and
photographically while they lose nothing of interest on this
account.

KOSMIK *films are clean films.* Stories of rape—seduction—
illegitimate children—infidelity—indecencies and obscenity are
barred—none to be found in KOSMIK films.

So dogged a preoccupation with morality only served to emphasize
the medium's potential for immorality. Was there behind that overriding fear of corruption a parallel desire *for* it?

The subject of sex had been so long suppressed that when newspapers in 1911 broke the story of the Rockefeller White Slave Report
and the city's subsequent vice investigations, the public was simultaneously shocked and utterly titillated. Like voyeurs who had not yet
had the opportunity to participate, they followed the news stories
with lascivious enthusiasm.

And shrewd producers once again tempted skittish moralists by
"borrowing" from life and moving in on the picture show's most
salable commodity. But at least with movies like *Traffic in Souls*
(1913, one of the first), the subject was out in the open. This film was
so successful that it sold 30,000 tickets in the first week and at one
time played to twenty theaters simultaneously in New York's metropolitan area. It was followed by others such as *The Inside of White
Slave Traffic* (1913) which proved so daring that police and church-
men alike intiated action against it. This despite the fact that the film
featured testimonials from public "authorities" and high-minded
citizens. Then *Damaged Goods* carried the series to new heights of
sensationalism, employing a flesh-and-blood doctor to lecture moviegoers on the dangers of syphilis.

When in 1914 *Variety* reported that Whitfield McGrath, "a moving
picture man," had been charged by Mrs. Dorothy Liban as being a
"white slaver" under the Mann Act, it seemed a natural outgrowth of

the media's flirtation with this delightfully illegal matter. The woman in question claimed that McGrath had transported her from her Milwaukee home to Chicago for "that purpose," but both were held in bail—he for $3,000; she for $1,000.

Fantastic allegations like Mrs. Liban's, and swelling box-office receipts, attested to the potency of sex on screen. Ironically, at about the same time it was beginning to play a significant part in the industry behind the scenes. For movies, apart from the rash of slave trade pictures, were already taking on a semblance of respectability, and their players were earning then-stupendous sums of money. Also, a certain prestige.

In fact, in 1910 producer Carl Laemmle, who was to found Universal Pictures, had made the first attempt to create a star—that is, to market a woman as a profitable commodity. In hiring the Biograph Girl, Florence Lawrence, for his own I.M.P. Company, he staged a fantastic publicity stunt by claiming Florence had been killed in an accident on New York's streets. Newspaper accounts were vague, but no one thought to question them—not until suddenly and conveniently she was found in St. Louis, where delighted fans besieged her, ripped her clothing into shreds, and fought for her autograph. The Lawrence celebrity, however, was short-lived. She was overtaken by a group of leading ladies—Blanche Sweet, Pearl White, Marguerite Clark, Beverly Baynes, Mae Marsh, Lillian Gish, and especially Mary Pickford, the movies' first real star with a star-type following, salary, and longevity—whose dramatic roles exalted purity and innocence.

And fan magazines like Motion Picture World (1911) and Photoplay (1912) gave personalities to the faces on the screen so that adoring female fans could respond as if to familiar friends. This curiosity about actresses' glamorous backstage lives combined with readers' adulation, as even then the industry showed signs of becoming what sociologist Hortense Powdermaker has so aptly tagged "the dream factory."

And such a "factory" was attracting impoverished girls who saw a chance for relief from the steel-and-sweet factories which would otherwise have been their destinies. In movies the pay was good; conditions more pleasant. And the necessary skills, aside from a pretty face, were nil. After all, by 1911 Mary Pickford was earning $275 a week; $500 by 1912. Money was a great seducer. Young women, desperate to change their dreary lives, discovered a new means of mobility. Without becoming prostitutes, they could cleverly use their physical assets to buy their way into the movies and, possibly, careers more fantastic than any their modest fantasies could have conjured. Sex, for so long taboo, became a weapon, a means to an end for girls outside the "trade."

Moviemakers at first were skeptical and outraged by the possibilities of sexual blackmail. Even the most powerful and influential of them, D. W. Griffith, was inordinately careful of his reputation. He would rarely interview a girl without a third party present, and with good reason. Tales were rife of executives hounded by desperate women desiring relief from menial labor and drab routines. Occasionally one of these girls would corner a producer or director and insist he give her a movie role. If he refused, she cried rape.

Yet sexual persuasion was not reserved for desperate women. If films were these girls' salvation, it would be the men with their godlike favors who determined just who would be saved, and who seduced.

On July 10, 1914, while the Dolly Sisters preened and pranced to the tune of $600 per week at the New York Roof, and while theaters were enticing movie customers with rice cakes and iced tea, *Variety* carried this item:

PICTURE MEN WORKING IN "RAW"

Raw is the term applied by many girls to the attempts of the men connected with moving pictures to "flirt" with them. Young women say the craze of many of the males in the industry to become better acquainted with girls playing in stock companies or looking for work has spread to office boys, the youngsters in the outer realms following the examples set before them, and "warming up" to beginners. . . . In one New York studio it is asserted that no woman can work in that particular place unless countenancing the advances of "the boss," who has nothing to recommend himself for female fancy excepting an official position.

Sexual bartering and bondage had not, obviously, been invented by the industry; during the first decade of the twentieth century an estimated 50 to 75 percent of all married men patronized houses of prostitution, an inevitable outgrowth of the Victorian principle of keeping women innocent. But within the industry and without, it was

—for the women being bartered—related to economics and dissatis-factions with traditional alternatives. But the move to ameliorate social conditions, and thus prostitution, would occur as females united to strengthen their self-image. Feminist Emma Goldman wrote in her essay *The Traffic in Women*: "As to a thorough eradication of prosti-tution, nothing can accomplish that save a complete transvaluation of all accepted values—especially the moral ones—coupled with the abolition of industrial slavery."[3]

In the early part of 1910 an amazing event took place—one which may have given men cause for alarm. More than 40,000 shirtwaist makers went on strike. They were supported by both the leaders of the Women's Movement and the wealthy women of New York, who formed a coalition and stood by the laborers until their demands for better pay and more amenable conditions were met. It was the first time that women had transcended class barriers to band together in concern for outrages borne by their less fortunate sisters. It was the first time they cried out for the dignity of womankind. Women's rights had won a small victory.

The veil of servitude began to lift.

And the realignment of power bolstered the cause of suffrage. As a parlor issue it was even achieving some degree of legitimacy, and in 1910 Ida Husted Harper wrote in *Harper's Bazaar*:

> There is no abatement of the interest in woman suffrage and a peculiar feature is the foothold it has gained in the eastern part of the country. Heretofore, it has found the strongest support in the Western states, where' prejudices are not so crystallized and the legal and educational advantages of women are much broader. . . .

The male populace immediately became apprehensive: "Of course the suffrage should be given to women as a matter of right, but great heavens! It would let loose a tremendous force which would sweep all before it, and we cannot afford this," said one member of the New York legislature.

Another Congressman vowed he'd rather see his daughter dead than in a voting booth.

And the women's magazines cautiously tempered their support with energetic homilies like this 1910 *Harper's Bazaar* editorial:

A well-known woman writer has announced that she has discovered woman's vocation . . . to earn a living, to make a home, to
run the house, to bear and train and teach children. In fact, it is
to do a giant's share on all sides of the world's work, and it is
lucky that there are a good many more women than men in the
world to meet the demands.

The more impetus the movement gained, the greater the masculine
backlash. In 1912 Alice Paul organized the Congressional Union and
embarked on a high-powered campaign for federal women's suffrage.
Characteristically, Congress—despite a petition of 500,000 names—
dashed female hopes the following year by defeating what had come
to be known as the Susan B. Anthony Amendment. It was the third
time the men of the nation refused to recognize women as their
equals.

The pervasive male atittude toward suffrage was reflected in films.
As early as 1901 novice moviemakers, with typically boyish antics,
turned out occasional one-minute jokes poking fun at Mrs. Carry
Nation, the prohibitionist who also championed women's rights. *The
Kansas City Saloon Smashers* has Carry bursting into a saloon with her
hatchet, only to be hustled out along with the guzzlers during a police
raid. *Why Mr. Nation Wants a Divorce*, also in 1901, is sophomorically
vicious humor, depicting Mr. Nation in their bedroom tending to the
kids. Frustrated, he turns to the bottle just as his wife enters. In
horror, Carry throws the booze to the floor and takes him over her
knee for a spanking.

Ten years later, however, when the subject of woman's right to
vote had evolved into more than a joke, many movies had not. The
bulk of them were sly and satirical, treating suffrage lightly. *Oh!
You Suffragette* (1911) was a typical farce, which used not men, but
mice as the ludicrous ploy; when the stoical revolutionary ladies spot
these tiny creatures, they "send the women scurrying home." *Women
Go on the War Path* (1913) was Vitagraph's updated version of
Lysistrata, a comedy in which suffragettes, by hiding their husbands'
trousers, prevent them from voting and thus win an election.

The more serious pictures of this genre are of special interest
because they were among the first cinematic efforts which used film
as educational tools for disseminating information and creating sym-

pathy and understanding for the movement. *Independent Votes for Women* (1912) starred Hull House devotee Jane Addams (who in 1931 won a Nobel Prize), Dr. Anna Shaw, and the principal officer of the National American Woman Suffrage Association enacting key roles. This clever propaganda drama is about suffragettes who enlist the help of their Senator's fiancée to persuade him to support them; the job done, he astonishes even himself and becomes their strongest advocate. *Votes* also incorporates, documentary-style, a real-life Fifth Avenue Suffrage Parade as its smashing finale. Interestingly, it was praised by critics, thanks in part to the dignity of the women involved in the production. Yet *Moving Picture World* managed to single out not the ideology, but "a word of commendation" for the suffragettes as actresses.

Eighty Million Women Want—? (1913) starred Sylvia Pankhurst and Harriot Stanton Blatch, president of the Women's Political Union. Again, it was widely commended as much for its public appeal as for its seriousness of purpose. Said *Moving Picture World*:

> Those who have looked upon the Votes-for-Women movement as the last refuge for old maids and cranks are due for a most pleasant and agreeable disillusionment. The heroine of the story, though a staunch enough suffragette, is womanly from top to toe, and both she and the hero look and act their best when they gaze upon the marriage license which forms the finale of the story. There is no more modern and interesting topic than the great change that has come over the political consciences of our people, and this feature gives a most attractive picture of the defeat of the old and the victory of the new in politics.

Considering the date and the source, this review was overwhelmingly supportive. And credit must go to the suffragettes who had become quite shrewd in handling their feminist films. They oversaw all aspects of the production, made sure that attractive women played leading roles, and subversively enhanced their feminist messages by setting them within lively "acceptable" stories of love and marriage.

One of the most ambitious films on women's rights was *Your Girl and Mine* (1914). Sometimes referred to as the *Uncle Tom's Cabin* of the suffrage movement because of its powerfully melodramatic theme,

Your Girl concerned innocently rich Olive Wyndham, who is victimized by a spendthrift husband. Because of the story's inherent drama and because of the audience's sympathy with Olive (who has no legal recourse to prevent her ruination), this was a meaningful bid for equality of social status for women, pointing out the injustices of 1914 laws regarding women's property rights (few) and parental privileges (even fewer). Produced in cooperation with the Congressional Committee of the National American Woman Suffrage Association and with the support of leading feminists, the film won superlative reviews, but a small following. Reported critic James S. McQuade, "The near future, I firmly believe, will reveal to those who advocate equal suffrage that moving pictures, as shown in *Your Girl and Mine*, will accomplish more for the cause than all that eloquent tongues have done since the movement was started."[4]

McQuade's evaluation was perhaps too accurate and also shortsighted, for this film marked a final major feminist excursion into cinema-for-propaganda. Since the Women's Movement had five more years of struggle before the nation would embrace suffrage and begin legislating more justly for females, it is curious that the medium was not further utilized.

The frivolous tone of the majority of suffrage films made in America is, however, the strongest comment on how the nation in the years 1910–14 viewed the birth of autonomous woman. Indeed, it took a world war to bring about a climate in which women might assert themselves as useful, productive citizens.

Although the United States didn't become directly involved in the war until 1917, men were going off to Europe to join the Allies long before America did; in 1914 and 1915 war was a glamorous and thoroughly masculine adventure. With boys leaving their jobs for the front, women volunteered to replace them in factories or offices—out of either patriotic zeal, economic necessity, or the pure pleasure of finally being able to participate in territory once forbidden.

The country was charged with excitement. Before long, even ladies of leisure had discovered a new sense of purpose. According to *Harper's Bazaar* in March, 1915:

Then when there is nothing else to do, the girls go in for First Aid courses. 'Tis a mad world indeed. Last year it was fancy dancing; the year before, our madness lay in "auction." This year, it's bandages and antiseptics. In the last analysis, therefore, it was the declaration of war, and not horrible examples that killed the dance.

Consistent with the prevailing attitude toward women, however, the press chuckled over female involvement in the war effort, reporting only the most trivial incidents. In August, 1915, a female patron of the arts presented to France an ambulance with its paneled walls painted peacock green "to a height of four feet with the rest of the surface the color of a lemon. Such a color scheme," *Bazaar* observed, "would make most well people feel sick and dizzy, but the giver of the ambulance is sure that the wounded soldiers will be delightfully amused; they will, perhaps, be made to forget their injuries by the nightmare effect."

Nevertheless, 1915 was a landmark year for women. On Broadway Elsie Janis was appearing in *Miss Information*; Emily Stevens was right in step with the emerging feminine freedom as the *Unchastened Woman*; Ethel Barrymore won hearts in *Our Mrs. McChesney*. This last, a play about an indomitable saleswoman for the T. A. Buck featherloom petticoat company, however modest, reflected the growing awareness that middle-class women were finally finding a semblance of respectability doing honest work.

The same year Margaret Sanger began publishing *The Woman Rebel*, which later became the *Birth Control Review*, an official organ of the American Birth Control League. James Montgomery Flagg's series of short film subjects, *Girls Who Know*, glorified the working girl. And D. W. Griffith premiered *The Birth of a Nation*. A simultaneous blaze of radical controversy and enthusiastic acclaim greeted it, and by the end of the year it had returned almost forty times its original $100,000 cost. But its significance goes far deeper. *Birth* not only indicated the astronomical profit potential of movies; it enticed audiences from all classes who were spellbound by the scope, the characters, and the brilliant detail of its Civil War tapestry. No one who saw it could deny its potency. With *The Birth of a Nation* the movies came of age. And more than that, they became an art.

Power to films—new and sure and vital.

Power to women—floundering but slowly awakening.

Only nineteen years had passed since Edison's lady had undulated across the screen at Koster and Bial's Broadway Music Hall. How would this new medium, in the hands of fearful, exploitative and money-hungry men, manipulate the image of emerging womankind? Could it preserve, against the tide of feminine opinion, man's cherished eternal girl-child?

3

MARY'S CURLS, GRIFFITH'S GIRLS
eternal girl-children, sugar 'n' slurps

She was our first star, "America's Sweetheart." And she was Everyman's notion of the eternal little girl. Mary Pickford, in a decade aching with feminine growing pains, couldn't have happened at a better time to stultify the growth of women's self-image.

With her thick golden curls, her cherubic body and pretty face, she was, from the beginning, the incarnation of angelic sweetness and childlike innocence. In 1909, when Mary, only sweet sixteen, drew attention in her first movies, *The Violin Maker of Cremona* and *To Save Her Soul*, those were just the qualities that appealed to our first generation of moviegoers.

Alexander Walker writes in his excellent book *The Celluloid Sacrifice*: "Mary Pickford was certainly assisted to stardom by the same idolizing of prepubertal girlhood which is so persistent, and at times sinister, a strain in Victorian popular sentiment. Her first director was a Tennysonian romantic. Her first fans were still nineteenth-century working-class folk."[1] And her first claim to fame was that mass of ringlets, the childlike halo framing her face. It was a symbol that would haunt her in future years, but in those days when no players received billing and when actors were strangers on screen, Mary quickly won friends; audiences recognized and loved her as "The Girl with the Curl." Soon studios cashed in on the tag, including it in their promotions of her films; to everyone's amazement, the phrase was box-office magic.

And so was the image that Mary began to carve for herself. Her specialty was the winsome waif, the sweet and sturdy ragamuffin who

37

would not disturb the status quo, flirt with immorality, or exude sexuality. Who would not, in short, emerge a woman.

Mary Pickford had, indeed, everything Victorian audiences wanted. And she knew it. It is no coincidence that Mary's screen credits read like a child's garden of verses: the public *circa* 1910 fancied her "flickers" like *Ramona, An Arcadian Maid, Lena and the Geese, Artful Kate, In the Sultan's Garden, Little Red Riding Hood,* and *A Little Princess.* In return she received their patronage—and a salary which escalated from $40 a week with Biograph studios in 1909 to $275 in 1911. By 1917 she was commanding $350,000 a year plus bonuses, and her star and her salary were still rising.

Only her age was decreasing—on screen. Mary made *Rebecca of Sunnybrook Farm* (1917) when she was twenty-four; at twenty-six she played the orphaned child in *Daddy Long Legs*; at twenty-seven she glowed as twelve-year-old *Pollyanna*; at twenty-eight she donned velvet knickers as *Little Lord Fauntleroy*, while at the same time playing his mother; at twenty-nine she performed her exuberantly childish skating scene on scrub brushes in *Through the Back Door* (1921); and at thirty-two she breathed life into twelve-year-old *Little Annie Rooney* (1925). By this time her considerable artistry and talent for mimicry were apparent.

Yet childhood meant more to her than mere playacting for money. Her bizarre preoccupation with the theme reflects her own deprived youth, when she was required to support her little brother, Jack, and sister, Lottie. Mary herself has explained her persuasion this way: "I was forced to live far beyond my years when just a child, now I have reversed the order and I intend to remain young indefinitely."[2] Those very qualities which meant so much to her were also important to her audience. Especially at the beginning. Up until 1920 Mary was the darling of the working class; because of her own working-class background, she intuitively knew what would delight the majority of film patrons. "Inspiring, consoling, and entertaining them in that order, Mary Pickford had the shrewdness to see the commercial value of humor and optimism without overt sermonizing,"[3] theorizes Walker.

Men adored her. She was vivacious, virginal, and, above all, *young*. Workingwomen identified with her. Happily, Mary's philosophy of love and loyalty harmonized not only with their needs, but with the values of middle- and upper-class females whose interest in moving pictures was just beginning to develop. While the nature of womanhood, by 1913, was subtly changing, with women throwing away their corsets, elevating their hemlines one or two inches from the floor, and bringing down their necklines to accommodate romantically clinging chiffons with sheer floating sleeves, while the daring tango, imported from Deauville, was the rage, these virtuous ladies subscribed to a morality no different from the one our heroine evoked on the screen. Did they not want to mother her? To sympathize with her dilemmas of poverty or preying men? To possess her ebullient youth themselves?

In September, 1913, Elinor Glyn captured the flavor of female life so well with her "Letters to Caroline" in *Harper's Bazaar*. Caroline was Elinor's goddaughter, but these were obviously essays on conduct for all young girls. "Marriage is the aim and end of all sensible girls, because it is the meaning of life," Glyn confidently affirms. Then she proceeds:

If the husband you select has a stronger character than you have, and if he is also extremely desirable to other women, the only way you will be able to keep him through all the years to come will be by being invariably sweet, loving, and gentle to him so that no matter what tempers and caprices he experiences in his encounters with the many others of your sex who will fling themselves at his head, he will never have a memory but of love and peace at home. Never mind what he does, if you really love him and want to keep him, this is the only method to use.

This attitude of clenched-teeth stoicism, rooted in Glyn's later Hollywood writing, was like an ingrown toenail; the double standard hurt, but women had lived with it for years. And familiar pain, as is often the case, gave comfort. So did Mary, the embodiment of Victorianism. For those frightened or puzzled by the new wartime morality, she offered solace and reaffirmed faith in tradition.

For instance, in *Hearts Adrift* (1914), as a Latin girl shipwrecked on a desert island, she "marries" the only other survivor "under the stars." They have a child, but when her "husband's" family arrives with a rescue party, Mary, true to her Victorian heritage, throws herself and the illegitimate baby into the heart of a volcano.

Tess of the Storm Country, that same year and on a similar theme, catapulted her to even greater fame. A triple-barreled moral magnet, *Tess*'s elements—religion, sin, and love—were all neatly beribboned;

the cleansing factor was Mary's purity and her humanity throughout her perils. The audience response was overwhelming.

Her next films played variations. *Behind the Scenes* (1914) proposed the dilemma of a girl who finally chooses marriage over a career. *Cinderella* (1914) was a more ethereal version of her rags-to-riches stories *Rags* (1915), *The Foundling* (1916), and *Poor Little Peppina* (1916), in which even mountain children and ragamuffins were transformed, not by financial wealth, but by the riches of their overflowing, overglowing hearts. *The Eternal Grind* (1916) had Mary toiling in a sweatshop by day and literally holding a shotgun at her fallen sister's wedding by night. This film, interestingly, was restricted in many cities as a "For Adults Only"!

A Poor Little Rich Girl, released in 1917, was the first full-length movie in which twenty-four-year-old Mary played a young child from beginning to end; previously she had been confined to adolescent maidens or to youngsters who in the course of the film blossomed into teen-agers. It was followed by *Rebecca of Sunnybrook Farm*, which forever branded her child-woman image on the public consciousness. It is strikingly in keeping with the times that as she developed her curly-haired orphan into an independent little virago, she could exercise directness and make silly, outrageous demands which, coming from a real woman, would have been too aggressive and threatening. Which is perhaps another reason why her female fans adored her. Her unladylike spontaneity was an outlet for all their repressed energies and fantasies.

Mary was, however, too much *Rebecca* or *Pollyanna* (1920) to be taken seriously in "immoral" roles. Sophisticated pieces such as *Madame Butterfly* (1915), where as Cio-Cio-San she walked into high water, drowning herself for love, were treated coolly. For Mary Pickford had promised our nation happily-ever-after immortality. If she would give the world what it wanted, it would deify her.

The prospect was compelling. Far from being brainless, Mary was shrewd, ambitious, and not averse to the fortune her girlish locks were reaping. But that very ambition may have clouded her judgement. With the approaching twenties Mary was already becoming a prisoner of her own myth. Yet she was too accustomed to power to risk losing it, and although she had complete artistic control over her films and surrounded herself with a coterie of clever writers and directors, the real strings were pulled at the box office.

Her image began encroaching on her life. Mary, who loved fine clothes and fashionable accessories, found that for personal appearances and photographs she needed a double wardrobe: her own sophisticated apparel and the youthful, plain and styleless dresses her fans expected her to wear. When in 1920 she divorced actor Owen Moore to marry Douglas Fairbanks, both she and the studios trembled with fear over how deeply the scandal would hurt her image. But the public gave Mary its blessing. A marriage between their favorite sweetheart and America's swashbuckling hero couldn't have been made anywhere but in heaven.

Which, of course, it wasn't. The peculiar aspect of Mary Pickford's saga is that while her career was a grotesque distortion of post-Victorian fantasies, she was actually very much a woman. She knew her share of emotional sorrows, first with Moore, who couldn't keep up with her, then with Fairbanks, who, after the initial excitement of their marriage and the period of complacency that followed, fell in love with Lady Sylvia Ashley. He and Mary were divorced in 1935. Two years later she married Charles "Buddy" Rogers, a former actor and orchestra leader. Today they still live at Pickfair, the mansion where Mary and Douglas once reigned as Hollywood's king and queen.

Mary's life experience might have given her infinitely more interesting and complex material to draw on, yet she chose the surefire box-office route. She was too intelligent to do so, though, without great ambivalence and, at times, frustration. In 1971 she revealed with more than a trace of irritation: "I can't stand that sticky stuff, you know. I got so tired of being Pollyanna. When I was making *Pollyanna*, a fly lit on the tablecloth and I scooped it up and said, 'Do you want to go to heaven, little fly?' And I smashed it. 'Well, now you have, little fly,' I said. And they left it in the picture."[4]

If Pickford's *Pollyanna* seems offensive today, it was hardly considered so then. Significant, however, and surprising considering his own romantic notions, is D. W. Griffith's scathing and accurate appraisal.

I firmly believe that the mental age of the average audience is about nine years. . . . Consider *Pollyanna* for instance. I personally think *Pollyanna* is the most immoral story ever produced on the screen. It takes a fake philosophy of gilded bunkum. Its reasoning, if applied to actual life conditions, will handicap its believers and leave them actually menaced.[5]

Pickford's fans disagreed. Her performance in *Pollyanna* prompted *Photoplay* to send her this valentine in March, 1920: "Way back in the minds of all of us are dreams—the dreams we started with, the dreams that came to grief when we encountered life as it really is. You have the ability—indeed, we should say genius—to stir those latent memories, to sweep back the years, to give us faith again . . ." wrote enraptured editor Frederick James Smith.

Indeed, the most provocative aspect of Mary's success during this period concerns her relationship to her audience—to those countless women of the Jazz Age unquestionably more cosmopolitan than their sisters had been twenty or even five years earlier. For her portrayals were largely dishonest, and in the light of our changing culture this has become glaringly evident. Whatever the sorrows or burdens or new freedoms of women, they had neither the option for happily-ever-after endings nor the access to Mary's fountain of youth. Why, then, did they continue to idolize her? How could her fairy-tale heroines endure (through 1925) against sophisticated competition from Norma Shearer, Gloria Swanson, Pola Negri, and the young Garbo?

Perhaps it is a moot point, like questioning how Mother Goose could coexist with Stendhal. Fairy tales, nourishing fantasies, are indigenous to every culture; their tradition is inherited by generations who enlarge their own worlds through this fiction. Mary's storybook creations closely resembled the optimistic attitudes, and primitive characters, and occasionally gruesome situations of such fables but were unique in that their appeal was *not* to children. *They appealed to adults who had long ago grown up.*

This paradox may have many explanations. Most obviously, Mary was, by the late twenties, an old pal the public refused to abandon. But that is too simplistic; besides, audiences are fickle friends. It may be more valid to point out that the middle-aged women of the twenties who became Mary's very first fans in 1912 or 1914 had lived rigidly structured lives. First obedient children, then dignified, domestic women who prepared for and got married as quickly as possible, they had never enjoyed the intermediary teen-aged freedom which society was now permitting. They had no identification with the wild young creatures in cloche hats, working hard, living fast, who were popular movie subjects. The spunkiness-*cum*-virtue of Mary's *Rebecca* or *Pollyanna* was clearly more within their understanding, and her characters' childish liberties supplied emancipation enough to assure these women that they were still in tune with the times. For this reassuring gift from Mary, they were willing to overlook the fact that their favorite was, at thirty-two, lallygagging about in a twelve-year-old's pinafore and curls—that their Eternal Child had metamorphosized into a preposterous girl-monster as out of date as the horse and buggy.

Nevertheless, Mary could not overlook it. She was tormented by agonizing conflict over her image and tried to break out of the mold as the gypsy heroine of Lubitsch's *Rosita* in 1923. She called it the worst experience of her career because the strong-willed director would not allow the strong-willed star to interfere with his conception. The movie was mediocre. And the public was unimpressed. The following year it was just as unimpressed by the pretentious *Dorothy Vernon of Hadden Hall*, Mary's original concept of modernizing a drama of the Elizabethan court for the Jazz Age mentality.

In desperation over the direction her career should take, she appealed in 1925 to *Photoplay* readers, asking what parts they would like to see her play. The overwhelming response—more than 25,000 letters—were requests for her to appear in such fluff as *Heidi*, *Anne of Green Gables*, *Cinderella*. She was thirty-two then, and the image in which she'd become entrapped was finally beginning to suffocate her.

Mary at last understood that if she didn't grow up, she'd soon grow out of a career. In 1929, now thirty-seven and blaming her predicament on her curls, she defiantly had them shorn into a flapper bob. Her public was outraged. She had cut the umbilical cord.

With her new more womanly hairdo, Mary made four more films. *Coquette* (1929), her first talkie, won her an Academy Award, but no box-office plaudits. *The Taming of the Shrew*, costarring Fairbanks, was a public disappointment and a personal disaster for Mary whose confidence was completely shaken by her husband's constant petty criticism. *Kiki* (1931) and *Secrets* (1933) marked the end of her career. Neither did exceptional business. The public lost interest when their moppet-goddess dared to grow up.

In defense of her retirement at the age of forty, when she should have been in her prime as both a woman and an artist, Mary Pickford has explained, "I always said I would retire when I couldn't play little girls any more, when I couldn't do what I wanted to."[6] Yet that is only half the truth, and in more introspective—and perhaps more painful—moments she admitted:

> I left the screen because I didn't want what happened to Chaplin to happen to me. When he discarded the little tramp, the little tramp turned around and killed him. The little girl made me. I'd already been pigeonholed. I know I'm an artist. . . . I could have done more dramatic performances than the ones I gave in *Coquette* and *Secrets*, but I was already typed.[7]

It was her final irony. For two decades she and the public had played on each other's fears and fantasies. But her myth was an insult. In abhorring age and repressing sexuality she had created a freak who denied—in fact, made repugnant—all that was inevitable about womanhood.

If Mary Pickford was the Eternal Child of Victorian fantasies, David Wark Griffith was the embodiment of the male conscience that idealized her. His contributions to the art and industry of filmmaking were enormous, but at best his treatment of women was naïve; at worst it revealed a strain of perversity and perhaps even distaste.

Already claiming ascendancy to the industry throne by 1912, Griffith, at thirty-seven, had in four years as a Biograph director turned out more than 400 one- and two-reelers of between six and fifteen minutes apiece. Even then the penchant for young beauties which was to influence his life and his work was apparent. He gathered a stable of girl-children as his leading ladies. Blanche Sweet (seventeen), Mary Pickford (nineteen), Lillian and Dorothy Gish (sixteen and fourteen), and Mae Marsh (seventeen) all were nymphets over whom he reigned with paternalistic pride.

Indeed, to separate Griffith's attitudes to his actresses and to the heroines they played is folly. On screen he extolled delicate, virginal maidens, slim and blond and naïve. "We don't know enough to get married," Lillian Gish tells her sweetheart in *The Greatest Question* (1919, on the eve of the Roaring Twenties), shortly after escaping from a rapist. Off screen he adored the same shy, girlish teenagers who were no longer children and not yet women; the same (kind of) girls over whom he reigned at Biograph.

A concerned teacher, the tall, wiry director, who was never without his wide-brimmed felt hat, presented an austere image to the budding actresses who idolized him. Anita Loos remembers: "He was very handsome . . . very serious. . . . None of us except Lillian Gish ever got close to him."[8]

And with good reason. His inconstancies and worries began at home. An early marriage to actress Linda Arvidson in 1905 had ended in bitter separation in 1911. According to Robert Henderson's *The Life and Times of D. W. Griffith*, Arvidson, refusing a divorce, threatened to expose Griffith's liaisons with certain of his youthful leading ladies if he did not pay her considerable alimony. Linda made it perfectly clear that she had no intention of divorcing him while his star was rising. Any hopes that Griffith had entertained about securing his personal freedom were now gone. This precluded his making any obvious alliances with other women.[9]

In 1935, finally free, the director, consistent with his lifelong tendency, married a twenty-six-year-old girl whom he had known since she was thirteen. He was then sixty-one.

In the early days, however, he managed to shroud his private life in secrecy. Eileen Bowser at the Museum of Modern Art in New York City suggests that he quickly learned discretion, making sure his personal correspondence with enamored females was handled through his cousin Willard. In fact, if he was a womanizer, he disguised it well, going to extremes to instill in his prodigies the fastidious morality which was a heritage of his Kentucky-Southern upbringing; those chivalrous virtues were still sacred to him. And never, not even in the twenties, would he be able to distance himself from them sufficiently to adapt to the changing morality.

Often he was maniacal, even ridiculous about the moral atmosphere in his studio. Yet this is not an uncommon pattern of behavior for individuals who repress, as Griffith apparently did, their true impulses and dwell relentlessly on pious ideals—such as virtue, chastity, and youth. At work his propriety was almost fetishistic: Love scenes on the set were faked by carefully set-up camera angles; kissing, he explained, was not hygienic. In one early film in which Lillian Gish's passionate embrace seemed too convincing, he proposed inserting a line in the title assuring audiences that her mother had chaperoned the film. Fortunately, he was persuaded not to.

Conscientious moralist that he was, he went so far as to direct a film, *The Escape* (1914), that was concerned with the problems and dangers of syphilis.

But more specifically, his puritanism was usually reflected in the conservative manner in which he handled his female characters, and the way he balked at other directors' handling of them. He reputedly was indignant that Marguerite Clark, a well-known film actress had peeled off her stockings in the movie *Wildflower*. And he abhorred the opulent on-screen Biblical pageantry, later polished up by De Mille, which permitted nudity under the guise of religious depiction.

Generally Griffith, because of his genteel Southern upbringing and Victorian heritage, gravitated toward and was most comfortable with the same sexless doll-women the Victorians extolled; the pure and purely ornamental children that excited Torvald Helmer in Henrik Ibsen's *A Doll's House*:

> Ah, you don't know a man's heart, Nora. For a man there's something indescribably sweet and satisfying in knowing he's forgiven his wife—and forgiven her out of a full and open heart. It's as if she belongs to him in two ways now: in a sense he's given her fresh into the world again, and she's become his wife and his child as well. From now on that's what you'll be to me —you little, bewildered helpless thing. Don't be afraid of anything, Nora; just open your heart to me, and I'll be conscience and will to you both.[10]

Griffith was of the same world, and similarly he was both conscience and will to his heroines, imbuing them with the determination to resist temptation and the conscience for infinite self-chastisement if they didn't. With few exceptions his females existed as childish love objects. Rarely did they behave as fully developed women with identities other than sexual, and rarely were they allowed to fulfill their sexuality without negative consequences. It is paradoxical and significant that Griffith, with so slight a vision of woman's capacity as a

human being, earned distinction as the first "woman's director." Ironically, though most of his heroines had but the flimsiest, most passive
connection to life, his artful visual concentration on them, the way his
camera played on their youthful beauty, gave them a strength and
universality that eluded his male characters.

A Svengali to his actresses, Griffith possessed a deep, persuasive
voice and an air of mystery that made him formidable. "Anything he
told me to do, I did," Blanche Sweet once remarked. "Anything to
win his praises."[11]

Griffith's indignation at *Wildflower* is ironic in light of his earlier
Man's Genesis. In this ambitious 1912 movie billed as a "Psychological
Comedy Based upon the Darwin Theory of the Evolution of Man,"
the director displayed an almost schizophrenic dual morality by
enlisting his leading lady to appear as a bare-legged cavegirl. This was
so daring that all his established actresses were aghast at the impropriety of the suggestion and refused the part. Their reluctance in fact
prompted Griffith to promise the plum in his next movie, *The Sands
of Dee*, to the girl who would agree to appear with limbs exposed.
Only newcomer Mae Marsh would do so.

For Griffith, Mae's naked legs were a strange moment of flamboyance. Yet this was part of his contradictory nature. Once, according
to Anita Loos, he instructed a young actress to give up panties, convincing her that underwear restricted sex appeal. On the other hand,
his adoration of childish girls, perhaps in tune with the times, was
obsessive and infantile, bordering on nymphophilia (as in *Broken
Blossoms* where an adult Chinese lusts after a child). This proclivity
indicated a revulsion and fear of adult females, not unlike that of
Humbert Humbert in Nabokov's *Lolita*:

No wonder, then, that my adult life during the European
period of my existence proved monstrously twofold. Overtly, I
had so-called normal relationships with a number of terrestrial
women having pumpkins or pears for breasts; inly, I was consumed by a hell furnace of localized lust for every nymphet whom
as a law-abiding poltroon I never dared approach. . . .[12]

Explains Nabokov: "Humbert was perfectly capable of intercourse
with Eve, but it was Lilith he longed for."[13] She appealed to him
physically and artistically:

You have to be an artist and a madman, a creature of infinite melancholy, with a bubble of hot poison in your loins and a super-voluptuous flame permanently aglow in your subtle spine (oh, how you have to cringe and hide!) in order to discern at once, by ineffable signs—the slightly feline outline of a cheekbone, the slenderness of a downy limb, and other indices which despair and shame and tears of tenderness forbid me to tabulate. . . .[14]

Griffith exalted heroines with slim, almost boyish frames and sweet, plump faces. In his projected autobiography he remembered fondly the first girl with whom he fell in love. He was twelve and she was "a beautiful girl, just what type I don't know, but she was very thin and could run like hell." Decades later the image of her spindly but agile child-legs was still with him. Not just Mae Marsh, but also Lillian Gish and Carol Dempster, with whom he was to do most of his work, were similarly built. It is of further interest that few of Griffith's films are at all concerned with heroines *not* of the nubile and virginal variety.

Judith of Bethulia (1913) is one of the rare exceptions. As a wealthy widow, Judith saves her people by dressing as a courtesan, seducing the Assyrian general Holofernes, and then beheading him. Unique among Griffith's heroines in her strength of purpose and in her overt sexuality, Judith, as portrayed by Blanche Sweet, is neither frail nor young. Nor is she, after inadvertently falling in love with the general, deterred from her original mission. More likely than not, Griffith, as well as the audience, was oblivious to his radically profeminist approach; and none of his female characters after Judith was allowed her independence or power.

Much closer to his heart was *The Birth of a Nation* (1915), on the grand scale inspired as much by *Judith*'s success as by the childhood sagas told him by his dad, old "Roaring Jake," a Civil War hero. *Birth* displayed more accurately Griffith's feminine ideals. Within the inherently racist framework of a Civil War story told from the Southern point of view, he drew an oversentimentalized cartoon of ripe girls willing to die for their honor—and men willing to kill for it.

The single unchaste female in *Birth* was neither white nor honorable; with his simplistic views on blacks and sexuality, Griffith's treatment of Lydia, the mulatto housekeeper who seduces her boss, white liberal leader Stoneman, borders on buffoonery. She is the film's Evil

Woman. As with *Judith*, sex is her weapon, and Stoneman's submission to her charms directly affects his inability to see the blacks' misuse of power. Later we see Lydia elevated to the role of full-fledged mistress of the house while the whites are virtually imprisoned by a Black Terror. Here sexuality (as she personifies it) is not an end, but a perverse tool for the debasement of society. It is equated with omnipotence which seems important in view of Griffith's own fears and his denial of sexuality to the female characters he considered ideal.

Elsie Stoneman (Lillian Gish), a pure and beautiful belle, never once suspects another evil mulatto's (Lynch's) lascivious intentions. When he corners her, simultaneously proposing marriage and rape, she resists with every frail breath—and finally faints. Rescue, naturally, impedes violation, but not before the audience is on the edge of its seats rooting for the safety of Elsie's hymen.

If Griffith allowed Elsie Stoneman's virginity to heighten suspense, he did so even more mercilessly with Flora Cameron, the Little Sister (Mae Marsh). Accosted in the woods by Gus, another wicked black, she flees, terrified. As he closes in, Little Sister, rather than succumb, hurls herself from a cliff. It is the "stern lesson of honor," Griffith eulogizes in his titles, and "we should not grieve that she found sweeter the opal gates of death." Or that the Klan found equally sweet the white sheets of revenge.

It is this theme of honor to which Griffith returns time and again. Whether delicate Gish is resisting the Hun's attempt to rape her in *Hearts of the World* (1917) or the marquis' advances in *Orphans of the Storm* (1921), whether she in *Way Down East* (1920) and then Mae Marsh in *The White Rose* (1923) are paying the price for *not* resisting is almost irrelevant. It is Griffith's preoccupation with the moral code in all his work which is important. Had he been less skillful eliciting sensitive, emotional performances from his actresses, these antiquated stories might never have been so enthusiastically acclaimed.

For as early as 1916 and *Intolerance*, it was evident Griffith was no longer in step with the times. The financial results of this lush Biblical sermon on man's inhumanity to man, according to MOMA's Eileen Bowser, "made him painfully aware of the need to cater more to popular taste, yet he was never sure of what popular taste was."[15]

With Lillian Gish, however, he thought he could find it—and perhaps without compromising his own romantic notions. For Lillian was the perfect Griffith heroine. Griffith exclaimed that with her "exquisite, ethereal beauty," she was "the most beautiful blonde in the world." On-screen her delicacy and virtue offset an irresistible promise of sexuality. Off-screen she matched Griffith in her devotion to her work.

The next three years are known as the director's Gish Period. Griffith starred Lillian in all but two of his films: Of these, *Broken Blossoms* (1919) was the most successful—and sexual. An Oriental falls in love with a mistreated twelve-year-old (Gish). When her father beats her to death, "the Chinaman," enraged, shoots the father, then carries her limp body home and stabs himself. The photography is murky, the atmosphere poetically misty and ominous. And Griffith, as never before, allows his camera to linger erotically on the beautiful Lucy and on Cheng Hua, whose every expression brims with desire. Even before Lucy and Chinky (as she calls him) are brought together, the opium-sated Oriental and his limehouse den ("the scarlet house of sin") establish the incredibly sensual mood.

What is so reflective of Griffith's own taste is the fact that not a woman, but a twelve-year-old child evokes intense lust. Not a woman, but a child brings the Oriental, once a peaceful Buddhist, to murder and suicide, and provokes her own father to constant cruel beatings.

Blossoms, because of the heroine's age, allowed Griffith free rein in exploring the male's sexual longings. When Lucy first collapses in his shop, Cheng, seeing she's a mere child, resists kissing her. Then, as she sleeps in his Oriental finery upstairs, he caresses the sleeve of her kimono, his eyes wander over her face and body. "Her dreams, her prattle, her sweet self are all his own," the titles tell us. And Lucy, grateful as only a child without sexual awareness can be, asks him, "Why are you so good to me, Chinky?"

But eventually Cheng's passion unnerves even the little girl. At one point, his face glazed, his control lessening, he is only a hair's breadth away from satisfying his desires; but Lucy instinctively recoils, and the Oriental is adequately chastised. We are told, deceptively, "His love remains a pure and holy thing—even his worst foes say this." For while he has won the struggle for propriety, he has also revealed his very physical lust. Are actions the barometer of purity, or are thoughts and desires? Griffith evades the issue, absolving himself through Lucy's naïveté of the implications of his self-indulgent fantasy. And his work became that of the poet, as well as the pervert.

However, in *Way Down East* (1920) the girl, Anna, is grown up. For her sexuality, she has been punished. And deceived. A mock marriage and an illegitimate child (who conveniently dies) are the heavy burdens she must bear. When an honorable man proposes, Anna (Gish) demurs. When his father discovers her past, he sends her away, his finger classically pointed toward the door. Into the storm the wronged woman plunges; frozen, nearly blinded by the blizzard, she stumbles onto the ice floes and endures symbolic flagellation by the elements.

Way Down East was one of the most profitable films of all times and brought to a trite story suspense and pathos. It gave Griffith a chance to sermonize against feminine sexual transgressions and to applaud the blessed state of monogamy and purity between man and woman. Yet he is harsher with Anna than with any of his previous female characters—her child dies; her scoundrel deserts her; her patrons cast her away; her fragile and impure body must defy the winter. And all because of that contrivance, a mock wedding ceremony. As the culmination of Griffith's romance with Victorian ideals, this hackneyed subject was what he knew best and, perhaps more important, what he *executed* best.

Orphans of the Storm (1921) ended the working liaison between Griffith and Gish. Set during the French Revolution, it is a wonderfully sentimental bit of tripe. Two modest country stepsisters, Henriette (Lillian) and the blind Louise (Dorothy Gish), on their way to Paris to find an eye doctor, are separated when a lascivious marquis, "inflamed by Henriette's virginal beauty," abducts her. The rest reads like the perils of twin Paulines, with prisons, dungeons, shackles, attempted rapes, slavery, love, and even a near beheading (Henriette's) thrown in before the sisters are reunited in love and riches.

Much of the beauty and life of *Orphans* is derived from the puppyish affection of the Gish sisters. When Louise kisses Henriette goodbye forever before she is led to the guillotine, it is straight on the lips and full of filial loss. One wonders if, had they not been sisters offscreen, the girls would have projected such strong emotion.

It is a rare screen portrait for female siblings to be drawn without jealousy or viciousness. Women throughout history have endured the myth of their own animosity toward other women. Here, however, Henriette and Louise are each other's love objects (in the most innocent sense). Whatever Griffith's hostilities toward certain aspects of womanhood, it is to his credit that here he allowed his youthful girls the graciousness of open, warm hearts; it may even have been as a result of this penchant for untainted—*ergo*, loving—youth. And it brought *Orphans* into focus as a piece of more than melodramatic dimensions.

After this film Griffith and Gish went their separate ways. But this beneficent mentor had taught his student well. A mere sixteen when she first began to work for him (*The Unseen Enemy*—1912), Lillian, now twenty-five and perhaps the greatest actress on the screen, was very much like him in many ways. Friends and coworkers have recalled each of them as devoted to their craft, aloof in relationships, moralists at heart. Yet the twenties was an era impatient with moralists. By the end of the decade the great man had been left behind. And so had his star.

Of Griffith, Anita Loos surmised, "Unfortunately, his attitude was pretty corny. And as his perspectives on everything got cornier and cornier, his pictures began to reflect those views."[16]

Of Gish, Louise Brooks, well-known flapper actress of the twenties, commented, "Stigmatized as a grasping, silly, sexless antique, at the age of 31, the great Lillian Gish left Hollywood forever, without a head turned to mark her departure."[17]

The master had perhaps taught her too well. His philosophy had in fact become hers. Lillian's post-Griffith films all display her striking acting talents, but *The White Sister* (1923), *Romola* (1925), *La Bohème* (1926), *The Scarlet Letter* (1926), *Annie Laurie* (1926), and *The Wind* (1928) all were rooted in the chaste Victorian terrain he had mapped out for her.

By 1930 Lillian Gish was beginning to feel uncomfortable in Hollywood, the community she had helped establish seventeen years earlier. After making her "talking" debut that year in an uninteresting film, *One Romantic Night*, she claims that she asked to be released from her movie contract, despite fierce opposition from the studio brass, and at the urging of close friends like critic George Jean Nathan. But looking back, this seems a rationalization. Lillian went on to make a name for herself in legitimate theater and occasionally returned to films as a character actress. But the more penetrating reason for her departure, is obviously the more painful one: By 1930, with Crawford, Garbo, Shearer, and Davis just over the horizon, Gish had exhausted the dimensions of her character. She was now hopelessly old-fashioned. And smart girl that she was, she recognized it too and bid farewell as a leading lady of the screen.

She had long before bid good-bye to her mentor. Griffith had been the most important influence in her life, and it is not unlikely that Lillian had fallen more than a little in love with him. Her autobiography, *The Movies, Mr. Griffith & Me*, is laden with reverent and wistful allusions to him, and to their friendship. And it was a fondness that Griffith apparently reciprocated. Historian Robert M. Henderson writes:

> When Lillian approached Griffith and told him of her own impending departure (for a Broadway play), Griffith became very confused. At first he didn't quite know how to react. . . . Griffith seemed unsure what advice to give this beautiful elfin-faced girl. Perhaps he felt emotionally involved with her in a way that conflicted with his image as the leader of the Biograph acting company. Maybe if he was away from her for a time, he might be able to sort out his reactions.[18]

There is no documentation that their relationship was anything but proper. It was, however, close. Lillian was Griffith's confidential friend and working companion, and even during her earliest years at Biograph, the other actresses were in awe of their intimacy. Lillian was "teacher's pet," and jealously, the other girls kept their distance. Anita Loos, who found Griffith terribly attractive, discovered that he was too immersed in his work (then *The Birth of a Nation*) to notice her. Yet:

> In those days the one girl D.W. ever appeared with outside the studio was Lillian Gish, although none of us ever dared whisper that their association was anything but platonic. . . . I remember seeing them enter the grand ballroom of the old Alexandria Hotel in Los Angeles one night, when D.W. looked like one of his own Southern aristocrats of *Birth of a Nation* and Lillian, in her pink ball gown and black lace mitts, was so breathtakingly beautiful

that for a man not to be in love with her seemed inhuman. Astoundingly enough, D.W. seemed almost inhuman; he was of Welsh extraction, and the Welsh are a very peculiar breed, poetic, unpredictable, remote, and fiercely independent. For such a man to be in love must be terribly frustrating, because his deepest instinct is to be a loner.[19]

Griffith may have been enraptured by the lovely Lillian, but while she looked like the child-woman of his fantasies, she was in fact a brilliant and dedicated artist, and a woman of great strength and independence. And independence was not one of the attributes of Griffith's ideal female.

It is far more plausible, though, that Lillian was in love with him. Griffith was her elusive master. She gave him the most impressionable ten years of her adult female life (sixteen to twenty-six). And what she took when she left him was, first, a devotion to her career so strong it precluded the possibilities of marriage or children. And then a fierce and total devotion to his memory.

Gish's post-Griffith life-style was shaped additionally by the same kind of loyalty she bestowed on him. Deeply religious, she at one time flirted with the idea of becoming a nun, but chose instead to devote herself to her aging mother. "When, after years of self-sacrifice, the death of her mother removed that obstacle to marriage," remarked Anita Loos, "Lillian preferred to continue the even tenor of spinster-hood."[20]

It is extraordinary that Gish, who had played the ideal Victorian female serving, adoring, loving, and resisting her men, in the last analysis rejected the most cherished Victorian goals, matrimony and motherhood, and preferred—with stainless steel conviction—a career and a life that was unique and individually hers.

Griffith, after their separation, felt more keenly than Lillian the need to change. The free-swinging twenties were closing in on him, but he lacked the flexibility to adapt comfortably. And awkwardly, shortsightedly, he reached out in a vain attempt to make the transition to the Jazz Age.

Carol Dempster was her name. In almost every way she was the antithesis of Lillian Gish. Where Gish was blond and fragile, Carol was dark, athletic, and boyishly attractive. Where Gish was feminine and passive, Carol was a dark flash of kinetic energy not unlike Pickford's virago-child, but without Mary's little-girl piquancy. And where Gish's every gesture was a testament to her as an actress, Carol was no actress at all, and her emotional range had a broad burlesque quality to it. Yet Griffith mistook her tomboyishness for flapper charm, expecting her nubile hypervitality to bridge the gap between the new and old morality. As the heroine of eleven Griffith films, Dempster is nevertheless all but ignored by historians and critics in discussions of the director's career. Yet his relationship with her is the most significant element of Griffith's work in the twenties. For in true Svengali fashion, not only did he believe that he could turn her into an actress like Marsh, Gish, or the talented girls he once worked with, but his own personal attraction blinded him to her more obvious faults. In short, "He was in love with her and obsessed with her; and as this fact became increasingly apparent, Lillian Gish became increasingly interested in becoming an autonomous artist,"[21] explains John Dorr, a serious student of Griffith.

The truth of his remark is supported in part by the chronology of Dempster's films. *The Love Flower* (1920), marking Carol's first starring role (*Orphans*, Gish's exit film, was completed in 1921), exploited her natural athleticism. She jumps, swims, throws rocks and hatchets. Griffith's so often giving her free rein implies that he associated the new woman of the twenties in some feeble way with this kind of frenetic activity. Despite his own austerity and aloofness, he had always been particularly fond of dancing and physical dexterity, and Carol's gyrations obviouly fascinated him. For in *Dream Street* (1921), an expressionistic allegory about three amoral wanderers—the dancer Gypsy (Dempster), "gay, swift, and restless as a bird," and two slow-witted brothers—the master again permits Carol to dart around like a frantic sparrow. The film, an unsuccessful attempt to symbolize good, evil, and the range of gray in between, was darkly melodramatic. Three times Griffith interrupted the story so that his star might dance, and always at incredibly inappropriate moments— when her father dies, when she hears that her idiot beau may be (and in fact is) a killer, and, earlier, to calm a panicky audience when a theater fire breaks out. Historian Edward Wageknecht called this last "certainly one of the most absurd dance sequences ever filmed."[22]

Interestingly, Dempster gave her best performance for Griffith in a grim and serious film controlled by the material rather than by the director's idea of a showcase for his heroine. In *Isn't Life Wonderful?* (1924) Carol was for once restrained, believable, and poignant. Portraying a postwar refugee in war-torn Poland, she rises to the challenge of emotional responsibilities and physical work in order to survive. Griffith severely curbs Dempster's buoyant nature; her hair pulled back, her clothes tattered, she is subdued, impressive, and finally a woman of purpose. Not since *Judith of Bethulia* in 1913 had he attempted to dignify women so, by providing his heroine with an identity other than that of a silly ornament.

Nevertheless, Griffith hadn't made a profitable film since *Way Down East*. In 1925 *Life* echoed popular sentiment by regretting that he had fallen behind the progress of movies. The following year, as if to challenge that statement, Dempster starred as Griffith's ideal flapper in *That Royle Girl*, a modern story desperately attempting to reflect the vogue. No prints of the film have survived, but Griffith reportedly had constant fights with the producers because of his many close-ups of Carol. The film was an elegy to her and her "modernity," and his prerelease comments were enthusiastic.

Neither Paramount, which had spent $100,000 tacking on a final hurricane sequence to liven up what amounted to a dull production, nor Griffith himself liked it. Not, at least, according to Lillian Gish.

Yet John Dorr aptly points out that by this time Lillian may have been feeling the irritation of a displaced heroine and of a neglected woman. In 1926 she released to the press statements about her former Pygmalion making "potboilers for the mobs"[23] and about his precarious financial position. In fact, notes Dorr, on occasion she lent Griffith money to pay his debts; but in view of her usual discretion with reporters, these particular remarks appear to be deliberately unflattering.

If she had any fears that Griffith and Carol would settle into a more permanent arrangement, however, they were needless. With the completion of *Sorrows of Satan* (1926) their relationship and the collaboration ended.

Because Carol Dempster, was so influential a part of Griffith's life and art between 1920 and 1926, it is not only strange but pertinent that she is omitted from discussions of both his private affairs and his films. Lillian Gish avoids her. Most critics, as if in a conspiracy to protect Griffith's image, gloss her over. Dempster may have been a mediocre actress, but if one is to understand Griffith, his heroines and his artistic decline fully, she must be acknowledged.

Typically, historian Edward Wageknecht, in one of the few Griffith-
Dempster recollections in print, makes no allusions to their involvement, but manages to convey disdain for the girl and (if one is aware
of the relationship) also subtle condemnation of her effect on the man:

My last glimpse of him was at the Roosevelt Theatre—a
motion-picture theatre this time—to which he had brought Carol
Dempster in the summer of 1925 for the first local showing of
Sally of the Sawdust; but now he was a different man . . . so bluff
and hearty that he was a little brash. The principal bit of enlightenment he now conveyed to us was that he hoped we had liked
the picture but that he himself didn't have a "damn bit of brains."
Then he called Carol Dempster out from the wings. "Say good
evening to the ladies and gentlemen," he told her, as if she had
been a little girl appearing at the last-day-of-school exercises in
the second grade. Carol responded in character by piping, "Good
evening, ladies and gentlemen," and that was about it. It was a
strange Griffith to contemplate, but one thing was quite clear.
He was well aware that he was bringing no *Broken Blossoms* to
Chicago this time, nor any *Orphans of the Storm* either.[24]

The truth was that Griffith, muddling through the decade with his
brash flapper Dempster in a bravura attempt after attempt to keep
up with the times and its confusing new morality, was still a child of
the bygone South. His ideal heroine was still the Victorian one. And
this Dempster Period reflects his lack of conviction in the females and
films he created.

The Griffith Records at the Museum of Modern Art in New York
City indicate 1927 as the beginning of his personal correspondence
with Evelyn Baldwin, then seventeen. The following year, with
renewed optimism, the great director delivered this radio speech:

What is there in the world but love? What is the most potent
power, but love. . . ?
Never since the beginning of time have there been so many
beautiful women as there are today, and it is all nonsense about
flapperism and the going away from the old morals. Girls were
never so straight, so clean, so high-class, and certainly never half
so beautiful. They cultivate their beauty, they cultivate their

minds, they are graceful, they are sweet—why, to win the dearest
thing there is in the world, love from mankind. That is the motive
that differentiates our civilization from dirty savages—love to win
this great approval, adolescent love.[25]

The public in the frenzied pre-Depression days of 1928 wasn't having any of Griffith's idealism or of his "love from mankind." His last
five films were failures.

In 1936 Griffith, as if to capture those same qualities of fragile
"adolescent love" he'd been exploring on the screen, married Evelyn
Baldwin who was thirty-five years his junior. The union, miraculously,
lasted eleven years before she sought divorce. For without his work
and without his art, the Great Man had taken to drink and solitude.

David Wark Griffith, even if perversely preoccupied, had been a
beneficent Svengali. To Lillian, to Carol, and then, even when his
power had waned, to Evelyn. Also to the scores of little girls who
began their career under his aegis. But when they and the century
grew up, they found they'd been created not in the world's image, but
in the image of their god alone.

By 1920 his heroines were but vestigial virgins. By 1930, with
women fighting for recognition of their very flesh and blood, they
were of another time, another place.

4

OLD MORES FOR NEW
thou shalt not commit (too much) adultery

As if to slake the rising tide of feminine autonomy, Congress in a burst of sentiment on May 7, 1914, proclaimed a national holiday, Mother's Day, to be celebrated the second Sunday every May. It was a vote for Mom and an apple pie in every home. The following month the General Federation of Women's Clubs at their biennial convention banned such suggestive dances as the tango and the hesitation and suggestive stories that were currently appearing in popular magazines.

At the same time *Theatre Arts* magazine chastized a Broadway comedy, *The Rule of Three*, which made light of a delicate matter: "Divorce as a subject for farcical treatment would hardly in any circumstances command itself to audiences of the kind managers would seek to bring to their theatres."

But by 1915 the world was opening up. The Wright brothers had already patented and flown their airplane. Transcontinental telephone service was available. And on December 10, Henry Ford made his millionth automobile.

The motorcar was to alter the nature of courtship drastically. For while the war gave women jobs and the Women's Movement brought them a new sense of identity, automobiles bridged distance for couples who otherwise might never have met. They also offered privacy; girls found themselves alone with boys for longer periods of time than ever before. Sexuality became more insistent than ever.

The year 1915 also marked the screen debut of Theda Bara with *A Fool There Was*—and the "vamp" was born. She told her man, "Kiss me, my fool"—and he did! Her silent command cut through the rubble of Victorian sentiment like a stiletto and an enthralled America par-roted her.

Even before Theda's debut, she was on her way, thanks to a sweep-ing publicity campaign. Billed as an exotic "daughter of Egypt," she granted interviews in incense-choked hotel rooms, alluding to a mys-terious, manufactured past. Even her name, her agent was quick to point out, was an Oriental anagram (death of Arab). Her image was the first specifically tailor-made to sell movies.

With her waist-length black hair, her darkly kohled eyes, and crude, exotic makeup, Theda Bara embodied still-primitive but enticing notions of depravity and wanton lust. She postured triumphantly as the poor male on whom she drew a bead was driven to drink, ruin, and slavery. Her success was so stunning that between 1915 and 1918 she made forty films, all capitalizing on this predatory female image. *The Serpent, The Vixen, The She-Devil, Purgatory's Ivory Angel* are just a few. Theda also gave her renditions of Camille, Salome, Cleo-patra, Carmen, Du Barry—and even Juliet.

In no way did her creation resemble a woman—unless one wants to give credence to full hips and bare nipples protruding from serpentine bras. Theda's image had more in common with the vampire, that ghoulish creature defined by Oxford Universal as "1. A preternatural being of a malignant nature . . . supposed to seek nourishment or do harm, by sucking the blood of sleeping persons. 2. transf. A person of a malignant and loathsome character, esp. one who preys ruthlessly on others; a vile and cruel exactor or extortioner."

Yet she was not, in 1915, a figure of ridicule. On the contrary, she was *sex*, blatant and overt and so far removed from reality that she could not possibly be a threat to audiences newly probing their own sexuality. For as repression usually breeds extremism, her vamp had its roots firmly founded in Victorian denial. She was an absurd sexual distortion. She was unnatural; therefore, she was *safe*. The movie-going public could ogle without feeling guilt and discomfort—and most of all, without feeling desire.

For there was no confusing Theda Bara with the girl next door. Not even with the *bad* girl next door. No woman at the time could have looked like her without being locked up or laughed off the street. If Lillian Gish or Mary Pickford had posed in such outrageously flimsy costumes, the vice squad and Gerry Society would have been appalled. But Theda's exaggeration gave her amazing license.

Bara, however—like Pickford and Gish—became a prisoner of her own legend. Three years later the vamp, as she had created it, had burned out. And so had the Bara star. For by 1918 postwar women were too serious-minded and sophisticated to take her absurd creature seriously. Yet she had served a purpose by bridging the gap between sexual austerity and sexual flamboyance.

And in so doing, she managed a permanent disservice to women. Before Freud's theories of behavior had become popularized, she cast that ominous shadow, the vagina with teeth. She sucked the blood from her lovers; she deprived them of self-respect. For her they groveled. And while by the mid-twenties her vamp aroused ridicule, was she not the mother of the *femmes fatales*, the Mysterious Women, the Impenetrable Bitches of later screen generations?

Bara inspired imitators: Betty Blythe, Vilma Banky, Nita Naldi, Valeska Suratt, Louise Glaum, Lya de Putti and, perhaps the most deserving heiress of the twenties, Pola Negri—all shared in the spoils. But theirs were more finely honed portraits that brought the art of vamping into the more human realm of the monetarily motivated *femme fatale*. Theda, however, by remaining crude and overblown, earned speedy extinction.

One challenger deserves notice for the mileage she reaped from an equally unattractive characterization. Nita Naldi, who billed herself as "The Queen of the Vampires," attained distinction opposite Valentino in films such as *A Sainted Devil* (1924) and *Cobra* (1925). *Blood and Sand* (1922) introduced her as a lusty widow whose ample proportions drove bullfighter Valentino to infidelity and ruin. She, too, however, defused sexuality by her sheer bulk. In one remarkably perverse scene amid the opulent splendor of her chiffoned, pillowed boudoir, she whispers, before biting her lover provocatively, "Someday you will beat me with these strong hands—I'd like to know what it feels like." In revulsion, Valentino throws her 180 pounds to the floor and stalks out while she laughs with unbridled sexual pleasure. We laugh, too; as a sex object today, Nita is, as they say in Spain, *nada*.

The Bara school of exotics made motion-picture sex into potent drawing power and reflected a changing moral climate out of which postwar directors could make their statements freely, less hampered by social or sexual restrictions than ever before.

And as had been the case in the period following 1910, postwar freedom in films was paralleled by a rise in the activities of the

Women's Movement. By 1917 suffragettes were conducting an all-out campaign for national recognition. That August, ten women were arrested while picketing in front of the White House, four receiving six-month sentences. In November the picketing resumed; forty women were arrested and sentenced. This, despite the encouragement of President Wilson, who on October 25 addressed a delegation from the New York State Woman Suffrage Party in the White House and enthusiastically announced his support of their platform: "I am very glad to add my voice to those which are urging the people of the great state of New York to set a great example by voting for Woman Suffrage."[1]

His plea went unheeded. In January, 1918, the Susan B. Anthony resolution for women's suffrage was adopted by the House, only to be defeated by a two-vote margin in the Senate. Its passage, however, was inevitable. Women were changing too drastically.

War production had lured females into the labor force; automobiles had given them mobility. In February, 1918, an epidemic of Spanish influenza swept the nation, creating an additional need for nurses and laborers. In 1916 Congress had passed a bill raising the pensions of Civil War and Mexican War widows who'd reached the age of seventy from $12 to $20 per month. Now, however, there were youthful widows who had lost their husbands to war and disease. If they didn't provide for themselves and their families, no one would.

Going out into the motorized, urbane working world meant autonomy and thus sophistication. It also meant a greater appreciation of the new sexuality movies were offering.

Theda Bara had begun the trend. In 1916 Annette Kellerman added another dimension to it when she graced the screen, *sans habillement*, as the mermaid in *Daughter of the Gods* and then *Neptune's Daughter*. Annette's beauty was classic, and her nude body was a sculptor's delight. With extravagant athleticism and strategically placed tresses, this oceanic Godiva popularized the concept of bathing beauties. Films began including obligatory beach scenes much as today's movies have obligatory love scenes. A new category was initiated: women as sex objects.

Sex was beginning to permeate every aspect of modern living.

A rash of educational films admonished our soldiers on the dangers of veneral disease and the evils of masturbation. Women were prepared for the new morality with enlightening celluloid sermons like

The Girl Who Didn't Know, The Price She Paid, or *The Girl Who Didn't Think.* But the glittering allure of previously forbidden fruits outweighed these instructive homilies.

By the end of the war a restless, maturing female population began demanding, in addition to frilly virgins and monstrous vamps, more worldly heroines—girls with dignity and spirit. Spellbound, women had read of the legendary escapes of the beautiful dancer Mata Hari, who had lived a wicked and exciting life in Paris as a German spy. And of Louise de Bettignes, a French agent who once carried a 3,000-word message in invisible ink on her spectacles. They'd read of the election of Jeannette Rankin, a gutsy Montana girl, to the House of Representatives in 1916. They were ready for females of style and substance, as well as sexuality.

Heroines such as the Talmadge sisters (Norma and Constance), Elsie Ferguson, Ethel Clayton, and Alla Nazimova more accurately reflected this independent new woman and were especially favored by female moviegoers. Nazimova, perhaps the most dignified and talented of all, was a pale, regal Russian beauty whose ripe good looks were real, not manufactured. A luminous stage presence as well, she was equally at ease playing Ibsen on Broadway as she was playing pacifists (*War Brides*, 1916), religious devotees (*Revelations*, 1918), or classical leading ladies (*Camille*, 1921; *Salome*, 1922) on film. Her downfall, however, was that she wasn't satisfied with adult roles. She couldn't resist Pickfordesque children and tomboyish comediennes, types for which she was embarrassingly unsuited. And her image was virtually damaged. The public wanted her to play mature women of the world and were willing to accept nothing less.

Postwar sophistication encouraged the creative giants, Cecil B. De Mille and Erich von Stroheim, men who were to personify most accurately the new Jazz Age freedom. If Theda Bara had emancipated sex, they were to modernize and homogenize it for daily use.

Cecil Blount De Mille, whose career was to prosper until his death in 1959, had by 1920 made thirty-seven films. *Carmen* (1915), *Joan the Woman* (1917), and *The Woman God Forgot* (1917) gave an early indication of his love for the spectacular, and *The Little American* (1916) and *Till I Come Back to You* (1918), both wartime films, precisely reflected the patriotic sentiment of a nation. But it was his sensational *Old Wives for New* in 1918 which captivated the moviegoer's fancy and so aptly anticipated the country's changing sexual orientation. In detailing a restless marriage in which the wife was so sloppy and unkempt that she drove her husband to another woman, De Mille righteously defended his work as one which would "suggest to both wives and husbands that marriages, though proverbially made in heaven, are woven on earth of many strands, among which such elementary things as cleanliness and good housekeeping can be of great importance."[2] Unwittingly or not, with this bright comedy, he sanctioned, even glorified, infidelity.

The film was so daring for 1918—it even contained filmdom's first bathroom scene, a bold concession to bodily functions other than eating—that the final print was almost shelved. But De Mille had faith:

> I took a print of the picture to a theater in a small town near Los Angeles late one afternoon and asked the manager to put it on his screen, no announcement, no rental, either. I just wanted to see how it would play. It had not been playing long when people began to get up and go out to telephone their friends to hurry down to see it. Husbands particularly, I was told, telephoned wives to come down: let supper go, but come down and see *Old Wives for New*. When the screening was finished, there was so much new audience in the theater that the manager had to screen it again. He was still screening it well after midnight. When I reported that to New York, opposition crumbled.[3]

One outraged critic called it "disgusting debauchery . . . most immoral episodes."[4] The public, however, loved it. *Old Wives* heralded a cycle of smart and sassy De Mille essays on emancipated living such as *Don't Change Your Husband* (1919), *For Better or for Worse* (1919), *Male and Female* (1919), *Why Change Your Wife?* (1920), *Something to Think About* (1920), *Forbidden Fruit* (1920), *The Affairs of Anatol* (1921), *Fool's Paradise* (1922), and *Saturday Night* (1922)—all variations on the daring theme of adultery, although always framed by a preachy final affirmation of the fruits of wedlock.

For instance, in *Don't Change Your Husband*, Gloria Swanson, a brassy and angular young woman who was to personify the flapper vogue of the twenties, plays a bored shrew who stops nagging her husband long enough to run off with another man; with a sudden change of heart she returns to find that her mate, left in peace, has developed into a stronger, more attractive fellow. Then in *Why*

Change Your Wife? she is a drab and harping *Hausfrau* who sends her husband into the arms of another more stylish woman. Spurred on by the challenge to win him back, she splurges on a new wardrobe, new hairstyle, and new image. Her husband is of course attracted to this luscious "new" female—and they reconcile.

The tone of De Mille's marital romps is fashionable and good-natured, yet a patronizing and alarmingly cheap philosophy pervades them. As with the pernicious vamp personality of Theda Bara, a sexually aggressive woman was a threat of sufficient dimension to necessitate portraying her as lacking in other ways. Thus, De Mille hobbled his women with shrewishness or slovenliness.

De Mille's philosophy for a happy home was whimsically simplistic. Extramarital dalliances were quickly forgotten, and superficial salves assuaged problem relationships. Chic wardrobes and stunning coiffures were balms that cemented his movie marriages; lack of them sent his men and women into others' arms. This De Mille predilection was occasionally noticeable off-screen also. "Never go across the alley even to dump garbage unless you are dressed to the teeth,"[5] he once told Paulette Goddard. "Cassocks are for altar boys who have nothing engaging to exhibit, but not for women,"[6] he would reaffirm. His females were vain, provocative, and outfitted for seduction. But what he originally endorsed he ultimately condemned; in later years he would construct plots around the theory that "feminine allure is a ruthless tool that has changed the course of civilization."[7] Perhaps that is why the *Samson and Delilah* story so attracted him in 1949. Indeed, he himself had created that "tool" for his heroines in his own early films. The De Mille marital farces of 1919 were, however, essentially moral. In fact, De Mille's philosophy for patching up marital rifts was thought so clever that many a woman was advised to heed him in order to ensure a happy hearth. As *Motion Picture* magazine in 1920 sanctimoniously pronounced, he was "the apostle of domesticity."

But his chief talent was in the less saintly realm of commercialization. His keen nose scented trends almost before they had happened. As gimmicky and avant-garde as his productions seemed, they were steeped in his own hybrid moral concepts. Historian David Robinson explains: ". . . his work was founded upon a duality of values . . . the irresistible urge to succeed combined with a comforting, if preposterous certainty of his own concept of God and the Christian ethic."[8]

For De Mille's private life was quite different from the image of the extravagant showman he presented to the public. Brought up in a close-knit and religious home, he followed his father's devout example and attended the Episcopal Christ Church throughout his childhood. Maintaining close and loving family relationships, he was a devoted and faithful husband until his death, adoring his wife and four children (three of whom were adopted). And most surprisingly, his conduct toward women was marked by a wholesome respect; the group on whom he relied professionally—his lifelong film editor, Annie Bauchens, his scriptwriter, Jeanie MacPherson, his confidante and secretary, Gladys Rosson—indicates his esteem for female intelligence. De Mille himself claimed that his attitude toward women was shaped by an incident that occurred when he was thirteen, on the death of his baby sister Agnes:

> As mother had done when father died, so she did again: she brought Bill and me into the parlor where our little sister's body was lying in its pathetic small white coffin. Mother made each of us boys put our hand over the dead child's heart and pledge that we would never treat any woman other than we would have wanted Agnes treated, if she had lived.[9]

It was a pledge he never forgot—off-screen. In his films, however, he favored a less elevated concept of womanhood and fancied high drama and gaudy mass appeal. He was, according to critic Paul Rotha, "a pseudo-artist with a flair for the spectacular and the tremendous; with a shrewd sense of the bad taste of the lower types of the general public, to which he panders; and a fondness for the daring, vulgar, and pretentious."[10]

De Mille was the man who dared to put Hollywood in tune with the Roaring Twenties.

Credit, however, does not go to De Mille alone. European-born actor-director Erich Von Stroheim had also, by the time the decade moved into full swing, produced three of the industry's most sensational early films: *Blind Husbands* (1918), *The Devil's Pass Key* (1919), and *Foolish Wives* (1922) were his trilogy paying homage to adultery.

Superficially, these films differ little from De Mille's. Yet where De Mille's were benevolent chastisements of lazy women and boorish

men, Von Stroheim's were more complex and less moralistic. Consequently, they were more dangerous. For they seriously explored the
rights of married women to sex after marriage and even more seriously condemned men whose neglect had in fact brought about their
wives' corruption. This view was more radical than even the postwar
generation was prepared for, and critics scathingly indicted his "sly
little thrusts at our tradition and sentiments."[11] Von Stroheim was
uncomfortably honest and immorally funny. And the films were illicit
enough to tempt a curious public.

There is a duality in Von Stroheim's moral philosophy of women,
however, which undermines the tone of his films. For while on one
hand his trilogy appears sympathetic and daringly profeminist, on
closer examination one senses in the director a perverse disdain. In
Foolish Wives, the last and strongest of the three, a bored and foolishly innocent, Mae Busch, falls victim to the money-mad scheming
of Von Stroheim (who also acted in his films). As a gigolo in the guise
of a recently deposed Russian court, he preys on Mae's ennui—and
her husband's fortune—with gusto. Of this silly woman's naïveté, he
moralizes: "A uniform and a continental title—they make fools of
American women." His sexual advances toward her are, for the sake
of propriety, constantly interrupted—by a priest, by the maid, by a
fire—but it is clear that with time, the officer would extract what he
wants, monetarily or sexually.

For women are his tools. Sex is, for him, merely a means to acquire
money. What could be more derisive? The count's two female accom-
plices clearly lust after him, but he returns their affections only in
order to retain them as partners in deception. He treats the idiot
maid to his virile charm and manages to wrest her savings from her.
When Mae resists a liaison, he courts her compassion with a plea for
money as a life or death matter. Finally, he is victorious.

Von Stroheim's personality dominates the film. He is the star on
camera, as well as off, and the film's most flagrant sexual allusions
come from his ominous presence. With strong Prussian features and
a shorn head like a gigantic goose egg, he suggests illicit, perverse sexuality. His psychological perception of women, his bold appeal to
their animal instinct, is unremitting and exact. Had he been of this
generation, his sexual presence might have brought him great stardom. But in 1920 he was "the man you love to hate." Women were
comfortable fantasizing about the suave, romantic allure of a Valen-

tino. Von Stroheim's iron Prussian, however, promising fetishistic interludes, was too much the predator.

In this way Von Stroheim resembled Bara's vamp. Just as Bara was the ultimate exaggeration of aggressive female libido, Von Stroheim's uniformed gigolo was the extreme masculine distortion. Indeed, his prototype was even more—it was a reaction to the emancipated post-war woman, to the female who acknowledged and acted on her sexual instincts. Men were losing their greatest source of control, and the implications were threatening, even emasculating. So Von Stroheim's seducer affected a virility impossible to destroy. *All* women were his prey; his calculated seductions were a universal leveler in that they were impersonal and mechanical and therefore insulting to women.

Beneath his contempt Von Stroheim revealed glimpses of concealed fear and bitterness. When the count warns Mae, "Monte Carlo is quite feminine—charming and dangerous," we understand that this is Von Stroheim's definition of women, too. This man who encourages infidelity and then laughs because the woman is unchaste; whose masculinity is defined by jodhpurs and high leather boots; who in later films delves even deeper into impersonal and unusual sex orientations (the famous orgy and bordello scenes cut from *The Merry Widow* and The *Wedding March* hinting at homosexuality; the scene cut from *Queen Kelly* in which Swanson loses her panties and an officer lingeringly caresses them before tossing them to her)—reflects in his screen work very personal preferences, preferences which perhaps gave him courage to explore aspects of sex no one else dared touch, but which were also instrumental in prematurely terminating his filmmaking career in Hollywood.

For as his prestige grew, Von Stroheim began to alienate producers, not merely because of his extravagance, but because of the harsh way he treated female characters. In 1926 this acid exchange allegedly took place in Louis B. Mayer's MGM office:

In arguing with Mayer about the portrayal of women in *The Merry Widow*, Von Stroheim casually remarked, "Well, all women are whores, anyway."

Mayer stared at him incredulously. "What did you say?" he demanded.

"I said, all women are whores," the director repeated.

"You have a mother?"

"Of course."

"And still you say that?"

"Yes."

"Why, you filthy Hun!" Mayer exclaimed, and he landed a fist in Von Stroheim's face. Before he could recover from the blow, the director found himself being thrown out the office door by Mayer, who then threw out Von Stroheim's hat and cane after him.[12]

The man himself was of a chameleonlike complexity, capable of calling his mother a whore one moment and the next of dedicating a movie (*Greed*, 1925) "To my mother"—a filmic first. Sentimentally, he treasured an inscribed cigarette case, a gift from *The Merry Widow* cast. He laughed off as *Weltschmerz* the symbolic mourning armband he usually wore on-screen. And he dabbled in mysticism with the encouragement of a reader and adviser, Madame Ora. Swathing himself in mystery, perhaps to conceal the mundane, if real, problems of an unhappy marriage and a sickly child, Von Stroheim was successful enough so that those who didn't know him were taken aback by his severity. God-fearing men were suspicious of him. Girls crossed the street to avoid him. Yet at least once he cried like a baby when a part he wanted went to another. However, his intensity and perverse emotionalism finally worked against him.

A master ahead of his times, Von Stroheim was too controversial to last long in Hollywood. His films, infused with arrogant and inverted sexuality, finally shocked more than they appealed. Still, he produced masterpieces—memorable and magnificent tracts like *Greed* (1925) ones like *Merry Go Round* (1922), *Queen Kelly* (1928), and *Walking* and *The Wedding March* (1928) and less memorable but interesting *Down Broadway* (1932). But never did he capture more explicitly for public tastes the undercurrents of a budding decade, the frantic desires and curiosity of a society in flux as in his first trilogy.

Von Stroheim himself, in a discussion on director Ernst Lubitsch, located the source of his special powers: "Lubitsch shows you first the king on his throne, then as he is in his bedroom," he said. "I show you the king first in his bedroom so you'll know just what he is when you see him on the throne."[13]

To a restless generation of postwar women, Von Stroheim's preoccupations were infinitely more enticing than Lubitsch's. The Nineteenth

Amendment, ratified in January, 1919, finally granted them the right to vote. Since 1900, the number of workingwomen had virtually doubled, and now, with a total of 8,229,000, they represented more than one-fifth of both the adult female population and the *total* working population.

Wives were bringing home the bacon, as well as frying it. If there was an apple pie in every home, one-fifth of them were store-bought. Stoves lay cold, and socks unmended.

Women, who had been confined for too long on Victorian pedestals, now had little patience for male-occupied thrones.

TWO

THE TWENTIES—WET DREAMS
IN A DRY LAND

Since Katy the waitress became an aviatress
The boys are all up in the air;
She used to give the fellows a smile now and then
But since she took to flying
She looks down on the men....

—from *Since Katy the Waitress Became an Aviatress*

5

DELINEATING THE FLAPPER
youth flamed and beauty fluttered

Woman especially made the twenties roar. She had exacted legislative changes and now triumphantly plunged into the heady victory celebration that was both economically and socially hers. But it was a conflicting and sometimes deceptive atmosphere in which she took that first autonomous step.

As of January 16, 1920, the country was dry. The Volstead Act, passed the previous year, decreed Prohibition the law of the land. Yet enforcement was doomed from the beginning, as a spirited self-indulgence replaced wartime sobriety. Crossword puzzles, mah-jongg, and flagpole sitting would become the rage. Flappers, already humming "A Pretty Girl Is Like a Melody" and "You Cannot Make Your Shimmy Shake on Tea" would take up the Charleston and the teacup brimming with whiskey, playing themselves into an exhausted stupor by night and working themselves toward promised equality by day. Possibilities were electric in the air, but before the decade was over, women would find themselves short-circuited.

In the beginning, however, optimism reigned.

The era glorified business as "the New American Religion." On April 16, 1921, Edward Earl Purinton, in the *Independent*, purred that it was "the finest game," "the soundest science," "the truest art," and "the fullest education." Women, while not holding positions of sufficient leverage to be in on the spoils, had since the war been carving their small but tenacious niches. Their number had escalated in manufacturing and mechanical industries, in professional services, and it had more than doubled in clerical occupations since 1910. They outnumbered men by a ratio of twelve to one in the corset factories in

1920 and were also in the majority in clothing, candy, envelope, paper bag, knitting, lace, linen mill, silk mill, and paper box factories. There were twice as many female designers as ever before; three times as many chemists, assayers, metallurgists, lawyers, judges, justices, college presidents, professors, athletics and dancing teachers, and religious, charity, and welfare workers. Five times as many female draftsmen were working. But the number of fortune-tellers, hypnotists, and spiritualists had been cut in half—from 1,220 in 1910 to 698 in 1920. Perhaps now that women had some small control over their own destinies, they did not feel the need to run interference for others'. With 1 out of every 4 workers female, a broader world of interaction awaited, as well as a broader cash base with which to participate in that world.

For the first time woman had money of her own. She could choose how and where to spend it.

And she certainly didn't squander it on bras and girdles. By 1922 corset sales had shrunk 25 percent so that manufacturers, clucking with desperation, worked out new designs and fabrics. By 1924 the first rubber girdle "for weight reduction" had been marketed, and the Gossard Company brought out six competing garments it labeled "the flimsiest excuses for girdles."

The flapper did, however, adore fashion. Short skirts, comfortable fabrics, stockings, and close-fitting hats consumed her earnings. Since her life expectancy as a single gal had lengthened and since in the working world she often met fierce competition from her peers, beautifying products, once considered the exclusive property of tarts, became necessities. Girls rouged themselves and painted on lipstick of brightest vermilion. They bought antiperspirants, antifreckle cream, rubber reducing garments for the bust, neck, chin, and ankles, devices suddenly inundating the women's magazines. In 1922 *Harper's Bazaar* permitted the intimacy of Kotex ads and accepted others in which men smoked. Cigarettes, pro and con, were still the core of controversy, yet while righteous local film censorship boards across the country agreed at one time or another to delete scenes or reject films showing women smoking, feminine defiance produced soaring sales.

And soaring hopes. The twenties exuded democracy. Automobiles, speakeasies, roadhouses, and office situations increased physical and social mobility and cut across class barriers; if a pretty girl scrimped and saved, she could purchase an elegant dress, put on saucy airs, and hobnob with the rich, near rich, and wishfully rich. Money could be had by anyone; so could good times. Dreams, the Jazz Age told its women, did indeed come true.

Nowhere was this promise more evident than in the movies. Films had become more than a hatch for escapist fantasies; they were reflecting the challenging new situations of females, reinforcing the new chic and bravado of the times, and evolving into the last word in style setting and moral dictating. One important movie trend was the portrayal of the flapper. Popular films such as *Dangerous Business, In Search of Sinners, Jazzmania, The Flappers,* and *Wine of Youth* deluged the screen, instructing single folk, especially girls, just as *Old Wives for New* had redirected values for married couples a few years earlier.

Flaming Youth (1923), one of the most influential of this genre, attracted great popular attention, as well as stardom, for its heroine, Colleen Moore. Looking back in 1971, Colleen recalled how she chopped off the mop of dark curls which as late as 1920 had typed her in such roles as the tomboyish girl-woman of King Vidor's *The Sky Pilot* (in which she hugged her rag doll to her bosom only days before marrying the film's hero): "Here was a chance for a girl who had straight hair, who was not buxom and not a great beauty. A new type was born—the American girl."[1]

Colleen epitomized her. Newly bobbed in a glistening Dutch boy "cut with a bang on the forehead, whose eyes are full of mischief and whose arms are long and slender,"[2] she played the beguiling twenties' innocent, captivating with her clothes, her dancing, and her flirtations. Before long, *Flaming Youth* created a mild revolution in feminine fashion, and unsophisticated country girls, as well as cosmopolitans, bobbed their hair and slipped into slim, skimpy dresses. By 1925 Colleen had become a national style setter and was advising her fans: "Don't worry, girls. No edict of fashion arbiters will ever swathe you in long and cumbersome skirts. . . . Long skirts, corsets, and flowing tresses have gone. . . . The American girl will see to this. She is independent, a thinker [who] will not follow slavishly the ordinances of those who in the past have decreed this or that for her to wear."[3]

The Flapper Revolution, however, was essentially one of style and surface. Girls primped and preened outrageously, but the primary purpose was the traditional one: alluring a husband. In 1971 Colleen laughed about her headstrong jazz baby: "Actually all she did was drink a cocktail and smoke a cigarette in public. Underneath she was a good girl."[4] Her character, Patricia Fentriss, in *Flaming Youth* bears out this observation: She teases and wiggles her rump, she dances and mingles with swells, but a mere kiss from an admirer triggers rage. This "independent" Pat, this "thinker," may rebel regarding nail polish or hemlines, but her sexual and moral leaning is violently Victorian. Witness the film's conclusion: As guest on a yacht, our carefree flapper, pursued too ardently by a demanding gentleman, escapes by jumping into the sea. This gesture, strongly reminiscent of Little Sister hurling herself over a cliff in *The Birth of a Nation*, is at least rewarded here by a sailor's fortunate rescue, but the message is clear. Even the most forward-looking and flashy gal must protect her virtue. Reported the New York *Times*: "The moral of the picture is to show the emptiness of the pace-killing life."

Exactly. The myth of the twenties is that of its daughters petting and partying in total sexual abandon. Women's economic and social position during this decade *did* change extraordinarily, but when it came to sex, moral judgments were still stringent. No man wanted a harlot for a wife although now she could *look* like one; women, whose goals were still marriage and children, generally refused to jeopardize their future. Beneath its surface vitality, the nation was carefully guarding a prudish heart. Challengers required squelching.

In 1921 Margaret Sanger organized the First American Birth Control Conference at Town Hall. The meeting was shut down by police who, according to subsequent investigation, had acted on instructions from Monsignor Dineen, secretary to Archbishop Patrick Hayes. Although she was able to open New York City's first permanent birth control clinic in 1923, the following year Sanger described her continuing legal hassles in *The American Mercury*—including seven federal indictments, the banning of her journal *Birth Control* in the mails, and her exposure to being "denounced, condemned, and hounded out of the country." "Custom," she concluded, "controls the sexual impulse as it controls no other."

She might have added, "And the movies." For films had the ultimate propagandistic power to sanction or snip out sexuality, and almost all screen efforts portraying modern life and the New Morality subtly sermonized *against* female promiscuity and *for* old-fashioned values. Occasionally, to be fair, they did serve the community well by explaining the "unique" predilictions of the young in simple, comprehensible terms.

King Vidor's *Wine of Youth* (1924) exemplifies this genre, one that appears to straddle the moral fence but, ultimately opts for time-honored virtues. In a lighthearted prologue Vidor sets up a comparison between girls of the twenties and their mothers and grandmothers; these last two we see in flashbacks, sitting on the family's Victorian sofa with their fiancés, swooning delicately: "There's never been so great a love as ours."

Then we meet the liberated flapper Mary (Eleanor Boardman, Vidor's not-yet second wife), who can't decide which of two beaux to marry, her lively friend Tish, and their boy friends. The two and a half couples propose a camping trip as a "trial honeymoon" in order "to know . . . how man is in everyday life before you give him your all." Despite provocative, even obligatory flapper sequences—a wild party and the abortive co-ed camping trip—our "liberated" daughter resists compromise and ends by snuggling up to her man on the family sofa, murmuring, "There's never been so great a love as ours."

Interestingly, four years earlier, in January, 1920, Vidor, just embarking on his career, took space in *Variety* where he set forth *A Creed and a Pledge*:

1. I believe in the motion picture that carries a message to humanity.
2. I believe in the picture that will help humanity to free itself from the shackles of fear and suffering that have so long bound it with iron chains.
3. I will not knowingly produce a picture that contains anything I do not believe to be absolutely true to human nature, anything that could injure anyone nor anything unclean in thought and action.
4. Nor will I deliberately portray anything to cause fright, suggest fear, glorify mischief, condone cruelty, or extenuate malice.
5. I will never picture evil or wrong, except to prove the fallacy of its line.
6. So long as I direct pictures, I will make only those founded upon principles of right, and I will endeavor to draw upon the inexhaustible source of good for my stories, my guidance, and my inspiration.

Vidor was essentially a liberal who in the future would deal with social issues in a vulnerable and honest, if naïve, way, but his piety in *Wine* suggests, as does his early credo, the moral and social obligation directors (and studios) of the Jazz Age felt toward a conservative public.

Morally, messages were embarrassingly simplistic. As late as 1929 Colleen Moore in *Why Be Good?* played a poor but lively maiden whose chief qualification for marriage to a wealthy boy lay in one virtuous accomplishment—that she was that rare creature who would not be corrupted by going to a roadhouse. For that she transcended class and culture.

Socially, films embraced the same tremendous class flexibility that life was suddenly offering. Middle- or upper-class flappers portrayed by Swanson, Eleanor Boardman, Moore, and Constance Talmadge did not seem to have much advantage over the smart working girl from a lower-class background—*if* that working girl treasured her scruples and used her appeal cannily. An astounding number of pictures found their way to the local movie houses reflecting and extolling her mobility: The American Film Institute Catalogue lists DIME STORE CLERKS (Alice White in *The Girl from Woolworth's*, 1929; Louise Fazenda in *Five and Ten Cent Annie*, 1928; Mary Pickford in *My Best Girl*, 1927); CHAMBERMAIDS (Aileen Pringle in *Body and Soul*, 1927; Natalie Moorhead in *The Runaway Bride*, 1930); HOUSEMAIDS (Sally O'Neill in *Broadway Fever*, 1929; Constance Bennett in *Common Clay*, 1930; Mary Miles Minter in *Her Winning Way*, 1921; Louise Fazenda in *The Gay Old Bird*, 1927; Colleen Moore in *Painted People*, 1924); FACTORY WORKERS (Grace Davidson in *When Destiny Wills*, 1921; Lassie Lou Ahern in *Little Mickey Grogan*, 1927; Bartine Burkett in *Don't Write Letters*, 1922); as well as GOVERNESSES, HOUSE-KEEPERS, NURSES, COOKS, DISHWASHERS, HATCHECK GIRLS, and STENOG-RAPHERS—all represented in formula flicks where the grimy waif, transformed into a cheeky beauty, wins (a) the rich boss or (b) the poor, handsome hero with the bright future.

While generous in its characterizations of workingwomen during the twenties, Hollywood concentrated almost exclusively on gals in blue-collar occupations. But by stressing these and excluding most others (one exception: chorus girls), the industry held a warped mirror up to life. Numerous women in the twenties had jobs which were not merely means to an end—jobs requiring skill, aggressiveness, education. Jobs that ranged from the ridiculous to the sublime. Delia Akeley, embarking on two solo zoological expeditions to Africa for the Brooklyn Museum, discovered important new species of antelopes and birds. Annette Adams, a San Francisco lawyer and the first woman ever appointed (by President Wilson) to the post of Assistant Attorney General, served from July, 1920, to August, 1921. She was followed by Mabel Walker Willebrandt, a Harding appointee often nicknamed the Prohibition Portia, as it was her impossible task to enforce liquor regulations during her term in office (1921–29). New York City's Bureau of Policewomen, organized in April, 1926, was a specialized branch whose members concentrated on attending suspect or convicted women and children, detecting shoplifters, and performing other delicate tasks.

On August 6 of that same year Gertrude Ederle swam the English Channel in fourteen and a half hours. The first woman to attempt that distance, she shattered by almost two hours the world record of the five men who had already made the crossing, and was accorded the most spectacular reception New York had ever seen. Mayor Jimmy Walker applauded her: "When history records the great crossings, they will speak of Moses crossing the Red Sea, Caesar crossing the Rubicon, and Washington crossing the Delaware, but frankly, your crossing of the British Channel must take its place alongside of these."[5]

Moses, Caesar, and Washington all had been portrayed in films, so why not Gertrude? Why not other outstanding women: authors like Willa Cather, who won the Pulitzer Prize in 1922 for *One of Ours*, or Isadora Duncan who early in the century had changed thoughts on the scope of modern dance and raised eyebrows with her unorthodox life-style, before dying tragically in 1927? Contrary to movie myths, female contributions in the twenties were steadily growing. Georgia O'Keeffe held her first major exhibition of "One Hundred Pictures" at the Anderson Galleries in New York on January 29, 1923. Expatriate Gertrude Stein, already something of a celebrity, presided regally over her *salon des artistes* in Paris, with dozens of brilliant men seeking her approval and invitations. Dancer Martha Graham debuted in 1920 with Ted Shawn; another young woman, Doris Humphrey, was already a member of the troupe. Both would profoundly influence the dynamics and form of modern dance as a means of personal, abstract, and highly theatrical art.

Of the ten best-selling books of 1925, eight were written by women:

Anne Douglas Sedgwick's *The Little French Girl*, Edna Ferber's *So Big*, Kathleen Norris' *Rose of the World*, Margaret Kennedy's *The Constant Nymph*, Edith Wharton's *A Mother's Recompense*, Ellen Glasgow's *Barren Ground*, *The Red Lamp* by Mary Roberts Rinehart, and *Professor's House* by Willa Cather. In 1928 the youthful Margaret Mead published her startling *Coming of Age in Samoa*. Dorothy Parker, who between 1917 and 1920 was an editor of the prestigious literary magazine *Vanity Fair*, had early in the decade cultivated a reputation as the wittiest woman in New York, quoted and misquoted obsessively by metropolitan and national columnists.

Although recently released from second-class citizen status, women contributed to art, industry, and twenties' culture with a significant zealousness and resilience considering how carefully and completely they had been excluded from those realms for generations. The spirit of liberation, coupled with industrialization, was contagious. In the ten-year period between 1911 and 1921, women had been granted more than 5,000 patents for inventions as varied as "typical" ladies' products (multiple skirt gauges, curlers, hairpins, and personal and household gadgets) and as "unpredictable" as poultry harnesses, roost disinfectors, time-controlled dam gates, and automobile spark plugs and body parts. Although less than 2 percent of the total number of patents accepted during those years, they totaled more than those attributed to women over a 105-year span ending in 1895 and showed a rate of increase more than three times that of male patent grants.

Womanpower's ascendancy naturally met with tremendous consternation from male forces. In 1920 Calvin Coolidge labeled women's colleges "hotbeds of radicalism." *Photoplay*'s editor, James R. Quirk, had his say about women and education, also. In the November, 1921, issue of filmdom's bible, his "Are Women's Colleges Old Maid Factories?" contained this observation:

Man, even the average college man, will fall in love with a beautiful "dumbbell" more quickly than with a spectacled feminine professor of psychology. It is not that he fears the intellectual equality or superiority of the woman. He is following the natural instinct to seek beauty. Nature knew more about the promotion of the birth rate than all the scientists that ever lived.

In 1924 *Photoplay* printed a rather cockeyed concession to the revolutionary idea that feminine brains have value. Said Hubert Howe in "What Kind of Women Attract Men Most?":

> That beauty isn't the first essential is obvious. It helps. Oh, how it does help some block-head baby-dolls! . . . Consider brains. The aggressively brainy woman is a horror. A woman so intellectual that it hurts is out of the question. But a typically feminine intelligence, a subtle hint of knowledge, a lively logic full of unexpected loop-holes, brilliance with just a vague hint of superficiality, these qualities in an exceptional feminine brain are interest-compelling and often quite attractive. . . .
>
> Sincerity, for one thing, or a convincing semblance of it, is essential. . . . Flattery applied with a shovel is distasteful. But gently spread on with the tip of one magnetic finger, it is irresistible. . . . She must have warmth. She must neither act nor look like an icicle. . . . A woman must have amiability. . . . All men like vivacity. . . . She must be well-sexed. She must be essentially woman. She must not emulate the manner nor voice nor outlook of a man. . . . Magnetism! That is the word which tells the whole story.

Masculine apprehension such as the above consistently accompanied feminine progress. By 1929 the rate of college-educated women had trebled. In that year 40 percent of all master's degrees and 15 percent of all PhD's were awarded to females, figures equal to today's. What's more, the proportion of academic women personnel at universities had increased from 26.3 percent in 1920 (a solid figure in itself) to 27.1 percent.

That March, in response to W. A. Neilson's sound appraisal of the positive aspects of higher education for women in the previous month's *Forum*, W. Beran Wolfe, apparently a licensed psychiatrist, scathingly criticized the institution of women's colleges. His embarrassing *Forum* piece, "Why Educate Women?," observed not only that our culture "is maintained by man-made laws. Our institutions give preference to men. Our theology and philosophy are permeated with the concept that the male is a superior being," but referred to the college woman as a "belligerent female struggling to attain her rights."

Wolfe cloaked his scorn for female education in a blast at women's colleges. Coeducational institutions, he noted, failed, too, because they intensified sexual struggle. The solution? Vaguely, "to prepare men and women for their communal life," to recognize intellectual equality of women because "civilization will *eventually* readjust itself to provide an equitable division of labor and opportunity between the sexes."

In other words: LADIES, WAIT!

Representing an elitist group of physicians-psychoanalysts-educators, Wolfe did not, however, stand alone. Business interests—and men everywhere—echoed his jitters. In 1922 Rudolph Valentino told *Photoplay* what Hollywood at large already knew: "I do not like women who know too much." And "Let her be your inferior, if possible. Then she will be happy with you." And "We Europeans do not expect too much of one woman."

Fitting, is it not, that the axioms held by the screen's most romantic hero (whose first wife reportedly accused him of never consummating the marriage and, even worse, whose second wife spread malicious gossip that his performance made her wish he *hadn't*) should unconsciously echo the studios' portrayals of women in the twenties? Certainly, working girls *must* be glorified—otherwise the gap between reality and "art" might prove unbridgeable (at least at the box office). Films hadn't succeeded in keeping woman in the kitchen—in fact, they'd unwittingly hastened her departure—but now the industry had a fair chance of stopping her at the factory gates, beauty salon doors, lingerie counters. Her godhead would be won with her maidenhead, and her gold wedding band would signify attainment of the goal she'd dreamed of. *Marriage.* Working and flapping, she could sow her wild oats, but marriage was the *real happy ending*.

It was enforcement through repetition.

The screen abounded with working-girl themes during the twenties, and every well-known actress offered her version of the stenographic Cinderella. Louise Brooks in *It's The Old Army Game* (1926) ran W. C. Fields' drugstore and persuaded him to sell her con man boyfriend's High and Dry realty stock. Gladys Walton did double cashier duty in *All Dolled Up* (1921) and then in *The Wise Kid*. Even Hungarian siren Vilma Banky played a cook in *This Is Heaven*, while in *Stage Struck* (1924) reigning queen Swanson slung hash in a beanery, did Lawrence Gray's laundry, and took a correspondence course in acting because he found actresses so irresistible. Then, in *Man-*

handled (1924), as a department store salesgirl, Swanson had a fling with a wealthy Pygmalion before returning to her first boyfriend, a poor inventor who in her absence had made a million.

Perhaps the most proletarian voice of this idiom was Norma Shearer's in *Main Street* (1923). As impatient Carol Kennicott, she echoes Sinclair Lewis' dissatisfaction: "Solitary dishing isn't enough to satisfy me—or many other women. We're going to chuck it. We're going to wash 'em by machinery, and come out and play with you men in the offices and clubs and politics you've cleverly kept for yourselves! Oh, we're hopeless, we dissatisfied women!"

True to her promise, the twenties' heroine finally did come out and play with the men, and although her territory was more limited than that envisioned by Carol Kennicott, she was, in the person of Clara Bow, by no means hopeless—or helpless. Of all the decade's actresses, Bow perhaps illustrates most stylishly the cult of the star-kissed working girl who with considerable aplomb leaps out of the slums and into her hero's heart. While by no means ordinary, Bow's red-haired beauty sat so right, was, in an extraordinary way, so average, that her rise as the kittenish twenties' flapper who cut across cultural boundaries to grasp her future was altogether fitting. Among Bow's outstanding vehicles were *Kid Boots* (1926), in which she portrayed a swimming instructor; *Red Hair* (1928), as a manicurist; *Mantrap* (1926); and then *The Saturday Night Kid* (1929), as shopgirls; *Wings* (1929), opposite Gary Cooper, as an ambulance driver in the war; *Rough House Rosie* (1927), as a flirtatious cabaret dancer; and *Three Weekends* (1928), as a chorus girl.

She also did justice to less typical roles, such as that of the flapper daughter Catherine in Herbert Brenon's interesting and popular *Dancing Mothers* (1926). Brenon gave Clara an opportunity to display her range, proving she could as deftly handle the character of a much-indulged upper-middle-class socialite as that of a salesgirl. Here she juggles beaux, dates womanizers, and stays out dancing and drinking all night; by virtue of her breeding (i.e. money), she is freer than her blue-collar heroines, but still possesses an almost childlike naughtiness. In one fine scene, she roguishly gulps liquor from a flask, her fingers tracing its burning path from chest to stomach, her eyes brightening with mischief. This is Clara at her mercurial best.

Her talent, naturalness, and sensual beauty found their perfect showcase in 1927 with *It*, the Elinor Glyn ode to pizazz and the working girl, which catapulted Clara to stardom. An excellent example of the working-flapper genre, *It* grossed more than $1,000,000 at the box office, quite a sum in those days, and stands testament to its leading lady. For the plot itself was so slight that it is impossible to extricate Clara's special magnetism from its remarkable success.

Based loosely on Glyn's widely read romantic novella published in *Cosmopolitan* magazine, IT, the movie tells us immediately, "is that quality possessed by some which draws all others with its magnetic force. With IT you win all men if you are a woman—and all women if you are a man. IT can be a quality of the mind as well as a physical attraction."

Clara, the lingerie salesgal so graced, takes one look at the handsome owner of the department store where she works. "Hot socks— the new boss!" exclaims her friend. Bow's response is more commanding: "Sweet Santa Claus, give him to me." Whereupon she proceeds to get him, first by wangling a date from his comic crony Monty, then insisting on dinner at the Ritz, having heard that Waltham, the boss (Antonio Moreno), will be there. Even after she reveals her lowly position in his employ, Waltham asks for a date, and Clara replies with egalitarian unpretentiousness, "Let's go to the beach and do it up right." The beach being Coney Island, she has great leeway to cuddle, giggle, reveal her pantalets, and be flirtatiously tactile. Just as the swank supper club was Waltham's turf, the amusement park is hers, and the working girl's pride and self-sufficiency are properly emphasized. From altering a simple frock into a sexy dinner dress to insisting on a prime table at the Ritz—"When I'm in the swim, I want to be with the goldfish"—she responds intuitively, aggressively to her circumstances.

But where Clara Bow makes the role and the idiom completely her own is in the minute gestures and thoughtless touches—a hand on a man's lapel, on his sleeve. A playful pout. An alert, mischievous glance or toss of the head. The way she kisses puppies and cuddles children or descends from cars, her tiny feet in perpetual jazz-baby motion. It's endearing, and her warmth and unself-conscious sensuality as an actress seem natural even today.

Her career was short-lived, however, partially because of the advent of sound and a new type of thirties heroine. Although in her first talkie, Paramount's *The Wild Party* (1929), Clara's Brooklyn-nasal voice surprised without flattering, the film's director, Dorothy Arzner, attributes its rawness to the fact that she was "thrown into dialogue without being groomed as MGM had done with Garbo, Norma Shearer, and others."[6]

More relevant, however, to the demise of her celebrity was her own colorful, yet tragic personal life. A sensational series of romantic scandals first amused, then outraged a condemning public. In 1926 an ex-Yale football player slashed his wrists after Clara had spurned him, and gossip redoubled when he accused her of kissing him so hard his lips ached for two days.

Headlines erupted again when, allegedly returning from a party in Agua Caliente, she arrived at a local hospital clad only in a nightie, a $5,000 fur, and dripping blood. The staff suspected attempted suicide, but the incident was written off as an auto accident.

Gossip columnists followed her relationships with boxer Slapsie Maxie Rosenbloom, millionaire vaudevillian Harry Richman, and Gary Cooper (to whom she was reportedly engaged). By 1931 she had paid $30,000 to the wife of a Dallas physician to halt an aliena-tion of affections suit, and shortly afterward she brought charges of embezzlement against her personal secretary. Daisy DeVoe. Daisy retaliated by flinging the intimate details of Clara's love affairs before the court—and the nation. Later that year Bow married former cow-boy star Rex Bell, who was to become lieutenant governor of Nevada. Though they never divorced, the couple, who had two sons, were separated for many years.

Perhaps Clara Bow might have withstood both the transition to sound and her publicity had she not also been in poor mental health. Suffering her first nervous breakdown during production of *It*, she returned to a sanitarium in 1932 for a lengthy stay and spent the rest of her life in and out of similar institutions, suffering from fainting spells and melancholia, and was finally barely able to recognize friends or speak coherently. Nevertheless, during the rare lucid periods of her almost three decades of illness, she completed a few inconsequential films, operated a Los Angeles coffeehouse called, appropriately, It, guested on *Truth or Consequences*, and appeared in 1947 as radio's first "Mrs. Hush."

At the height of her career, in November, 1927, she gave an interview to *Theatre Arts* magazine reflecting the rigors of stardom. In retrospect her candor is touching and perhaps prophetic:

> I know that everyone looking at me on the screen says: "I'll bet she's never unhappy." The truth is that I haven't been happy for many, many months. The person you see on the screen is not my true self at all; it's my screen self. . . .
> The public likes me best in wild, fiery roles; those are the ones that take the greatest amount of energy from me, and I can tell you it is not easy. My nerves are at their peak now.
> The "it" Mme. Glyn attributes to me is something of which I am not aware. As far as I know, I think it must be my vivacity, my fearlessness and perhaps the fact that I'm just a regular girl or a tom-girl; one that doesn't think of men much; maybe it's my indifference to them. I really don't care particularly about men. I know four whom I rather like. Each one possesses some one thing that appeals to me—but not one possesses the combination. . . .

Alone in a sanitarium, Clara Bow died of a heart attack in 1965. Yet she left us her legacy, giving depth and breadth to the screen image of the lower-class flapper. Her heroines were all things to all men—erotic, zany, charming, impudent, strong, smart, and joyous. Despite predictable moral endings which were the fate of all twenties' characters, hers embodied the most attractive elements of that decade's principles of democratization. But most of all, the Bow ideal translated brilliantly into flesh and blood. Finally, movies had a woman approachable, attainable, and, happily, enough like the girl next door to be very, very real.

But was she too real? Did her very proximity violate a prime law of audience-celebrity adulation and contribute to her loss of favor as the decade closed, the stock market crashed, and the Depression put a lid on youthful energies? Perhaps.

For such energies had been exploited by society's newfound idolatry of youth and beauty. In 1918 H. L. Mencken wrote:

> To tell a man flatly that his wife is not beautiful is so harsh and intolerable an insult that even an enemy seldom ventures upon it. One would offend him far less by arguing that his wife is an idiot. One would, relatively speaking, almost caress him by spitting into

his eye. The ego of the male is simply unable to stomach such an affront.[7]

By the mid-twenties such speculations were reserved not only for wives, but for intended fiancées. Girls in dating and social situations were rated mercilessly. They competed with each other. They obeyed advertisements calling on them to bind their breasts and make themselves more attractive in any one of a hundred ways. Now that women were "on the loose" for longer periods of time, male criticism jumped from gentle and appreciative to brutal. Women had, by virtue of certain dating and working freedoms, become predators; combative males responded by setting up standards with which to "appreciate" their appearances. Pitted directly against one another for that vital golden band, women submitted meekly to a new institution, the beauty contest.

In 1921 the first Miss America Pageant was held in Atlantic City during the week following Labor Day. Its alleged purpose was "to develop a higher appreciation of the beautiful in young womanhood by the American public." The more important goal was the mercenary one, however. Wrote Charles Merz in *The Great American Bandwagon* (1928): "One hundred thousand visitors is the average estimate of the number of people who remain for the four days of the carnival, and at the low estimate of $10 spent per day per person this means four million dollars."[8] To distinguish this inherently vulgar flesh parade from a carny sideshow, the organizers cloaked themselves with respectability by banning such young women of dubious character as "actresses and artist's models," also "widows and divorcees."

Soon Miss American Rodeo, Miss Prune Trees and Cherry Blossoms —you name it and they crowned her—was being led, victorious, around the ring.

It is ironic that actresses were barred from the original contests. After all, the public idolized and mimicked film beauties; the industry paid them fortunes women had never before commanded; and film critics extolled, dissected, and detailed screen queens' topographies with endless delight. Films had evolved into one vast Miss America contest; only the contestants, absent at the judging, couldn't thumb their noses at spurious or embarrassingly ardent critics. Not even the sedate New York *Times* bothered to curb its reviews:

Of Louise Brooks, whose sleek bob and stylishness temporarily rivaled Colleen Moore's in *Evening Clothes*, 1927:

Miss Brooks, with a change in her eyebrows and curly hair, is stunning.

Of Mae Murray in *Circe the Enchantress* (1924):

Miss Murray's lips are made up in a futuristic shape and her eyebrows are diagonal. Altogether she is exotic, graceful, dainty and lithe. . . .

Of elegant Norma Talmadge in *Du Barry, Woman of Passion* (1930):

Miss Talmadge is at her best in the scenes where her dark hair is covered with a powdered wig, which offers a most pleasing contrast to her bright brown eyes.

Of Greta Garbo in *Streets of Sorrow* (a German import by Pabst), reviewed in 1927:

Greta Garbo, who has since become a finished screen actress, at the time this picture was produced did not know the elementary rudiments of make-up. She has spoiled her own attractive features through her efforts to add to the languidness of her eyes.

But best of all is the review of vivacious flapper Constance Talmadge in the 1924 comedy, *The Goldfish*:

Miss Talmadge is obviously proud of her barber, for there are close-ups which show the cut at the back of her head and also at the sides. It is quite a charming head, and one does not wonder that even such an astute person as the Duke of Middlesex (Frank Elliott) should eventually succumb to the permanently waved shock of hair. Miss Talmadge never moves her head slowly, but gives it a jerk, which sends the abbreviated tresses over her eyes. In the event that during any part of this performance one should forget the Talmadge hair in what's happening to other people, Miss Talmadge as Jenny arranges to have certain situations which elicit applause for the "bob." In one sequence she is shown shampooing the short hair.

Certainly, no matter how appearance-conscious the public was, reviewers outdid them. Unnecessary inspection of minutiae exaggerated the importance of good looks. Movie companies were soon plucking actresses from beauty contests and sponsoring their own as publicity stunts. Blanche Sweet was one of a number of stars who headed a "Bobbed Hair Club" for women, and local theater owners were advised to perk up business by advertising "Most Beautiful Bobbed Head," "Most Beautiful Hair," "Most Beautiful Baby" contests. Ladies were invited to match their bodies, or simply their legs, against pop-out silhouettes of current celebrities. If it was a "Most Beautiful Legs" contest, the winner would occasionally have a new design for hose named after her.

Emphasizing beauty and youth implied disdaining homeliness and age with its inevitable "ravishes." When Norma Talmadge starred in *Secrets*, a popular 1925 film in which she was required to age from young girl to old woman, the *Times'* reviewer noted with double-edged attention:

> Miss Talmadge sacrifices beauty and youth to appear as the aged mother and wife. . . . But when she is a wee bit past 40, Miss Talmadge appears to have been reluctant to do anything more than submit to gray hair. There are no signs of sunken eyes or thinnish neck, nor wrinkled forehead, or lines of laughter. She is 40! A beautiful woman with hair tinged with signs of age.

Talmadge's courage in performing the role *at all* couldn't deter the critic; her head was on the chopping block.

As was Mabel Normand's. By the mid-twenties this boisterous, tomboyish comedienne's career was lagging, and her appearance in *The Extra Girl* (1924), a comedy making merry of young ladies trying to break into the movies, received this review: "In the beginning one or two scenes are mildly amusing, but for quite a long spell one sits and thinks that Mabel Normand is a little too old to play the part of a screen-struck daughter."

Hollywood and the twenties would not tolerate age—not even middle age. Which is why *Dancing Mothers* was so unusual, portraying as it did the anguish of a dutiful, middle-aged wife who waits patiently at home each night while her husband and daughter philander in clubs and speakeasies till the wee hours. Fortunately, the mother in question (Alice Joyce) is so lovely that when, fed up and encouraged by a friend, she challenges her family at their own game, she does not seem ludicrous. Most thoughtful and provocative about *Dancing Mothers*, however, is the mutation of the mother's loneliness, first into pain and then disillusionment, on which she is finally permitted to act. She is swayed neither by honest declarations of love from the elegant man-about-town who prefers her to daughter (Clara Bow)—in itself a modest salute—nor by her husband and daughter who view her new mode of living so jealously that they renounce their social lives to win her back. In the unique final resolution, her husband assures her condescendingly, "Don't worry, I'll never reproach you for what you've done"—although the sexual implication is merely *his* fantasy. "After all, I'm still young. I still need your care," the daughter whines —which is *her* fantasy. But mother, wounded and having had a taste of independence, will have none of them. "How could I [return]," she says, "when the two of you are still so far away from thinking of anything but yourselves?" For the first time aware of her own rights and needs, she leaves them, her boyfriend, and her past and walks out the door on the way to a European cruise and some undefined new life. For all its flapper gaiety, *Dancing Mothers*' serious undertone refused to be compromised.

Most middle-aged women, lacking the beauty of the serene, dark-haired Alice Joyce, would not have fared so well or been given the choices at her disposal. Often, however, they submitted to desperate schemes to ward off years. In 1926 Elinor Glyn, influential author of romantic fiction such as *It*, felt pressured enough to preserve her looks that she subjected herself to a facial treatment so agonizing that her arms had to be strapped to her sides for ten days. At the time she was sixty-two.

Few films, however, would deal with age or its related problems; those that did, such as *Black Oxen* (1924), were fantastic enough to relieve any grim reality that a more direct handling would impose. Starring lovely dark-haired Corinne Griffith, it concerned a fifty-eight-year-old woman, rejuvenated by an X-ray operation to look and feel young again. Transformed, she lures a new lover from under the nose of a smug little flapper. This popular wish fantasy of stopping time did well, and critics reveled in the contrast between Corinne's old-world "elegance" and the flapper's tawdry aggressiveness. But in terms of an exploration of a specific societal malaise—the impact on woman of aging—it helped not at all.

Nor did on-screen treatment of homely or older women. Almost *all* young women were pretty; *all* older women were crotchety, finicky, funny—buffoons, the butts of sight gags, sources of title writers' most vitriolic indulgences. For instance, in *It's the Old Army Game* (1926) the camera catches middle-aged Blanche Ring, and we are told, "One look at her and all trains stop." Or in *The Patsy* (1928) Marie Dressler, overbearing mother to Marion Davies, is the subject of this exchange:

FATHER: Your mother has her good points, Pat.

PAT (Marion): She sure has—and they stick out all over her!

Everyone is fair game for humor in comedies, but in twenties films —which set the precedent for those of subsequent decades—older and dowdy women were a little less fair and more game than others. Zasu Pitts, who starred in Von Stronheim's *Greed* (1925), was given her first break as the result of a malicious joke. When Mary Pickford needed a beautiful second lead for *The Little Princess* (1917), a cruel studio messenger boy showed up with Zasu, all eyes, gawky body, and gesticulating hands. Out of pity, Pickford and writer Frances Marion signed her to a role anyway. Zasu capitalized on her bizarre appearance in films like *Seed* (1930) and *Bad Sister* (1931) and worked as a supporting character actress until her death in 1963. Best remembered for her TV series *Oh, Susanna*, Pitts always mocked her own lack of femininity and often sacrificed her humanity. Critics were not always kind either, as this 1928 *Times* comment on *Buck Private* indicates: "Zasu Pitts does some good comic work, but even she might have been guided to act more like the average human being."

Among the most exploited female buffoons of the Jazz Age, however, were Polly Moran and Marie Dressler, both vaudeville comediennes and fine actresses whose roles were limited not by talent, but by public attitudes. Marie Dressler, an early Sennett comedienne, did outstanding work in *Tillie's Punctured Romance* (1914) with Chaplin. But because she was stout, craggy, and "unattractive" by dint of her years and full figure, she was forced out of Hollywood and onto the vaudeville circuit until Frances Marion sent for her to star in *The Callahans and the Murphys* (with Moran). The picture received rave reviews but was immediately shelved owing to protests from the Irish community. A few films allowed her a small measure of dignity: *Anna Christie* (1930), in which she played the crusty, sympathetic mistress of Greta Garbo's father; *Min and Bill* (1930), for which she won an Academy Award as the keeper of a seedy waterfront hotel who battles authorities for the right to raise her daughter; *Dinner at Eight* (1933), in which she stole the show as an indomitable old dowager; and *Tugboat Annie* (1933), as the salty, spirited riverboat rival of Wallace Beery. These roles presented themselves too infrequently, and in between Dressler was usually cast as a character who milked laughs solely with her physical awkwardness. To make sure audiences would be rolling in the aisles, directors would pair her with pop-eyed, plastic-faced Polly Moran, who also slipped in and out of countless comedies as the maid, cook, or addlepated housekeeper.

The quality of these vehicles was so poor that even critics writhed. When *Reducing* was released in 1931, it was greeted severely by the New York *Times*:

Marie Dressler and Polly Moran are featured at the Capitol this week in a curious hodge-podge called "*Reducing*" which suggests that her employers are determined to bury Miss Dressler's talents under tons of grotesque slapstick. There is a genuine laugh or two in the current film sandwiched between reels of stale wheezes. The assumption throughout is that the spectacle of two unattractive women of advanced years fighting about matters of a personal nature constitutes a good basis for comedy.

For once, a critic was displaying humanity and righteous indignation. But that meant little in an era that doted on it. Canonizing false values and polarizing reality, films projected a surface veneer and refused to deal with controversial, troublesome, or depressing aspects of modern life. Influential producer Max Graf reflected the industry's attitude in the *Film Daily Yearbook* of 1924: "I . . . firmly believe that the public wants AMUSEMENT. The museums are the place for ART"—ART being anything that disturbs, mirrors unpleasant truths, or rejects predictable niches, AMUSEMENT being simply box office.

And women were splendid box office in the Jazz Age. As long as they were funny, frivolous, silly, helpless—and above all, young and pretty—they were the best amusement around.

Hollywood had prospered by simultaneously peddling and putting down flapper freedom. Its glossy ladies, living in the celluloid shadows of a changing society, were at once enhanced by male fantasy and repressed by male prejudices. Beauty and youth, the propagandists whispered, would take a girl far, and goodness would definitely have something to do with it.

So glamor was apotheosized—exaggerated, distorted, and dangerously overvalued.

6

REVAMPING THE VAMP

or comeuppance for the chorus girl, the whore and other ladies of the evening

Glamor had turned America's head. By 1920 Hollywood's opulence was beckoning star-struck girls, while nervous mothers, confronting bloodcurdling tales in the popular press, attempted to restrain them. Scandal smeared the front pages of the nation's papers.

Small-time seduction, like the courtroom confession of director Harry McRae Webster, was tame enough stuff. Battling the U.S. Photoplay Corporation in May, 1921, Webster admitted that he had asked a seventeen-year-old girl to pose nude. "Most movie directors do," he said brazenly. "If we're to show a rather bold picture of a woman's form, it is necessary that we make certain the form is worth exhibiting."[1]

But when starlet Olive Thomas, while on a Paris vacation with her husband Jack Pickford (Mary's brother), committed suicide in 1920, it was a scandal of a different color—black. Across the Atlantic floated gossip alluding to narcotics involvement and Jack's extramarital excesses as her motives.

One by one, other idols crumbled, and drugs were blamed. First Wallace Reid—and then later Lew Cody, Barbara La Marr, Alma Rubens, and Mabel Normand.

Director William Desmond Taylor, who reportedly had a penchant for collecting his ladyloves' panties, was murdered under strange circumstances in 1922. Suspicion fell on the director's former valet, his missing brother, two of the screen's most wholesome heroines, and one of the heroine's mothers. Mary Miles Minter, having originally gained fame as rival to Pickford, had written Taylor flowery letters declaring her love, love which had apparently gone unrequited. Her mother, who had attempted to destroy the romance because (said Mary) she, too, was interested in the director, had been practicing with a .38-caliber pistol—coincidentally, the same type which had sent two bullets into the back of Taylor's head; finally, Mabel Normand, whose love letters were also among the dead man's possessions, had been the last person to see him alive that night. The murder was never solved, but both girls' careers were ruined by their entanglement.

Ugliest of all, however, was the notorious 1921 Fatty Arbuckle orgy in the St. Francis Hotel in San Francisco which resulted in the death of starlet Virginia Rappe. Sources claimed that amorous Fatty had ruptured her bladder with his weight, then mistaking subsequent throes of acute peritonitis for heated passion, had considerately inserted an ice cube in her vagina to cool her off. Acquitted of rape and involuntary manslaughter after three trials, he nevertheless did himself out of a career.

Hideous fates like these, moralists assured eager Hollywood-bound adventuresses, undoubtedly lay ahead.

In 1921 on hearing of her plan to leave for Hollywood, Clara Bow's mother went to her daughter's room clutching a large kitchen knife in a vain attempt to dissuade her. The impending family disgrace she felt would be unbearable.

However, neither fascinatingly lewd stories nor frantic mothers could dim show business' allure. In Hollywood's democratic studios family didn't matter, nor did background or education. Only obvious physical attributes, some talent and some luck, would determine a girl's success.

At the same time, what could be a more potent antidote to the vicious immorality of these bizarre incidents than the work of impresarios like George White and Florenz Ziegfeld? *George White's Scandals* and *The Ziegfeld Follies*, long-running and ever-changing Broadway revues, had won their popularity by "glorifying the American girl"—and consequently legitimizing the beautiful chorine. Slowly she was becoming an accepted figure in café society. Women's magazines were including her secret fashion tips and blow-by-blow accounts of her luxurious and exciting private life. The exquisite likes of Olive Thomas, Mae Murray, and Marion Davies had already climbed the rungs to stardom; others, like Louise Brooks and Marilyn

Miller, would follow. All proved that extravagant sums of money could be commanded by a pretty face and figure. Nothing white-washed the disrepute of the profession quite so quickly or thoroughly as that money.

By 1920, 14,354 women listed their profession as "actress," according to the U.S. Labor Department. That number, seemingly small, looms more significant when one considers that it is almost equal to the number of women earning undergraduate college degrees that year. The ranks of actresses had taken a marked upswing since 1910 (whereas similar statistics for men revealed a sharp drop): Hollywood was their Mecca; glamor, their god.

Paralleling this migration, a curious movie genre mushroomed: chorus girl films. Ground out with endless variations in which the "chorus girl" might be an Apache, exotic, or even hootchy-kootch dancer, cabaret hostess, cigarette or hatcheck girl, the genre also served endless purposes. It contained every ingredient necessary for success: It moralized; it titillated with its voyeuristic glimpses of "backstage life"; it offered its heroines up for glamorous seduction. And if they fell, then, as thinly disguised border-line prostitutes or gold diggers, they would be disposed of during the final reel—falling off the stage or down a flight of stairs, getting run over by a trolley, or being sold into white slavery. If they chose to deny temptation and suppress ambition, they were rewarded by a handsome hero, who would remove them from that sordid world altogether. The sound of babies, not applause, would fill their ears and satisfy their egos.

With this idiom, Hollywood not only baked its cake, but ate it, too; chorines wore *au courant* clothes, drank and danced the night away in roadhouses like other flappers. But where it was difficult and unsym-pathetic to indict a stenographer for working, the cabaret dancer's trade implied a built-in obsolescence; if a husband, corruption, or greed didn't get her, age certainly would. Her on-screen image, a logical concession to upward mobility, presented the most dramatic of all possible worlds in the most allegorically negative and pious manner.

The genre was tailor-made to alleviate other problems as well. Hollywood in 1921, as a result of big-money reorganizing, diverse censorship pressures, and interest in superior European products (like

Passion and *The Cabinet of Dr. Caligari*), was undergoing its first real slump. The chorus girl was a live antidote.

And so the deluge. The American Film Institute Catalogue lists 101 entries between 1920 and 1930 for chorus girls alone (with barely any overlap into cabaret hostess, cigarette girl, etc.). Titles usually flaunted subject matter, and such efforts as *Broadway Lady*, *Broadway Gold*, *At the Stage Door*, *An Affair of the Follies*, *After the Show*, *A Broadway Butterfly*, *Broadway Babies*, *The Gold Diggers*, *Gold Diggers of Broadway*, *The Princess on Broadway*, *Stage Kisses*, *Sally of the Scandals*, *Queen of the Chorus*, and *Peacock Alley* became national staples. This idiom would alter and grow with the sound era, molded into kaleidoscopic stage-door love stories by Busby Berkeley and Rouben Mamoulian in the thirties; reflecting frenetic show-must-go-on camaraderie in the forties (with Garland, Kelly, and Eleanor Powell). It would even be cleaned up for family fare with vaudevillians Grable and Dailey in *Mother Wore Tights*; then Dailey, Merman, and O'Connor in *There's No Business Like Show Business*. But as a biased comment on feminine frailty, the chorus genre would remain unsurpassed.

It was also, however, a major source of roles. Every well-known actress, not to mention tens of minor ones, impersonated her share of dancing girls. In 1920 the great Nazimova appeared in *Stronger Than Death* as a French dancer in British East India whose weak heart and sense of adventure are cured by the man of her dreams. Clara Kimball Young, whose image was deliberately sophisticated and mysterious, appeared that same year in *The Forbidden Woman*, also as a French dancer whose past comes to haunt her after a rejected suitor commits suicide. Effervescent baby-vamp Bebe Daniels starred in *You Never Can Tell* (1920) as a coat-check gal, parading around in luscious furs to alert wealthy male patrons to her potential; in *The Affairs of Anatol* (1921) she played exotic showgirl and heartbreaker Satan Synne, whose diamond-studded black batwoman's cape hides a good-natured, grieving heart.

Former showgirl Mae Murray, whose "bee-stung lips," blowsy blond bob, and dancer's training made her a natural for this genre which the era liked to term "terpsichorean," appeared in *Jazzmania* (1923) as Ninon, queen of a small country who ditches her responsibilities and runs off to reign instead as a dancing queen of an American jazz palace. In Von Stroheim's *The Merry Widow* (1925) she's the poor dancing girl who waltzes off with the king's heart; earlier, *The Gilded Lily* (1921), directed by her then-husband Robert Z. Leonard, concerned a cabaret dancer saved in the nick of time from a destructive lover.

Pola Negri, once a member of the Imperial Ballet School in Warsaw, made her chorus contribution with *Men* (1924), as a waitress-Apache dancer stepping up in Parisian society. Constance Talmadge in *Two Weeks* (1926) played a chorine who, choosing virtue over ambition, escapes from an evil-intentioned suitor and finds refuge with three bachelors. She persuades the most eligible, who dislikes women, to overcome his aversion, and together they find love. And Marion Davies, in King Vidor's *Show People* (1928), goes Hollywood, where in a parody of the Sennett bathing beauty crowd (and perhaps of Swanson), she rises from slapstick foil to grandiose movie star.

Gloria Swanson, who established herself as the paragon of De Millean sophistication, also dabbled in the chorus idiom. A carefree Parisian soubrette in *Zaza* (1923), she later created a bumptiously innocent chorus girl in the comedy *Fine Manners* (1926). As Orchid, whose upper-crust fiancé stashes her away with spinster Aunt Agatha to learn discretion and etiquette, she loses not only her coarse ways, but her lover. "Brian had sought his Orchid—and had found a pale white flower," the titles mourn. The shrew had been tamed too well. Miserable, the engagement now broken, Orchid reverts to her brash self—which intrigues Brian anew. "I have been a snob and a fool. I want you just as you are—forgive me," he apologizes.

Oddly enough, however, the actress whose vibrant chorines and dancing flappers most vividly catch the tone of the Jazz Age is Joan Crawford. Indeed, for no less a chronicler of the twenties than Scott Fitzgerald, Crawford—perhaps because in her roles she reminded him so much of Zelda—represented the flapper at her most headstrong and desirable. With her dark hair and strong features not yet harnessed by the bitch girdle Hollywood later strapped on, Crawford the chorine danced her way to stardom in such Jazz Age vehicles as *Pretty Ladies*, *Sally, Irene and Mary*, *Paris*, *The Taxi Dancer*, and *Our Dancing Daughters*. In *Sally, Irene and Mary* (1925) she is money-hungry and impetuous chorus girl Irene who exploits the love of a millionaire, then dies in an automobile wreck. Her role as Diana Merrick, the willful dancing girl in Our Dancing Daughters (1928) was somewhat more complicated, for Joan stops dancing and drinking long enough to fall in love.

Crawford's impact in Our Dancing Daughters and other similar roles—while perhaps difficult for us, having been deprived of her youthful vivacity, to imagine today—was stunning. In a group of studies made between 1929 and 1933 by the Payne Fund to determine the influence of movies on children (more than 17,000,000 between the ages of fourteen and twenty-one attended regularly in the twenties), she was repeatedly cited as a behavioral model by teen-age girls. One high-school sixteen-year-old wrote: "When I go to see a modern picture like Our Dancing Daughters, I am thrilled. These modern pictures give me a feeling to imitate their ways. I believe that nothing will happen to the carefree girl like Joan Crawford but it is the quiet girl who is always getting into trouble and making trouble."[2]

Another said of her character Diana Merrick: "No matter what happened she played fair. She even lost her man and in the eyes of the older generation; they think that when a modern young miss wants her man back, she'd even be a cutthroat, but Joan Crawford showed that even in a crisis like that she was sport enough to play fair! And 'play fair' is really the motto of the better class of young Americans."[3]

A fifteen-year-old delinquent girl noted, "The movies make me want to have a good time, but what kind of a good time is the question." After seeing Our Dancing Daughters, she went to a party and, "Of course I mingled with the drinks as she had done. I also sang the theme song of Our Dancing Daughters."[4]

Impressionable adolescents obviously extrapolated from this and other films according to their needs, occasionally oblivious to the grim fates of the heroines. In Our Movie Made Children (1935), a composite study of a number of Payne Fund research projects on the effects of films on youngsters, the names Joan Crawford and Clara Bow crop up most often. Girls, delinquent or not, modeled hairstyles, mannerisms, clothing, and saucy behavior after their heroines. They admitted discontent after viewing their favorite films, which emphasized glamor, material wealth, and the importance of irresistibility to men. Studying 115 major films of the decade, Edgar Dale of the Bureau of Educational Research at Ohio State University noted that 33 percent of the heroes, 44 percent of the heroines, 54 percent of the villains, and 63 percent of the villainesses were either wealthy or ultrawealthy (which infers that it is the *men* who are really the subtle gold diggers!). Also, at least 70 percent of these films had as their main theme "the winning of another's love."

Movies, then, contributed concretely to developing false values in life and overemphasizing the worth of secondary ones. Henry James Forman in *Our Movie Made Children* explains:

> What we call morality is conformity to the mores. . . . Failure to conform to the existing standard of mores is immorality. We have seen to what an astonishing extent the attitudes of the young are modified by pictures seen on the screen. What is a good picture? A picture, leaving aside the quality of its art, is good if it complies with the national mores and bad if it conflicts.[5]

But what could be more idealistic and impossible than to reward every "good," "pure," and "vivacious" heroine with Prince Charming? To revile and kill off every immoral "villainess"? To insist on black/white, good/evil characters so that delineations—the steps in getting to know oneself, others, and working toward (or being deterred from) a goal—are discarded. The process of learning about the world became inverted; expectations rose; and audiences adopted more egocentric views of life. While superattractive heroines in optimum-appeal situations had numerous alternatives, each of them attractive, how many were so fortunate in real life? How many teen-aged girls weaned on *good*-chorus-girl-gets-her-man and *good*-flapper-gets-her-boss dreams were shattered by confronting reality? Where was that absolute system of rewards and punishments that Hollywood had promised?

And why did screen heroines covet "winning the love of another" above all else? Why did they not value themselves? Their work? An independent future? Or dedication beyond that of their heart? Clearly films of the twenties attempted to squash feminine self-determination whose seeds were rooted in the reality of events. It is interesting to speculate what the strength of the Women's Movement would have been if it had been positively reaffirmed by intelligent female screen images during the formative and crucial twenties.

Ironically, the Hollywood product, because of its limited philosophy of justice, harmed women in unexpected ways. Professor Herbert Blumer of the University of Chicago in his research on *Movies, Delinquency, and Crime* (1933) studied 252 delinquent teen-age girls, all of whom admitted they had played truant from school to attend movies. One hundred and twenty-one confessed that after having seen a passionate love picture, they "felt like having a man make love to them."[6] Forty-three percent of the girls admitted "that movies gave them the itch to make money easily." Fourteen percent declared they had been influenced by movies toward "gold-digging" men; 25 percent, to living with a man and letting him support them. "No less than seventy-two percent of them admit having improved their attractiveness by imitating the movies. But what is more important, nearly forty percent admit that they were moved to invite men to make love to them after seeing passionate sex pictures."[7]

An alluring heroine, the vivacity with which she approached life, and the lavish clothes, furs and jewels she wore apparently affected these girls far more profoundly than the moral outcome of the movie. The escapist thrust of films presented as glamorous or seductive situations which in fact may have been disappointing and difficult in real life. How many chorus girls worked so hard that they were too tired to go out at night? How many sat alone because they were not meeting the kind of men they wanted to date? How many could not sustain a relationship because their work took them from one city to another where they stayed in squalid hotels and ate wretched food paid for out of criminally low salaries? The discrepancy between life and "art" was vast, yet both Hollywood and its moral overseers opted for glitter-and-glamor portrayals and were forced by popular and industry pressure to tack on silly moral endings—equating chorus girls and cabaret hostesses with women of easy virtue; bringing a hero-savior on the scene in the nick of time; making redemption by a handsome millionaire obligatory.

They promised women anything. . . .

No wonder that, according to Professor Blumer, movies taught delinquent girls to barter their sex for money. For this largely lower-class underprivileged group lacking not only strong behavioral models, but judgment about the (indifferent) nature of the real world, films impressed too deeply.

The overwhelming majority of middle- and upper-class women

were not immune, either. They too reordered values by Hollywood standards. Gorgeous clothes. Beauty. Magnetism. "Winning another's love"—*ergo*, marrying wealth. And especially, the promise that if a woman were "good," all would be right with her world.

To ensure such goodness in aspiring actresses, the National Board of the Young Women's Christian Association, in conjunction with Hollywood's industry and its citizens, in 1926 set up a Studio Club where women employed in the movies might obtain inexpensive lodgings and be safe from preying men. By the mid-twenties, however, intimations of chorus girls' and hostesses' evil ways had crystallized vividly on-screen. Life was shortly to catch up with art.

"The Night Clubs of New York," a 1929 article in *Survey* magazine, noted that prostitution, which had been on the downswing in the city until 1923, had slowly picked up between 1923 and 1926—whereupon it became rampant:

> The Committee of Fourteen reports the investigation of 373 nightclubs and speakeasies in the past eighteen months. Of these, 52 are believed to be "respectable." From the remaining 321, there are reports on 806 hostesses and other women employees, of whom 487 acknowledged that they were prostitutes. In addition, there are reports on 418 other prostitutes who were permitted to solicit customers and 260 procurers, connected with the business of commercialized prostitution, who were found in these clubs.

At the same time *The New Republic* claimed that 3294 women had been charged with prostitution in New York in 1929, and of these 2225 were convicted.

These statistics, paralleling flapper freedom, budding female autonomy, and substantial achievements in the working world, could be (and probably were) misread as woman's bizarre and rebellious way of usurping a major freedom that the twenties would not permit her —sexual freedom. But the roots of the growth in prostitution were more complex. External flamboyance—liquor, jazz, and a more fluid mingling of men and women at work and play—conflicted with an underlying puritanism, creating an atmosphere so highly charged that prostitution alone could assuage it. The twenties bred dissolution and lawlessness at every level, and as near universal as the cry for Prohibition had been, so too was it near universally ignored. President Harding himself reportedly had liquor stashed away in the White House. Like men, women who had never before cared about alcohol now drank because it was stylish; the number of drunken arrests multiplied compared to those made during the wet years.

Then, too, the flapper just didn't deliver. Not sexually. She dared to work, to smoke and pet, having discovered that the period between girlhood and wifedom need not be spent in demure angst. However, for all her teasing, she surrendered her chastity only for a marriage contract. Sex was in the air, and prostitution the most available release.

Finally, the twenties celebrated high living, installment buying, and conspicuous consumption. Seventy-seven million people attended the movies every week. For the first time "jest folk" could glimpse silken drapes, Louis Quinze sofas, and gilded society lilies. Why prostitution? In the twenties, working women's wages were 60 percent less than men's for performing the same job; yet money meant glamor, beauty and entrée to the right people. Why not? Working roadhouses and nightclubs, hardly distinguishable from the madcap flapper crowd surrounding her, the professional could make easy money. Lots of money. And quickly. No culture could have been a more perfect breeding ground for her.

Again, however, the screen presented an image divorced from reality. Hollywood, having moralized on the chorus girl and cabaret hostess, treated the prostitute more severely. Only those ladies who had attained classical, almost-mythological stature because of historical and literary context were portrayed with any depth. *Anna Christie* (performed by Blanche Sweet in 1923 and Garbo in 1930), *Camille* (Nazimova in 1921; Norma Talmadge in 1927), kept women *Madame Du Barry* (Pola Negri in *Passion*, 1919; Norma Talmadge in *Madame Du Barry*, *Woman of Passion*, 1930), and *Sadie Thompson* (Gloria Swanson, 1928), given life by stellar actresses in elaborate productions, nevertheless reflected the two alternatives allowed their more modern incarnations—redemption or death. Anna and Sadie meet good men and, despite difficulties, create pure new lives for themselves; they survive. Camille, less fortunate, consumes herself with tuberculosis and guilt that not even love can allay, and Du Barry loses her head on the guillotine.

The majority of modern-dress prostitute films in the twenties were, however, flimsier, sordid affairs, rarely, if ever, handled with any truth or sensitivity. It is little surprise that important actresses almost never undertook these roles. Prostitutes *rarely* enjoyed their life or the luxury of their earnings and ended up happily only when they latched onto the first respectable male—and that after a trial of excruciating pain, poverty, and penitence. Should a woman be thrown back to the gutter, it was a destiny determined by her own weakness of character. Thus, Hollywood absolved itself and society of any need for further investigation of a major social problem.

One film however deserves notice as a delightful departure in style and tone: Norma Talmadge's *The Woman Disputed* (1928). As a prostitute, she is befriended and reformed by two friends—Paul, an Austrian officer, and Nika, a Russian lieutenant. War is declared, and before the men leave for enemy camps, she promises to marry Paul. Nika, jealous, seeks vengeance when his troops march through her town by forcing her to have sex with him in exchange for the freedom of a captured Austrian spy. The information the spy has procured frees the town, but Paul, hearing of Norma's role in the proceedings, leaves her. Only when 10,000 Austrian soldiers gratefully kneel at her feet in thanks does he reconsider.

This tribute is at once comical, moving, and provincial. Essentially, Norma was not short-changed in the bartering; even the most priggish would accept a rape-for-ten-thousand lives as a commonsense exchange. One questions, however, the price one man puts on a woman's body and the stupidity of another in rejecting, rather than having compassion for, her compromised position.

Sweet, however, is Norma's triumph. This army represented every man who had put her in business and reviled her for it. Now they grovel in gratitude; her heroic act of submission has not only redeemed her (in their eyes), but more important has brought *them* redemption—of their lives and of their compassion.

The humanity and finesse of *The Woman Disputed* seem worthier of the extravagant free-living twenties than the usual odes on sin and streetwalking like *Scarlet Seas*, *Red Kimono*, *The Singapore Mutiny*, *Stormy Waters*, and *West of Zanzibar*. Yet in order to comprehend the industry's rudimentary and harsh approach to sin and female morality, one must consider the censorship situation at the time. By 1920 there existed substantial opposition to Hollywood's "degeneration" on-screen and off. State censorship boards sprang up to elucidate what would *not* be permitted in their theaters. While limitations varied somewhat from state to state, it wasn't by much. Pennsylvania in 1922 "disapproved" of exhibiting films dealing with abortions, eugenics, birth control, race, suicide, and similar subjects; also barred were scenes showing men and women living together without marriage, sensual kissing, lovemaking, bathing scenes which "go too far." Discussions of the consummation of the marriage were frowned on. In addition: "Views of women smoking will not be disapproved as such, but when women are shown in suggestive positions or their manner of smoking is suggestive or degrading, such scenes will be disapproved." Finally, "Themes or incidents in picture stories, which are designed to inflame the mind to improper adventures, or to establish false standards of conduct . . . will be disapproved."[8]

Kansas, whose censors in 1921 were considering whether to allow scenes of women smoking, had a rule that a kiss could last no longer than thirty feet of film!

An ordinance in Port Arthur, Texas, forbade the *audience* "making goo-goo eyes at the flappers."

But the greatest indignities were among those detailed by Frederick James Smith in Photoplay in October, 1922.

> Consider the censor in Ohio who objected to Stevenson's *Treasure Island* because it might teach children piracy! Or the Pennsylvania censors who wanted to marry *Camille* to Armand. The western guardians of public morals who insisted that a legal marriage be inserted in Kipling's *Without Benefit of Clergy*, and the Kansas censors who refused to permit *Carmen*, the cigarette girl, to smoke her own. Poor Carmen has suffered, for Ohio took the bull ring away, too.

Aware that in order to keep all channels of distribution open for movies to obtain maximum circulation (and thus box office), the industry had to censor itself. Famous Players-Lasky (Paramount), then the kingpin of studios, made the first move early in 1921 with its Fourteen Points:

1. No sex attraction in a suggestive or improper manner.
2. No white slavery pictures. These were justifiable only when that evil was present.
3. No stories with illicit love affairs as a theme *unless* they convey a moral lesson.
4. Nakedness is banned, except for long shots of small children.
5. No inciting dances, no closeups of stomach dancing.
6. No unnecessarily prolonged passionate love scenes. No "man-handling."
7. No stories predominantly concerned with crime unless part of the essential conflict between good and evil.
8. No drunkenness or gambling should be made attractive.
9. No pictures which instruct morally feeble in crime-committing methods.
10. No needless religious offenses.
11. No disrespect for religion.
12. Suggestive comedy business eliminated, including winks, gestures, postures.
13. No unnecessary bloodshed, closeups of bloody faces, or wounds.
14. No salacious titles, stills, and ads.

While the studio's publicity staff assured that its Fourteen Points for cleaner movies were voluntary and "in no manner a direct influence brought to bear by the recent agitation in favor of eliminating sex stuff," they were an omen. Later in 1921 Attorney General Will Hays, a laconic man and an efficient administrator, was invited to leave his post in order to take on the $100,000-a-year task of keeping the silver screen clean. Shrewd studio heads felt that he would make a quiet, attractive figurehead while they worked out regulations among themselves; in this they were mistaken. Will Hays and his Hays Office ruled Hollywood with an iron hand while headstrong moguls bowed in obeisance.

The National Board of Review and the Better Films Committtee, allies of Hays' Motion Picture Producers and Distributors Association, eventually included their share of female voices—as did local censorship boards. Simply pawns and token appointees, however, these out-of-touch women doddered out of Women's Christian Temperance

Union meetings and took their tatting and moral outrage into the viewing rooms.

One ought not underestimate the narrowmindedness of the moguls themselves. Undoubtedly the subject deserves a book of its own, yet the chastely Christian interpretation of female mores to which Carl Laemmle of Universal, William Fox of Fox Film Corporation, Sam Goldwyn of Goldwyn Studios, Adolph Zukor and Jesse Lasky of Paramount, Jack and Harry Warner, Harry Cohn, and Louis Mayer and Irving Thalberg of Metro subscribed is consistent with their obsessive concern for respectability.

All were Jewish immigrants from Eastern Europe or first-generation children who hustled furs, fruit, rags, gloves to make their first pennies. All subscribed to that Southeastern European ethic in which woman was either madonna or whore, a mother to be revered while she stirred the chicken soup but discarded if she succumbed to an unsanctified libido. As these men came to money and power, they exorcised their Jewishness through the companionship of elegant, fine-boned, and fair-haired females. (Thalberg, who dated Corinne Griffith before marrying Norma Shearer, reportedly disdained Jean Harlow as vulgar.) Class and containment, not sensuality, made ladies sexy. But most important, the double standard existed. Heartily disapproving of women challenging marital bonds, Hollywood's moguls strongly believed in the institution—but modified its precepts for their own use. The industry is rife with tales of Warner, Cohn, or Mayer chasing stars and starlets around their desks.

Studio chiefs had few compunctions about misusing their power. They had even fewer about condemning such behavior in others. Louis B. Mayer, rumored to be one of the worst offenders, vilified "salacious pictures," expounding his uplifting moral philosophy in the Hearst press:

> As long as we have men and women in the world, we will have sex. And I approve of it. We'll have sex in motion pictures and I want it there. But it will be normal, real, beautiful sex—the sex that is common to the people in the audience, to me, and to you. A man and a woman are in love with one another. That's sex and it is beautiful, in the movies and in life.[9]

And "ugly" sex—illicit, immoral gold digging—was inevitably punished. Almost always films doled out these punishments not to the

men, but to transgressing women, and especially to those most bla-
tantly sexual or evil females—vamps. Faring far worse than their
sister prostitutes who were pathetic creatures of circumstance, vamps
were self-centered women whose desire for luxuries and other women's
men motivated their every action and propelled them to total destruction. More human and less otherworldly than Bara's early creations,
they were therefore more deadly. And more suitable as targets for
preaching against the idea of aggressive, self-serving women. Often
vamps died for their sins in melodramatic accidents: In *Rose of the
World* (1925) Pauline Garon expires in childbirth after making her
husband miserable, while Estelle Taylor in *A Fool There Was* (1922)
dies after causing the death of a businessman trying to strangle her;
she is responsible as well for his partner's suicide. Nita Naldi in *Cobra*
(1925) burns to death in a hotel fire where she has arranged to meet
former lover Valentino behind her husband's back. A few vamps,
managing to get through their films without perishing, suffer on other
levels: In *A Wonderful Wife* (1922) Miss Du Pont, having trifled
with the commissioner, discovers that her husband is a cad; in *What
Price Beauty* (1928) Nita Naldi loses her man to a natural country
gal; and Barbara La Marr in *Heart of a Siren* (1925) tries to poison
herself when her lover walks out.

It is strikingly significant that most of the twenties vamps, like
prostitutes, were played by second- and third-magnitude actresses.
Betty Blythe and Nita Naldi continued to play out female parodies
and to reap comfortable livelihoods from them. Other less predatory
vamps included Margaret Livingston, Laura La Plante, Marcia Manon,
and Alma Bennett. Topnotch stars, however, avoided the image with
good reason. The role was hardly sympathetic, and no leading lady
could expect to cultivate a steady following within the genre.

Jazz Age vamps had, in addition, lost the bite of the serpentine
Theda Bara primitive. Only in the realm of pure fantasy or comedy
would this aggressive female be truly enjoyed. Audiences were too
sophisticated now. For them, the vamp was more successful and credible when her edges were softened, her image overhauled, and she
emerged as the *femme fatale*. She would come to radiate subtle mystery as embodied by Garbo, Dietrich, and others in the talking thirties,
but during the Jazz Age she knew a crude and shaky genesis, perhaps
because the era itself and the Hollywood products reflecting it were
hardly prone to nuance.

The woman most responsible for bridging the gap and allowing the female heartbreaker a range of recognizable human emotions was Pola Negri. A legend even in her own time, Pola Negri conjures up all the exoticism that was Hollywood's in the twenties. Yet we overlook her talent and forget her considerable positive contributions to this genre simply because most of us immediately assume that Negri, the last of the Bara heirs, was cast from the same kohl-and-asp mold.

Nothing could be further from the truth. First of all, she was a facile actress whose face and body could register a considerable range of emotions. Born Appolonia Chalupec in Poland in 1899, Negri had trained at Warsaw's Imperial Ballet School and Academy of Dramatic Arts, receiving acclaim for her work with their National Theater and then with the great Max Reinhardt before she even entered films. When she arrived in the United States for her first Hollywood role, *Bella Donna*, in 1920, she had completed such films as *The Eyes of the Mummy Ma*, *Madame Du Barry*, *The Loves of Carmen*, and *The Flame* (all for Lubitsch) and had been hailed as Europe's greatest dramatic actress.

Yet even before she had set foot on American soil, she was being exploited. *Carmen* was released here as *Gypsy Blood*. *Madame Du Barry* created quite a flood in 1921 as *Passion*, a typical industry misnomer for this historical spectacular about Du Barry's rise and fall. It must have dashed expectant audiences filing in to see a French Revolution Theda Bara; instead, they got a vivid costume pageant which intelligently and tastefully romanticized the tragic story of hat-shop apprentice Jeanne Berçu who climbed from the peasant ranks by charming first Don Diego, then the Comte Du Barry, and finally the king. Negri, as Du Barry, is alternately vixenish and childlike, miserable and brokenhearted. Rarely does she scheme. In this version she is victim, not vulture.

Hollywood, adamant about its preconceived notions, was not easily deterred from this stereotype. They had imported Negri—and she was at their mercy. In her autobiography, *Memoirs of a Star*, she recalls her skepticism almost immediately after being handed *Bella Donna*:

The more I studied the book, the more uneasy I was about the role of Mrs. Chepstowe. I had gained recognition in America playing *Du Barry*. I did not feel that my first role in this country

should be of another woman devoid of morals or any of the other
qualities an audience found sympathetic. Everything I had done
until then in my career had been carefully selected to avoid the
mistake of type-casting. It would be terrible if Hollywood thought
of me only in terms of playing "vamps."[10]

The studio had carved a niche for her, and her second film, *The
Cheat*, would reinforce it:

> . . . I was again unhappy with the story and the treatment of
> the part I was to play. I wanted to play interesting roles with some
> depth and instead found myself once more cast as a clothes horse
> wearing a series of lavish gowns and an exotic make-up that had
> little to do with either the character I was playing or the real me.
> With the exception of one dramatic scene where I was branded as
> *The Cheat*, there was no more call on my abilities as an actress
> than there was on one of Ziegfeld's showgirls.
>
> The studio tried to quiet all my artistic worries with evidence of
> my popularity at the box office and the fantastic amount of fan
> mail I received. Why should I complain when, in an amazingly
> short time, I had become the largest financial asset of the Famous
> Players Corporation? All I could think was that the public who
> had so admired my work in *Du Barry*, *Carmen*, and other Euro-
> pean films was being extraordinarily kind and tolerant in accept-
> ing *Bella Donna*.[11]

Her high-spirited gypsy, Maritana, in *The Spanish Dancer* (originally written for Valentino), her bitter, social-climbing dancer in
Men, and her amorous, seductive czarina in Lubitsch's *Forbidden
Paradise* (which was actually a satire on royal and feminine lust)
would continue to enhance Negri's vamp legend.

But it was a myth that did the actress a great disservice. She herself
protested to the New York *Times* in 1970, "I was never the vamp. I
was the great dramatic actress. Would you call the chambermaid I
played in *Hotel Imperial* a vamp? Or the peasant in *Barbed Wire* a
vamp? Definitely not. As far as I'm concerned, vamps went down the
drain with the market in 1929."

Negri's attitude to the genre was best illustrated by her witty film

Woman of the World, produced in 1925 when she was at the peak of her acclaim. It was a lighthearted poke at the pretense of vamps and a sly tweak at Middle American naïveté. First we were greeted by Negri, the cosmopolitan countess who only a week earlier was tattooed with her lover's crest. Now he is dallying with another woman, which the titles tells us is only "a moment's diversion—a woman of the world should understand." But she doesn't and so runs off to the other side of the world—to rural Maple Valley in the American Midwest. There the country bumpkins stare, gossip, and elect her Queen of the Bazaar; for 25 cents anyone can step up to her booth and "talk to a real countess." But Granger, the town's stern law-and-order councilman, views her less congenially. While he considers her morally indecent, he is falling in love with her. Fearing his emotions, he runs her out of town, but not before Negri, worldly enough to know his heart, also flares up at his unjust persecution. Grabbing a bullwhip, she confronts him in front of the other councilmen, lashing Granger's face with the whip, and he—humbled in a comic recall of the vamp's masochistic prey—shivers with pain, passion, and delight. In the next scene the couple marry, and we have their supreme concessions: The rigid law officer offers a cigarette to the bride he once almost arrested for smoking, and the woman of the world gracefully and happily slips into the role of Maple Valley housewife. At heart she is—Hollywood shows us—Everywoman.

Overcaricaturized and corn-fed, *Woman of the World* appeased all moral camps and gave its star an opportunity to display herself once more as a warm comedienne, capable of self-mockery and droll comedy. Despite garish outfits emphasizing her stocky Rubensesque figure and a severely cropped bob, she projects a surprising pre-Mae West Mother Earth, as with eyelids lowered and mouth pursed, she notes her hayseed friends with wry amusement. No doubt Negri spoofing the vamp did much to encourage that creature's demise.

Cleverly Negri realized that displaying her versatility as an actress not only increased her own satisfaction with her work, but also endeared her to her public, enhancing her stardom and longevity. Certainly *Hotel Imperial* was one of her least glamorous and best-regarded films. Directed in 1927 by Mauritz Stiller (the man who discovered Garbo), Negri played a grimy Austrian chambermaid who, in a hotel taken over by the Russians during the war, submits to a Russian general's advances to shield a countryman.

The film is embarassing in its abusive treatment of the maid. Believing that she has also slept with the hero, the general explodes: "He can have you, but not in the clothes I paid for." Ripping off her gown and humbling her in front of hundreds of partying Russian officers, he hurls his last, most devastating insult at her: "You want to be a servant—then down on your knees where I found you." Whereupon he throws cigarette butts and garbage at her feet.

The effect is brutal. Stiller makes his point with unabashed and revealing glee. Having brought Garbo with him from Sweden, insisting that she receive a movie contract, too, he was responsible for her celebrity and reportedly fell entirely in love with her. But with fame, she had turned to John Gilbert and shut Stiller out of her life. When he died in 1928, friends dramatically attributed it to a broken heart. Was the convincing hostility he brought down on Negri's character born—like the general's—of the bitterness or rejection?

Furthermore, Stiller attributes remarkable power to the girl he humbles. Like Talmadge in *The Woman Disputed*, Negri's physical desirability controls the fate of a man (and a nation), enabling her to convince the general that the hero, who lacks an identity card, is no threat.

If Negri as a chambermaid could embody such subtle sexual powers, perhaps even so humble a role contributed to her myth as a *femme fatale*. Yet very probably her private life influenced her legend as much, if not more, than her screen portrayals. Wrote scenarist Frances Marion in her memoirs, *Off with Their Heads!*: "Young men talked about her like amateur poets, while elderly gents hied themselves to Max Factor's and were fitted for toupees. Such was the devastating effect on our males when La Negri descended upon Hollywood."[12]

By the time of her arrival Negri had already divorced one Count Dambski. Alleged love affairs with both Chaplin and Valentino, photos of her grieving at Valentino's funeral in 1926, stories of her vast jewelry collection and the Roman plunge in her living room inflamed audiences and perhaps confused her screen image with her personality. In addition, Negri herself flaunted her exotic influence: "I invented red toenails, I invented turbans, I invented boots. I wore boots in

Poland, it was so cold. So I wore them in Hollywood," she explained to the New York *Times* in 1970.

Valiantly struggling against exploitation by the Hollywood system, Negri suffered too from the pressures of stardom and of being a woman in a world where youth, money, and that shopworn you're-as-good-as-your-last-picture credo prevailed. Marriage to a money-grubbing deposed Georgian prince, Serge Mdivani, brought temporary retirement —and devastation. Serge squandered and mishandled the stupendous fortune she had earned in Hollywood. The stock market crashed. The marriage shattered. A short bout with alcohol incapacitated. Yet Negri triumphed over these grave setbacks, pulled herself together, and returned to work whenever roles interested her. And wherever they were offered. But her reign had ended. In 1930, at thirty-one, Pola Negri was indeed a legend; but as far as the industry in America was concerned, she was well past her prime.

She was, however, in good company. Mae Murray amassed a similar fortune and a strong popular following, then retired to make an unhappy marriage with Serge Mdivani's dilettante brother David. Later, on returning to Hollywood to work, she discovered that Louis B. Mayer had never forgiven her for breaking her MGM contract after *Valencia*. Mayer blackballed her, and no studio, not even an independent, would give her work.

Gloria Swanson, once the screen's reigning star, also overstayed her welcome. Although her singing voice was colorful and operatic, her shrill speech in such early talkies as *Music in the Air* (1934) contributed as much to her demise as the fact that she, too, was no longer an ingenue; she too had been overexposed. Swanson, who put up the money for, yet suppressed, her last silent, Von Stroheim's *Queen Kelly*, because she loathed it and thought it wouldn't get past the censors, is today, at seventy-five, a woman of great stamina and candor. Yet she too was vulnerable to exploitation during her most potent years.

"I never thought I spent any of my money foolishly," she said in 1971. "But I did have hundreds of thousands of dollars stolen from me because I was so innocent. I didn't even know what a homosexual was until I was 30. Can you imagine in Hollywood? I had a secretary who got $90,000 once, but that was just peanuts compared to some of the others."[13]

In 1950 she told the *Saturday Evening Post:*

The mess I made of marriage was all my fault. I can smell the character of a woman when she enters the room, but I have the world's worst judgment in men. Maybe the odds were against me. When I was young, no man my age made enough money to support me in the style expected of me. There's no sense kidding myself. I love all the pomp and luxury and style. When I die, my epitaph should read: *She Paid the Bills*. That's the story of my private life.

Is it not, also, a bizarre reversal? The Chorus Girl had come out of the line to become the Leading Lady; the fickle lover—the callous gold digger—was the industry.

7

THE LOVE PARADE LIMPS ALONG
starring glyn, lubitsch and a cast of
thousands, from a scenario by de mille

Had the war, the vote, short skirts, and a supposition of equality banished romance? Elinor Glyn thought so. What the world needed now, she felt, was great love, noble and aristocratic. She tapped a hidden vein and came up with pure gold.

For the Jazz Age soul may have been proletarian, but its spirit promised tomorrow's wealth and romance. Audiences, in their installment-bought sophistication, were tiring not only of De Mille—who at least gave them extravagantly mounted productions—but also of his imitators. Lackluster attempts like *Hairpins* (1920), in which Enid Bennett played yet another slovenly wife, taxed the screen. In *The Primitive Lover* (1922) Constance Talmadge's man won her obedience and respect by treating her "like a squaw" with a kidnapping and a good spanking. Then Pauline Frederick and Lou Tellegin in *Let Not Man Put Asunder* (1924) played a divorced couple who, after brief flings with other partners, reconciled. Dozens of similar photoplays followed.

Combating the tendency of De Mille and his disciples to milk farce from what might have been romance (or even drama) was a responsibility Glyn undertook almost single-handedly. The British novelist took the opposite tack, spinning romance out of farce—or what today appears like it. She had, however, in common with De Mille a devout, if unconscious, adherence to the Wildean epigram that style, not sincerity, was the foremost virtue.

Glyn had created a small sensation when *Three Weeks*, her florid novel of passion and perfect, if adulterous, love, was published in 1907. In that and other novels like *Beyond the Rocks, His Hour, The Career of Katherine Bush*; in treatises like *The Philosophy of Love*; and in stories like *It* she had won a certain reputation which put her in a unique position: By 1920—having endured an unhappy marriage and three other liaisons of some consequence—Elinor Glyn, despite the fact that she was fifty-six and of another era and culture, had become the nation's arbiter of love, our directrice of feminine *affaires de coeur*.

Yet her subject matter was as concerned with deportment and modern manners (*ergo*, style) as it was with passion, and she most often stressed aristocratic lineage and glorified the nobility of sacrifice. Sex became secondary to magnetism (*It*). Women, she advised, ought to remain mysterious and elusive in order to keep their men interested, even after marriage. Touching was a special consideration for loved ones (recall Bow in *It*); to touch too often not only took away the "thrills," but descended into cheap pawing. As silly as some of her rhetoric sounds, Glyn was so popular that she supplemented her written counsel with cross-country lecture tours.

Perhaps her usefulness was in providing a safe span between turn-of-the-century innocence and a modern world in which men and women dealt with each other not only as creatures of fancy, but as friends, business acquaintances, and potential sex partners; however, the romantic notions that pervade her creations seem laughably escapist, appallingly indirect, and, most important, sexually binding ideals that limited rather than freed women for meaningful experience. The public, always associating her with *Three Weeks*, considered her something of a revolutionary, though. And Hollywood bought her confections, packaged them prettily for mass consumption, and sent them into movie houses from coast to coast.

Her first film, written especially for the screen, was *The Great Moment* (1920), which starred Gloria Swanson as a British aristocrat who falls in love with a rugged Westerner. He plies her with whiskey, unleashing her wild streak of gypsy blood (Mother was a Russian gypsy). Rescued by Daddy, she becomes engaged to a millionaire who throws lavish parties at which she, in her misery, repeatedly makes a spectacle of herself. But the commoner turns up, they are united in love, and he surprises her with the fact that he has become wealthy.

Beyond the Rocks (1922) again starred Swanson as an innocent aristocrat. Married to a vulgar millionaire, she falls in love with a dashing young man of her own class (Valentino as Lord Bracondale); but eventually her honor prevails, and she breaks off the relationship.

Three Weeks (1924), like the novel seventeen years before, received much notoriety, being the story of a beautiful but unhappily married queen (Aileen Pringle) who shares three weeks of adulterous bliss with a young man (Conrad Nagel), then dutifully returns to her evil husband; eventually she bears her lover's son but dies at the hands of the maniacal king. Then *His Hour* (1924) had John Gilbert and the regal Aileen Pringle enacting a love story set at the Russian imperial court. *Man and Maid* (1925) was different in that it dealt with a poor typist who marries a rich hero, but *Love's Blindness* (1925) reverted to Glyn's preoccupation with aristocratic lineage. *Ritzy* (1927), a ridiculous farce, concerned a girl combing Paris for a duke, and a duke—in love with her—parading as a commoner to teach her a lesson.

Quite understandably, Glyn's best and most successful films were her last two, *It* (1927) and *Red Hair* (1928)—both about fiery working girls who experience upward mobility (with well-to-do commoners) via their wit, charm, and pride. These films, with Bow as their leading lady, flaunted a modernity of spirit and a modicum of common sense lacking in Glyn's past achievements. They even featured the author herself in cameo appearances which allow us a brief glimpse of the imperious dowager at her most powerful.

Samuel Goldwyn, who once claimed that a history of films would not be complete without a portion being devoted to Glyn's contributions, also wrote, "Elinor Glyn's name is synonymous with the discovery of sex appeal in the cinema."[1] What more perfectly timed grist could the industry's fantasy mill have asked for? Providing monarchy for the masses and a delicate restraining hand on the hard-and-fast twenties, the Glyn heroine was a prisoner of her sex and of the bedtime stories handed down to girl-children for centuries. To the twenties' female working out her own confusion regarding new opportunities and old taboos, this escapist dream, the passive-female equivalent of the Fairbanks swashbucker, offered comfort, even relief. In addition, Glyn's manor-bred maidens were human enough—they had love problems, too, and invariably unhappy marriages. Their indiscretions, moreover, could be forgiven as divine errors; their honorable sacrifices as the painful burden of duty.

Glyn's common women of her Bow Phase fared even better. As aware of the money they didn't have as her aristocrats were oblivious to their wealth, these girls adventured, too, but on familiar territory. Never before had a manicurist been quite so glamorous. Or a saleslady.

Stumbling into splendid (if temporary) affairs, Glyn's women, rich and poor, offered an appealing alternative to the De Mille wives who in constantly being made over or in scheming to make over their husbands, endured less than ideal (and worse, less than noble) situations.

The unique aspect of Glyn's work, however, was her remarkable ability to appear superficially and flamboyantly risqué while actually expounding a conservative philosophy which cautioned against common lust while glorifying honor, loyalty, and silent suffering. The public, as well as the industry, bought these obsessions with a fascination that only a people without royal heritage and very recently removed from Victorianism could exhibit. Soon a variety of sentimental marshmallows dealing with the titled and the wealthy sated the market. Lubitsch, too, would play on the aristocratic theme, but he would counterbalance it with an acerbic wit and absolute disregard for sentiment.

Whether the bent of these films was romantic or comic, they were jewel cases for the most sophisticated heroines of the screen, Norma Talmadge, Norma Shearer, Florence Vidor, and the omnipresent Swanson.

An aside: Had it not been for the combined influence of De Mille, Glyn, and finally Lubitsch, who legitimized marital farce, farcically aristocratic romance, and then aristocratic farce, many female stars might have avoided comedy altogether. Even as late as 1917, some believed it cheapened an actress and permanently stereotyped her. That year when Mack Sennett proposed molding Gloria Swanson into another Mabel Normand, she indignantly refused. "I hated comedy because I thought it was ruining my chances for dramatic parts,"[2] she later admitted. Earlier, when Chaplin rejected her for a role, she drew herself up to her full four feet eleven inches and huffed: "Thank you. I think it's vulgar anyway."[3]

William Randolph Hearst agreed. His Cosmopolitan Pictures lavished millions on his mistress Marion Davies' elaborate costume epics, nearly ruining her career. Davies, an awkward dramatic actress at best, who could barely contain her gestures and looked even sillier than she felt in the gaudy period pieces Hearst hoped would dazzle critics and audiences, did have, however, a supreme gift for whimsy and pantomime and an unerring sense of timing. She was a talented mimic and an endearing, spontaneous comedienne. Although she was restricted by her mentor, such fine Vidor films as *Show People* (1928) and *The Patsy* (1928) give every indication that without Hearst Marion Davies might have been a truly great comic star.

Appropriately enough, society comedy in the twenties would earn a new respectability. In the hands of Ernst Lubitsch more than either of his colleagues, it would become a deft, searing, and uproarious indictment of human foibles. Yet in his handling of sex, Lubitsch, like Von Stroheim, would be direct, and while as psychologically astute, he would emphasize not the perversity, but the light and human side. It would be his special mark, his "Lubitsch touch." He would also allow his screen heroines a degree of sexual freedom they had never known before. But this, too, would have its price.

Ernst Lubitsch began his theatrical career as a ham actor in German music halls, cabarets, and vaudeville. By 1918, having already directed a number of short comedies, he teamed up with the then-unknown Pola Negri to make *The Eyes of the Mummy Ma*, an exotic love story whose murky expressionistic technique prompted Berlin critics to hail it as the first artistic German film. With Negri he brought to life *The Loves of Carmen* (1918) and *Madame du Barry* (1919) which established both their reputations in Europe and America. He completed a number of projects including *The Oyster Princess* and *The Doll* (1919); *Romeo and Juliet in the Snow*, *Sumurun* (with Negri), *Anna Boleyn* (1920); *The Mountain Cat*, *The Wild Cat*, *The Wife of Pharaoh*, and *The Flame* (1923—all with Negri) before arriving in the United States to work with Mary Pickford at her invitation.

The working relationship floundered. As much as he admired Pickford, Lubitsch's predilection was for strong characters and films stressing sexual and psychological interrelationships. He admired *Broken Blossoms* and De Mille's *Forbidden Fruit*. Von Stroheim intrigued him. Chaplin's *A Woman of Paris* would later profoundly influence the body of his work. After seeing *Foolish Wives* in 1922, Lubitsch, echoing Griffith two years before him, commented, "The American moviegoing public has the mind of a 12-year-old child: it must have life as it isn't. That's the only handicap of the American screen; you have everything else."[4] Yet if he thought he'd change that mind by starting with Little Mary, he was mistaken. She immediately rejected his first-choice project—*Faust* (which he must have proposed with a sly sense of humor)—and they settled on *Rosita*, about a nineteenth-century Spanish street singer who is reluctant to become mistress to the king. Reviews were kind, audiences showed interest; but Mary fled back to her waifs, and Lubitsch, relieved, went on to explore his own sensibilities regarding women, sex, and love.

But first, as Herman Weinberg in his excellent study *The Lubitsch Touch* points out, he saw *A Woman of Paris* (1923). Chaplin did not appear in this film, and its stark, unrelieved drama startlingly counterpoints his major comic efforts.

Admirable in its controlled handling of a melodramatic situation, *A Woman of Paris* unsparingly carved a cruel destiny for Marie, a woman whose insecurities and emotional paralysis blight her life and that of her lover. Chaplin kept a cool distance but at the same time he stripped her of a very real and unsentimental womanliness, a softness. In view of his own penchant for nymphets and very young girls, he may have been uncomfortable with an adult female protagonist in a feature unrelieved by laughter. For Chaplin's proclivity was not unlike Griffith's, although he was less discreet in avoiding scandal and shotgun marriages: His first wife, Mildred Harris, was sixteen and pregnant when they married in 1918 (Chaplin was then twenty-nine). Ironically Lita Grey, his second wife, was called Lolita long before Nabokov's novel was published. She was seven when they met (according to Kenneth Anger in *Hollywood Babylon*), fourteen when they dated, barely sixteen and very pregnant when they married in 1924. Both unions ended quickly, with large divorce settlements and much bitterness, especially on the part of Lita Grey and her mother, both vicious in their court testimonies regarding the comedian's sexual preferences.

Whatever his personal reasons for remaining aloof from or uncomfortable with her, Chaplin somehow made of Edna Purviance's Marie a dreary matron sapped of all vitality. From her first moment of indecision, when she telephones her lover from the railway station, receives a hurried response of "One minute—" but hangs up and admits defeat before investigating the situation, Chaplin telegraphs that he is stacking his cards. No woman in love and in the midst of leaving her family and her home at her beau's urging would be so lethargic. Since all future action hinges on that telephone call—or "fate," as Chaplin would have us believe—this initial motivational error invalidates all that follows.

A Woman of Paris, however, was innovative enough to stir Lubitsch to a new filmic and psychological consciousness. What absorbed him here was Chaplin's understatement and his utilization of telling detail to further plot and fill out characters. When Revel goes to Marie's dresser and pulls out one of his handkerchiefs, we are aware of their affair. When John sees Marie in Paris, he feels the silk of her slip, and his eyes move across the opulence of her apartment; he, too—word-lessly—comprehends her situation. Gestures rather than exposition, nuances rather than clumsy titles or overwritten situations, indicate relationships. Lubitsch responded to the maturity of these revelations and adopted them for his own. Only he applied them differently, utilizing comedy rather than drama, lively aggressive females rather than retiring ones.

Herman Weinberg notes:

. . . In America, with its taboos and repressions, its surface puritanism, he became facetious on the subject and decided to make American audiences laugh at something they took so seriously. Actually, there were two American fetishes he satirized—sex and money. Like those Restoration wits and gallants, Congreve et al., Lubitsch was almost as obsessed with money as he was of sex, as a fact of life.[5]

Until 1924, De Mille and Glyn had held center stage in portraying sex among the upper classes—he with his colorful plots in which temporary perfidy rejuvenated sloppy wives; she with her chaste romanticism as passive women suffered indiscretions played with passion, starry-eyed, and opted for honor. Lubitsch would have none of this. He utilized marital themes similar to De Mille's and picked up on Glyn's preoccupation with high society, its poses and manners. Yet in an era where surface glitter concealed solid propriety, he was irreverently scandalous. Veiling male-female role reversals in laughter, couching adulterous intent in civility and wit, he slipped through the censors and gifted audiences with pictures in which women were finally able to express their libidinous thoughts—and sometimes even act on them—without paying the usual painful penalties of banishment or death.

The Marriage Circle initiated this syndrome. It was 1924 when Lubitsch created his first ribald comedy of sexual manners in which a bored and neglected wife wreaks havoc with her best friend's ideal marriage, then drives happily off into the sunset with a new suitor, a snappy auto, and the blush of youth and money still on her cheek. The films which followed would toy with and elaborate on the theme of the dominant, triumphant woman: *Three Women* (1924), *Forbidden Paradise* (1924), *Kiss Me Again* (1925), and *So This Is Paris.*

Lubitsch's women in the silent era were indeed aggressive, as Weinberg points out. They were rarely sentimental and certainly not moral in the traditional sense. For a Jazz Age consciousness, his treatment seemed quite avant-garde, and perhaps just what was needed for a new, healthy perspective on sex. For coloring public sanctimony was a flagrant fascination with the subject.

In 1926 the New York *Evening Graphic*, running the divorce story of Frances "Peaches" Heenan and Edward West "Daddy" Browning with Peaches' confession on one page and Daddy's on the one opposite, so outraged the Society for the Suppression of Vice that the tabloid's editors were arrested. But the public, for all its mock horror, lapped up the affair of the fifteen-year-old schoolgirl and the fifty-one-year-old New York millionaire who divorced after a three-month courtship and six-month honeymoon. Daddy, claiming they had never consummated their relationship since his child-bride's mother lived with them, sighed that, despite her epilepsylike convulsions, "I want Peaches back. I want to be her father." Peaches, less chivalrous, offered that the convulsions began during their union because Daddy did such things as "growl Woof! Woof! like a bear in my ear." She further stated that he married her to protect himself from an imminent investigation concerning his affection for little girls and concluded with finality: "My dream of love has turned into a hideous revolting nightmare."

Simultaneously, New York's acting mayor, "Holy Joe" McKee, inaugurated a clean-up campaign on Broadway. A play entitled *Sex* opened to good reviews but was quickly shut down when the playwright-star was summoned to stand trial on a morals charge. Mae West, the young woman in question, challenged the court, which could find nothing indecent about the show's plot or dialogue. Still, the assistant district attorney asserted that "her personality, looks, walk, mannerisms, and gestures made the lines and situations suggestive." The arresting officer corroborated this testimony, claiming that she "moved her navel up and down and from right to left." Although under cross-examination, he admitted he did not actually see her navel, but "something in her middle that moved from east to west,"[6]

Mae was convicted and sentenced to ten days in the Welfare Island jail. She served eight, two days off for good behavior.

On June 10, 1927, agents for the Society for the Suppression of Vice, again disregarding constitutional freedoms as well as the public's right to be informed, armed themselves with search-and-seize warrants, invaded a printing plant, and confiscated galleys of the book *The President's Daughter*, which recalled what was perhaps the supreme moral irony of the decade. Written by Nan Britton, mistress of the late President Harding, it related the inflammatory details of their affair, including the revelation that the couple's illegitimate daughter, Elizabeth Ann, born on October 22, 1919, had been conceived in the Senate Office Building chambers. The author, who won a small victory nineteen days later when the case was dismissed and all printing plates were returned to her, was eventually forced to publish the book herself with the aid of the Elizabeth Ann League, a society formed to work for the rights of illegitimate children.

It was into this highly charged atmosphere where speakeasies, racketeers, and dances like the shimmy spoke of "sex" and where sententious censors retorted "filth" that Lubitsch moved, with his amoral confections. Not once did the censors or the public roar— except in laughter. Through his first eleven Hollywood pictures, Lubitsch contributed importantly to maturing America into a new sexual understanding. He also enlarged our vision of woman's role in this provocative new arena.

But not by much. Despite his optimal use of female aggressors who escaped scarlet branding, Lubitsch nevertheless encumbered them with doltish or unattractive characteristics. At once they became less threatening, relinquishing any real challenge to the sociosexual status quo. Consider *The Marriage Circle*, which at first glance appears revolutionary in portraying women acting on their impulses. Mizzi (Marie Prevost), the villainess of the piece who, rebuffed by her own husband, persists in her attempt to seduce Dr. Braun, may be pretty and charming, but she is also sulking, selfish, and deceitful. In attempting to compromise Dr. Braun, callously threatening her best friend's marriage, she reveals herself as a stupid and petty woman ready to destroy anyone who interferes with her plan. Within a comic frame, Mizzi is no more endearing than the vamp. Her interests go no farther than allaying her loneliness; her methods—trickery, groveling, dishonesty, and force—emerge as scheming and pitiful. Because there is so little of Mizzi with which female audiences can identify, she is ultimately useless as a symbol of feminine liberation.

Lubitsch's superficially radical, sexually demanding females weave in and out of his work until *The Love Parade*, in which, as Herman Weinberg emphasizes, "Lubitsch finally sums up all this female dominance and makes a wry comment on it."[7] That wry comment, as might be expected, is also a negative one, which is unfortunate, for the story builds from a game of good-natured innuendo and sexual one-upmanship in which male and female are equally matched. Unquestionably, it helped for that female (Jeanette MacDonald) to be a queen of the make-believe kingdom of Sylvania (queens always have more fun), but as the film opens and playfully pokes fun at convention and social order, hers is an aristocracy bearing little resemblance to Glyn's. The queen is exasperated by her counselors' daily suggestions of a possible husband. She finally meets her match: Maurice Chevalier, a philandering officer she must punish for his scandalous activities. For once, her arrogant self-assurance is equaled by another's. They marry—and with the final "I pronounce you wife—and man," her cheeky independence begins to harden into shrewish thoughtlessness.

Each morning the queen flurries off to her royal duties, and her husband is left to idleness and boredom. Chevalier, stripped of his masculinity, relegated to the position of queen's plaything, decides to leave. First through a series of incidents, he repeatedly humiliates her —which is just what she really wants—and then prepares to depart. Reduced to a humble slave, the queen cries in despair, "I'm going with you. Wherever you go, I'll follow. You can't get rid of me." He has succeeded in taming his royal shrew.

Lubitsch's "wry comment" on female domination turns out to be that familiar cliché about the aggression-emasculation syndrome, nullifying whatever spirit and upfront sexuality he allows his screen women. Furthermore, the queen, so clever at captivating her man, is, on the contrary, so boorish and insensitive after marriage that the situation becomes (like Chaplin's) hopelessly contrived. Chevalier, required to obey, wrings sympathy from the audience, and she—the comically well-meaning fishwife—elicits laughs. Like Mizzi in *The Marriage Circle*, the queen evolves into the villain of the piece.

And Lubitsch's sabotage is done. Two selfish female buffoons, softened by laughter, are the moving spirits of these stories. Undoubtedly Lubitsch supporters would argue that in radicalizing sex and women's roles on- and off-screen, humor was—and still is—essential. They point to Bernard Shaw and mutter: *"If you want to tell people the truth, you'd better make them laugh or they'll kill you."*[8] But that depends on the kind of truth being propagated. Is the aggressive buffoon the only alternative to passive, traditional femininity? The laughter these characters evoke suggests not truth, but Mark Twain's "The secret source of humor is not joy but sorrow; there is no humor in heaven"[9] (which Herman Weinberg thoughtfully included in his prologue on Lubitsch). Sorrow and perhaps fear. For certainly there is little that is funny about Lubitsch's silly females. Nor did Lubitsch think it funny when (in an ironic switch of *The Marriage Circle*) in the thirties his first wife, Irni Kraus, fell in love with his dear friend and screenwriter Hans Kräly. Not only did the marriage disintegrate, but the on-screen civility and cool, cynical humor were absent. Kräly never wrote for Lubitsch again, although their partnership had until that time been sweetly rewarding.

As for the Lubitschean humor as a potent weapon in the struggle toward acceptance of a newly defined female, this, too, has been exaggerated. Dorothy Parker, writing from Spain in 1937, made this observation:

The only group I have ever been affiliated with is that not particularly brave little band that hid its nakedness of heart and mind under the out-of-date garment of a sense of humor. I heard someone say, and so I said it too, that ridicule is the most effective weapon. Well, now I know. I know that there are things that never have been funny, and never will be. And I know that ridicule may be a shield, but it is not a weapon."[10]

For the men making movies in the twenties, ridicule (*ergo*, humor) shielded them and their masculine audiences from inevitable feminine demands for equality, social and otherwise. It squelched a treacherous usurping of their positions in the boudoirs and boardrooms, in the factories and on the campuses. Since the female uprising had to be put down, what a pleasant discovery that humor was at least as effective a method as pious moralizing.

What had been an imperceptible backlash in male social attitudes was creeping toward visibility.

On the eve of the Depression, on July 28, 1929, the New York *Times* held a happy little wake for the bygone flapper:

> Paris, endlessly resourceful in feminine inventions, is busily engaged in sending New York a new siren. . . . With her clothes molded to her figure, her draperies that veil line and curve only to accentuate them, her air of knowing much and saying little, her mysterious allure that is at once the oldest and the newest of feminine accomplishments, she spells the death sentence of the flapper. . . .
>
> Ancient wisdom teaches her to be a confidante, but seldom to confide, to understand rather than to seek to be understood, to charm and delight rather than to demand amusement. Newer, franker ways have abolished any "slave complex" she might have inherited along with that knowledge. . . .
>
> She no longer has to bother about smashing tradition or demonstrating her superiority to convention. In this she is the flappers' debtor, for that young person abolishes surplus clothes and surplus manners with the same enthusiasm she devoted to acquiring gin and cigarettes. By sheer force of violence she established the feminine right to equal representation in such hitherto masculine fields of endeavor as smoking and drinking, swearing, petting, and disturbing the community peace. They need no longer to be the subject of crusades. Indeed the incurable flappers who go on fighting for them are as absurd as the good ladies who still carry the hysteric air of martyrs in the cause of woman's rights.

Sandwiched between descriptions of clothing and makeup, comparisons between tweeds and tulle, the message was clear: Our noisy, demanding women were shutting up and slowing down. How comforting that they should *listen*—and in their "mysterious," relieving silence, seek "to understand rather than seek to be understood."

Even in films there was the reappearance of the old-fashioned girl with turn-of-the-century values. Lillian Gish in *The Wind* (1928) and especially Janet Gaynor in Frank Borzage's *Street Angel* (1928) and *Seventh Heaven* (1927) and in Murnau's *Sunrise* (1927) won surprising acclaim resurrecting this Victorian madonna. Janet even received the industry's first Oscar for her role in *Seventh Heaven*, that of a wide-eyed urchin sprung from the Paris streets by Charles Farrell,

VICTORIANA

ary Pickford in *Poor Little Rich rl* (1917).

Lillian (left) and Dorothy Gish on set of *Remodeling Her Husband* (1920). *Courtesy of Paramount Pictures*

d Wark Griffith
esy of the
um of Modern Art
MA)

ian Gish and Robert Harron
True Heart Susie (1919).
rtesy of Paramount Pictures

Carol Dempster in *Sally of the Sawdust* (1925). *Courtesy of MOMA*

Above, Theda Bara in *Cleopatra* (1917).

Right, Nita Naldi in *The Ten Commandments* (1923). *Courtesy of Paramount Pictures*

THE VAMPS

Pola Negri in *The Cheat* (1923). *Courtesy of Paramount Pictures*

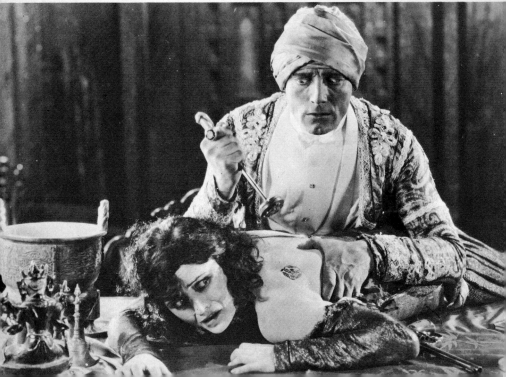

THE FLAPPERS

Colleen Moore *Courtesy of Warner Brothers/United Artists*

Above, Joan Crawford and Conrad Nagel in *Hollywood Revue of 1929. From the MGM release, The Hollywood Revue of 1929,* © *1929, Loew's, Inc.*

Below, Gloria Swanson (left) and Elinor Glyn. *Courtesy of Paramount Pictures*

Clara Bow in *IT* (1927).

Louise Brooks *Courtesy of Paramount Pictures*

WOMEN OF MYSTERY .

Marlene Dietrich in *Blonde Venus* (1932). *Courtesy of Universal Pictures*

Greta Garbo as Queen Christina (1933). *From the MGM release Queen Christina © 1934, Metro-Goldwyn-Mayer Corporation*

... And Wit

Jean Harlow

Mae West and Soo Yong in *Klondike Annie* (1936). *Courtesy of Universal Pictures*

Shirley Temple
Courtesy of 20th Century-Fox

Jane Withers
Courtesy of 20th Century-Fox

DEPRESSION BABIES . . .

Deanna Durbin in *100 Men and a Girl*
1937 *Courtesy of Universal Pictures*

ana Turner in *They Won't Forget*
1937). *Courtesy of Warner Brothers*

... AND BABES

an Blondell in *Gold Diggers of 1933*.
*ourtesy of Warner Brothers / United
rtists*

Ginger Rogers in *Sitting Pretty* (1933).
Courtesy of Universal Pictures

Alice Faye
Courtesy of 20th Century-Fox

THE PINUPS

Rita Hayworth in *Gilda* (1946).
Courtesy of Columbia Pictures

Betty Grable in *Coney Island*
1943, Courtesy of 20th-Century Fox

subsequently cooking, cleaning, and waiting for him to return home from the trenches. She was the first star of any consequence who seemed capable of inheriting the mantle of Pickfordian innocence. Her heroine was the least threatening and most refreshing in a long time. In return for reaffirming its masculine ego, Hollywood would keep her around for a while. Janet Gaynor, with huge doe eyes and a madonna face, would have the distinction of being one of the few stars to survive the transition to talkies.

By 1929 movie theaters had converted almost entirely to sound systems. Technicolor, one more fascination, would bring in audiences despite the Depression. More than 92 percent of the moviegoers were adults paying $2,000,000 daily to America's box offices. And Hollywood, having released over 820 features in 1928, was presenting its women in a light precisely paralleling the avoidance-approach-avoidance tack with which men in life responded to female progress. Upheaval wrought by women had been, if not shattering, then discomforting. The familiar values of a Janet Gaynor comforted like an old-fashioned balm on open wounds.

And in life, as in movies, women were forced to wonder about the contradictions of their partial freedom. Where did it lead? What would they do with it? What *could* they do with it?

Where would their educations take them if men required them to stay home and have babies?

What would a decade of working do for them if their take-home pay barely covered expenses, and employers refused to equalize it with male salaries for similar jobs?

Why should they kiss and pet, smoke and drink, if finally they would be branded cheap and easy? No wonder, as the *Times* pointed out, they retreated into a pose of "mysterious allure." Was this enigmatic suspension the answer to a perplexing no-exit situation?

Was liberation worth anything, after all?

As early as 1922 Zelda Fitzgerald sensed this ambiguity in her essay *Eulogy on the Flapper*: "Women," she noted, "despite the fact that nine out of ten of them go through life with a death-bed air either of snatching-the-last-moment or with martry-resignation, do not die tomorrow—or the next day. They have to live on to any one of many bitter ends. . . ."[11]

She had a point.

One of these bitter ends was the thirties.

THREE

THE THIRTIES—SACRIFICIAL LAMBS
& THE POLITICS OF FANTASY

*And therein lies the wondrous hope
that man has often put in woman: he
hopes to fulfill himself as a being
by carnally possessing a being, but at
the same time confirming his sense of
freedom through the docility of a free
person.*

—SIMONE DE BEAUVOIR,
The Second Sex

8

THE WHOLE TOWN'S TALKING...

but why are they lying to me?

"Silence gives the proper grace to women," Sophocles mused centuries ago in the golden age of Greece. He could not have known that in 1927 Jolson's "Mammy" would shatter the muteness of the silent screen.

Or that in 1929 the stock market would topple; deafening Depression poverty would obliterate the enthusiasm with which women had taken their first tentative steps toward an integrated society.

As prophesied, the Golden Age of Hollywood—and the advent of the talkies—exorcised a fair amount of feminine grace from the screen: Gish, Pickford, Swanson, Banky, Bow faded just as fast as their post-Victorian child-women and flashing flappers were expelled from sitting rooms and salons.

And in their place? "Talkies." Jean Harlow brashly wisecracking. Mae West mutttering, "I like a man who takes his time." Graceful? Not always. But then Sophocles hadn't heard Garbo's "I vant to be alone." Norma Shearer's "A new kind of man—a new kind of life."

And Dietrich falling in love again.

Sound created a new dynamics on the screen. Characters, now vocal, were also more real. Brittle edges fascinated. Exotic, almost effeminate romantic heroes like Valentino, Ramon Novarro, and Richard Barthelmess were shunted aside for the craggy masculinity of Gable, the Irish brogue of Richard Dix, the quiet drawl of Gary Cooper, or the clipped elegance of Cary Grant. Their female counterparts were alert, direct dames or throaty, provocative enigmas. Lingerie salesgirls and hash slingers were on the decline, and not only because few in Depression audiences could afford peignoirs or corned beef; lines like "Draw one, light on the cream," or "Fry two eggs

133

over, hold the bacon" were short on wit and murderous on plot. On the other hand, giving the heroine an assertive job and a telling retort livened up celluloid proceedings.

And so Depression movies portrayed women working by their wits. Or at least by their wit. A curious conglomeration of detectives, spies, con artists, private secretaries, molls, and especially reporters and editors constituted a new genre, and the screen was—yes—graced with some of its breeziest comedies and gutsiest dramas. Unfortunately, if films were to truly reflect the image of women in society, this development ought to have occurred a decade earlier when it was directly relevant. Now it was a belated distortion of the truth of woman's social role. In the name of escapism, films were guilty of extravagant misrepresentations, exuding a sense of well-being to the nation in general and women in particular. In fact, precisely the opposite was true.

Women were the sacrificial lambs of the Depression, but amid the collective pain of the nation's empty bellies, they scarcely felt the knife. Hysteria earmarked those first years. While Broadway offered comic relief with Cole Porter's *Anything Goes* (1934), Jerome Kern's *Roberta* (1933), and George Gershwin's *Girl Crazy* (1930), Tin Pan Alley reflected mass despair, even helplessness in the lush, dreamy ironies of "Lazybones," "Time on My Hands," or "Stormy Weather;" the wail of "Brother, Can You Spare a Dime?"; the fatalism of "Life Is Just a Bowl of Cherries." Marathon dances, trials by endurance, tested how much energy couples could expend for a few extra dollars and free meals. As early as 1928 New York City's Board of Health ordered the "Dance Derby of the Century" at Madison Square Garden closed after 481 hours. Four years later antimarathon legislation was passed in Tacoma, Boston, San Francisco, Los Angeles, Portland (Oregon), Seattle, and Philadelphia; in New York Governor Herbert Lehman signed a bill limiting such dances to eight hours.

In 1930, with the worst of hard times yet to come, woman's position was one of desperation. While more than 10,000,000 women were working, one-fifth of those employed would soon be jobless. By the end of the year the toll approximated 2,000,000, the greatest mortality first those between twenty and twenty-four, then blacks, and finally the foreign-born. Considering that in 1 out of 6 urban families, women were the sole wage earners and that 10 percent of out-of-work females were "heads of families," these facts indicate not just unfortunate necessity, but they stand as a monument to discrimination. Since females were performing the same tasks as men for considerably lower wages, economics alone would have challenged their early removal from the labor force.

Indeed, this backlash against twenties' female accomplishments extended beyond the blue-collar realm. Professional women, whose ranks had doubled, tripled, and quadrupled during the Jazz Age, were now fighting simply to maintain their status quo. By 1940 the number of women chemists had declined, and the ranks of elementary and high school teachers dropped by over 50,000. Schools in the United States and Canada, in order to justify prejudicial dismissal procedures, drafted regulations disqualifying married women from eligibility within their systems and firing single women who married during the term of employment. Thus, the forties' and fifties' Miss Grundy mythology surrounding crusty spinster teachers was laced with truth; certainly any bitterness these women harbored was in response to that patriarchal inhumanity commanding females to choose between bread in their mouths and a man in their beds: Woman's inalienable right to work and eat became less precious in consideration of masculine welfare.

Either this harsh treatment eluded moviemakers, who because of sound and Technicolor experiments were among the last to feel the money pinch, or they expediently ignored it, launching instead a bright new genre—girl reporter.

By 1930 almost 15,000 women were so employed, a figure comparable to that of the ranks of actresses and college graduates in 1920; yet in the next decade only 1,000 more females would be recruited into journalism. Many others would be temporarily laid off, as jobs and wages dwindled and men received preference. Never mind the facts. The milieu was too richly suited to the talkies to bypass on grounds of accuracy.

Hollywood's front-page ladies dressed well, ate well, bowing to neither hard times nor biased hiring practices. And dozens of these films with small plot, character, or career variations were released. Joan Crawford appeared in 1931 (in what was an atypical role for her then) in *Dance, Fools, Dance* as a cub who steps in when the newspaper's ace reporter is murdered. By engaging gangland chief

Clark Gable, she obtains pertinent information to solve the murder and clear the case. Her resourcefulness also wins the love of a wealthy heir who had wrongly dismissed her as a flightly playgirl.

Loretta Young paid her dues in Frank Capra's *Platinum Blonde* as Gallagher, a reporter in more comfortably feminine style, whose chief function it is to moon after the city desk's star, Robert Williams. Williams has been her pal, and not until he runs off with his front-page story—heiress Jean Harlow—does Harlow point out for him Gallagher's obvious attributes. Gallagher mops up after the disastrous Williams-Harlow marriage, helps unblock him as a playwright (all but *writes* his play for him), but only when she's serving up bacon and eggs does love triumph.

Too passive and ethereally lovely to do justice to her reportorial assignment, Loretta Young's martyr weakened the comedy of *Platinum Blonde*. A less glamorous and more utilitarian choice, Jean Arthur adeptly handled the role of feisty editor-reporter. Although she had been acting in silent films since 1923, playing one interchangeable sweet young thing after another, sound gave Arthur a definite advantage since her unique, scratchy little voice lent definition and credibility to her casting as an updated Pickfordian dynamo. As early as 1930 she appeared as a counterspy in William Wellman's *Young Eagles*, and by 1934 and *Whirlpool* she had given the first of her many captivating performances as the nosy go-getter who smokescreens her astuteness in a cloud of dizzy, offhand conversation.

Arthur's most famous films, *Mr. Deeds Goes to Town* and *Mr. Smith Goes to Washington*, both directed by Frank Capra, amplified this image and enhanced it with the wacky comic touch Capra did so well. In *Deeds* (1936), Arthur, an aggressive sob sister, cops an exclusive series of stories about hayseed millionaire Gary Cooper by posing as a naïve country girl in the big city; complications arise when they fall in love and Arthur must reveal she's written the pieces painting him an idealistic boob. Then in *Mr. Smith* (1939), a variation on *Deeds*, she's the secretary who cleverly guides another country boy, Senator James Stewart, to expose the corrupt graftmongers. Well suited to these roles, Arthur, small and breathy, impressed as a warm little bird; her sexlessness minimized predatory assumptions, but her concealed strength allowed her freedom of activity. Her snoop carried the seeds of the matriarchal myth—the myth of the diminutive mother hen who arranged men's lives, was responsible for their successes, thrived as the woman behind their democratic thrones. And of course basked in *their* worldly accomplishments, not her own.

With World War II this myth would find nourishment in the inescapable reality that females *had* to keep families together and industry moving. It would climax in a monstrous condemnation of the aggressive woman at the hands of Philip Wylie who in *Generation of Vipers* (1942) would warn of "Momism" as the dire consequence of womanpower. But it was a myth, smelling of fear, even in the Depression era.

However, *Fortune* magazine, in a dishonest attempt to pass over the despairing state of the female labor force, included in its August, 1935, issue devoted to "Women in Business" an editorial applauding not executive business positions, but "the humbler roles" occupied by females, roles which so perfectly complemented man's creative ability. Laboring over the importance of female precision, the editor also noted:

> In the field of the office it was not the *work* of the home which was carried over into the industrial setting, but the *setting* of the home which was carried over to the industrial work. . . .
>
> Many of the best-paid secretaries are so literally their employers' daytime wives that their employers' death would mean painful widowhood. . . .
>
> The American office, to a great part of its female workers, is not a career but a device by which a woman works her own way through maidenhood.

So perfectly does this describe Jean Arthur's image as secretary-editor-general-factotum-busybody; perfectly, too, it prescribes the invariable denouement of her films. Inevitably, she gets her man—the same man she has mothered, smothered, and achieved victory for—and crosses the golden threshold from maiden to matron.

Granted, her image was that of a strong lady. Strong, but meddlesome, bossy. A setup for Momism. In addition, if one considers that by 1935 women's previously-meager wages had dropped 20 percent, that in New York City alone females who five years earlier were earning $35 to $60 weekly wages now scraped by with $25 to $35, Hollywood compounded its disservice by insulating feminine minds with a false, even obscene sense of well-being, suggesting possibilities which life, for the most part, did not. Perhaps because the Depression was treating its women so cruelly, the screen could afford to offer comfort in some small way. And constructive escapism, the kind Jean Arthur provided, is certainly not the worst of all evils.

Yet escapism it was. Although her light touch was apt for this image, the genre was not reserved to Jean Arthur alone. Bette Davis, during the interim period between her apprenticeship as docile ingenue (*Bad Sister*, 1931; *Way Back Home*, 1932) and her emergence as a self-centered vulture (*Of Human Bondage*, 1934; *Bordertown* and *Dangerous*, 1935; *Jezebel*, 1938) created a number of career-girl roles. A stenographer in *Three on a Match* (1932), political campaigner in *Dark Horse* (1932), copywriter in *Housewife* (1934), assistant to an insurance probator in *Jimmy the Gent* (1934), and underworld bookkeeper who double-crosses the mob for the government in *Special Agent* (1934), she—by the dramatic intensity of her performances—was much more a threat as a workingwoman. First, she was sexy. Second, she was dead serious about herself. These qualities, combined with an imposing, unadorned self-awareness, created an alarmingly competent creature who inevitably encountered difficulty in her male-female relationships.

In *Front Page Woman* (1935) Davis is a reporter for a city newspaper, whose job simply provides the bone of contention between her and fiancé George Brent, star reporter for a rival paper. Brent snickers at her reportorial attempts—"women are bum newspaperwomen," he insists—and Davis refuses to marry him until he retracts. In grand style she proves herself by clearing an innocent man of a murder charge and getting a confession from the killer. Her *real* satisfaction comes, though, when Brent grudgingly admits that women reporters are not always inept.

Such distortion of emphasis is as typical of Hollywood as the flamboyantly romanticized lady journalists. But in reality, not only were the pickings slim for females entering the profession, but very few scaled the journalistic heights to achieve the respectability and glamor of a writer like Adela Rogers St. John or talented photojournalist Margaret Bourke-White whose photo of Fort Peck Dam graced the first *Life* cover in 1936. In 1935, the same year *Front Page Woman* and other sassy-smart lady-editor stories slicked across the screen, the Assembly of the League of Nations pleaded in an official statement to the International Labor Organization for "equality under labor legislation—and that it will, in the first place, examine the question of legislation which effects discriminations, some of which may be detrimental to women's right to work."[1] In a destitute economy, woman's plight was the most destitute of all. Life was a test of strength. Females required resilience to survive, which in some backhanded way fed right into, and was supported by, a number of films related to the reporter-working-girl genre.

Detective films. Undercover agents. Spies. Con artists. Insignificant in the Hollywood scheme of things where lavish biographies and musicals reigned supreme, these B movies, as plentiful as the variations on the reporter-editor theme, allowed women to act positively; they *created* the action rather than simply languish as helpless victims, well-lubricated vessels, or family stabilizers.

In 1930 Carolyn Keene's *Nancy Drew* mystery series began publication, its heroine a smart, right-thinking teen-ager who drove around in a beat-up blue coupé and was bailed out of treacherous predicaments by two girlfriends, Bess and George(!). The male characters (her lawyer father and boyfriend) were peripheral and flimsily sketched. Quickly, these books (which succeeded the *Hardy Boys* series by three years), became staples for preteen girls who today still admire the blond adventuress' daring and relative freedom. In 1932 Margaret Sutton created the *Judy Bolton* series, about a more conservative auburn-haired amateur sleuth, who provided another escapist solution to restraints now clamping down on feminine destinies. Like the books, adventuress-movies captivated public interest. Although most were not of the sterling technical and comic quality of the Arthur-Capra epics, certain bravado qualities redeemed them. Motivated by personal curiosity or obligation, women acted on their *own* impulses—through most of the film at least. In *Miss Pinkerton* (1932) Joan Blondell is a nurse investigating a murder on the Gothic estate where she is employed. Myrna Loy's low-keyed elegance and common sense repartee graced *The Thin Man* (1934) and its five sequels; playing detective evolved into a social, amusing romp for the securely married lady, as well as for the floundering husband seeker. In 1938 a number of *Nancy Drew* mysteries were even adapted for the screen, starring Bonita Granville, but they were ground out without thought or style and failed to capture the innocent excitement of the books.

The screen was laden too with female undercover agents. Garbo dabbled in capricious espionage first in *The Mysterious Lady* (1928), then in *Mata Hari* (1931), and finally in Lubitsch's comic delight, *Ninotchka* (1939). Dietrich gave an additional, passionate dimension to the genre in Von Sternberg's *Dishonored* (1932), where her heart ultimately bests her head; unflinchingly, she gives her life for her lover's freedom and is shot down by a firing squad.

Interestingly, espionage agents whose primary affliction was susceptibility to love (which interfered with sleuthing and loyalty) had a harder time of it than the garden-variety con girls. Like detectives and spies, the con girls lived by their wits, were activators rather than reactors, and excelled at steely-nerved calm. But their goals were petty and simple—money. Whether Joan Blondell and James Cagney were fleecing racketeers and lecherous old men in *Blonde Crazy* (1931), Norma Shearer (and in a later version, Joan Crawford) was elegantly setting up a society jewel caper in *The Last of Mrs. Cheyney* (1929), or jewel thief Miriam Hopkins in Lubitsch's *Trouble in Paradise* (1932) was outfoxing mellow professional Herbert Marshall, the stress was hardly on their morality, but on the gambol—and the cleverness of these spunky ladies. Love would regenerate them; at any rate the crime, Robin-Hood fashion, hardly hurt anyone not worth hurting in the first place.

It's unfortunate that Hollywood could not visualize a woman of mental acumen *unless* she was fixing up a mess her man/boss had made, covering a scoop to prove herself to a man, or deftly forging a life of dishonesty. Nevertheless, these females with engaging ingenuity, derring-do, and some confusion of motives, offered refreshing relief from the passive doll-women of the pre-twenties or the peripatetic husband hunters of the Jazz Age.

An important distinction also existed between saucy con girls and vicious predators like Olga Baclanova in Todd Browning's *Freaks* (1932), who turns her charms on a hapless but wealthy circus midget. Or like Glenda Farrell, the merciless landlady in *I Am a Fugitive from a Chain Gang* (1932), who, by reading Paul Muni's mail, discovers his past, blackmails him into marriage, and bleeds him dry while flaunting her decadent life. These females, modern neorealistic heirs to the vamp, antedated the full-blown and bitterly realized Evil Women who would become a staple of late thirties' melodrama.

An entirely different breed were those likable gun molls scattered throughout Depression movies. The cinema's gun moll had moxie, rather than a conscienceless sense of violence. For just as Hollywood

refused to recognize the best in female potential, it rarely acknowledged the worst, which—as the times explicitly depicted—was ripe
for expression.

The rise of the gun moll, and the underworld racketeer story was a
natural. D. W. Griffith had brought a gangster's girl to the screen as
far back as *Intolerance* (1916). Von Sternberg's *Underworld* and *The
Docks of New York* had furthered her development. With Prohibition,
organized crime had become a persistent reality, and because gangster
pictures provided such root-'em-toot-'em action, for once art did reflect
life. But John Dillinger, "Pretty Boy" Floyd, and Al Capone were not
the only public enemies. A good number of women found their place
in the sun of ignominy. Back in 1924 Celia Cooney, "the Bobbed-hair
Bandit," had been captured and sentenced to from ten to twenty years
in prison for committing ten robberies netting her $1,600. In 1931
Winnie Ruth Judd killed two women friends, dismembering them and
shipping them in suitcases to Los Angeles. That same year Mrs. Irene
Schroeder earned notoriety as the first woman to be electrocuted in
Pennsylvania.

Even more sensational was the 1934 shootout in which Bonnie
Parker, with her effeminate lover, Clyde Barrow, was killed by Texas
deputies. The following year, Ma Barker, who had taught her sons
everything they knew about kidnapping, thievery, and murder, was
similarly cut down in a shootout in her Florida hideout. Machine Gun
Kelly, apprehended in 1933, gave credit where it was due—to his wife,
Katherine, an ex-manicurist who goaded him into big-time robbery
and murder, then distributed empty shell casings from his gun as little
mementos.

Depression life created for women a climate in which frustrations
spilled over into deadly aggressions; perhaps female anger even surpassed that of men, since their oppression was more stifling, and it's a
wonder that more women didn't act out frustrations in similar fashion.

Underworld molls would earn equal notoriety in this decade through
screen portrayals, especially the early brash Jean Harlow in *Hell's
Angels* (1930) and in 1931's *The Public Enemy*, *The Secret Six*, and
The Iron Man, but the strength of this image depended on a combination of circumstances. Sound presented the moll as shrill, her man as
gruff, gravelly and "virile." The early thirties' relaxation of the
Production Code (until 1933–34) permitted more than innuendos; it
defined mistress-lover relationship. The money-mad slut wore flimsy,

revealing clothes, was naughty, brazen and street-smart. Glossing over her depravity with the excitement and adventure of her life, as well as with the good looks of the particular actress, films saw Depression hard times as a peculiar vindication for the poor-girl-in-bad-company, whose basic strength was in her loyalty to her hoodlum master.

What it boiled down to was that Hollywood didn't even give unscrupulous women the right to be evil and mercenary without hanging feminine motivation on the old hat of loving servility. At least run-of-the-mill gold diggers like show girls Aline MacMahon and Joan Blondell in *Gold Diggers of 1933* have a fair chance of enjoying life on their own terms. These girls find walking gold mines—and milk them for their own good times, not out of obeisance to a male. Mac-Mahon especially gratifies herself and plunges into life on her own terms, refusing to be a satellite to masculine whim. In fact, she demands that men exist as *her* satellite.

In life female independence fashioned itself from more humanitarian cloth. Proof positive was women's increasing contribution to society: Pauline Sabin in 1929 organized the Women's Organization for Prohibition Reform, one of the most militant groups working for repeal (which was finally won in 1933); Frances Perkins, appointed by President Roosevelt as his Secretary of Labor, was the first female Cabinet member in history; another Roosevelt appointee, Georgia Neese Clark became the first U.S. Treasurer, a post which has since consistently gone to women. In 1931 Jane Addams won the Nobel Peace Prize; the founder of Hull House had devoted more than four decades to working for social justice and improved conditions for women, children, immigrants, and blacks. Where in the thirties' literature of the screen do we see this reflected? Or is a meddlesome Jean Arthur-manipulator the only remotely related candidate?

And where do we see women of the stature of a Pearl Buck, who grew up among missionaries in China and later won the 1931 Pulitzer Prize and 1938 Nobel Prize in Literature for her moving *The Good Earth*? Is white missionary Barbara Stanwyck falling in love with an Oriental in *The Bitter Tea of General Yen* (1933) the best Hollywood could do?

What about women's contributions to aviation? The Wright brothers, Howard Hughes, and Charles Lindbergh were not the only daring young people in flying machines. Harriet Quimby had been the first woman to fly the English Channel in 1912. In 1928 Amelia Earhart flew the Atlantic, then four years later became the first female to perform that feat solo. In March, 1937, she was on a solo around-the-world flight when she and her aircraft vanished. Another aviation innovation occurred in May, 1930, when United Airlines began employing flight stewardesses, much to the distress of the airmen. Until World War II these "Florence Nightingales of the Airways" were required to be registered nurses, and on the unendurably lengthy and turbulence-filled flights, courage and stamina, as well as first aid, were invariably required.

Hollywood, however, ignored such activities, save for a few comical attempts like *Wings in the Dark* (1935) in which blinded pilot Cary Grant invents a new instrument panel enabling him to fly sightless; therefore, he can save aviatrix Myrna Loy, who gets lost returning from a solo New York-Moscow flight. "It's too hard, too dangerous. I wouldn't like to see any woman do it," he warned her. Now, blind, he's better equipped to cope than she, with two good eyes. But since the crash which caused this affliction, neither his panel nor even her love can bring meaning to his life, and after the rescue he plans to fly off into the blue yonder. On the airfield Loy gently collides with him to keep him earthbound. No one is hurt, and the jolt restores his sight.

Another entry into the airborne sweepstakes, Dorothy Arzner's *Christopher Strong* (1933) starred Katharine Hepburn as an aviatrix who finds herself pregnant by one Sir Christopher Strong, unfortunately someone else's faithful husband for twenty years. On a record-altitude flight our otherwise-liberated heroine removes her oxygen mask and commits suicide. Intriguing because it kills two birds with one stone, so to speak, *Christopher Strong* manages to turn a willful, independent woman who has chosen an unusual life-style into a "noble" coward who refuses to compromise her honor. Flying becomes a means of disposal here, and the real issue is that Katharine's Lady Cynthia discards other possibilities such as having the child or an abortion in order to punish herself for this, her first indiscretion. "Courage can conquer love," she writes Sir Christopher. However, perhaps a parachute jump-to-abort would have been preferable, and it's surprising no one at RKO thought of it.

Despite advances in women's rights, the nation in the thirties persisted in a Dark Ages philosophy toward abortion and birth control. In 1937 Margaret Sanger was finally victorious, as the dissemination of birth control information by doctors was legalized. But abortions themselves were still outlawed, although in the Depression thousands of women, unable to feed an extra mouth, underwent illegal operations. The issue was a grave one—and still is—but Hollywood confronted it so rarely and with such clumsy antipathy or hokiness that it might not have bothered at all.

For instance, *Little Man, What Now?* (1934), a curious Depression comedy, starred Margaret Sullavan and Douglass Montgomery as an improverished couple in Germany (a European setting gave license to portray certain uncomfortable truths) who learn to make do despite his hard luck in finding work. At the very beginning of the film, they are seen entering a (German) doctor's office. She is pregnant and wants an abortion—very practical considering the circumstances. Montgomery sympathetically tells the gynecologist's nurse, "Women do have it worse than men, don't they?" But this lady will have none of his pity and plays it for laughs: "I don't know. I'm not a man." Then Margaret leaves the specialist's office, crying, while the good doctor, savior of yet another unborn life, gives solace. "Don't worry. Three can live on the money you make—a hundred and eighty marks a month." With tremendous flexibility, the weeping mother-to-be walks outside and needs only to see a child playing in the puddle to be elated about the blessed event.

Wild embellishments like *Wings in the Dark*, dramatic displays of theatrical honor like *Christopher Strong*, or happily-ever-after nonsense muffling explosively realistic conditions—like *Little Man*—rendered life-art adaptations useless. Hollywood would not permit its films to refine or consolidate the image of women, nor, with its conservatism, would it even attempt to educate or offer females alternatives (other than journalism!). On-screen, woman's potential was sloughed aside, and her only sensible outlet was love.

Just as in the twenties Hollywood's moguls appointed themselves guardians of women's morals, so now did they become wardens of their minds. In the MGM universe so carefully ordered by Louis Mayer and Irving Thalberg women were irrelevant, elegant mannequins or drawing-room fops. This emphasis was no accident, stemming from the producers' own attitudes toward feminine social roles. When Mayer's daughter Irene told him she intended to enroll in college, his reaction, reported Bosley Crowther in Mayer's biography *Hollywood Rajah*, was vehement:

"A daughter of mine go to college?" he [Mayer] scoffed. "Become an *intellectual?*" He flung the word with a sneer. His contempt for that category of people—"intellectuals"—was frequently proclaimed.

Instead he encouraged Irene in the wholesome outdoor pursuits of horseback riding, swimming, and tennis. . . . There were those who strongly suspected that Mayer secretly wished Irene were a boy and consequently tended to treat her with a sort of masculine camaraderie.[2]

Obviously scorning education for women, Mayer would have scorned presenting heroines whose life-styles were determined by their education. In all fairness to him, he occasionally recognized and employed female talent. Ida Koverman was his most influential administrative assistant, and Mabel Walker Willebrandt, after her service as Assistant Attorney General, became one of MGM's top lawyers.

Thalberg's bias was of a different order. A self-educated man, he appreciated culture and higher learning in women, disdaining the earthier, more sexual variety (like Harlow). But even so, he evidently could not regard such women as *people.* Bob Thomas in his study *Thalberg* explains:

Although Thalberg could work in complete harmony with female writers, he seemed incapable of establishing any deep friendships with women. He had known periodic infatuations with Hollywood beauties, and he enjoyed the pleasure of their company on social occasions. But he appeared not to *like* women for themselves. He worked in a world that was intensely masculine, despite his employment of actresses and female writers. The studio world was everything to him, and he was devoted to the men who helped him build and maintain it. . . .

The pleasures Thalberg sought were male pleasures. . . .[3]

Another comment by Thalberg revealing his attitude toward women occurred in a discussion with the Marx Brothers after seeing their *Duck Soup.* Advising the brothers to interweave romance even if it meant sacrificing laughs, he observed, "Men like your comedy, but women don't. They don't have as much sense of humor. So we'll give women a romance to become interested in."[4]

It would have been useless to note, as Germaine Greer did in *The Female Eunuch*, that women through history *had* to have a sense of humor to survive not just men's jokes, but their more serious attempts at defining females. Or to point out that few women became screen comedians, first because the universally held notion was that a woman stooping to burlesque and slapstick was stigmatized as unfeminine, and second because fewer women had the years of vaudeville exposure in which to perfect their timing and image. When finally they did so, they had passed the age of being useful to Hollywood as anything more than a parody of female deficiencies like Marie Dressler and Polly Moran.

Nevertheless, if one assumes that *comediennes* must have a sense of humor to perform successfully, Thalberg, in making this comment, failed to scan his own stable. In 1930 Dressler, her buffoonery intact, outgrossed all other stars, male and female, at the box office. Jean Harlow would display her comic flexibility in roles bringing her tremendous popularity—and audiences' delight. In the past both Mabel Normand and Mary Pickford had been compared with Chaplin.

If anything conclusively proved Thalberg wrong, it was a film that opened in 1933, the same year as *Duck Soup*. *She Done Him Wrong* drew crowds who hardly needed the lure of free dishes or housewares that theater chains were offering to stave off Depression losses. Mae West certainly convinced that women were funny—also very, very bright.

But thirties' films accomplished the paradoxical feat of showing vigorous working gals whose independence was a ruse, a passage to traditional marriage and social success. Most important, by refusing to show existing conditions they packaged a lie insulating females from the facts of their social and economic undermining.

Talkies had indeed opened up new possibilities. Stars were larger than life—and more memorable. Audiences could now mimic accents, as well as appearances. But studios, purporting to ease the anguish of Depression reality, began hawking, not truth, but distortions. Celluloid aphrodisiacs—talking, walking, and comforting a patriarchal society recently emasculated by the dollar devaluation—transformed movies into the politics of fantasy, the great black-and-white opiate for the masses.

And who could combat national pallor more adeptly than the blond bombshells bursting onto the screen?

9

GENTLEMEN PREFER BLONDES
and ladies become 'em

I wish I had a dollar for every bottle of peroxide sold during the thirties. That was the decade when blondes had the most fun, at least on-screen—and angel hair, no longer reserved for Christmas trees, glowed brighter than tinsel atop the heads of Jean Harlow, Mae West, Shirley Temple, Joan Blondell, Ginger Rogers, Alice Faye, Marion Davies, Constance Bennett, Miriam Hopkins, Carole Lombard (and occasionally Dietrich, Irene Dunne, Bette Davis, Stanwyck, Shearer and Crawford). If proof were needed of the power of woman's film image on women in life, the number of platinum heads tells the story.

The transition from golden silence to sound had transformed the blonde. Where prior to 1929 she was the virginal heroine of Gish-Pickford-madonna inspiration, in the early thirties she was the temptress, a silken-white Lilith draped and devastatingly alluring. But as sculptured and sublime as her body appeared, her voice provided a perfect counterpoint in which heaven and earth collided. Brash, brassy, brittle, the sound echoed as worldly-common as the goddess herself was extraordinary. But rather than be an alienating force, this vocal equalizer humanized her. For men, the goddess proved fallible and not as aloof as her image promised. For women, the voice made the image at once humorous, vulgar, and trashy enough, dumb enough to be touchingly real.

With Jean Harlow, this blond deity approached earthly incarnation. But Harlow's career registered the fluctuating regard of the studios and public alike for the sexy "broad" or "dame," terms popularized by talkies' vernacular. Her first starring role, in Howard Hughes' *Hell's Angels* (1930) presented nineteen-year-old Jean as a

147

self-centered, faithless dynamo, dividing her affections between two brothers and then dumping them both for another man. Critics panned her acting, but audiences remembered her "star quality"—the marshmallow hair, sharp features, and uncompromising presence. In the next two years, Harlow rose as the Number One Bad Girl of the screen, making seven more films in which her morals and virtue were unquestionable—unquestionably amiss. *The Secret Six* (1931), *The Iron Man* (1931), *The Public Enemy* (1931), *Goldie* (1931), *Platinum Blonde* (1931), *The Beast of the City* (1932), and *Red-Headed Women* (1932) all fell within this mold, although in *The Secret Six*, as a Depression Dolly of Poverty Row, she eventually cooperates with police after her gangster-boyfriend cold-bloodedly commits murder. Another picture, *Three Wise Girls*, sandwiched in during 1932, strained public credulity by casting her as a naïve small-town gal who falls for a married man.

The most interesting of the above, however, were *Platinum Blonde* and *Red-Headed Woman*, which heralded the direction Harlow's career would take in the next few years. *Platinum Blonde*, an early Capra comedy, though heavy-handed, showed glints of the director's knack for outrageous situations and cast Harlow in the improbable role of hoi-polloi socialite. Later, under MGM's opulent aegis, she would take on other such parts (*Dinner at Eight*, *Saratoga*), and although there was nothing even remotely suggesting class about her either vocally, physically, or in the flashy skimp of her costumes, in an era of economic hardship she made the socialite fantasy accessible—a moneyed lady wearing her vulgarity like a proud, friendly badge on her bosom. This gimmick sold Harlow as a vulnerable commodity— any gal brought up with so much dough acting so crassly had to be either impetuous and rebellious or pitiably stupid. So her behavior was excusable.

Platinum Blonde, however, plowed newer ground, even while it reinforced (with Loretta Young's performance) the career-girl myth. Rather than simply break a man's heart and betray him with another, Harlow's emasculation of her ace-reporter husband challenged not his sexuality, but his role as independent provider. Socialite Harlow views his livelihood and his playwrighting aspirations both as an inconvenience and a blight on leisure-class dilettantism. Indefatigable and insensitive shrew that she is, she strips him of all that has been essential to his self-definition; insisting on setting up house in her parents' mansion, she insults his friends and belittles his work. The final below-the-belt blow occurs when a rival newspaper headline documents their front-page marriage: "I WEAR THE PANTS," SAYS CINDERELLA MAN. In so insisting, he wears out the marriage.

If *Platinum Blonde* gave Harlow the opportunity to hold the purse strings to castration, *Red-Headed Woman* allowed her to use her body to obtain and manipulate those purse strings. First marrying for wealth, she then tries to blackmail and bed her way toward social acceptance by her husband's peers. But one too many indiscretions—with the chauffeur—takes the bloom off her rich man's bud, and not even reconciliation with her husband works now. Thwarted, Harlow shoots him but is later freed. Although her role resembles that of the early vamp, Anita Loos' script is fast and funny; the gold digger's ruthlessness is toned down by comic lines and lighthearted direction, and eventually she skips off scot free to a charmed future as a noble concubine—with a racehorse, a titled lover, and (the same) chauffeur all her very own.

During the early thirties of slackened production codes, Jean Harlow found her métier as a funny, sexy tart whose sensuality heightened crude humor and whose humor gave added depth to her formerly one-dimensional image. In 1932 critics and audiences alike raved at *Red-Headed Woman*'s double wallop, and Bland Johaneson in the New York *Daily Mirror* exulted:

> Filled with laughs and loaded with dynamite, it exposes the males as chumps and convincingly describes what the tired businessman likes. The answer is Harlow. This shapely beauty gives a performance which will amaze you, out-Bowing the famed Bow as an exponent of elemental lure and crude man-baiting technique.

Jean Harlow was to make thirteen more pictures in her brief but glowing career. Her next, *Red Dust* (1932), and then later *China Seas* (1935), both with Clark Gable, were the only ones in which her brazen, tough-minded amoral heroine, having met her match in Gable, pursues him with a shady, if droll, tenacity worthy of her early moll experience. The body of the remainder of her work—*Hold Your Man*, *Bombshell*, *Dinner at Eight*, *The Girl from Missouri*, *Reckless*, *Riffraff*, *Wife Vs. Secretary*, *Suzy*, *Libeled Lady*, *Personal Property*, and *Saratoga*—acquiesced in the new stringency in censorship, presenting Harlow not as shady lady, but as a delectable heroine, often abused, misused, and misled by men, but never relinquishing her feistiness. Now that men's pocket's weren't hurting so much, they could vanquish even the toughest cookie on-screen. When she goes to a reformatory for Gable's crime in *Hold Your Man*, is unjustly accused of scandal after her husband's suicide in *Reckless*, or steals money for her sick husband in *Riffraff*, she is being put in her place for flaunting her sexuality. Nevertheless, her wonderful vulnerability/resiliency and basically appealing cheapness constituted a unique feminine image on film. MGM, the studio which vehemently supported "taste" and "refinement," had unwittingly provided an ideal climate for Harlow's growth, opening up the vistas for her comic and dramatic talents and pulling her out of the B's into an assortment of well-mounted escapist productions, where she took guff but could and did dish it out as well— and in the rawest, most straight-from-the-shoulder manner.

In life Jean Harlow's difficulties were legendary, however, and eerily like her 1933 hit, *Bombshell*, in which she is a leading lady plagued by selfish family, inconstant lovers, and a manipulative press agent. Similarly, Harlow's mother and stepfather controlled and dominated her; her marriage to brilliant scriptwriter Paul Bern collapsed with his suicide and a cryptic note begging her to forgive him because "you understand last night was only a comedy." Informed speculators have suggested as Bern's motives medical reports of his underdeveloped genitalia, as well as alleged impotence and sadistic sexual predilections. Irving Shulman in his controversial biography *Harlow* states even more dramatically that during the marriage, Jean's kidneys were permanently damaged by Bern's beatings; deteriorating over the years, they became diseased—and eventually were responsible for the uremic poisoning that spilled into her system. It was during the production of *Saratoga* that Jean fell fatally ill. Her mother, a Christian Scientist, refused to have her daughter removed to the hospital until her condition had advanced beyond salvation. Jean Harlow died of a cerebral edema on June 7, 1937, at the age of twenty-six.

Her tragic private life contained a double irony. The sexiest woman on the screen who had been so eager for a man who would love her for her mind married one woefully inadequate to her body. Then, that an actress who had been supporting her family in the grand style since she was nineteen, with no interest in her mother's religious beliefs and three marriages behind her, was subject—like a little girl

—to Mommy's will in a life-or-death matter was incredible. For all the living Harlow had packed into her young adulthood, Hollywood stardom and her family's dubiously intentioned pampering had kept her a child rather than a woman determining her own actions. The consequences devastated needlessly.

Yet in her seven lustrous years on screen the image of female sexuality she presented blended glorious physical appeal, earthy vulgarity, and ribald comedy. Only one other bombshell matched her in influence: Mae West. Perhaps even more than Harlow, Mae was responsible for tickling the fancy of Depression audiences with a ribbon of sexual innuendos as irresistible as they were pointed. "I like a man who takes his time," West drawled out of the corner of her wide mouth. "It's not the men in my life, but the life in my men that counts." And "I used to be Snow White, but I drifted." Knowing what the proper intonations of her nasal delivery would do, Mae West heftily swaggered from one costume epic to another, making nine films between 1932 and 1943—a small number, really, but enough to create a lasting legend.

Her second film and first starring role, *She Done Him Wrong*, a 1933 adaptation of her stage success *Diamond Lil*, broke all box-office records and saved Paramount, which had once been the reigning film studio, from bankruptcy. A tepid story of the Bowery in the 1890's and of indomitable, irresistible saloonkeeper Lou who gets involved with bad company but is bailed out by Cary Grant, it contained Westicisms such as "It ain't bad having a girl that all the men are after. It shows I must be pretty good, heh?" and "When women go wrong, men go right after them." But visually and in terms of plot, nothing smoldered; even Mae's embraces were parodies, and with every clinch came an inevitable interruption by a character walking in a door, out a door, through the room. She brought sex to the box office with nary a passionate kiss, yet, as with her play *Sex* in 1926, her frank and challenging delivery alone was enough to get the censors' dander up. When the Hays Office, spurred on to save the nation (with a little help from the Catholic Church and later the Episcopalian Committee on Motion Pictures), organized the Legion of Decency, it was a mere six months after *She Done Him Wrong* premiered—and the pressure groups made no secret that Mae was a chief reason for the Legion's genesis.

The furor to suppress Mae West intrigues even further when one recognizes that in her circus picture *I'm No Angel* and in *Belle of the Nineties* (1934), *Klondike Annie* (1936), *Go West Young Man* (1936), *Every Day's a Holiday* (1937), *My Little Chickadee* (1940), and *The Heat's On* (1943), her last film until the travesty of *Myra Breckinridge* (1970), Mae distills and disguises the same *Done Him Wrong* plot. Whether she's serving drinks in the Yukon, warding off men backstage or in a turn-of-the century saloon, she—the writer of all her scripts, as well as the star—sets up a harmless situation in which appointed admirers are directed to exalt her; in case anyone forgets, we are told how irresistible she is. Then, moving in on a room, benignly, sarcastically, she fends off the chorus, but basks in their love and finally allows individual reinforcement. Says Gilbert Roland in *She Done Him Wrong*: "You're a fine woman, Lou. One of the finest women that ever walked the streets."

And here is the inexplicable: West's presence makes a contrapuntal mockery of her double entendres, exonerating the star from salacious behavior—for audiences, at least. In the mouths of Harlow or Crawford, her delicious provocations might indeed have seemed indecent. But there stood Mae, age forty in 1933, boned and corseted and looking uncomfortably like a turn-of-the-century sausage, barely able to move because her skirt was too tight and heels too high; posturing with pouting mouth and radiating allure with a burlesque of rolling eyes. To point out that then (as well as in *Myra Breckinridge*) she resembled a robust drag queen is nothing new; in 1934 George Davis wrote in *Vanity Fair* that she was "the greatest female impersonator of all time." More recently a TV producer commented, "She's really played a leading man all these years."

This camp quality was Mae's greatest asset—and perhaps her liability, too. As a parody, she didn't take herself seriously; therefore, few others did. Men could laugh good-naturedly at her audacity; it wasn't threatening because Mae was *not* a potential conquest—she was one of the boys, and her banter borrowed from and elevated locker-room sass. For women, she had neither the beauty nor the youth to pose a moral threat on example, and furthermore she deliberately made certain that no dialogue or action would disenchant her female audiences. On the other hand, as the powerhouse, the aggressor, she controlled plots and manipulated males with the deftness of a puppeteer, as dispassionate and calculating as any woman might dream of becoming. Mae herself admitted that she existed as "the woman's ego." It is this aspect of her screen image more than her sardonic sexual cynicism which so aggravated her detractors.

Never before, and never since, has a woman in films been so thoroughly in control of her destiny. First of all, she was usually self-employed and self-supporting. Mae's character adored herself with a passion that didn't leave room for men. They were interchangeable; she could afford the luxury of showering kindness on them but always remained diffident, distant, even if—as in the end of *She Done Him Wrong*—she bows to Cary Grant's charms and they go off together. Her age and self-styled drag queen enervated the sexual aspect of her wit, a wit which nevertheless might have been less consequential had she also been *less* capable of ordering and insulating her own on-screen world. For her boldness—*not* for her innuendo—she was punished.

By the time production began on *Belle of the Nineties*, the Hays Office had stationed a guard on the set, checking out every line and piece of business Mae inserted. After *Klondike Annie*, a picture in which she played the incongruous part of a police fugitive disguised as a Salvation Army missionary, William Randolph Hearst—who had been keeping both a wife and Marion Davies for more than a quarter of a century—began heckling her in the editorials of his thirty-five newspapers. Today these read like foils for her act, but in 1936, when he tagged her a "monster of lubricity," and "a menace to the Sacred Institution of the American Family," finally asking Congress "to do something" about her, his seriousness caught on. The following year she was banned from radio after appearing as Eve on an NBC program opposite Don Ameche (Adam) and Charlie McCarthy-Edgar Bergen (The Snake). "Would you, honey, like to try this apple?" she asked. The censors bit. And she left.

Although her films were tremendous moneymakers (*I'm No Angel* quickly breaking even more box-office records than *She Done Him Wrong*), Paramount, unwilling to support her censorship hassles, dropped Mae's contract in 1938. It was the beginning of the end for her. One picture for Universal and one for Columbia in 1943 followed before she returned to the theater and her nightclub acts. But by the end of the decade Mae had truthfully outlived her usefulness. She had shown the world how to laugh at sex, but as films became more romantic, more dramatic, and modern, her material was old-hat. She had played out every angle of her one-line joke.

Today many hail Mae the First Lady of Liberation on the screen.

While she embodied certain aspects of the strong, independent female, this is a comforting delusion more than a clear-cut reality. It's nice to think that somebody way-back-when represented feminine strength and took up the torch as the shadow play's fem-lib messiah. But Mae West was uncomfortable with her femininity. She girdled and minced and pouted and purred, posturing and gesticulating so that she did in fact mirror the transvestites whom she had studied thoroughly and written about in a 1927 play called *The Drag*. This inhibited her freedom and functional ability in a manner Simone de Beauvoir pinpoints perfectly in *The Second Sex*:

> Costumes and styles are often devoted to cutting off the feminine body from any possible transcendence: Chinese women with bound feet could scarcely walk, the polished fingernails of the Hollywood star deprive her of her hands; high heels, corsets, panniers, farthingales, crinolines were intended less to accentuate the curves of the feminine body than to augment its incapacity. Weighted down with fat, or on the contrary so thin as to forbid all effort, paralyzed by inconvenient clothing and by the rules of propriety—then woman's body seems to man to be his property, his thing.[1]

But the irony is that while all females suffer and starve to some extent for fashion, Mae's was an unnecessarily masochistic kind of extreme vanity which she overworked as her trademark. Veneer may have been all she was about; she rarely let us see her with her hair—or shoes or corset—down. Good business practice, it may have been. But while the image was well served, the human qualities were as constricted as her flesh, and the person underneath must have endured inordinate discomfort.

If, however, Mae presented certain other characteristics of a fem-lib antecedent, she did so with the same nonthreatening, overextended crudeness and relish that embellished Bara's vamp (whom she satirized). In other words, she was all fantasy. Mae controlled her situations too thoroughly just as, with too many artifacts, she controlled her appearance and other characters' opinions. Audiences knew that West would provide a gutsy, robust show. She had balls. But never for one moment would a man take her eccentric character seriously as a *real woman*; never would a woman fantasize about *becoming* Mae

West, though she might well copy her dramatic cartwheel hats and plumes, her boas and diamonds.

Of the two bombshells, Harlow's impact was the happier. She didn't have the West wit or studied style, but she was spontaneously willful, going after the money or man she wanted *with commitment*. Her *desires mattered*. Her context was modern. Her common denominator was the vulgarity of her elegance. When Harlow walked, dressed, or even talked—"You can take your Bostons, Bunker Hills and bloodlines and stuff codfish with them," she tells a stuffy beau in *Bombshell*, "and then you know what you can do with the codfish!"—she freed herself from all inhibitions of passive female upbringing. And she held the trump card, one West had consciously disdained to play in her writing and characterizations. Harlow's ace was her vulnerability. In happy combination with her salty sexuality, this swept her flashy babes right across the credibility gap.

Together, however, the duo wrought havoc with existing notions of femininity. Mae West, firing off vocal salvos with imperious self-assurance, and Jean Harlow, merchandising her physical allure for the masses, transformed the idea of passive feminine sexuality into an aggressive statement of fact. They were the cinema's truly explosive bombshells. Of the blondes, they were the first—and definitely the best.

For Hollywood, seeing a good thing, converted sass to sugar and taught the blonde to dance. Paralleling the Harlow-West phase, a plump well-rounded young gal, who given free rein might also have given West a run for her money, was under contract to Warner Brothers. Later Joan Blondell would even come to resemble Mae West, but Blondell's warmth and earthiness, infinitely more natural, was proportionately more threatening. In her first thirty-two months in Hollywood she made twenty-seven films—Depression musicals such as *Penny Arcade*, *Footlight Parade*, and *Gold Diggers of 1933*, comedy-dramas like *Blonde Crazy*. Blondell usually played an adoring, efficient production secretary (to Cagney's prologue producer in *Footlight Parade*) or employed chorine (*Gold Diggers*). Even when her characters indulged in dubious pursuits—such as impersonating a friend in *Gold Diggers* to extract money from a wealthy snob or conning con men out of ill-gained cash in *Blonde Crazy*—she bared a heart of gold and a sly intelligence which was restricted by the simplistic early-thirties' Warner's story lines. Not as brassy or flashy as Harlow, her versatile image, much like that of Gloria Grahame almost two decades later, nevertheless fit no Hollywood peg, and by the late thirties when those snappy revues had run their course, Blondell was relegated to B movies. Later she took on character roles of blowsy, slovenly boozers and loose women.

Another blond second fiddle in early musicals, Ginger Rogers usually played the sleazy "heavy," the feline trouper waiting to dig her teeth into some other woman's man or show number. In *Gold Diggers of 1933*, she had the dubious distinction of singing "We're in the Money" in pig latin, then attempting to horn in on Aline MacMahon's aging moneybags. But Ginger packed a then-veiled triple punch: She could sing passably; she could dance, eventually, like a dream; and as with Harlow, her pudgy-floozy baby face would open up like an innocent shopgirl sitting on her sensuality. When RKO executives unsuspectingly teamed her up with an ascetic, angular gentleman whose feet floated with the elegance of sapphires, the pair clicked. His unbendable smoothness was haute couture; her puttylike pliability was Everygirl, a scrubbed-up, pre-Tennessee Williams *Baby Doll*. The film was *Flying Down to Rio* (1933); Rogers and Astaire were only second leads. The dance, however, was the carioca. With the release of *Rio*, Depression audiences were cariocaing like crazy and clamoring for more of the ingenuous chic the couple provided. Rogers made ten films with Astaire: *The Gay Divorcee* (in which they introduced the continental), *Roberta*, *Top Hat*, *Follow the Fleet*, *Swing Time*, *Shall We Dance?*, *Carefree*, *The Story of Irene and Vernon Castle*, and *The Barkleys of Broadway*. Leaving behind the chorus bitch, she polished her dancing, twinklingly defended her honor, and made love on screen with beautiful music and breathtaking grace. It was always boy-meets-girl and, after certain foolish interference, boy-dazzles-and-marries-girl. The public went wild. By 1936 Astaire and Rogers were the third-biggest draw at the box office, surpassed only by Shirley Temple and Clark Gable. In 1937 they placed seventh. This coupling was a perfect tonic, a Depression diversion which enchanted with its rich sets, gorgeous chiffony costumes, and lilting romantic numbers like "The Way You Look Tonight" and "They Can't Take That Away from Me." A delicate hint of sex hovered in the air, made all the more intricate by the taut hardness of Astaire flowering under the fleshy blond femininity of Rogers.

The Hays Office couldn't and wouldn't have thought of faulting them. But movies found another vehicle for their blondes which implied sex not in word or action, but in appearance. Cast a blonde in a musical or comedy, make her ever so pouty and sentimental, and the audience will ogle. They'll imagine. They'll get the picture.

Early in the decade musicals had been the vehicles for glorious naïveté. Ruby Keeler had tapped in and out of *42nd Street*, *Gold Diggers of 1933*, *Footlight Parade*, and *Dames*, usually as the ingenue lead opposite Dick Powell. Always the good girl, she was wooden and hollow and, even when immersed in her dance routines, uniquely sexless.

Then songstress Jeanette MacDonald replaced her as the musicals' purest darling, although at first under Lubitsch's sly direction, she displayed promise and sophistication, as well as a lovely voice. But when MGM took over her contract and teamed her up with Nelson Eddy, MacDonald became to the costumed operetta what Keeler was to the time step. Which is unfortunate, for her persona had promised much better. A handsome redhead with fine cheekbones, lovely eyes registering rare humor and intelligence, and a full, sensuous mouth, she might have been guided toward a wide range of dramatic and comic roles (like *San Francisco* in 1936 opposite Gable). Instead her first Eddy pairing, *Naughty Marietta* (1935), and its seven replicas (*Bittersweet*, *Sweethearts*, *New Moon*, *Maytime*, among others) infused the couple's wooing—and her honor—with a cloying, infantile unreality. By 1942 and *I Married an Angel*, these courtships-over-high-C seemed antiquated, and former fans—saturated and more sophisticated—dubbed them "The Iron Butterfly" and "The Singing Capon."

But all that sexlessness would soon be altered.

In 1938, the same year that a Rogers look-alike, a sixteen-year-old blonde named Lana Turner, caused Mickey Rooney's pulse to palpitate more rapidly in *Love Finds Andy Hardy*, Little Miss Alice Faye made the top ten box-office elite. It was the era of the big bands. Teen-agers were learning the big apple and dancing it while Benny Goodman, Artie Shaw, the Dorsey brothers and Harry James' orchestras swung. Youthful canaries Helen O'Connell, Ella Fitzgerald, Billie Holliday, and Marian Hutton and groups such as the Andrews Sisters interpreted popular tunes like "Three Little Fishies" and "A-Tisket, A-Tasket"; after years of Kate Smith's booming radio interpretations, their velvety styles sounded a welcome relief, and the business of jive and swing, which Goodman had first toyed with in 1936, signaled reemerging prosperity. Alice Faye, who had at one time been a band vocalist, began her movie career as an abysmally warmed-over Jean Harlow. Then Darryl Zanuck, the youthful Twentieth Century-Fox tycoon, cleaned up and restyled her image, utilizing her band experience and making her the studio's resident blonde. Faye played romantic leading ladies in a number of late-Thirties' musicals like *King of Burlesque*, *On the Avenue*, *Alexander's Ragtime Band*, *That Night in Rio*, and *The Gang's All Here*, always blubberingly earnest and in love, often crooning in the tropics and heaving her buxom bosom until the minimal plot complications were worked through, sometimes in Technicolor. The burden of her adult ardor—*what's a grown-up lady like you doing mooning 'neath a moon like that?* one wonders—was quickly inherited by Betty Grable in 1940, when Faye's box office began to falter. Twentieth's new golden girlie, Grable played *Down Argentine Way* as the mirror image of her predecessor, although her legs were a bit longer and breasts slimmer. But always offensive was that feeling of stifling maternal warmth, out of kilter with the heroine's aging innocence. Grable was to win fame as World War II's favorite pinup, boosting the boys in the barracks by perching jauntily on their footlockers. Her legs, some say, won the war for the Allies. By then no newcomer as a sex object, Betty had primed for it in these late-thirties' musical marketplaces—marketplaces in which grown women behaved like dewy-eyed ingenues, where puffed-up lips and puffed-out breasts spelled arrested seduction.

And where the tart directness of a Mae West or Jean Harlow had gone soft and saccharine.

10

AH, SWEET MYSTERY OF WOMENHOOD GOES SOUR

garbo, dietrich, davis: a passage to infamy

"The threadbare vocabulary of the serial novels describing woman as a sorceress, an enchantress, fascinating and casting a spell over man, reflects the most ancient and universal myths," writes Simone de Beauvoir in *The Second Sex.* "Woman is dedicated to magic. Alain said that magic is spirit drooping down among things; an action is magical when, instead of being produced by an agent, it emanates from something passive. . . ."[1]

Woman, the passive sex. And on-screen, the most passive women of all cast shadows as mythological Circes. Garbo and Dietrich. Each inscrutable. Each haunting in her embodiment of the yin-yang of opposites. Aloof, yet inviting. Passionate, but impassive. Direct though elusive. Extravagantly beautiful—almost masculine.

Distinctly different from each other, each a fascinating creature of strange and subtle textures, Greta Garbo and Marlene Dietrich shared however that special enduring fame which they gained as enigmatic incarnations of all that is mysterious to man—all that he wants to conquer, subjugate, and destroy. Divinely untouchable, often unworldly, their allure lay in their denial of that humdrum destiny reserved for woman. Rarely did they seek or want love, perhaps because it would be their ruin or demystification. For once a man imposed himself on them, he consumed them.

Greta Garbo had arrived in the United States in 1925 with an MGM contract obtained at the insistence of director Mauritz Stiller. Privately, Louis Mayer thought her legs too heavy, her frame too broad and tall, her face plain and unfashionable. A screen test made by Stiller hinted at an individual quality like no other actress, and on a gamble, MGM's frail producer Thalberg cast her opposite their Valentino-like star Ricardo Cortez in *The Torrent*. Electrified audiences held the film over at the Capitol in New York, unconcerned about the slight plot or well-known male leads. It was Garbo they wanted to see.

Like the twenty-three other films she would make before retiring in 1941, *The Torrent* was a variation on the time-honored theme of the vamp, a stereotype the actress ironically disdained. But because of her own ineffable on-screen fascination, she softened and brought credibility to it. *The Temptress* (1926), *Flesh and the Devil* (1927), *The Single Standard* (1929), and *The Painted Veil* (1934), as well as her two espionage sojourns, *The Mysterious Lady* (1928) and *Mata Hari* (1931), subscribed to this image. As the demimondaine reformed by love in *Anna Christie* (1930) and *Camille* (1936), the lovely young wife cuckolding an older husband (*Wild Orchids* and *The Kiss*, 1929), or the impenetrable woman who, when the ramparts of her heart are ravished by love, is either ruined (*Anna Karenina*, 1935; *Conquest*, 1937) or brought great pain (*Susan Lenox*, 1931; *Grand Hotel*, 1932; *Queen Christina*, 1933), Garbo superbly enlarged the myth.

Her talking films especially brought out the duality of her *femme fatale* character. That husky, accented voice, so private in its utterances, whispered the pain of passion and was almost childlike in its joy. The kaleidoscope of ambiguities that was Garbo defies description, yet what it brought about was the subtle victimization of the siren. First of all, Garbo of the thirties was rarely, if ever, evil; she didn't gobble men up voraciously, as was the vamp's wont on the silent screen. She drew them like magnets in spite of herself. She said no; they said yes—and ultimately they changed her mind:

• In *Susan Lenox, Her Fall and Rise*, because she is forced to submit to advances by her carny boss, lover Clark Gable walks out. After a brief turn as mistress to some powerful men, Garbo—desolate and in love—spends her days following him into the steamy tropics to beg forgiveness.

• In *Grand Hotel*, as an aging ballerina, she wants to be alone until gentleman-thief John Barrymore extracts her love; leaving the hotel, she prepares for their assignation without knowing that he, simultaneously, has been killed while robbing another guest.

• As Ninotchka, the Russian spy, Garbo's resistance to Melvyn

Douglas evaporates after he plies her with capitalistic amour in Paris.

• *Queen Christina* reveals her as the masculine seventeenth-century Swedish queen who, disguised as a man, meets and falls in love with John Gilbert, a Spanish envoy to her court. Despite the protestations of her nation, she abdicates her throne for him, only to discover as their ship readies to sail that he has foolishly got himself killed in a duel.

• And of course, as Anna Karenina she forsakes her child and reputation to run off with persistent Fredric March; when he tires of her, she hurls herself in front of a train.

Whatever the outcome, it was not just a man's breaking down of Garbo's resistance and her total commitment to him afterward which was so extraordinary. Nor was it merely that her streak of honesty, her intelligent self, augmented the challenge the way a woman who holds herself as precious conveys her worth to the male (his desire for possession parallels her own evaluation). We are moved knowing that the extent of her grief will correspond to her reluctance to capitulate. Once she has offered up that rare gift of herself—and loses (by his death, rejection, or forced separation), the gash on the already-open wound of her self deepens.

Garbo excelled at conveying this soulful, hurting fragility, simply because she maintained control, examining with exquisite precision the complexities and minutiae of her emotions. Consequently, on-screen all others paled. When Garbo made love, her partner seemed invisible. Words would stick in her throat fluid and full, but not seeming to be directed toward anyone in particular. It was as if she were caught up on a crest of autoerotic intimacy, a self-caress, with her public as keyhole voyeurs.

Her curious duality served to appease and compel men and women alike. For men, her aloofness made the effort of conquest (*ergo*, her destruction) worthwhile. Indeed, isn't' the man who tames the temptress infinitely virile? Isn't her imprisonment his freedom? For women, she suggested—with her large, awkward grace and andro-gynous qualities—a sense of strength, a quiet self-awareness usually equated with masculinity. Women admired her toughness and were fascinated by her willingness to acknowledge her sensuality, not through clothes or nakedness, but through her voice and eyes and the slackness in her mouth. Hers was an adult passion, quite different, infinitely more real than the flapper winks and vamp basilisk stares.

It consumed, even frightened in its intensity, but also gave great, slow pleasure—the pleasure afforded by a mature, receptive woman. (Nowhere is there a scene of more sensual beauty than that of Garbo, lit by the fire, lying beside lover John Gilbert and nuzzling a bunch of grapes in *Queen Christina*. Or one of more breathtaking ambiguity than that film's end—a lengthy close-up which finally freezes her face in exquisite barrenness.)

One might finally, however, point out that the seesaw was weighted in Hollywood's (rather than woman's) favor. Women the world over might don Garbo berets, pluck their eyebrows to copy her wide forehead and fine penciled wings, chop their hair into straight short Garbo bobs, and summon expressions emulating her sphinxlike impassivity, but inevitably the Garbo character's ephemeral spirit was broken and her bravado punctured. She exuded splendid élan and soul while going down, but her ship always sank. Love was inevitably the vehicle of catastrophe and ruin. (However, she never existed outside of or apart from a love relationship, after her initial diffidence had faded.)

Why, one might ask, was she so well suited to thirties' audiences? What did this timeless creature have in common with the nation's poverty or with the handful of silk-clad ladies pouring tea in upper-class salons? Very subtly Garbo whispered of the best and worst in woman's nature so that ultimately her image haunted but evaded real definition. In *As You Desire Me* (1932), the film version of Pirandello's play about a woman who may or may not be the long-lost wife of the man who is now her lover, she says: "There is nothing in me, nothing of me; take me, take me and make me as you desire me."

Such elasticity explicitly reflects the historical crux of the woman's role just as it explains our attraction to Mysterious Females. After all, how cleverly the trappings of mystery and illusion cloak a vacuum, the embryo of a personality that has never developed—or been allowed to. And how expiating of man to elevate mystery if he is the force which has prevented (in fact, even abhorred) the embryo's development. Or is the answer more his boredom, mystery finally being a relief from ordinariness—the ordinariness of the women he had allowed (or caused) to stultify?

In the hands of Marlene Dietrich, the woman shrouded in mystery would emerge as a creature of stronger definition, neither as pliable nor as otherworldly as her exemplar. Much of what Garbo suggested, Dietrich carried to extremes. She could be more sultry, more masculine. More warmhearted, more deadly. Even her appearance exaggerated the original—wider mouth, more veiled eyes, angular cheekbones, and arched brows. If Garbo whispered, Dietrich surged, and in so doing she brought additional credibility and life to her characters and hence to her image. Yet she and Garbo differed more acutely in that Garbo, until her entrapment in a tragic liaison, acted without consciousness of the men around her and according to her own whims; Dietrich remained from the first —with *The Blue Angel*—the calculating serpent, ever aware of the men, their follies and weaknesses, ever ready to spring. Thus her characters had a greater capacity not only for living, but for castrating. Her denial of her self to men evolved into a game: Who would subjugate whom? Who would crack the whip? Whose will would break first? But whether this was the conflict point of a Dietrich script (*The Blue Angel*, 1930; *Morocco*, 1930; *Dishonored*, 1931; *The Devil Is a Woman*, 1935) or a subtle aside enriching the proceedings (*The Scarlet Empress*, 1934; *Shanghai Express*, 1932), such an aura definitely existed. And it existed more profoundly in the first American films Marlene made under the direction of Josef von Sternberg, an eccentric egoistic director of great visual and dramatic acuity whose perceptions of female psychology in 1930 were painfully accurate. In his autobiography, *Fun in a Chinese Laundry*, Von Sternberg explains:

It is the nature of a woman to be passive, receptive, dependent on male aggression, and capable of enduring pain. In other words, she is not normally outraged by being manipulated; on the contrary, she usually enjoys it. I have plenty of evidence to assume that no woman, as opposed to the male, has ever failed to enjoy this possibly mortifying experience of being reorganized in the course of incarnating my version of her.[2]

When he met Dietrich in Berlin in the late twenties, neither her plumpness nor her poorly photographed appearances in former films deterred Von Sternberg from envisioning the Ideal Woman he could mold on that exquisite bone structure. He ordered her to take off weight, made her up, and rehearsed every glance and inflection she would need as the treacherous but cajoling Lola Lola. He dramatically proved his expertise, and Dietrich's scornful emasculation of the fat and pathetically eager Professor Rath in his German-made *The Blue Angel* brought her fame before the team even began working in America.

Her canonization as the Von Sternberg ideal was completed with their next six films: *Morocco*, *Dishonored*, *Shanghai Express*, *Blonde Venus*, *The Scarlet Empress*, and *The Devil Is a Woman*. Here Von Sternberg's expressionistic lighting and sensitive camera would probe the depths of her marvelous countenance; his ability to create and sustain mood would develop her sexuality. His rudimentary plots, combined with instinct (*i.e.*, his fantasy) about where woman must deny and tease, where she must submit (and who can judge that more cannily than a man?), reinforced her image as Deadly Mystery Woman, so much so that *Vanity Fair* magazine noticed that he had turned her into "a paramount slut." And in order to make her "mortifying experience" more searing, he imbued her with greater strength—witness the tantalizing tension between her and men—so that her ultimate groveling for her lover also symbolized her own humiliation.

Morocco typifies this in its closing shot as Dietrich, shoes in hand, her independence forfeit, struggles through the sand—one of the droves of wretched women in will-less pursuit of her lover.

This formula seemed to be Von Sternberg's talisman. It worked well, if not at the box office (where their last collaborations lay dying), then in the building of the Dietrich legend. And it worked in their personal union as well. Dietrich has always claimed that without Sternie (as he was called in his days as a cutter, before "von" was added by a confused journalist), she would have been nothing. Feeling the lack of guidance on assorted disorganized sets in later years, she would often repeat, when anguished, "Oh, Josef, Jo, where are you? Where are you now when I need you?"

Ironically, however, Von Sternberg himself terminated their alliance. Though Marlene protested loudly, he felt that the symbiotic give-and-take had been long overdrawn; in addition, his prestige and box office had dangerously ebbed. But without his star creation, he faltered (his 1937 *I, Claudius* with Charles Laughton and Merle Oberon showed promise but was never finished; only *The Shanghai Gesture* in 1941 earned distinction). Dietrich, on the other hand, kept active as a star of twenty-nine more films spanning almost three decades, and her nightclub and recording work still draws cults of worshipers.

Except for *Blonde Venus* (1932), in which her few scenes with her small son brought out a touching, mature and completely generous aspect of her nature, Dietrich in Von Sternberg's hands was, if legendary, also limited. Perhaps without him, she would never have achieved her decadently sexual magnificence, but in the hands of other less fanatic directors, she exuded a warmth and piquant humor which displayed her range as an actress and as a personality. In Rouben Mamoulian's *Song of Songs* (1933), a highly romantic exercise, Marlene gets a chance to play first—and beautifully—a naïve country *Fräulein* transformed by the ignorance and mistreatment of men into a divinely angry baroness and then another paramount slut.

In *Destry Rides Again* (1939) as a hard-boiled dance hall girl in the old West, she nobly saves Sheriff Destry (James Stewart) by throwing herself in front of a flying bullet. The contrived sinner-must-be-punished ending was forgivable only for the sight of a flailing, fiery, and comic Marlene free of the restraining Sternbergian artifice at last.

Or rather, free in the most conventional sense—to work with other directors whose lighter material and own psychological preferences were less steeped in concepts of bondage-cum-humiliation. For Dietrich never really departed from, nor did she want to depart from, the initial image of Mysterious Woman which Von Sternberg had honed for her at the expense of his own career. So pervasive was it that just by being on-screen (regardless of her material or its characterization), she suggested perverse passion. Heightening the dichotomy of her male-female (control-subjugation) nature by tailored, severe clothes and slacks (in Von Sternberg's films, she repeatedly appeared in male attire), she promised every man excruciating ecstasy if he could tame her or annihilation if—like the female spider who in mating kills her partner—she struck back.

If Dietrich's screen efforts finally disappointed or failed to deliver all they had hinted at, it was, however, a built-in hitch in the genre; she could not possibly be Everywoman. For a Mysterious Being by definition possesses a certain mystique or power of attraction that normal women lack, but she is also relegated to the position of outsider.

Because men have set up such an ideal, women—whose age-old task it has been to preen for and please them—have also set premiums on similar characteristics. And for what? Why enigmatic allure, why the perfume of mystery? For voluntary exile in affairs of the heart and head. One of the few tactical defenses left to women, the posture of mystery is a self-defeating cycle in the end.

But that was the ultimate fantasy from which Marlene Dietrich's image drew breath. She had transformed Garbo's more passive, wounded image into a subtle but deliberate and potentially malignant threat. If she, the predator, were enslaved at the end of a film, so what—she deserved it. Masculine audiences, relieved, could thus reaffirm their virility; women could imagine a desirability that would see men kneeling at their feet, too, but eventual capitulation on screen delivered them from unknown responsibilities. Submission, after all, was a familiar friend.

Rebellion without submission meant further alienation. Movies interpreted this as connivance, neurosis, psychosis, paranoia. By the time the mysteries that were Garbo and Dietrich had gelled in the public consciousness, Hollywood had already stuck in its thumb and pulled out a successor as self-aware as the Swede, as unyielding as the German, and more calculating than either. The quintessential Evil Woman. Homegrown Bette Davis. Floundering in a succession of second-banana sweet-girl parts, Davis in the early thirties graduated to tough but vulnerable molls or career chicks and was a natural as the missing link who could combine stardom with malevolence, at the same time—by sheer uncompromising force of personality—propelling the romantic allure of Dietrich and Garbo into obsolescence. First of all, although she was sexy, she was not classically or even commercially beautiful. Second, rather than curry a velvet accent, she spat out her dialogue with clipped, almost British clarity. Third, her startling eyes and disdainful mouth rang up every raging emotion her character felt—anger, lust, madness, cruelty, and pain. No understatements. Like a violent interruption, the Davis presence could have been harnessed (and in the forties occasionally was) into an exemplary female image had she not so quickly found the Evil Woman niche. It was invaluable, to her and to Hollywood. For no other first-magnitude thirties' star would dare entrench herself repeatedly in thankless, unsympathetic roles—and return triumphant to tell the tale.

Of Human Bondage (1934), a Somerset Maugham classic in which the heroine is a venomous sloven, was Bette's first venture into undisguised ruthlessness. As Mildred, the illiterate waitress to whom medical student Leslie Howard is attracted, she methodically, irrationally devours him. By the time she burns the last few bonds enabling Howard to afford medical school the only mystery is why this malicious tart has enslaved him at all. Her death of that creeping corrosion attacking all nasty streetwomen relieves all concerned.

Not unlike Von Sternberg, Maugham bases his treatment of women on his fear of their sexuality and its crushing, binding tentacles. But rather than deal with complexities of the female nature and sociosexual jockeying for power or freedom, he simplifies his women, dismissing them as emotional and moral Frankensteins (e.g. *Rain,* adapted for the screen in 1928, 1932, and 1956 as *Miss Sadie Thompson; The Letter,* adapted in 1929 and 1940). Bette Davis' *Bondage* impersonation firmly recalls the base of power wielded by the Mysterious Woman, but she flails her sexuality with a psychotic irrationality, laying bare (without motivation) every possible *human* flaw, which is then passed off as a *female* shortcoming.

Before the decade closed, Bette Davis would expand her repertoire of bitches, doing so with such finesse that she picked up two Academy Awards on the way. *Dangerous,* the first, made in 1935, was the story of a declining stage star, self-centered and immoral, who attempts to kill her husband by crashing their car into a tree after he refuses to divorce her. He survives, a cripple for life; she escapes injury but—fortified with a new play written by the man she had intended to marry—repents, staying with her invalid husband.

Jezebel (1938) won her a second Oscar for her tempestuous and vain Southern-belle heartbreaker (whom Warner's rushed onto the screen as their low-budget answer to Scarlett O'Hara). Arriving a year earlier than Vivien Leigh's consummate Southern bitch, Bette's Jezebel was equally reckless (though, in truth, less evil), inadvertently causing the death of one suitor after being scorned by another. Between these she managed to play a murderess in both

Satan Was a Lady (an adaption of *The Maltese Falcon*) and *The Letter* (1940). Then in *The Little Foxes* (1941) she let her husband die of a heart seizure on the stairwell in order to wrest control of the family's business interests. During *In This Our Life* (1942) she steals her sister's boyfriend, eggs him on to suicide, kills a child in a hit-and-run accident, and drives to her death. Quite a deal of nasty business for a woman young, lovely, and at the height of her power.

This is significant because actresses whose jowls and bags become more pronounced in their middle years are commonly relegated to one of two roles: Evil Old Bag or Mother. Bette would later play many more neurotics. In all fairness, she balanced these with beautiful, compassionate roles in *Now, Voyager* (1943), *Dark Victory* (1939), *Watch on the Rhine* (1943). But in the mid thirties she seethed with rage and, more than any actress, signed, sealed, and delivered for general gloating the myth equating feminine strength with evil passion. She must have been doing something the public wanted; from 1938 through 1941 Bette Davis joined that elite circle of the year's ten top-grossing stars.

Her rage may well have been the collective fury of all women who felt powerless and passive in love and life. The Women's Movement had sputtered and ground to a halt with the Depression; by 1938 the economy may have been returning to "normal"—but that merely implied that *men* were beginning to reorder their lives. How easy for women to watch Bette vent frustration for them and then nod: "What a lousy broad." How comforting for men to see that female strength implied lack of scruples. And how sensational! The cycle of gangster films had ended; no longer a passive moll and hardly a mystery, the Evil Woman revealed a driving, malignant will when her passion was crossed. The world could pass judgment on her smugly and without delving too deeply.

Bette Davis did not play Scarlett O'Hara in *Gone with the Wind*, and it's just as well. As bitchy as Scarlett was, the more humane Hollywood gods were in her favor. And well they might have been, for it was the most coveted female role in movie history; every major actress tested for it, and a three-year talent search proved fruitless. But Vivien Leigh, assigned to impersonate Scarlett at the last moment, was perfection. She looked like a dream; she played in Technicolor; and Rhett-Gable, about whom the audience cared tremendously, was a fortress of strength, charm, and romance fighting her infantilism. Petty and self-centered, Scarlett missed out on mystery, even neuroticism. Her evil was merely an open childlike petulance which brought additional rewards for its spunk and self-sufficiency. We rooted for her regeneration—that she would finally mature, if not for her own sake, then for Rhett's. "After all, tomorrow is another day," she sobbed in her empty mansion after he'd had enough.

And we believed it. *We wanted to...*

That was 1939. Scarlett, gracious belle, bowed at the portals of the forties—the era of "women's pictures."

Tomorrow, surely the sun would shine.

11

THE LANDSCAPE OF SOCIAL FANTASY
idle riches, baby bitches

While Dorothea Lange traveled across the country for the Farm Security Administration, photographing the searing poverty of rural United States, fantasy-starved Americans gorged on headlines reporting real-life romance and riches. A twice-divorced Baltimore socialite, Wallis Warfield Simpson, shook the British Empire and the world in December, 1936, when her paramour, Edward VIII, abdicated his throne to marry "the woman I love."

The following May 12, the concept of royalty again took on fairytale charm when the new King George VI's small daughters, Princess Elizabeth, eleven, and Margaret Rose, six, practically stole the coronation show. Shortly children's crayon books and paper dolls with robes and scepters flooded the market as their mothers' dreams were exploited and handed down.

Deprived of indigenous royalty, we manufactured our own, and not only in paper cutouts. In the mid-thirties so desperate was the thirst for diversion that our absurd absorption with Hollywood's kings and queens intensified. Café society mesmerized. Clubs like El Morocco, Sherman Billingsley's Stork, the 21, all speakeasies during Prohibition, emerged post-1933 as chic watering spots where money gleamed and personalities glittered. The world followed Woolworth heiress Barbara Hutton through her 1933 marriage to Prince Alexis Mdivani (brother of Serge and David, the fortune-hunter-husbands of Pola Negri and Mae Murray) and its subsequent debacle. It followed the divorce and her marriage to Danish Count von Haugwitz-Reventlow, but was enchanted most of all by beautiful dark-haired debutante Brenda Frazier. At seventeen

171

1938's most glorious Glamor Girl posed for Woodbury Soap ads, was honored at an extravagant $60,000 debut, and ran around town with actors Bruce Cabot and Douglas Fairbanks, Jr. Other heiresses like Mimi Baker and Cobina Wright, Jr. (who embarked on a short-lived movie career), sparked similar interest as the nation avidly watched how the other half lived.

But the self-appointed mother hen of the smart set was a fat nonsocialite who clucked around the moneyed and powerful, stumbling on a unique vehicle for becoming the high priestess of their social scene. Elsa Maxwell gave parties. Lavish, exclusive parties. She also spoke candidly about her energies and life-style: "My social whirl was purely a labor of love in pursuit of pleasure." Sex, however, did not count as one of these pleasures. "I wouldn't subject myself to it. I married the world—the world is my husband. That is why I'm so young. No sex. Sex is the most tiring thing in the world."[1]

Probably Elsa's attitude, a welcome relief, did more than all else to endear her to elitist darlings. In the New York *Mirror* in 1938 she elaborated on the qualities required of her female guests:

First I want a woman guest to be beautiful.

Second, I want her to be beautifully dressed.

Third, I demand animation and vivacity.

Fourth, not too many brains. Brains are always awkward at a gay and festive party. Brains are only a requisite when the party is limited to a handful of persons, say six or eight.

And fifth, I expect obedience. . . .

Discerning women might have considered a Maxwell invitation an insult, but she unfortunately trotted right in step with the prevailing attitude of the times. And of the screen. For while 76,954 socially ostracized women graduated from college in 1939; while Katharine Anne Porter was being acclaimed for two brilliant volumes of short stories, *Flowering Judas* in 1931 and *Pale Horse, Pale Rider* in 1939; while field agency investigators like Lorena Hickok and Martha Gellhorn, having toured the country in 1933 for Roosevelt's Federal Emergency Relief Administration, reported on conditions of relief workers in order to provide jobs via a $500,000,000 grant-in-aid program for states and local public agencies, movies suffered both from the fashionable antifeminist backlash brought on by the Depression and from a warped vision of American life.

If Hollywood's idea of portraying Depression hardship was for gangster Jimmy Cagney in *The Public Enemy* to squash a grape-fruit in Mae Clarke's face (vicarious vengeance, admitted director William Wellman recently, on the wife he was soon to divorce), or for ex-millionaire William Powell in *My Man Godfrey* to wander around as a butler, viewing the good life from the servant's shoes, how could we expect the industry to serve females any less exploitatively? Only a very few films—like Chaplin's *Modern Times* (1936) and Vidor's *Our Daily Bread* (1934)—chose to deal with the grim realities of existence without typical Hollywood white-wash (even though *Modern Times* was a comedy, it spoke poignantly of starvation, unemployment, and the sterility of mechanization). Vidor's *Our Daily Bread*—which he had to finance himself because no studio would touch its dismal and "Communistic" theme—was a naïve but probing tale of a couple who return to the earth and, enlisting the cooperation of others unemployed, make an abandoned farm into a collectivist unit. The women work right alongside the men (reminiscent of Carol Dempster in Griffith's *Isn't Life Won-derful?*) and are an integral part of the social fiber of the com-munity.

But in most of the films which touched on the Depression, women generally gave comfort to starving men (Loretta Young in *Heroes for Sale*, 1933). If they were affected personally, their milieus were limited—to chorus girls hustling men or hassling to secure jobs on a darkened Broadway (*Gold Diggers of 1933, 42nd Street, Footlight Parade*). Or to wives and mothers and mistresses descend-ing into prostitution in order to support their men and children.

The Depression provided a fine backdrop for this sort of female depravity-as-proof-of-devotion. Even virginal Helen Hayes in *The Sin of Madelon Claudet* (1931) has an illegitimate son. While the love relationship which produced him was essentially pure, her sub-sequent encounters, all in order to support the child, lead to prison, interminable separation, and the final burden—giving up all claim to the boy because her past will ruin his chances of a brilliant future in medicine. Hayes suffers stoically, but on her back, just as Dietrich did two years later in *Blonde Venus*.

Barbara Stanwyck's *Stella Dallas* (1937) is afflicted with a different strain of mother love. Having used her cunning and charm to cross over from the other side of the tracks into a middle-class marriage, Stella's obsession to "get in with the right people" is superseded only by a smother love for her daughter which insulates her completely from a life of her own, even from the reality of the world. "I don't think there's a man living could get me going anymore," she confides to a suitor. "Lolly just uses up all the feelings I got." In her isolation, Stella evolves into an embarrassingly gaudy buffoon who primes her daughter for high society—and then must relinquish her to that milieu. "I never knew anyone could be so unselfish," Stella's ex-husband's socialite wife tells her warmly. But Stella must be pitied more than admired. For as this grotesque hyperbole of mother love, she has sabotaged her own identity, stifled her fears and dreams, and assuaged her emptiness through a comically vigorous motherhood, which would in the end leave her alone.

The Depression, smelling of antifeminisim, gave Hollywood a perfect excuse for such ludicrous allegories of sacrifice, tears, and female humiliation. Therefore, audiences might have been fortunate that studio moguls like Mayer and Thalberg who had known extreme poverty as children and now had little tolerance for it preferred the veneer of films-as-entertainment. In his 1934 Annual Report, Will Hays bragged:

> No medium has contributed more greatly than the film to the maintenance of the national morale during a period featured by revolution, riot, and political turmoil in other countries. It has been the mission of the screen, without ignoring the serious social problems of the day, to reflect aspiration, optimism, and kindly humor in its entertainment.

Consequently, industry potentates preferred to etch a totally different Depression landscape: the landscape of society fantasy. Even during the early crisis years, this was a favorite theme and may have primed the public for its unnatural deification of Café Society later on. Not quite as overbearing as the Jazz Age's aristocratic romps, Society Maiden movies worked one of two themes. The first concerned a woman of extraordinary wealth and leisure whose stuffy husband absents himself too frequently on business trips. She succumbs—or evidence leads him to believe she does—to the charms of another. The ensuing alienation and reconciliation of spouses must then be worked out.

Kay Francis' elegant carriage made her a natural for such roles. A tall (five nine—then, *very* tall), dark-haired beauty with small, even features and large dark eyes, Kay made well over sixty films and exemplified this genre with *Transgression* (1931). Metamorphosing into a glamorous siren when her husband leaves for work in India, Kay is persuaded into a demi-affair that evolves into a murder and blackmail scandal from which she scurries and, still pure, returns to the fold.

Certainly the most popular and well-turned-out socialite was Norma Shearer. Not only did she head the list of MGM stars who specialized in glossy upper-crust photoplays, but as vice-president and production chief Irving Thalberg's wife, she received what he thought were plum roles. Occasionally even *she* protested at their uniformity, but Thalberg could not visualize cheapening his wife by characterizing her otherwise. So when Norma wasn't emoting as Juliet in *Romeo and Juliet* (1936) or as Elizabeth Barrett Browning in *The Barretts of Wimpole Street* (1934), she strutted through familiar paces in the equivalent of soap-operas-by-Suzy or Cholly Knickerbocker. *Their Own Desire* (1930); *The Divorcee* (1930), for which she won an Oscar; *Let Us Be Gay* (1930); *Strangers May Kiss* (1931); *Private Lives* (1931), from Noel Coward's comedy; and 1934's *Riptide* (which resembled *Strangers May Kiss* not only in plot conflict—a new man attempts seduction when work takes hubby across the ocean—but because Robert Montgomery was the interloper in both cases)—all played variations on this theme and seemed designed to set off Shearer's rather severe ambiance with gowns by Adrian and "classy" witticisms by MGM's dialogue wizards. Thalberg's efforts succeeded. Her rather homely elegance in well-directed, sophisticated vehicles placed her in the box office's top ten during 1933 and 1934 (Kay Francis was in the top thirty, also a good showing).

It is interesting that Shearer's most complex and colorful assignment came two years after her husband's death in 1936. In *Idiot's Delight* she portrayed a smart, manipulative vaudeville performer who falls for Clark Gable. Her bizarre overacting as a bogus Russian countess is high kitsch, but nevertheless compelling—and indicates the depth and range she might have attained had her roles not been so stringently channeled.

Movies about society matrons, superficial and insulting, implied that, given leisure, women lounged about salons, titillating their imaginations and libidos with illicit liaisons. Probably part of this assumption is true: Thirties' females, having been stripped of all usefulness if they were wealthy enough to hire maids and governesses and didn't care to roll bandages or plan April-in-Paris balls, *did* have paltry resources. But films were immutable in their unwillingness to probe the real source of feminine discontent and perhaps make precarious the status quo. Even indiscretion had its roots—in a husband's absence or inability to please his wife, intellectually, spiritually, or physically, and in her ennui. Yet in society as in films, traditional concepts of order, fidelity, and social role playing were idealized, with female dissatisfaction dismissed as deficiency of character.

This myth of the profligate socialite peaked, dramatically, with two early films. In *The Story of Temple Drake* (1933), blond Miriam Hopkins played a wealthy, heartless tease who's kidnapped and raped by Jack La Rue. Not only does he brutally subdue her, but he releases her pent-up drives—an illicit, almost-masochistic eroticism which responds even more willingly when he places her in a brothel. Observing her perverse, near-catatonic pleasure, La Rue gloats, "I spotted ya the minute I saw ya." Here applause for his ego, perception, and performance as the lady awakens into a sexual tigress—and the genre of heiress-commoner spins toward its outer limits.

But as always, contradictory needs prevail; Everyman conjures up a wildly rouged passion flower, but marriage redefines her as legal chattel. *The Kiss Before the Mirror* (1933) spelled out, almost as contractual exposition, man's expectation and fears. A husband is acquitted of killing his unfaithful mate, and his attorney is impassioned because *his* wife (Nancy Carroll) is similarly indulging. "Faith is the greatest element in love, and exclusiveness of possession is all that makes marriage worthwhile," says this lawyer, Frank Morgan. "Did the defendant love his wife so much that the murder can be explained by that love? . . . He murdered her *because* he loved her . . . a man has a right to avenge his honor. A husband is home."

This latter-day Othello, however, requires more than fidelity.

Throughout the film, director James Whale alludes to the woman potent in her cruel manipulation of men, deadly in her vanity. The murdering husband guessed his wife's secret by spying as she primped at the mirror. Similarly, Morgan warns his female assistant to smash all her mirrors and, on reconciling with his wife, throws his unused gun at her glass. For these men, the anointing and narcissistic rituals of the very rich or beautiful female challenge their possession of her. From her own vain recesses, she draws strength, becoming less the man's object and more her own person (whose capacities as temptress-emasculator increase accordingly).

This very bleak, self-consciously expressionistic drama with no humor, understanding or appreciation of women, seems silly, even quaint now. But *The Kiss Before the Mirror* persisted vigorously. "No matter how low a woman may fall, there's always a man waiting for her," Morgan mutters bitterly. Yet not one of these martyred husbands ponders the depths to which a man must sink to kill—and how silly adultery seems in comparison. (Or did one misread the message? How worthless a perfidious woman; she deserves death, the ultimate objectification!)

Fortunately, the fates of Miriam Hopkins and Nancy Carroll were excessive screen reactions—and warning—to upper-class females whose hyperactive libidos, stimulated by ennui, demanded censure. Single socialites, especially, were appointed a different, more flexible and less punitive niche. Unless a woman were shown in bed or, later, pregnant, an "affair" might mean a kiss, an embrace, a couple sleeping in the same room but never touching, or a deep platonic affection—all to be interpreted as the viewer fancied. But money and the single girl almost always combined to render our heiress spoiled, haughty—to be tamed by the crass commoner too rugged to let a bank account intimidate him, too coarse to let manners inhibit him. Sexual tension alone determined the most peculiar alliances.

When seedy gambler Clark Gable swept the refined Norma Shearer off her feet and out of the arms of her polo-playing fiancé in *A Free Soul* (1931), she was fascinated, murmuring passionately, "A new kind of man—a new kind of life." When he slammed her into a chair, the audience gulped. Talkies were just out of their infancy, and never before had a woman of culture been so enticingly maltreated on screen.

But *A Free Soul*, based on the real-life relationship of Adela Rogers

St. John and her famous criminal-lawyer father, was a heavy movie, as Gable died at the hands of the polo player, and the lawyer died acquitting him. The most enjoyable versions of the Heiress Vogue were the comedies in which the heroine seemed less offensive because she had moxie, if little else, to recommend her. Aside from Harlow's vulgarly rich dame of *Platinum Blonde* and down-at-the-heels socialite of *Saratoga*, one of the best-remembered roles of this genre was Claudette Colbert's in *It Happened One Night* (1934). Runaway heiress Colbert's taming by journalist Clark Gable brought her an Academy Award and status as the sixth biggest moneymaking star of 1935.

But the most stubbornly aristocratic madcap of the thirties was Katharine Hepburn. Bone-thin, imperious even in the full flower of her youthful beauty, Hepburn achieved greater success in thirties comedies like *Bringing Up Baby* (1938), *Holiday* (1938), and *The Philadelphia Story* (1940) than in her career-woman flings, *Christopher Strong* (1932), *Break of Hearts* (1935), or *Mary of Scotland* (1936). As the eccentric and wealthy owner of a pet leopard in *Baby*, she diligently pursues disinterested anthropologist Cary Grant. In *Holiday* she's a rich, rebellious girl who winds up with older sister's beau, Grant; he gives her the courage to act out the sybaritic philosophy of life they both believe in, but which she can't follow without him as her catalyst. Then in *The Philadelphia Story* (1940) a property which she herself bought and produced after triumphing in it on Broadway, she's a gloriously spoiled bride unable to recognize her true feelings until common-man reporter Jimmy Stewart and ex-hubby Grant shake her up with moonlight and liquor. But in this, Philip Barry's most fatuous homage to the moneyed and manored, while the groom is revealed as a fawning politician and self-made fraud, Stewart also loses the bride to Grant's elegant, amused condescension. As C. Dexter Haven, Grant alone is not intimidated by Hepburn; he alone enjoys her discomfort and finds humor in her arrogance. Like the unimpressed hucksters in most heiress fables, he breaks her stubborn will and thus becomes her master forever.

Grant, sufficiently charming and snide, sufficiently immovable as a force opposite women, managed the same ploy as husband to Irene Dunne in *The Awful Truth* (1938), *My Favorite Husband* (1940), and *Penny Serenade* (1941). Earlier, in *Joy of Living* (1937), Dunne's prima donna star and self-made woman succumbed to an absurdly insistent Douglas Fairbanks, Jr. But she was essentially a matronly, warm comic personality with neither Hepburn's stridency nor her depths of alertness that would in the forties find its most substantial material.

Hepburn's thirties' screen women possessed an abrasiveness and independence out of kilter with the decade. She could never submerge her unparalleled self-awareness, even in the lightest or most traditionally feminine roles, and although comedies sanded her brittleness for popular consumption, she enjoyed a fickle romance with her public. For they could not connect feminine wiles with her brand of stubborness or precocity. Beside the flaccid elegance of other Depression aristocrats, Hepburn's most positive qualities—honor, ambition (as in her aspiring actresses of *Morning Glory*, 1933, and *Stage Door*, 1937), intelligence, aggressiveness—acquired an obsessional ardor which didn't wear well.

Infinitely preferable was the dream of transportation—little old Apple Annie becomes a queen for a day in *Lady for a Day* (1933); Joan Crawford's slatternly cabaret dancer becomes society's darling for two weeks in *The Bride Wore Red* (1937). Or a fantasy of queenly idylls. If women were reading about Barbara Hutton and Brenda Frazier, why not then see their on-screen counterparts' intimate revelations? Not only did society comedy in the thirties win a place (beside Westerns, war movies, and gold diggers' songfests) in the tradition of movies, but so did society dramas. Joan Crawford was their busiest exponent, and during the decade the same actress who had been the quintessential flapper, now gowned and bejeweled by Adrian, evolved as the sophisticate beset by love. Between 1930 and 1940 she enacted a wealthy playgirl in *Montana Moon* (1930), *This Modern Age* (1931), *Letty Lynton*, *Today We Live* (1932), *Chained* (1934), *Forsaking All Others* (1934), *No More Ladies* (1935), *I Live My Life* (1935), *Love on the Run* (1936), *The Last of Mrs. Cheyney* (a 1936 remake of Shearer's 1929 film). In almost all she found love with the cowboy, reporter, jewel thief, or other ultimately worthy and dominating rogue. Finally, even the public was saturated, and although Crawford was the only female star to stay consistently within the top ten between 1930 and 1935, three years later she was considered box-office poison (along with Marlene Dietrich, Bette Davis, Hepburn, and a few others). Still, it was not until the forties, and her tooth-and-nail insistence on more challenging roles, that she would break this mold. As with many actresses saddled with playgirl stereotypes in the thirties, the transition would come in the reworking and expansion of the career-woman genre.

The most obvious reason for this was World War II and the advent of "women's pictures." The second was that it was, for a fortyish Crawford, a graceful and credible metamorphosis. But also, in a strange way the society genre paved the way for public acceptance of real-life career women. Although heiresses on screen generally frittered away their time and cared for little beyond their padded shoulders and sequined evening gowns, they—like businesswomen—were strong-willed, mercurial, and decisive, even if their areas of decision were limited. They conducted themselves with poise and managed servants like generals. Money brought egoism and a pathetically misguided waste of energy, but it often developed a self-assurance which—when seated behind a forties desk—worked positively as a professional asset.

It is impossible to discuss popular notions of upper-class females in films without mentioning *The Women*, Clare Boothe Luce's grotesque 1939 study in bitchery, pettiness, superficiality, and stupidity.* Quick on wit and studded with an MGM galaxy of females—Norma Shearer, Joan Fontaine, Joan Crawford, Paulette Goddard, Mary Boland, Rosalind Russell—it is the flimsy tale of wives who watch gleefully as Shearer's husband falls victim to money-hungry perfume salesgirl Joan Crawford. One, then another marriage declines, and although the men never materialize, the marital status of each wife is drawn (and altered) through malicious gossip and jealous confrontations. The women meet over lunch, at the manicurist, in exercise class, at a fashion show, and in Reno while awaiting final decrees—and each encounter provokes deft verbal sparring matches that flamboyantly confirm the myth of female cloying and clawing.

While many of the lines are funny today the way scathing bitchery usually is (as high camp), that *The Women* was ever written at all and that it was regarded as anything more than a laughable exploitation seem incredible. Yet more than any other film of the decade, it mercilessly illustrates the popular disregard for women, conveniently dismissing them, not just as inanities painting their nails with Jungle Red and dabbing their earlobes with Summer Rain, but as mean, stupid,

* Revived on Broadway in the spring of 1973.

destructive creatures. So crudely drawn are the characters that the film achieves dubious distinction as the apotheosis of female self-abasement.

Fortunately, the sulfuric acidity of *The Women* was atypical, although the portrait it presented of upper-class boredom was not. Most movie heiresses, fantasy figures, soothed a public wondering where the next dozen eggs were coming from. Women studied their favorite heroines and bought the first home permanent kits in 1934 to marcel their short waves and sweep them behind their ears like Shearer. They accentuated their eyes and wore wide-shouldered suits like Crawford, tweezed brows like Dietrich, bleached their hair into Harlow halos, and generally cast themselves in stars' molds. Perhaps because talkies added dimension and individuality to screen images, perhaps because the bleakness of daily life left ladies more susceptible than ever before, the superficial aspects of movie queens—their clothes, looks, gestures, and manner of speech—sparked daydreams and became goals to emulate.

Emphasis on female beauty, and how to attain it, ran high. In May, 1936, *Literary Digest* printed a piece, "Remolding Entire Lives by Surgery," in which the book *New Faces—New Futures* by Dr. Maxwell Malty was discussed. Malty noted: "Even slight facial distortions can cause the most acute suffering because of real or imagined social ostracism, particularly among women."

Hollywood's goddesses who were setting social standards for beauty in fact also set Hollywood's own standards! The studios sought to create from old patterns, and it was no coincidence that Jean Parker, an MGM feature player, looked, sounded, and even had a name similar to Jean Arthur. Or that Betty Grable and Alice Faye were interchangeable (after Faye's Harlow image had been refurbished). Think, too, of Claudette Colbert and Jane Wyman; Anne Baxter, Ann Sheridan, and Susan Hayward; Ruth Roman and Ruth Hussey. For the studios, beauty and economics worked hand in hand. A sure thing was a good thing; it spelled box office.

And for the woman in life, beauty insured admiration. She envied the clear complexions and perfect features on screen, just as her man would have been proud to have such look-alikes on his arm. The concept of individual attractiveness had vanished in favor of conformity to popular image. With the emphasis removed from woman's ability to create on her own, to work even menially (because jobs were in short supply), and to be an individual pursuing a life-style uniquely her own, concern with appearance mushroomed as an acceptable time filler, even an obsession.

In the fall of 1936 the neo-Victorian view of woman's place (or lack of same) was not confined to a masculine vision, either. Author Margaret Laurence produced an unconscionably antifeminist book, *The School of Femininity*, in which she described the normal female as "a vessel of the race . . . a still, deep sexual being . . . a biological force under a compelling instinct to find a safe place to lay her babes, and before that she is in subconscious search for a man who will give her the babies and help her to find a place to lay them."[2]

During the Depression some of these "vessels" were grabbing bread from their mates' mouths, seeking jobs their men wanted, and having babies their mates couldn't afford. Better that they should mimic goddesses of the screen, the passive, perfect objects of male dreams or tempestuous firebrands whose taming satisfied virile egos. A woman with an unbendable will of her own, reluctant to surrender to vesseldom, was rare in screen lore.

The only females with personalities and strength unfettered by genre expectations were, not surprisingly, those under fifteen. It was a remarkable but understandable phenomenon of the times that the reigning box-office figure (male or female) between 1935 and 1938 was Shirley Temple, who also placed eighth in 1934 and fifth in 1939. Jane Withers achieved sixth and eighth positions in the top ten circle during 1937 and 1938 respectively. A youthful Judy Garland barely made tenth place in 1940. They would be followed in the forties by excellent child stars Elizabeth Taylor, Margaret O'Brien, Natalie Wood, Gigi Perreau, and Peggy Ann Garner, but never again would so adoring a cult surround the lollipop set.

Undoubtedly the Shirley Temple phenomenon sprouted in part because of the small heroine's enormous charm and obvious talent. Originally appearing in the 1933 Baby Burlesque shorts, she stole *Stand Up and Cheer* from under the noses of all its adult stars and soon afterward debuted in her first starring role as *Little Miss Marker* (1934); here, as a waif adopted by a Runyonesque Broadway mug after her father commits suicide, five-year-old Shirley again completely captivated public fancy. By 1940 she had starred in twenty-one films, each a surefire success—and each with a similar formula. Moppet Temple, with infinite child's wisdom, endears herself to adults and restores or improves a crucial aspect of their lives (e.g., *The Little Colonel, Poor Little Rich Girl, Curly Top,* and *The Littlest Rebel*).

Shirley's feistiness resembled Pickford's but was less ludicrous since her roles suited her age. Yet precisely *because* she was young—and not yet a sexual being to control or fear—she could dictate her needs, act on her whims, and meddle in the business of all concerned. As a child—and therefore, a neuter—she possessed tremendous latitude; her opinions *counted* in areas where no adult woman would dare venture, much less be heeded. (Interestingly this antifeminist climate also resembled to a lesser degree the Victorian one from which Pickford emerged.) The tot presence, a transference of female energies, had its parallels in other media as well: comic strips and radio. In 1924 *Little Orphan Annie* first appeared on the pages of the nation's newspapers. With her short red bob, unseeing eyes, and pet mongrel Sandy by her side, Annie rescued "jest folks" from the perils of shady businessmen, criminals, and poverty (a pablum prototype of Nancy Drew?) and never aged a day. Along with a wealthy and domineering foster father, Daddy Warbucks, she became a virtual institution on the radio during the thirties, and kids everywhere sent in sponsor Ovaltine's seals in exchange for mugs, secret-code cards, rings, bracelets, buttons, and Orphan Annie's Secret Society badges.

But Annie couldn't approach the commercialism accompanying real-girl Shirley's stardom. Shirley Temple dolls, dolls' clothes (authorized and not), soap, ribbons, books, hairdos, and countless other toys were marketed. Mothers demanded that hairdressers style their daughters' hair with the fifty-six curl mop that Shirley had refashioned out of Pickford's cuttings. Look-alike contests were held. Studios cried for another miniature gold mine to put into circulation.

Jane Withers seemed an unlikely candidate. A pudgy, sloppy imp, whose chief screen accomplishment lay in asking Santa for a machine gun, she debuted in a secondary role as the jealous child of a wealthy couple in Shirley's *Bright Eyes* (1934). But she played it with such brattish, genderless venom, with as much mustard as Shirley had sugar, that she practically stole the show and was compared favorably to the reigning little-boy menace, Jackie Searle. However, by the time of *Ginger*, her first starring role in 1935, Jane, then nine, had been cleaned up and sweetened so distastefully that one critic wondered if the Hays Office had not run interference. The story—pure Temple

—concerned Ginger-Withers who is adopted by a rich family after her alcoholic uncle is jailed. On his release, he renounces her so that she'll have the opportunities of wealth, but Jane runs off and retrieves him. *Gentle Julia* (1936), *Little Miss Nobody*, *Pepper* (1936), and *Keep Smiling* (1938) followed suit.

In similar fashion Deanna Durbin, a sweet-faced, plain fifteen-year-old with an extraordinarily rich soprano voice, debuted in *Three Smart Girls* (1936), in which (with two smart sisters) she helps thwart her divorced father's plan to marry a money-hungry woman. Her next film, *100 Men and a Girl* (1937), established her as a top Universal star. Here little Deanna, through relentless persistence and obnoxious nerve, reordered the universe for 100 men by organizing an orchestra to give employment to her musician father and his destitute musician friends, then finagling a promise from Leopold Stokowski to conduct it. This was quite a coup which no grown-up film female could brag about.

The concept of child-as-good-fairy reaches its implausible apex here. Although *100 Men and a Girl* joyously, sentimentally entertains us as Deanna single-handedly conquers the logistics of hardship, her pubescence is disturbing, even grating. Without youth, which tempered the saccharin of the Temple and Withers vehicles, Durbin comes across as shrill and unpleasantly bossy, a teen-aged old lady marshaling a band of impotent men and dominating them as moral conscience, mother, manager, and promoter. How easy to imagine Deanna only a few years hence as the embodiment of another patriarchal nightmare—Momism!

Would tiny minds that connived and schemed grow into cunning adult ones? Where else would the Temple, Withers, and Durbin images have gone had they grown up on screen with their busybody personalities intact? During that period only Judy Garland managed to make the transition from the fourteen-year-old of *Pigskin Parade* (1936) to adult stardom. She alone had, from the beginning, that marvelously vulnerable quality—equate it with traditional femininity, if you will—which presented her as a very real human being. Something Hollywood forgot about when they cast their miniature steamrollers.

Consider, too, that while girl-children of the screen were patching up adults' vicissitudes, male child actors were discovering their *own* boyish identities. Mickey Rooney, who became the nation's top moneymaker with his Andy Hardy series for MGM, played a teen-ager concerned with *his* automobile, *his* girls, and *his* family. The family—and Judge Hardy in particular—existed to love and support *Andy* through his Carvel High tribulations; the boy did not engage in charity patchwork, so engrossed was he in living.

But audiences so loved the misguided independence of eerily midgetlike girl viragos that Darryl Zanuck, then head of Twentieth Century-Fox (where Temple did most of her work) was encouraged to sign the world's most famous girl-children, the Dionne quintuplets, who were only two at the time. Screen tests were made and insured for $2,000,000, but the Quints appeared only in the last ten minutes of *The Country Doctor*, then in *Reunion* and *Five of a Kind*. Zanuck was amazed that his brainstorm had burst, but obviously it was straining the formula: How much meddling, matchmaking and mischief could little girls just teething and barely talking accomplish—even on the principle that five heads were better than one?

Forties' movies, reflecting entirely different cultural needs, would not, however, endow their female children similarly or adore them unstintingly. Preteen wisdom would pale as the country, shaking off the emasculating effects of the Depression, stood stalling on the brink of World War.

With Johnny once again heading "over there," American women would once again *have* to grow up.

FOUR

THE FORTIES—NECESSITY AS THE MOTHER OF EMANCIPATION

*I have given the main part of
my life to my trade, plus a perfectly good nervous system I
could use now. I've traded in
all my illusions and a feminine
vocabulary and any softness that
might have been in my nature. . . .
But sister, when the war is over
and a gal can relax into planning her personal affairs again,
I'm going to heave a great big
sigh and see if I can really
get off and walk—in a ladylike
manner—I hope.*

—CONSTANCE ROE,
member of International
Typographical Union
"Can the Girls Hold Their
Jobs in Peacetime?"
Saturday Evening Post,
March 4, 1944

12

THE RISE AND FALL OF
ROSIE THE RIVETER

monkey wrenches and tears

On December 7, 1941, the Japanese bombed hell out of Pearl Harbor. Johnny got his gun. America mobilized. And social roles shifted with a speed that would have sent Wonder Woman into paroxysms of power pride.

It was a beautifully ambiguous, surprisingly satisfying period. Appropriate concern for the safety of the world required unification and integration; by 1943 more than 4,000,000 women were employed in munitions work alone. An additional 15,000,000 joined the labor force, doing such formerly masculine jobs as coal mining, operating mechanical hoists and cranes, swinging sledges, sorting ore, greasing machines, and firing and cleaning antiaircraft guns. Factories bowed to the needs of their new employees—installing ladies' washroom facilities, sanitary napkin disposals, providing pregnancy leave and child-care facilities, and disseminating birth control information from Planned Parenthood. (This soon halted when the Catholic Church protested.)

Necessity undoubtedly mothered emancipation. Working meant more than feeding one's self and family while the head of the house was fighting for democracy; it was a patriotic gesture. By late 1943 the only males who hadn't volunteered or been drafted were those too old or young, too infirm, or otherwise incapacitated. But the industrial world was shocked—and occasionally dismayed—that women, now 36 percent of the labor force, worked faster than men, required less supervision, had fewer industrial accidents, and did less damage

189

to tools and materials. On May 16, 1942, *Business Week* reported that airplane plants considered women 50 to 100 percent more efficient in wiring instrument panels. That they could perform 80 percent of all war-industry jobs (but only held 8.5 percent) and all but 80 out of 937 jobs in civilian industry. Boeing Aircraft in Seattle utilized squads of "superwomen" for moving and lifting heavy loads. Sperry Gyroscope announced that women could and did work in every possible capacity. And even though female participation was undercut by the press which attributed their astounding output to the fact that women "don't get bored as easily," "have less initiative," and are "creatures of habit,"[1] it was finally accepted, even welcomed, into the fiber of economic life.

In addition, the sobriety and purposefulness of the times lent dignity to woman's home front contributions. As they stoked the great American hearth, public opinion deified mothers as more maternal, daughters as more virginal, and businesswomen as more patriotic. Female independence was an unavoidable, if temporary expedient. At the beginning nobody, not even the women themselves, imagined they might want to make it permanent.

Hollywood could therefore afford to be temporarily indulgent. The forties, since dubbed the era of "women's pictures," for the first time concentrated heavily on films depicting women's lives and problems, probing their emotions, and displaying them against an enormous array of job backgrounds. Why? Audiences for the first time were almost entirely female. Most topflight male stars had enlisted or been called up for war (Gable, Stewart, Tyrone Power, William Holden, Robert Montgomery, and Wayne) and the only big box-office names left were women. And new female activities cried for reflection and imitation. Women, neither as bored, listless, nor depressed as they had been a decade earlier, were not as malleable either; hence, where the screen had not long before created a reality *for* them, now females created their own. The Hollywood product mirrored—and altered—it.

Rosie the Riveter, the lower-class working girl, queened it in forties' movies. This genre, functioning more as tribute to patriotism than to emancipation, nevertheless echoed real-life situations and also infused such participation with a sense of adventure, as well as duty. The vicissitudes of warmhearted, fast-talking Ann Sothern as an aircraft worker in *Swing Shift Maisie* (1943); the earnestness of *Government*

Girl Olivia de Havilland; the energetic duty of movie star Lucille Ball putting aside her minks to serve in a defense plant in *Meet the People* (1944); and even the peripheral sacrifice of Claudette Colbert, soiling her fireside and chintz by taking in an irascible boarder (Monty Woolley) and eventually becoming a welder in *Since You Went Away* (1944) stamped the equivalent of the Good Housekeeping Seal of Approval on woman's working endeavors. As often as not, actual scenes inside munitions factories or on assembly lines were eliminated or kept to a minimum, but heroines, uncomplaining, even cheerful, toiled away with gusto. Screen workers became heroic models for women in the audiences, women whose men had already gone off to fight or who would soon be alone and perhaps widowed. Women who had to learn to survive without men.

Appropriately, too, movies had their share of women in white. Jennifer Jones gave up the idea of college and became a nurse's aide in *Since You Went Away*. Claudette Colbert, Veronica Lake, and Paulette Goddard composed a trio of struggling nurses on Bataan in *So Proudly We Hail* (1943). Lana Turner matched nerves and deadliness with Clark Gable as a war correspondent in *Somewhere I'll Find You* (1942). WAC and WAVES received equal time. While even Uncle Sam acknowledged their usefulness, saturating landscapes with posters advertising the women's armed forces as "Soldiers without Guns," Betty Hutton slapsticked as twin sisters in *Here Come the Waves*; in *Keep Your Powder Dry* Lana Turner played a petulant heiress joining the WAC to prove she's more than just a pretty pocketbook—and receiving a commission at the film's end, she burst into tears.

Certainly, women in combat and nurses on the front idealized female bravery and participation. But the most affecting and meaningful films were the simpler, perhaps overly sentimental and trite "women's pictures" in which workers came to grips with their manless existences. Wartime provided Hollywood with irresistibly tear-jerking plots, yet they were not without purpose, offering catharsis to their anxious, lonely audiences. Bitchery and frivolity gave place to female strength: strength and love and support between mother and daughter, mother and daughter-in-law, sister and sister—and woman and woman.

Camaraderie's lighter moments glowed with silly, bland humor, as in *Something for the Boys* (1944), in which Carmen Miranda, Vivian

Blaine, and Phil Silvers converted a decrepit mansion into a home for war wives. The housing shortage, a much-used theme, was the foundation for Jean Arthur's *The More the Merrier*; romance and slapstick and innuendo arose from the fact that she shared a Washington apartment with Charles Coburn and Joel McCrea. In *The Doughgirls* (1944) Ann Sheridan played one of a number of unmarried women who pretend to marriage in order to keep her Washington hotel room. And in *Tender Comrade* (1943) Ginger Rogers, Ruth Hussey, and two others pool their money, rent a large house rather than live alone in ratholes, and, while "running the joint like a democracy," comfort one another. Ginger, pregnant, with her husband at war, leans most heavily on their generosity and solicitude. The tearful, inevitable finale occurs after her little boy's birth—with a death telegram: "Little boy ... you two are never going to meet," she tells the infant. "Your father only left you the best world a boy could grow up in—he bought it with his life and he left it as your heritage . . . don't let anyone say your dad died for nothing."

Melodramatic, yes. Patriotic, yes. But Ginger does not whine for herself; she mourns for her man and her son. It is obvious that her friends will assuage her pain, that she has developed the resilience to cope.

Mrs. Miniver finds genteel Greer Garson with war at her once-elegant and pastoral doorstep. A bombed-out house, a wounded Nazi in the flowerbeds (whom she captures single-handed), and the deterioration of her luxurious life are taken in stride; Garson must cope with more pressing dangers—the possible death of her husband and flier son. Love unites her with her teen-aged daughter-in-law, Teresa Wright. Marrying with full knowledge she may soon be a widow, Wright confesses: "If I must lose him, there'll be time enough for tears, there'll be a lifetime for tears." Her vocalizing of the fear looming over the Minivers' heads relieves tension and brings the women closer together. Common experience and maturity spans age and disarms traditional rivalries.

Hollywood's flood of war-widow films, which also include *Watch on the Rhine* and *Since You Went Away*, might be looked on as exploitative soap opera, but the genre, however tentative, deserves more than quick dismissal. Too limp and self-indulgent to compete as "art," these movies were, however, highly touted popular culture which earned healthy sums at the box office and were relevant, even urgent, balm.

Bette Davis' *Watch on the Rhine* made the ten best films' list in 1943; Claudette Colbert's *Since You Went Away* was similarly honored the following year. Mass-marketing faith and fatalism, the cinema for the first time spoke as a priest whose ministrations were sought by millions of moviegoing women. Through their screen counterparts, they could assemble order out of chaos and sacrifice. Davis' stoic wife, losing her husband in the underground resistance movement and then allowing her oldest son to go off to continue his father's work, and Claudette Colbert, buoying the spirits of her teen-aged daughters, Shirley Temple and Jennifer Jones, while privately agonizing over her husband's whereabouts, emerge as heroines of epic dimension. They learn to live *without* their men. Their survival, not as hysterical, embittered martyrs, but as womanly, capable models of human adaptability, was a Hollywood screen first.

It is ironic that in modern industrial society the two major world wars have elicited a tremendous collective response from women, resulting in reforms by and for them, reforms reflected on the screen. Within a most maudlin framework World War II movies provided substantial and practical identification. The screen universe was an immensely flexible environment, where women had to rise to a challenge imposed by unalterable events. Since women workers had fallen into an abyss of obedience during the Depression, it is not surprising that they at the beginning of the war unanimously expressed their intent to work only temporarily until the veterans had returned home. By 1944, though, more than 85 percent had reconsidered and wanted to keep their jobs. Often, purely economic reasons dictated this choice: Women had been widowed; their husbands had been disabled; they had children to care for. But more common was the overriding conviction that even dull factory tasks were preferable to returning to the insulating responsibilities of housework and child care. New vistas had opened, female ambitions soared, and the media recognized and tentatively explored these alternatives.

One of the most dashing, female-glorifying comic strips, *Brenda Starr, Reporter*, conceived and drawn by a woman, Dale Messick, in 1940 romanticized the exploits of a fabulously dressed, titian-haired beauty who just happened to be her newspaper's brightest asset. Picked up by the Chicago *Tribune* and New York News Service, *Brenda Starr* (who's still going strong) went daily in 1945. The same year she was serialized on the screen in thirteen short adventure yarns, among them *Hot News!*, *The Blazing Trap*, and *The Mystery of the Payroll*, in which the heroine (Joan Woodbury) escapes danger, cracks her story, and gets the scoop.

Chic Young's *Blondie* had first appeared in the New York *American* in September, 1930, and even today she's trying to pull her dim-witted helpmeet Dagwood Bumstead out of business and domestic scrapes. She, too, was adapted for the movies, and Penny Singleton starred in twenty-seven short features between 1938 (*Blondie*) and 1949 (*Blondie's Hero*).

Other more exotic serial heroines of the forties—Kay Aldridge in *Perils of Nyoka*, Ruth Roman as Lothel in *Jungle Queen*; Marguerite Chapman in *Spy Smasher*, and Adrian Booth as *Daughter of Don Q.* —reflected this fresh attitude of female self-determination, translating it into the language of popular culture.

Commercial features, staid and comparatively realistic, also acknowledged that woman was finally more than an appendage to the masculine ego, and the industry dignified her as never before—or since. Of course, war films and patriotic reviews like *Cry Havoc*, *This Is the Army*, *A Yank in the RAF*, and *Thirty Seconds over Tokyo* saturated the market, as did period tearjerkers such as *Back Street*. But what Rosie the Riveter began and the B serials carried forward as naïve caricatures, Hollywood simultaneously glamorized and slicked up, breaking ground for their working women in elitist territory: In professions requiring brains and fortitude Claudette Colbert played a schoolmarm in *Boom Town* and *Remember the Day*, as did Bette Davis in *The Corn Is Green*. Novelists were portrayed by Colbert (*Without Reservations*), Davis (*Old Acquaintance*), Crawford (*When Ladies Meet*); business executives by Crawford (*They All Kissed The Bride*); lady editors by Ginger Rogers (*Lady in the Dark*); advertising executives by Roz Russell (*Take a Letter, Darling*); Congresswomen by Loretta Young (*The Farmer's Daughter*) and Jean Arthur (*A Foreign Affair*). This film form did not forsake love as its central point of conflict, but oftentimes self-awareness, profes-sional élan, and romance could exist side by side with the female as the healthy protagonist, the male as the needy one.

Spellbound (1945) subtly documents this. Ingrid Bergman as an intense iceberg psychiatrist, who is sexually awakened by her insti-tute's new chief, Gregory Peck, finds herself embroiled in a murder mystery revolving about him. An impostor suffering from amnesia,

Peck is everybody's prime suspect. But through a combination of love, psychological technique, and persistence, Bergman protects him and eventually solves the crime. She also shows up a gaggle of idiotic colleagues and is definitely the dominant, sane force. Although one detects undercurrents of the traditional attitude that "Miss Frozen Puss," as her patients call her, is simply waiting to be thawed by the right man, director Hitchcock (in a rare film where events are resolved by feminine strength) uses her to cure Peck of his memory lapse and in no way compromises her background, education, or career to effect happiness and dignity for both of them.

Hollywood's view of the career woman occasionally seemed crudely exaggerated, however, as though the workings of an ambitious female mind were too foreign, too enigmatic, to comprehend. Joan Crawford's *Mildred Pierce* (1945) and *Humoresque* (1946) played on unrealistic obsessions which eventually undermined the heroine's passionately committed existence. In her Oscar-winning *Mildred Pierce*, for instance, Crawford so devotes herself to her children, especially her spoiled older daughter, Ann Blyth, that she alienates her husband. Blatant ambition for the sole purpose of adorning the girl (and winning her love) drives Crawford to rise from waitress to restaurateur. But on the way to success, she sacrifices herself totally, marrying a cad and eventually attempting to take a murder rap when the daughter kills him. The story, full of melodramatic loopholes, deserves notice, for Crawford plays *Mildred Pierce* with a tremendous warmth and maturity which would be ill-served in her future pictures. The premise that Mildred, beautiful, bright, sensual, and dedicated, would confuse her obligations as a mother, leaning on her daughter to fulfill her own persona, is difficult to swallow simply because Crawford has so many attractive resources of her own. But mother love on that order becomes a joke. Unfortunately Warner Brothers took it seriously.

If her obsessive love was Mildred's chief flaw, so was it Crawford's downfall in *Humoresque*. As the wealthy patron of violinist John Garfield, her cool, calculating self-assurance erodes as she falls in love. Unable even to bear his devotion to his career, Crawford stylishly (in a sequin-encrusted gown) ends her pain in suicide. Again, that a vital and sophisticated female should collapse and kill herself seems incompatible with her very nature, just as her irrational possessiveness embodies the wish fulfillment of a society preferring to write off independence as shallow veneer. Underneath it, Hollywood implied, lies helpless, incapacitating desire and devouring, suffocating love which is hostile to life itself.

Fortunately, such exaggeration did not mar all forties' working-women's pictures. The cinema often juggled and balanced feminine interests with marvelous dexterity; individualistic heroines dignified good-natured plots, their exquisite humanity, humor, and intelligence giving added dimension to the image of woman in film and in life. Among forties' players, Katharine Hepburn stands alone. Or perhaps, more accurately, Hepburn vs. Tracy. By herself, she weathered fiascos like *Undercurrent* (as the aging, bookish bride who suspects her husband wants to kill her). But with Tracy, her films winked at the battle of the sexes, and the two gently wrestled and rearranged careers and egos toward a healthy, mutually satisfactory relationship. Hepburn, her mind as finely honed as her features, her career as fast-moving as her volatile body, would generally collide with the implacable bulk of Tracy's languid, stubborn maleness. There's more than a little taming of the shrew in their collaborations, but both hero and heroine worked from the peripheries of their individual eccentricities toward a common center of compatibility. Usually the seesaw of their attraction/relationship was based on give-and-take, and they were as scales equally weighted vis-à-vis intelligence, involvement in the world, and feeling for each other. Therefore, variations on *Pygmalion* or soapy love stories were avoided, while Hepburn and Tracy showed us—with flair and wit—how two productive beings can iron out male/ female conflicts while remaining true to themselves.

Woman of the Year (1941) was perhaps their funniest and most flawed collaboration. As rival headline-making reporters, Hepburn, a brilliant, self-centered political journalist, and Tracy, a cigar-chomping sports columnist, meet and fall in love. But because elegant Kate, engrossed in her career, hasn't the vaguest notion of domestic commitment or sharing, the marriage begins as a comic shambles with a UN delegation sharing their honeymoon. It ends the night Hepburn is to be honored as "Woman of the Year." Fed up with her selfishness, Tracy refuses to accompany her to the banquet. "I've got an angle that would be sensational. The outstanding woman of the year isn't a woman at all," he accuses, then moves out.

At this point the happy caricatures deteriorate, and the film stoops to proselytizing. Hepburn's liberated aunt marries ("I want to be the prize for a change"), and Hepburn sets out to win Tracy back. While he sleeps, unaware, in his new bachelor flat, she ritualizes a symbolic renunciation of her ambitious life-style: She makes breakfast. Unable to turn on the gas or perk coffee, separating eggs through a strainer, she then vows to her bemused, just-awakened hubby that being *just* his missus is what she wants.

Tempering, even redeeming, this silly ending, however, is the fact that finally Hepburn has come aware of another person's needs and dearly tries to cater to them. Also, one suspects that after a week of her in the kitchen, Tracy would send her packing back to her job. Because he has married this particular female in the first place, he obviously doesn't want a kitchen drudge, but an independent, busy wife who is merely willing to compromise for their dual happiness.

The culmination of the couple's trial-by-emancipation reached its most acid and delightful peak with *Adam's Rib*, the sparkling 1949 comedy pitting them against each other as man vs. woman, husband vs. wife, lawyer vs. lawyer. Tracy, the assistant DA, prosecutes a woman (Judy Holliday) who, having caught her faithless husband red-handed in his love nest, has shot him. Hepburn, sympathetic to her plight, decides to defend her as a symbol of downtrodden women everywhere. "Men have killed and proved a reason, and been set free," she tells the court. "Self-defense—defense of others, of wife or children or home. . . . An unwritten law stands back of a man who fights to defend his home. Apply the same to this maltreated wife and neglected mother." Tracy complains she's making a mockery of the law, turning the courtroom into a circus, and polarizing their marriage. When one of her witnesses, a hefty female weight lifter (testifying to prove female brawn can equal man's physical strength) lifts him over her head as a demonstration, his ego is dashed. Much to his—and the judge's—surprise, Hepburn wins the case. And Tracy demands a divorce. The next day in their accountant's office, they're beset by sentiment—a tear even trickles down *his* face—and rush off to renew their love in the country. The modernity of *Adam's Rib* rests in its repeated use of and pokes at role-playing nuances like this one: Later confessing that crying was a ploy, Tracy warns he will make such "female" tricks part of his behavior. "It shows what I say is true. No difference between the sexes," Kate pounces, but his kisses effect a compromise—a "little" difference. "Hurray for that little difference," he mumbles at fade-out.

However, Hepburn has won, professionally and privately. Having inconsiderately humiliated her husband, she nevertheless manages that impossible feat rarely allotted to screen females: She has her cake and eats it. Tracy, too, has learned a bit about humility and how much she means to him. This statement on love, careers, and competition seems remarkably fresh today. But in all fairness, credit must be paid to the authors of the screenplay, Garson Kanin and Ruth Gordon. Not only does the script read almost as well as it plays, but one can't help wondering whether a writer who didn't happen to have the youthful, lively, and intelligent Miss Gordon as his wife could understand as thoroughly the joys of living with so energetic a female.

Another equally delicious Hepburn-Tracy-Gordon-Kanin creation, *Pat and Mike* (1952) explored virgin turf in portraying the warm relationship between a female athlete (whose tennis and golf games go to pieces whenever her fiancé is present) and her manager-trainer. Mike-Tracy first views Pat-Hepburn as a prize racehorse: "Not much meat on her, but what there is is cherce." Her superb physical coordination, discipline, and forthright charm enamors Tracy. Still, as in *Adam's Rib*, Hepburn thoughtlessly manages to offend his pride: Here, she beats up two thugs ready to attack him. "I've built you up into some kind of Frankenstein monster. . . . Do you think I can show my face in Lindy's? I like a she to be a she and a he to be a he," he explodes, delightfully wounded. But mostly he likes Hepburn's inimitable self. Together they will compete with the world—and win.

Iconoclastically, *Pat and Mike* refused to compromise female athletic prowess, which aside from swimming (Esther Williams, Annette Kellerman) and ice skating (Sonja Henie) has always been depicted as masculine or unattractive. Hepburn-Pat's unrivaled competence at tennis and, after a few sessions, even golf, was not far-fetched, either. In 1932 Mildred "Babe" Didrikson at the age of nineteen triumphed at the Los Angeles Olympic Games, winning the 80-meter hurdle and setting a new world record with the javelin. An all-around athlete who later became a three-time winner of the U.S. Women's Open golf championship, Babe, who excelled at most other sports, too, would stride up to her opponents before the contest and announce: "Ah'm gonna lick yuh tomorrow."[2] In 1950, two years before *Pat and Mike*, she was declared by an Associated Press poll the greatest all-around woman athlete of the twentieth century. And she was the obvious inspiration for the film, the first in which a woman took herself seriously in sports, pushing her body to its limits to compete in a field cherished by men as their own territory.

Hepburn, with her spare, athletic body and sometimes bewildering style, somewhere between that of a prim schoolteacher and a mischievous boy, was a natural for the role. Yet if her nova was never as popular with the public as it should have been, it was in part because the spartan incandescence she emanated *was* athletic and therefore drastically altered the alchemy of screen sexuality—which took some getting used to. Opposite Tracy, however, this energy was transformed into a perfect *pas de deux*, an ideal relationship celebrating the most happily integrated emancipated woman of the era.

Another strong female personality of the period, Rosalind Russell, earned stardom in a number of sharp, fast-paced comedies as the high-powered executive sidelined by love. Like Hepburn, Russell conveyed imperiousness, but without the former's fragility or vulnerability, and Russell's solid, almost-matronly quality tends to encourage easy and unfair dismissal. Yet she was a fine actress and an accurate barometer of the forties' attitudes to women. Floundering around in second leads in the mid-thirties (with Harlow in *Reckless* and *China Seas*), she attempted the difficult, mature lead in Dorothy Arzner's *Craig's Wife* (1936) while a mere twenty-six—and received deserved plaudits. *The Women* brought her stardom, and Howard Hawks' *His Girl Friday* (1940) cemented it. Here, for the first time, as Hildy Parks, Russell was the tough newspaperwoman who parried gags with Cary Grant and Ralph Bellamy in what (Hawks says) was the fastest on-screen dialogue to date. Almost every other role that followed bore a resemblance to Hildy, and Russell's marvelous sense of comic timing, coupled with an almost incorruptible independence, set her up as an ideal professional woman in *No Time for Comedy* (1940), *Hired Wife* (1940), *This Thing Called Love* (1941), *Design for Scandal* (1941), *What a Woman* (1943), *She Wouldn't Say Yes* (1945), and *Tell It to the Judge* (1949).

If much of this material resorted to burlesque, there were enough strong characterizations to admire, as well as other courageous, if middling, attempts to bring worthwhile women to the screen. One must include among them *Flight for Freedom* (1943), an aviatrix yarn based loosely on the life of Amelia Earhart; *Roughly Speaking* (1945), an ambitious, unsuccessful biography of feminist Louise Randall Pierson; and *Sister Kenny* (1946). The last was perhaps the most moving for a number of reasons: First, it was remarkably timely; Sister Elizabeth Kenny, an Australian nurse, had been fighting to have her unique method of massage-as-physical therapy for polio victims recognized since World War I, but not until 1939 did Australian hospitals accept it. In 1940 the University of Minnesota Medical School adopted her methods as its preferred form of treatment, and soon afterward the Elizabeth Kenny Institute opened in Minneapolis. Second, it was a rare biography (unlike Greer Garson's *Madame Curie*, for instance), concentrating on her professional courage and commitment, playing down a love story (in this case, Sister Kenny renounced her lover to concentrate on work). Third, Russell forsook a glamor portrait and aged into a thoughtful, dowdy woman whose beauty lay in her dedication.

Often film students overlook or denigrate Rosalind Russell's role in American movies. Men see her as too tough; indeed, never for a moment does an audience doubt that she can't manage all by herself. Women, brought up to admire typical feminine qualities—wispy voices, helpless giggles, delicate appearances—discount her wry wit and handsome, tailored stature. But Russell may have been ahead of her time, creating an image most relevant today and belonging to an elite group of thirties and forties' stars (*i.e.*, Hepburn, Lana Turner) able to survive into the seventies and avoid the aging-actress-exile to ax murderess or vampire victim—an exile that plagued Bette Davis, Joan Crawford, Olivia de Havilland, Tallulah Bankhead, and Zsa Zsa Gabor. In fact, some of Russell's most facile moments—*Picnic* (1955); *Auntie Mame* (1958); *A Majority of One* (1961); *Five Finger Exercise* (1952); *Gypsy* (1962); *The Trouble with Angels* (1966) and its sequel, *Where Angels Go Trouble Follows* (1968); *Oh Dad, Poor Dad, Mama's Hung You in the Closet and I'm Feelin' So Sad* (1967); and *Mrs. Polifax—Spy* (1971)—proved her incredible durability and pertinence in roles ranging from that of a lonely spinster to daffy CIA agent. They proved, too, that a productive life can indeed exist for an actress over forty.

Had Hollywood built on its image of the career woman, films might have acted as a more positive force in shaping the role of women in years to come. But as the men returned home from the war, box-office—and social—demands changed. Slowly heroines moved into the background, becoming less aggressive or incapable of working out their own fates. Even professional screen women had difficulty. For instance, in *The Bachelor and the Bobbysoxer* (1949), Myrna Loy, a judge, develops a hankering for artist Cary Grant; but her profession works only as a one-line joke, and she is completely dependent on aggressive little sister Shirley Temple and wise old Gramps to activate her love life, the core of the story.

Loretta Young as *The Farmer's Daughter* in 1947 won an Oscar for her portrayal of the clever Norwegian-American who begins her career as maid to a Congressman and winds up as Congresswoman herself. The following year newly muddy, conflicting attitudes to professional women were implicit in *The Accused*. Here Young plays a sexually repressed psychology professor who tentatively encourages the attentions of a deranged student and murders him when he tries to rape her. Not only does her hysteria and inability to cope refute her life's work, and her career hinder her development as a female, but her accumulation of psychological data defies application in controlling both her emotions and behavior. Indeed, her work is the very source of her predicament.

Why?

GI Joe was home again. Reluctant to patronize films about women who ran their lives smoothly and competently without him, he needed reassurance about his own place in society. Moreover, a postwar upheaval had drastically pulled the linoleum and concrete floors out from under women and relegated them to the nubby, worn carpets of home. Displacing females from industry's stronghold was a major task whose tactics were being contemplated long before Hiroshima or Normandy.

As early as 1942 magazines began enumerating the "problems" caused by women undertaking war jobs. *Time* magazine, on September 14, 1942, ran an article complaining that women flirt at work and as evidence reported that Douglas Aircraft had to close its Santa Monica bomb shelter because of lovemaking during the lunch break. Furthermore, girls' transparent blouses and peekaboo sweaters distracted men. Smoking, powdering noses on company time, inordinate absenteeism for catching up on housework, and "gossiping in gangs of two or more" were all criticized.

The following October 17, *Business Week* reported: "Any effort to determine why the world's newest industries are at grips with the world's oldest profession should not discount the determination and ingenuity of the professional." The piece then mentioned that fifty women in Portland, Oregon, shipyards lost their AFL union cards for "plying their trade." Some prostitutes in that city solicited on the job as taxi drivers. One female welder was fired for distributing cards for a "vice den." But worst of all: "A collateral fear expressed by the Portland police is that the prostitutes may consort with Negroes, who then may try to take liberties with other white women and that this might lead to serious race complications."

In 1943 the New York *Times* Magazine wondered, "What About Women After the War?" Author Elinore M. Herrick, director of personnel and labor relations of Todd Shipyards Corporation (and obviously a career woman), pacified the nation:

> Different women want different things. I think most of them—whether they will admit it or not—want only to marry, have a home and children and a man to do their worrying (and sometimes their thinking) for them. Some marry wanting children and can't have them. Some simply want a life of ease—with a marriage license.

Miss Herrick gave comfort but added a note of warning that economic reorganization and provisions would be necessary. Otherwise, "The war will end with women a drug on the market, as they were twenty-five years ago."

That is precisely what happened. In June, 1945, 95 percent of the women war workers who originally had planned to quit after victory intended to stay with their jobs. All 80,000 females in a Chicago radio plant expressed their desire to remain at work, as did 85 percent of Detroit's auto workers. But with 11,000,000 veterans coming home to old jobs that had been reserved for them, the future promised chaos.

Fear was reflected in such magazine titles as "Getting Rid of the Women" (*Atlantic*, June, 1945). "What's Become of Rosie the Riveter?" asked the New York *Times* magazine in May, 1946. "From a humanitarian point of view, too many women should not stay in the labor force. The home is the basic American unit," stated Frederick C. Crawford, board chairman of the National Association of Manufacturers. He was echoed by Frieda S. Miller, director of the Woman's Bureau, waxing patriotic with: "Women workers do not want to get ahead at the expense of the veterans. In fact, they never have regarded their work as a substitute for that of men. Their own record of achievement over a long period of years obviates that need or desire." Obviously, Ms. Miller didn't look long enough at her statistics.

By September, 1945, the U.S. Department of Labor's *Monthly Labor Review* was laying down "Recommendations on Separation of Women from Wartime Jobs" in order "to cushion the effects of transition." It was suggested that requests for voluntary resignation and dismissal of split-shift workers be called for first. Then separations would be based on skill and seniority, with severance pay commensurate with length of service. Since most women had only stepped into their jobs at the beginning or during the war, their jobs were rarely insured; severance paid a pittance.

Industry overtaxed its ingenuity to rid itself of female workers. Shops shut down and converted; females, the newest employees, were the first fired and last rehired. Others were rehired at painfully low wages. As usual, women earned two-thirds that of men, sometimes less, and employers shrugged while they stated that if they were forced to pay equal wages, they would hire men only. Movements restoring old state restrictions forbidding women from lifting more than twenty-five pounds were used to discriminate, as were thinly veiled hiring requests for "first-class mechanics only." Females rated only third-class positions because of lack of seniority rather than lack of ability or experience.

To exacerbate the situation even further, unemployment compensation fanned discriminatory attitudes. Benefits, based on salary, were—for women—low to begin with. But women in service industries were without legal refuge, and married women were also deemed ineligible unless special petition proved their need to continue working. For the law simply assumed they would meekly resume their household duties.

Massive layoffs which began after V-J Day continued. By 1947 more than 3,000,000 women had resigned or been fired from their positions (more than during the Depression dip). And just as thirties' films ignored this societal shift, so did Hollywood refuse to deal with it as a postwar problem. Only the celluloid emphasis changed. Woman— professional or otherwise—was fading. The once-dominant, strong protagonist became the background buffoon, love object, or thorn in her man's side. Gone were attempts at re-creating lives of intriguing women. Gone with the war's end were most of those films where female intelligence, faith, and courage created interest and those where love was spiritual, universal, rather than personal (Jennifer Jones' Oscar-winning *The Song of Bernadette*, 1943; Ingrid Bergman's *The Bells of St. Mary's*, 1945). The few movies dealing with postwar readjustment spoke only from the male viewpoint. To the returning GI females seemed changelings.

Anne Leighton expressed the problem in *Harper's Magazine* in a December, 1946, piece on "The American Matron and the Lilies": "Many American war veterans are silently bearing some unexpected rehabilitation difficulties in coming home to what used to be a pleasantly pliable and even appealingly incompetent little woman and finding a quietly masterful creature recognizing no limitations to her own endurance."

The Best Years of Our Lives (1947) illustrates such one-sided thoughts of rehabilitation. Three soldiers come home. Harold Russell has lost his arms; his teen-aged fiancée is queasy about it. Dana Andrews' wife, now a nightclub singer, is two-timing him. She complains that she has been spoiled during the war, living on both his war pay and her own nightclub earnings—and she doesn't intend to alter this new life-style. Eventually, after she flaunts her lover in his face, they separate.

But the most telling postwar relationship in the film is that of banker Fredric March who confides to Andrews on returning home for the first time: "Feels like I were going in to hit a beach." The poignancy of reunion with his family evaporates and shadows cross his face when daughter Teresa Wright boasts, "You don't have to worry about us, Dad. We can handle the problems [on the home front]. We're tough." His dejected expression reveals how their toughness frightens him. When wife Myrna Loy receives a phone call shortly after he has arrived (unannounced and unexpected), that same uncertainty crosses his face. She is canceling perfectly legitimate plans; but they are *her* plans, *her* life—and March is the intruder. That evening he takes his women out, and while he gets drunk, the ladies patiently sit by, having set aside all their needs to try terribly to understand him. But that, perhaps, is the point: *The film portrays the readjustment of the returning soldier, and scarcely considers parallel problems of his woman.*

Instead, expectations demanded that females turn clocks back to situations that once were, that might have been, or that should have been. But in reality, demands and needs of women now cried out for novel solutions and sensitive examination. They were not forthcoming. Not in life. And certainly not on the neighborhood screen.

One gentleman, Victor Dallaire, a former correspondent for *Stars and Stripes*, voiced collective masculine confusion and hostility when he wrote of "The American Woman? Not for This G.I." in the *New York Times Magazine* on March 10, 1946:

> Being nice is almost a lost art among American women. They elbow their way through crowds, swipe your seat at bars and bump and push their way around regardless. Their idea of equality is to enjoy all the rights men are supposed to have with none of the responsibilities. . . .
>
> After three months in this land of challenging females, I feel that I should go back to France and tell them they're a heck of a lot better where they are just in case some of them believed us and are still waiting.

Similar vibrations and warnings were felt in the upper echelons of professional circles as well. In 1945 a judge told a young lawyer fresh out of Harvard Law School: "Tell your sisters of the Bar to forget the idea that they must be like men—using the much-vaunted 'cold logic' of the male that so often proves to be just that, leaving everyone cold who hears it. For me, I'll take a good shot of feminine intuition!"[3]

Such cocksure surfacing of GI Joe's wartime sexual exploits or the pointless flattering of woman's "intuition" at the expense of logic may dim the real urgency smoldering here—a plea for the return of the passive, "pleasantly pliable and even appealingly incompetent" female. A cry reminiscent of 1929's hailing the return of the unobtrusive, "mysterious" siren—that feminine ideal who had abdicated both brains and interest in active social participation.

This plea would be answered shortly. In fact, "return" imprecisely describes the situation, for in society's—and Hollywood's—heart the fluffy little lady had never really vanished. She had just lain dormant, carefully camouflaged on the screen by tuneful period musicals and suspense shockers.

And in footlockers and trenches she had not been concealed at all.

13

PIN THE TAIL ON THE PIN-UP

or the preening of grable, greening of hayworth,
and cleaning up of russell

Wartime opened a rich new area to GI jokes. More than 300,000 women served at home and overseas in the WAC, the WAVES, Coast Guard, and Women Marines, but never could they live down humorous speculation on the color of their underwear (khaki?), consequences of pregnancy (PWOP meant pregnant without permission), and the possible lesbian tendencies such spartan rigors implied. As if to purge this last impression, a 1944 Tangee lipstick ad displayed photos of seven uniformed female officers and this desperate slug: *"We are still the weaker sex.* It's still up to us to appear as alluring and lovely as possible."

The war also sanctified jovial masculine sexual self-expression. If the sailor had a girl in every port, OK; if the soldier in the foxhole starved for sexual release, OK, too. And while Norman Rockwell's grotesque drawing of Rosie the Riveter appeared on the cover of the *Saturday Evening Post* on May 29, 1943, boys plastered their barracks with inviting pinups of their favorite film stars. Lana peered down at them with moist cherry-red lips; Hedy Lamarr came hither with the same orgasmic half-lidded countenance that had brought her to fame with *Ecstasy* in 1936. But most popular of all were Rita Hayworth, kneeling on an unmade bed, her pale nightgown and black lace bodice carefully defining an ample bosom, and Betty Grable in a skintight swimsuit with her rump to the camera and a smile over her shoulder.

Men loved the pinup. Women, anesthetized by the idea of "glamor," couldn't care less. But Postmaster General Frank C. Walker, acting on behalf of the government, found it all rather demoralizing and in

1944 banned the ladies from the mails, determined, out of a puritan watchdoggism, to rescue the armed forces from depravity.

Hollywood had less heroic reasons for soft-pedaling sex during the war years. The most obvious was box office. It seemed at once un-diplomatic and unbusinesslike for movie queens to expose their limbs and lick their lips in darkened palaces full of frustrated, lonely women —women wearing last year's gray gabardine suits with wide shoulder pads and shorter skirts. Masculine styles and upswept hairdos, durable for easy and safe movement at work, reflected, too, the nation's mili-tary tone. Movies during these years cleverly played it safe and, con-tent with only a hint of sex, continued the trend of late-thirties' musi-cal songfests. The entire family could enjoy them, and sex could exist as subliminal suggestion, like a desirable but elusive perfume.

Furthermore, movie musicals of the forties exuded warmth, camara-derie, and nostalgia. Many served as historical monuments, tributes to patriotism, to Americana and the wonderful warmth of home. Films like Judy Garland's *For Me and My Gal* (1942), *Meet Me in St. Louis* (1944), and later *The Harvey Girls* (1946); Betty Grable's *The Dolly Sisters, Sweet Rosie O'Grady, Coney Island* (1942), and *Mother Wore Tights* (1947); Alice Faye's *Lillian Russell* (1940) and *Hello Frisco Hello* (1943) were just a few which recalled the tranquillity of yester-year. The stars of these vehicles, boned and corseted to set off their curves, existed as peaches-and-cream incarnations of the virtues of the American girl. Often themes centered on show business—and during vaudeville moments demure Grable or Garland would conveniently and respectably doff her bustle and display her legs. When the musicals left the turn of the century behind them, they were even more daring.

Betty Grable, the eighth biggest box-office draw in 1942, gained additional momentum after *Song of the Islands* costarred her with Victor Mature. As a local Pacific Island girl, replete with happy hula hips, lei, and gardenia, she sings, rebuffs the muscular, overly sensual Mature, and finally gives in to his persuasions. By 1943 Grable had jumped to Number One at the box office, and she maintained a place on the top ten list for thirteen years. Fox estimates that she alone was responsible for more than $5,000,000 of their annual profits, and in 1947 and 1948 she earned more money than any other woman in America ($208,000 per annum).

Grable's staggering success may be puzzling to those indifferent to her plumped-out face, plumped-up lips, and just plump body. Yet there was about her a directness—her virginal naïveté; her full, uncomplicated voice, always incredulous and vacantly girlish; her exuberance. Ardent in love and pertly angry when disappointed, she may have been (aside from Garland) the most feminine, uncomplicated, and ripe female on-screen during the war years. While all the grand dames —Davis, Crawford, Garson, Bergman, Rogers—were busy weeping their way through "women's pictures," Grable, blond and pink and glowingly healthy, celebrated the joy of being a girl untouched by war, work, gray serge, or brains. Because she so curiously embodied both familial and maternal warmth *and* "all-American sex appeal," she outdistanced all box-office competitors. Giving succor at the family level and in the trenches simultaneously was no easy trick, and it carved Grable's niche in the history of American movies. At the same time her pinup marked the rise of the modern sex symbol.

Grable would continue as Twentieth Century-Fox's Golden Girl until another, sexier blonde would usurp her crown: Marilyn Monroe. But the public had to be primed for Monroe, and a woman with a surplus of the real sensuality Grable lacked made the magical transition.

Rita Hayworth, born Margarita Cansino, was a lithe, tallish youngster when Fox talent scouts down in Agua Caliente caught an act in which she performed an Apache dance with her father, Eduardo. Ignoring Daddy, they signed Rita to a contract, but after a number of secondary roles of spitfires, Latin dancers, and leads in B movies, she was dropped. She did manage to pick up, however, Husband No. One, an automobile salesman named Edward Judson, who took Rita's career in hand. Negotiating a Columbia contract for her, Judson then put her in the charge of the studio beauty specialists. To dispel "Latin firebrand" stereotyping, they directed her to submit to eyectrolysis for a high and graceful forehead and tinted her locks a fiery auburn.

Harry Cohn soon began to sit up and take notice. His most celebrated leading lady, Jean Arthur, was itching to terminate her relationship with Columbia, and Cohn groomed Rita as his new box-office sensation. For an auspicious beginning, he starred her opposite Fred Astaire in two musicals, *You'll Never Get Rich* (1941) and *You Were Never Lovelier* (1942). With these films, and a loan-out to Twentieth for *My Gal Sal* (1942), her ability and prestige grew. But it was

Cover Girl (1944) which proved to Columbia that Rita had indeed arrived.

This time her costar was Gene Kelly, still too new to films to be a big box-office draw. But as Rusty Parker, the Brooklyn nightclub singer who almost leaves behind the man she loves (Kelly) when she soars from celebrated Cover Girl of the Year to Broadway leading lady, Rita established her stardom. Not only did she and Kelly dance superbly together, but their song "Long Ago and Far Away" has since become a movie musical classic. Also, in a highly publicized casting coup, the chicest models of the day (like Jinx Falkenberg) decorated the film with polished bandbox sophistication which provoked female interest. But preeminently, the star herself found her stride after nine years in movies. Sultry, she radiated sex. Yet just as Grable's duality included a Betty Crocker motherliness, Hayworth's was a frank and open beauty. Her smile dazzled; her strong, lithe body was amazingly fluid. Unabashedly sexual, she also possessed a playful abandon that the screen had never seen before. And if this escaped the notice of patrons of *Cover Girl*, it confronted them head on in *Gilda*.

As well it should have. The Japanese had formally surrendered aboard the battleship *Missouri* on September 2, 1945. Men, home from the Pacific and European fronts, looked for diversion and found instead *Mildred Pierce* and her quasi-liberated friends. But they patronized movies enthusiastically, and studio revenues, which had for a time during the war undergone a slump, reached an all-time peak in 1946. *Gilda*, released that year, was the kind of titillating attraction that the shrapneled nerves of GI Joe doted on.

First, it wasn't a musical, but a steamy melodrama of gangsters, spies, and world power monopolies set in Buenos Aires. As ex-lovers, Hayworth and Glenn Ford renew old flames and grudges when she, Gilda, becomes the bride of Baron Mundsen. Elaborate complications follow, and with the baron dead—or so they think—Johnny (Ford) takes over his worldwide tungsten monopoly. He takes over Gilda, too, and, after their marriage, wreaks revenge on her for once having thrown him over. A virtual prisoner, she is isolated from him, but unable to escape his control. Even a new lover is revealed as Johnny's stooge. Pushed to her limits, Gilda does the only thing that will provoke a reaction from him: She flaunts her sexuality. In a black strapless sheath and long black gloves she challenges him in his own club, singing her milestone "Put the Blame on Mame." Feline, fiery, her sexuality is no pose here. It's self-indulgent, seducing, an angry weapon. What *Gilda* explores so exactly is not just the blinding fires of passion, but the need for humiliation and subjugation that has been so much a part of our sexual mythology on-screen and off. Gilda and Johnny manipulate and feed on each other's discomfort. Contemptuous, he treats her like the whore she has been to him. When she prostrates herself in the casino as he forcibly halts her "Mame" exhibitionism, Gilda hysterically cries out, "Now they all know what I am. It's no use you just knowing it, Johnny. Now they all know that Johnny married a ——" In his embarrassment, he slaps her across the face.

Gilda's overt sensuality pulled out all the sexual stops that had been plugged since the demise of the Sternberg-Dietrich collaboration. Yet the difference was that while Hayworth could invite, purr, lick her lips, her sexuality was a very physical one—without mystery or pretense. The golden girl, the beautiful all-American hooker with flowing shoulder-length hair, reverberated in the public imagination, dispelling the intense I-am-nothing/your-perverse-pleasure-is-my-amusement ephemeralism of thirties' sirens. This ripe directness matched the needs of postwar audiences, and for the first time a heroine seemed to say, "This is my body. It's lovely and gives *me* pleasure. I rejoice in it just as you do."

In reality, Rita's rejoicing met with constant obstruction. One of these was studio boss Harry Cohn who saw his box office dwindle every time she decided to take pleasure as a woman and wife. Her first marriage had been quickly dissolved, and while Cohn was successful at heading off a binding relationship between his gold mine and Victor Mature, he failed dismally when Orson Welles came into her life. The brilliant young jack-of-all-trades, who was then also a slim, handsome raconteur, and Cohn's star were married in 1943. Five years and one daughter later, the relationship was dissolved. But before Cohn could breathe a sigh of proprietary relief, Rita was embroiled with playboy Prince Aly Khan.

This time the public and press were on Cohn's side since the heir to the Muslim throne had not yet divorced his wife. In the rigorously moral postwar years, Rita was the target of character assassination. But when Khan freed himself and made her his princess in 1949, all was forgiven. She, however, couldn't care less and didn't return to pictures until 1952; by that time her relationship with Khan had ended, she had borne her second daughter, and the public had newer, more golden girls. Rita's movies like *Salome* (1953), *Miss Sadie Thompson* (1954), *Fire Down Below* (1957), and *Pal Joey* (1957, a role Cohn originally wanted for Dietrich) warmed over her wide-open sex appeal, but never again could she rekindle the public's acclaim. She starred in films on-and-off throughout the sixties, tried marriage two more times —to singer Dick Haymes and film producer James Hill. Today there are rumors of alcoholic bouts, and although friends have begged her to try a comeback in their movies, her unreliability and mysterious disappearances prior to production have dimmed their enthusiasm. A most telling reflection of the inner wars she has waged may be a brutally honest confidence Hayworth once gave producer-writer Virginia Van Upp. Miss Van Upp had been sent by Columbia to Europe to dissuade the star from her liaison with Aly Khan, and Hayworth, after proclaiming her love for the prince, confessed that she was worried about the impending marriage. Why? "Because you wrote *Gilda*," she said to her friend. "And every man I've known has fallen in love with *Gilda* and awakened with me."[1]

This beautifully captures the undercurrents of the cinema's fantasy power, and the fears of every star or woman who is idealized or idolized as a mysterious mannequin. Her day of reckoning always comes, for her image boomerangs, too powerful to be reconciled with reality, no matter how superb or lovely she is. You see, she is also only human.

Movies were hastily exorcising humanity from sexuality. The industry separated the two traits as blithely as Julia Child would an egg yolk from a white. Pure, isolated screen sex was escalating like mercury on a humid summer day, and before long, it would practically obscure both Grable's rump-round legginess and Rita's languid-limbed celebration of self.

1946 emerged as a landmark for the female breast. It marked the brief release of Howard Hughes' controversial movie *The Outlaw*, which had been held up for more than three years because of censorship indignation over Jane Russell's endowments. Indeed, hers were the breasts that launched a thousand jokes, complaints, and letters from citizens' groups across the country. The story is both sad and funny. Hughes, who headed RKO and had launched Jean Harlow's stardom in 1930, decided in 1940 to film the simple story of Billy the Kid, Doc Holliday, and Rio, the spitfire whose favors the twosome shared. In the hands of a gentleman with less talent for publicity, this might have been a run-of-the-mill Western, but Hughes cast the 38-inch-bosomed Miss Russell as Rio, then proceeded to glue his camera to her chest as she bent down, reclined, was raped, rode a stallion, or gave comfort to the Kid. He deliberately photographed from her cleavage down to her navel and was so obsessed with the Russell anatomy that he engineered a specially built brassiere to keep her high, wide, and handsome, at the same time minimizing excess movement. "We're not getting enough production out of Jane's breasts,"[2] was his excuse.

The Hays Office's convulsions were nothing compared to the public's. A fetching billboard which accompanied the movie's original 1943 San Francisco opening caused so much furor that the police were readying action when the picture was discreetly withdrawn. But not, alas, forgotten.

At the war's end, Hughes—perhaps noting that with the men now home, Russell's curves would receive a warmer reception—began organizing an extensive, tasteless advertising campaign whose slogans went: "What are the two great reasons for Jane Russell's rise to stardom?" and "How would you like to tussle with Russell?"

But they provoked the wrong people. The Motion Picture Association of America, indignant again, revoked the seal of approval it had half-heartedly bestowed in the first place and its ban was upheld in a suit filed by Hughes in the U.S. district court in New York. But he released the film without a seal anyway, and overworked state censors heartily voiced their opinions on The Outlaw's salacious aspects. Almost as disgusting as Hughes' exploitation of Russell were rulings such as that of a Baltimore judge who complained that her breasts "hung over the picture like a thunderstorm spread out over a landscape."[3]

One can hardly speculate on the proclivities that made Howard Hughes take so stubborn a stance regarding a film that was mediocre at best. Was it spite? Lasciviousness? Self-indulgence? Crudeness? A protest against censorship? Simple greed? The lengthy delay damaged the box office and postponed the minor stardom of Jane Russell, whose physical attributes had become legend before anyone had actually seen her.

Russell, after making The Paleface with Hope in 1948, came into her own in the early fifties as the good-hearted, stacked dame. In keeping with her surly, Amazonian exterior (she looked amazingly like the incarnation of the 1943 comic strip *Wonder Woman*) there was a businesslike competence about her that perfectly complemented Monroe's daffy-wet little girl of *Gentlemen Prefer Blondes* (1953) and played down her own sexuality. Still, Russell, who married a football player, led a staid, religious life off-screen, and has recently appeared in bra commercials on television, learned something about the excesses of industry exploitation and humiliation via her Hughes experience. Years later she reminisced about *The Outlaw* fiasco: "Sometimes the photographers would pose me in a low-necked nightgown and tell me to bend down and pick up a couple of pails. They were not shooting the pails. Or else they would tell me to jump up and down in bed in the nightgown while they shot from above and below. I didn't realize what they were doing. I was green as grass."[4]

And more naïve than any woman had a right to be.

While the most flamboyantly sexual images of the forties were those of Hayworth and Russell, on-screen sex was more often white-washed and veiled in vague suggestion. Veronica Lake, petite and frail as the actress who minces about like a waif in hobo clothes in *Sullivan's Travels* (1941), played out peekaboo fantasies with her silky blond pageboy gliding like a curtain over one eye. Lana Turner popularized both Schwab's Drugstore and fuzzy sweaters, and in repose her icily distant beauty was transformed into a child-like, pouty invitation. More in keeping with Hollywood wholesome-ness, Esther Williams, a former swimming champion with a statuesque body, revealed her lean muscular form in a number of romantic comedies such as *Bathing Beauty* (1944), *Easy to Wed* (1945), *Fiesta* (1948), *On an Island With You* (1948), *Neptune's Daughter* (1949), and *Pagan Love Song* (1950). More fascinating even than her classical build was the fact that water never mussed her Grecian, seed-pearl or gardenia-studded hairdos. Esther Williams' mermaidery rightly became a target for smirks and ridicule. James Agee in a *Time* review of *Bathing Beauty* (1944) mused that when wet, "she suggests a porpoise amused by its own sex appeal." But his droll perceptions are even more acute in another review of the same film for the *Nation*:

Bathing Beauty swarms with bathing suits and their contents; most often and most carnally in focus is Esther Williams, lolloping in a friendly way before underwater cameras. Above water level Harry James and Xavier Cugat play, and Red Skelton for my leathery taste, is occasionally rather funny. I could not resist the wish that Metro-Goldwyn-Mayer had topped its aquatic climax—a huge pool full of girls, fountains, and spouts of flame—by suddenly draining the tank and ending the show with the entire company writhing like goldfish on a rug. But MGM resisted it.

One delightfully humorous exotic, a buffoon parodying all her sexy sisters, was Carmen Miranda. Known as "The Brazilian Bombshell," she became a staple in forties' musicals like *Down Argentine Way* (her debut, 1940), *The Gang's All Here* (1944), *That Night in Rio* (1941), *Weekend in Havana*, (1941) and *A Date with Judy* (1948). Her eyes twinkled like Garbo's, her mouth moved like Mickey Mouse's, and with her tutti-frutti hat and maracas she radiated an exuberant, if foolishly overdressed and purely decorative, charm. Debuting at a time when all the European exchange markets had been closed by the war, she was viewed as Hollywood's great Latin hope for attracting South American theater chains, and she inaugurated a Latin American explosion here with lively, tongue-twisting songs ("Mañana") and lavish South-of-the Border production numbers which Busby Berkeley and others built around her. Miranda, in many ways more fortunate than the seriously sexy ladies, could pursue a man, smothering him with hyperthyroid kisses and imitations of woo. But she was never a threat. Like Mae West, she projected as much sex appeal as a Christmas tree in July. Simply too ornate and broad, she remained a joke, a laugh machine vacant of nuances or emotional life. Enraged, she'd roll her eyes and spew forth epithets in volatile Spanish; happy, she'd roll her eyes and flash her cartoon smile. The most that could be said about her (which is a lot) is that she always seemed to be having a good time, and when she was on screen, so did the audience. But usually theirs was at her expense.

By the late forties box-office sex had thoroughly whetted Hollywood's appetite. The industry began decking out even highly touted dramatic stars as cylindrical-breasted tempests. In *Flamingo Road* (1949) Joan Crawford played an ex-carny girl trying to make good despite static from politico Sydney Greenstreet, who dislikes her because her pinched waistline, tight button-down sweater, and past work suggests a weak moral nature. Styles were changing, and fashion had been stripped of shoulder pads and serge; now yards of material, soft jerseys, raglan sleeves and cinch-belts entranced designers, and Crawford was just one of a long line of stars Hollywood trussed up in a highly exaggerated manner.

But it was Jennifer Jones in King Vidor's *Duel in the Sun* (1947) who postured and pouted in the most embarrassing interpretation of what Hollywood was beginning to consider sexy. Usually Vidor's work was conservative and controlled, but *Duel*, produced by David O. Selznick, Miss Jones' second husband, was an exercise in excess (Vidor eventually quit, unable to work under the producer's detailed scrutiny). Since Selznick in his endless memos admitted his preoccupation with his female stars—especially Jones—down to the shape of their eyebrows and length of their curls, he must bear a good deal of responsibility for this fiasco. One of his great early intuitive gifts had been to recognize and adorn female beauty and talent—and Vivien Leigh (*Gone with the Wind*, 1939), Ingrid Bergman (*Intermezzo*, 1939), and Joan Fontaine (*Rebecca*, 1940) received fortunate showcases under his sensitive aegis. But in the case of Miss Jones, love blinded both taste and critical judgment. Selznick's forties' career seemed dedicated to immortalizing her as the Perfect Woman: She was his Ideal Mystic in *The Song of Bernadette* (1943), his Ideal Aging Teen in *Since You Went Away* (1944), Ideal Ageless Beauty in *Portrait of Jennie* (1948), and Ideal Spitfire in *Duel*. Here, as Pearl, the half-breed, Jennifer Jones was also something of a joke. The story tells of Pearl, "a wildflower sprung from the hard clay, quick to blossom, ready to die." Irretrievably drawn to "bad" brother Gregory Peck whose savage seduction wins her heart forever, Jones-Pearl acts out every cliché associated with vamping. *Duel*'s dramatic thunder ends appropriately in a pistol duel. Liberated and honorable enough to kill the lover who has menaced her and society long enough, Pearl nevertheless sacrifices her own life. After a desperate last-gasp crawl over rocks and pebbles, under the blazing sun, she and Peck clench hands; in pools of their own blood, they die together.

Dwarfing the corn of the story, however, is the Jones-Selznick pre-fifties' concept of sexuality. Jones lounges in doorways, arching her back and tossing black tendrils and quivering (her) red gash of lips. The whole business might be overlooked as unfortunate error had the same excesses not been repeated in black and white five years later. *Ruby Gentry* was another Vidor vehicle in which Jones-Ruby—this time a swamp girl in checkered blouse and blue jeans—taunts (and brings about ruin for) Charlton Heston.

It was 1952, and her posture, fast being adapted as a staple of B melodrama, was unnatural, a fakery, although its real-life counterpart already existed in movie magazines' back-page ads for Frederick's of Hollywood. This mail-order dress house happily supplied (and still does!) pointy breasts and clover behinds to every wistful housewife and movie-mad teen-ager who'd learned from the screen's Pearls and Rubys, from its Russells and Hayworths, just what was truly "sexy."

Rendering woman a caricature of her own femaleness, Hollywood, however, was not content to dictate exteriors alone. Simultaneously, if surreptitiously, movies began probing the psychic root of woman's vulnerability.

For if the flesh was willing, and so susceptible to suggestion, would not the spirit be also?

And the mind? And soul?

14

SUSPICION STALKS!

Franklin Delano Roosevelt told the world during his first inaugural: "Let me assert my firm belief that the only thing we have to fear is fear itself." Possibilities like death, Nazism, loss of loved ones or limbs represented very real threats during the war years. But the terrors of the Meuse-Argonne or the forages through once green and lush foliage of the Pacific were nothing compared to the havoc wrought by and on women in one particular category of forties' films.

Women's pictures broadcast contradictory messages. Where the more affirmative genre for a time sympathetically depicted waiting or working wives and capable girlfriends, another, a peculiar strain of suspense film preyed on alleged female doubts and infirmities. Persecuted by an incurable disease, her own insanity, or by the person closest to her, the screen heroine had not been trapped in such perilous straits since Pearl White was tied to the railroad tracks in a *Perils of Pauline* or since Gish fled across the ice in *Way Down East*.

The most obvious method of undermining was physical. Bette Davis had died of a brain tumor in *Dark Victory* (1939). By comparison that was kind. She didn't have to fend off a murderous intruder sent by her husband the way bedridden Barbara Stanwyck did in *Sorry, Wrong Number* (1948). But the list of forties' female victims reads like a *Who's Who* hospital roster. It would be too ghoulish to list them all. Suffice it to mention that deafness was a favorite plague. If Loretta Young were able to hear, how could Don Ameche have invented the telephone (*The Story of Alexander*

Graham Bell, 1939)? Again, she was similarly afflicted in *And Now Tomorrow* (1944), as a result of meningitis, but while poor doctor Alan Ladd didn't invent a telephone for her, he did manage to perfect a serum which restored her faculties. Her inability also allowed Ladd, a frustrated suitor, to turn his face away (for rich-girl Loretta read lips with genius) and wisecrack such hostilities as "That's one round for you, baby"; to break all professional ethics by simultaneously courting and treating her medically; and to try the untested serum out, almost killing her in the process.

Both Dorothy McGuire and Jane Wyman were not so lucky, both being mute, and Wyman deaf as well. McGuire in *The Spiral Staircase* (1945) is a maid who is target for a maniac who preys on impaired girls. Fortunately, at the moment of her impending demise, she recovers her voice. Wyman's urchin *Johnny Belinda* (1948) is persecuted by a brute who rapes her, kills her father, and then tries to kidnap the illegitimate child she conceived by him; finally rallying, Wyman out of fury and frustration murders the man.

Slow poison, another favorite method of victimizing females, was intrinsic to the plot of *Notorious* (1946); here Ingrid Bergman would have been done in by her Nazi husband had Cary Grant not rescued her. In *The Two Mrs. Carrolls* (1947) Stanwyck found herself back in bed because of tiny doses delivered by mate Humphrey Bogart.

But the most popular means of terrorizing females in forties' movies was not simply to do away with them or present them as creatures with physical disabilities; movies played on their mental balance, presuming, first of all, that hysteria could overtake women at any time, second, that paranoia was practically their second nature, and, third, that men were arbiters of the sanity—or insanity.

Neurosis could even be glamorous and almost fun—as in Kurt Weill's *Lady in the Dark* (1941), in which Ginger Rogers, an irri-table top fashion editor, is pursued by private demons borne of an ugly-duckling childhood in the shadow of a gorgeous mother. After a number of gaudy musical dream numbers (in one, her mink coat is jewel-studded), Rogers, with the help of an analyst, makes a breakthrough, one which must have set psychiatry, as well as female autonomy, back a few light years:

SHRINK: You've had to prove you were superior to all men; you
       had to dominate them.
ROGERS: What's the answer?
SHRINK: Perhaps some man who'll dominate you.

Her cure is imminent when she confides to a friend: "It's over,
I'm giving it (the magazine) up. I'm going to live my life as a
woman—I want someone to lean on and take care of me. I want to
live my life as other women do."

For those who couldn't take psychiatry and Ginger seriously,
The Snake Pit (1947) had Olivia de Havilland as a real psychotic,
one whose childhood Electra impulses had been similarly, but more
severely, disarranged by a hostile mother and rejecting father. Her
adult dysfunction occurs when both Daddy and an ex-suitor die, and
Olivia goes bananas because she has not worked through and
accepted her father's behavior. The cheap Freudianism of *The
Snake Pit* was quite popular; additionally, the film reputedly helped
institute reforms in asylums which, prior to public enlightenment
and an important mid-fifties innovation, sedatives, did indeed treat
their patients as both inmates and animals.

But the most insidious films were those exploring the interiors
of female minds, minds where susceptibility to suggestion rather
than legitimate dysfunction took women to the brink of insanity.
Doubting herself and her senses endangered woman's very life. In
Gaslight (1944), Charles Boyer marries Ingrid Bergman to have
free access to search for her dead aunt's hidden jewels. By contra-
dicting her observations, flickering the lights when she's alone in
a room, and insisting that she's an invalid, he nearly induces a
nervous breakdown and is just about ready to commit her to a sanitarium forever when bystander Joseph Cotten intervenes. Almost
never during the long ordeal her husband imposes does Bergman
question him, refute this transparent insanity frame-up, or trust
her own instincts.

The queen of the mind benders, however, was Joan Fontaine,
Olivia de Havilland's sister. Both women could mask their faces
with incredulous serenity and naïveté, then adeptly wrack them
with terror, but Fontaine in *Rebecca* (1940) and *Suspicion* (1941),
both directed by Hitchcock, and also *Jane Eyre* (1943) reworked

the pattern of a genteel young woman who, in becoming part of a man's life, almost goes to pieces as inexplicable. events surrounding him terrorize her. For *Jane Eyre*, it's the booming, Byronic Mr. Rochester and the piercing screams from the unidentified animal-wife chained up in his attic that send her running. In *Rebecca* the ghost of her husband's first wife, the suspicious lesbianlike house-keeper, Mrs. Danvers, and mysterious husband Laurence Olivier nearly undo her. In *Suspicion* the strange circumstantial behavior and lies of impecunious hubby Cary Grant drive her obsessively. Is he poisoning her milk? Did he kill their friend Captain Melbeck? Is he trying to push her off the cliff? Fontaine is terrified, and director Hitchcock has fun making her paranoia real to us. But it's all the director's naughty game. At the end the couple drive off, and since Grant has not killed Fontaine when given the chance, we must conclude that her hysteria and insecurity about her mar-riage, as much as chance circumstances, created this climate of irrational fear.

Fontaine is a typical Hitchcock woman. If his females are not murderers (*The Paradine Case*, 1947), they are usually victims (*Notorious*, 1946; *Psycho*, 1960; *The Birds*, 1963; *Frenzy*, 1972). When Anthony Perkins gussies himself up as Grandma, by way of Hitchcock's providing a motive for stabbing Janet Leigh (and others) in *Psycho*, the director superficially links latent homosexu-ality, mother hate, and violence. When the milky-white female necks crumble one after another in the hands of another latent homo-sexual in *Frenzy*, and these ladies hardly put up a decent survival battle, it may not be realistic, but it reflects how thin his characters are and how much humanity he sacrifices for suspense. Yet Hitch-cock is so sneaky, such an irascible and wry craftsman that he wields his inscrutable, dry humor over men, as well as women; his insanely predatory males are hardly better off. Because he main-tains a careless aloofness from his characters, one might surmise that rather than exhibit a contempt for women, he simply seizes on them as the most pliable, passive victims available: If a female protagonist could be vulnerable to, and thus perpetrate, the irra-tional more credibly, the director and plot strategist need not work as hard in formulating plausible scenarios.

But Hitchcock wasn't the sole perpetrator of antifemale thrillers. During the war years this was an immensely popular genre, and the female public was especially drawn to it. Underscoring female helplessness, could these exuberant, almost-Victorian exercises in terror and woman's inability to cope be subtle reminders that they weren't as self-sufficient as all that? Did women enjoy—or require —masochistic stories? Most likely they merely accepted these films as distracting entertainment, simply unaware of the potential psychological damage of the content which violated, even insulted, their very natures.

Another curiosity about this genre is that rarely did these movies bother to draw any realistic portrait of the husband or of the male-female relationships. Both were generally left tentative and unfocused, while the female's neurosis was the point of vulnerability. Boyer in *Gaslight* is a caricature; Grant in *Suspicion* is deliberately vague.

One film of terror which formulates an unusual interaction is *Shadow of a Doubt* (1943), another Hitchcock thriller—with a difference: The female character is fleshed out with intelligence and insight by Teresa Wright, who is introduced to us as the teen-age alter ego of her uncle, Joseph Cotten. Both are named Charley, and Teresa worships him as one would an older brother, father, lover, and mentor all rolled into one. Cotten, a vagabond, represents the glamor and excitement she, a small-town girl, longs for. "I think we're both alike," she confides, and proof seems to be the ESP she has cultivated regarding him. When she sends him a telegram, his own, announcing his arrival in town, crosses hers. Then, later in the week she relates a dream where they say good-bye on a train. This is prophetic, but not until after Teresa painfully pieces together clues revealing Cotten as "The Merry Widow Murderer."

Facing the truth is no easy matter for a staunch girl who only days before indulged dazzling romantic and incestuous notions, but Teresa's weaning from Cotten is made possible by two factors. The first is the presence of a detective who has fallen in love with her. The second is the irrefutable evidence of Cotten's guilt. When asked to speak at a woman's club meeting, he launches into an explosive tirade against women—that old men die and "leave their money to their wives, foolish wives—and what do the wives do, these useless women? You see them drinking, eating, gambling—greedy women. Are they human or are they faded, fat wheezing animals? And what happens to animals when they get too fat and too old?"

Considering Hitchcock's filmography, it is impossible not to wonder how much of himself he is revealing in this discourse. But the director can almost be excused here, because he allows Wright to triumph—even if atypically. After a scuffle, this petite innocent throws the big grown-up uncle off a train—the "good-bye." This amounts to unique self-assertion in a genre whose success absolutely depends on female weakness, mental and physical. Even though a 1947 study of the endurance of prizefighters and chorus girls concluded that fighters tired more easily, sheer size and force gave man the advantages. Few of these female victims bothered to harness their brains, as incapacitated by love, they preferred to deny their instincts or sanity rather than disappoint their dreams.

Certainly, if woman could practically obliterate herself for love the converse might be true: She could obliterate others. The genre of the female victim occurred simultaneously with that of the Evil Woman. It may be no coincidence that the plethora of these films coincided with female acquisition of economic and social power in life. In fact, such movies may even have been in part a consequence, signifying that women were finally a threat to the status quo. Hollywood simplistically interpreted this shift in the only terms it could understand: power, the quest for love or money.

And by the time this genre had played itself out, Bette Davis, its first lady and pioneer, might as well have been Mary Poppins, so sinister were her successors.

Mary Astor's Brigid in *The Maltese Falcon* (1941), with her breathless, orgasmic voice, was a masterpiece of deception. Alida Valli in *The Paradine Case*, Geraldine Fitzgerald in *The Strange Affair of Uncle Harry* (1945), Joan Bennett in two Fritz Lang classics, *Woman in the Window* (1944) and *Scarlet Street* (1945), Lana Turner in *The Postman Always Rings Twice* (1945) and *The Three Musketeers* (1948), even Rosalind Russell in *The Velvet Touch* (1948) stooped to greedy duplicity or vicious rampage. Disposing of their victims by poison were Joan Fontaine in *Ivy* (1947), Merle Oberon in *Temptation* (1946), and Ann Todd, totally corrupted by love, in *So Evil, My Love* (1948). All these *films noirs*, with exquisitely expressionistic atmospheres (and often directed by European expatriates like Preminger, Siodmak, Curtiz, Lang), explored premeditated evil in which avarice and controlled loathing more often than passion dictated the carnage wrought by Fatal Women.

Nowhere did icy premeditation cast its pall more thoroughly than in Billy Wilder's *Double Indemnity* (1944), from a story by James M. Cain (who also wrote *The Postman Always Rings Twice* and *Mildred Pierce*). Barbara Stanwyck's cold, murderous Phyllis Dietrich seduces insurance agent Fred MacMurray into carrying out the murder of her husband, and it is through MacMurray's eyes and narrative that the story unfolds. Sex, greed, and violence combine. Racy exchanges or glances between MacMurray and Stanwyck purr with hokey sexuality. "I wanted to see her again close, without that silly staircase between us," MacMurray says. Then later, "I kept thinking . . . about the way that anklet of hers cut into her leg." Or, best of all, "How could I know that murder sometimes smells like honeysuckle?"

More desperate and believable evil was perpetrated by Bette Davis' Rosa Moline in King Vidor's overripe, ramblingly histrionic *Beyond the Forest* (1949). Rosa is so despairing, so consumed by the fires of her idle small-town life and so overwrought with slovenly rage that she is almost likable, and Vidor's naïve preface, quite ill-fitting. "This is the story of evil. Evil is headstrong—is puffed up. . . . It's salutary for us to view it in all its nakedness once in a while," he says, then draws a picture of a bored bitch who even shoots porcupines for fun because "they irritate me." This, a few smirks, and Rosa's volatile complaints prime us for the moment when she puts a bullet through an old man about to prevent her from running away with her lover. Acquitted, and with no luck at all, Rosa dies from the aftereffects of an abortion. Dragging herself to the train station in one of the cinema's all-time brilliantly overplayed scenes, she who can escape punishment for taking an adult life finds that killing a fetus (by throwing herself down a hill) is inexcusable: with peritonitis wracking her body, Rosa has thrown on clothes, spit out to her maid, "Excitement, Jenny, did you ever hear of excitement?" swabbed some lipstick across her mouth, and limped out. But in front of the train that might have carried her to a new life, she dies.

One critic commented that he never saw a woman so desperate to get to Chicago. Charles Silver's program notes at a recent showing of this film at the Museum of Modern Art in New York dismiss Rosa with: "It is similarly fruitless to try to excuse the character as some primitive manifestation of female liberation." She may be, as Silver—and playwright Edward Albee, before him—suggested, the essence of forties' camp, but for this one must thank Davis' flailing, truculent performance. Here the murderess evolves into a buffoon and is consumed by the same passions which have provoked her to extinguish others. Regardless, her frustrations speak in earnest now of a problem which in 1949 was immediately dismissed: a dead-end life which might well produce a hysterically off-center female.

Movies so adeptly commingled hysterical craving and evil, as if tacitly reprimanding women for indulging their emotional lives at all. And the thinnest of lines separated hysteria from insanity. In *Possessed* (1947) Joan Crawford's mental imbalance prodded her to murder; an insane Gene Tierney (*Leave Her to Heaven*, 1945), madly possessive of her husband, unblinkingly drowned his crippled younger brother, induced a miscarriage (a common preoccupation), and finally gave herself a lethal dose of poison. And then *Dark Mirror* (1946) wrapped up the scarred female psyche in a neat bundle of explanations, at the same time pitting female against female, sister against sister, and presenting woman as devil or angel.

Olivia de Havilland, whose paramount talent was in making transparent the most smothering or humiliating emotions and showing the process through which the mousy female character acquires and releases her fury, superbly enacted the role of twins, but even she could not make credible the simplistic psychological explanations *Dark Mirror* spouted for the psychotic killer-sister's motives. Says the psychiatrist who just happens to be falling in love with the good twin (which seems pretty stupid, and realistically revealing, considering that he has discovered that such favoritism has been the source of bad sister's problems from childhood): "All women are rivals fundamentally, but it never bothers them because they automatically discount the successes of others and alibi their own failures on the grounds of circumstances. Luck, they say. But between sisters, it's a little more serious." Since the evil twin, having committed one murder, is now preparing to do away with her sibling, this recitative limps along while the film itself cashes in on a comfortable myth.

Competition between sisters, especially twins, was a favorite Hollywood chestnut. Bette Davis' *A Stolen Life* (1946), not nearly as exaggerated, sick, or successful as *Dark Mirror*, similarly polarized twins, with the evil one marrying the other's boyfriend, then drowning conveniently to allow her more deserving relative to triumph. Interestingly, friendship between males has often been filmed with epic flourishes (Hawks' *Red River*, 1948), but in one-to-one female relationships, only the negative aspects are considered dramatic enough material. These were wrung dry in the forties' Evil Women cycle.

The intermingling notions of female evil and sensuality have fascinated men for centuries, and it is most fitting that Orson Welles, a brilliant master of mood and irony who just also happened to be Rita Hayworth's husband at the time (the marriage was floundering), should have utilized her talents to weld evil, sex, and fantasy in *The Lady from Shanghai* (1947). As Elsa Bannister, the sensual, emasculating spider, Rita flaunts her worldliness. The ports she's worked and the languages she speaks symbolize her experience, her brains. Her knowledge of Chinese sinisterly represents the dark worlds of evil she embodies. Languishing on a deck, as aware of her body as of the tunes she's singing, she's the incarnation of the decadent sybarite, barely flinching when she condemns others to death, losing control just briefly when she and her husband shoot it out in a hall of mirrors. What glory, death of beauty before the glass which gives beauty its strength!

And suddenly the fantasy female and fatal woman are embodied as one.

15

FANTASTIC ON-SCREEN IS FANATIC OFF

Fortunately, the fantasy creature of forties' drama was not always malice-laden. Often she existed as an amoral, noncommittal sensualist, an updated version of the Mystery Woman that echoed Garbo or Dietrich.

Lauren Bacall, independent, self-aware, represented the best of these new mysteries. Allegedly she was discovered by Mrs. Howard Hawks who spotted Bacall's photo in a fashion magazine. Coached by Hawks himself, who every day for a year had her work out in an empty lot, shouting until she was hoarse in order to lower the register of her voice, Betty (her real name) or "Baby," as husband Bogart affectionately called her, magnetically modernized the screen with her odd mixture of gossamer and lemon. Tall, rangy, she was the only screen female since Dietrich who had the resources, or chutzpah, to look as if she might be mentally undressing each male with her glance. And she could exude the same distant challenge of Dietrich, rumble with the wry sexual innuendo of West, finally capitulate with the grace of Garbo.

But Bacall earned her stars because she most perfectly complemented Bogart's diffidence. In *To Have and Have Not* (1944) she helped him run fishing boats for the Free French, but the original Hemingway plot was scrapped to allow their romance to take center stage. When Bogie kisses her, she, the cheeky dame, cracks, "It's even better when you help." Later she delivers her famous challenge: "If you need anything, just whistle. You know how to whistle, don't you? Just pucker up and blow."

The enigma of Bacall, in all their vehicles together (*To Have*

229

and Have Not, The Big Sleep, Dark Passage, and *Key Largo*),
sprang from the fact that she, a wandering soul with a vague but
tainted past, gave her heart in obeisance to Bogart, her affectionate
alter ego. So she fulfilled a dual fantasy role—the unbroken, unbreak-
able colt alive with wit and sexuality, and the prize fantasy won by a
man whose low-keyed cynicism might have proved him indifferent to
her charms in the first place.

Without Bogey, however, Bacall floundered. Alone, she was acid,
just a little too brittle and serpentine. This worked against sustained stardom, especially if the vehicles were unsuitable, and in
the early fifties her luminosity would seem diminished—or misused
—in *How to Marry a Millionaire* (1953), *Woman's World* (1954),
and even the highly successful and romantic *Written on the Wind*
(1956). Only in the marvelous 1957 *Designing Woman*, a reworking of the Tracy-Hepburn comedy *Woman of the Year*, did Bacall,
as a fashion designer matching wits with sportswriter-hubby Gregory Peck, find material sophisticated and stylish enough to engage
her attractively. Yet in those early postwar years she seemed a
happy combination of the New Woman and the Mona Lisa odalisque
whose smile-smirk held a note of irony at her own containment, her
own mystique.

Only one other screen heroine projected an image as self-possessed
and sexy as Bacall's. Ann Sheridan, the "Oomph Girl," freed of
traditional feminine wiles, glances, blinks, and pursed lips, was hampered by a corny publicity campaign ("oomph") and a succession of
B romantic melodramas like *Castle on the Hudson, San Quentin, City
for Conquest,* and *Juke Girl.* Yet whether she was bringing to life *Nora
Prentiss* (1947), in which as a brusque nightclub singer she remained
loyal to her pitiable and possessive lover, or deadpanning as Cary
Grant's efficient machine of a wife in Hawks' *I Was a Male War Bride*
(1949), Sheridan maintained an ascetic panache which resembled an
unmannered Katharine Hepburn. There was about her an almost
rugged pioneering spirit which after the war, and more bright endeavors like *Come Next Spring* and *Take Me to Town,* definitely
handicapped her. For movies were beginning to glorify the more
elusive and ephemeral fantasies of beauty. So ephemeral were they that
these fantasies often existed only in the mind or on the canvas of a
dreamer.

Jennifer Jones, under Selznick's tutelage, wandered through *Love Letters* (1945) as a magnificent amnesia victim whose lapse has been caused by the discovery that some love letters she received were written by someone other than the man she thought! With no past or future, just an etherally disconnected presence, she rises like Venus from the sea; no one need be burdened by anything more than her beauty and haunting, faltering half-memory. Then in *Portrait of Jennie* (1948) Jones awakens from death and is the subject for artist Joseph Cotten, who is falling in love as he paints; she runs through a whole lifetime (including a brief, predestined rendezvous with him) in order to make him a great painter.

In 1944 Otto Preminger presented Gene Tierney in *Laura*, another face in the misty night whose beauty haunted even while she, too, was supposedly dead. Certainly death—or amnesia, a form of release from life's bonds—plays as much part as beauty itself in immortalizing females. For in death, woman—who is often feared in life—can be deified and worshiped.

Ava Gardner would continue this syndrome on screen, and her Ideal Fantasy Creature would in the late forties be first an incarnation of a department store statue (*One Touch of Venus*, 1948). Then in *Pandora and the Flying Dutchman* (1951) she is again Everywoman, able to free the Flying Dutchman (James Mason) who is destined to sail his ghost ship into eternity unless he finds the woman who will love him enough to die for him. Since their initial meeting is fated—Mason has already painted Pandora-Ava's portrait and is waiting patiently for her—the breathtaking Everywoman Pandora willingly, graciously complies with the rest. Then, in *The Barefoot Contessa*, she again varies this theme, playing an untouchable Succuba writhing in her own beauty; defenseless against love, yet unlucky. Finally she is murdered by her impotent husband for her infidelity—and he possesses her at last.

This Ideal Fantasy Creature—like the Mystery Woman of Garbo or Dietrich—was just as sweetly and effectively relegated to the role of pariah. In order to fulfill her destiny, she was required to remain aloof, discombobulated, and most effectively, die. Again this final, precise objectification offered the most romantic proof possible of her love and of her existence as a positive, giving force.

The exploitation of women through fantasy heroines parallels the exploitation of movie stars, who are the public's fantasies, through the media and within the industry. Even stars' most fiercely private lives have been influenced by their work because in films, money and ego and power are virtually inseparable. And when a woman acquires these, she is often at a personal disadvantage.

In an interview with Rex Reed not long ago, Bette Davis confided:

> If I had to do it all over again, the only thing I'd change is that I would never get married. But then I wouldn't have my kids and without them I would die. But my biggest problem all my life was men. I never met one yet who could compete with the image the public made out of Bette Davis. You think being a well-bred Yankee girl brought up with a moral sense of right and wrong, it doesn't kill me to admit I was married five times? I am a woman meant for a man. I get very lonely sometimes at night in this big house—there's nothing glamorous about that. But I never found a man who could compete. I sat here two nights ago in my living room all alone and watched a film I made with Gary Merrill while we were married. Same billing, everything. At the end the announcer said, "Ladies and gentlemen, you've been watching *Phone Call from a Stranger* starring Bette Davis, Shelley Winters, and Gary Davis!!" So help me God. And that's what men had to put up with. And I don't blame the men. I was a good wife. But I don't know any other lady in my category who kept a husband either, unless she married for money or married a secretary-manager type where there was no competition. That's a price I've paid for success, and I've had a lot of it.[1]

Undoubtedly multimarried Joan Crawford, Lana Turner, Judy Garland, Elizabeth Taylor, and Joan Fontaine shared similar problems. Hollywood in the forties inflicted additional burdens on its stars by sharing them, perhaps indecently, with the world. Fan magazines had existed since before World War I, but now emphasis was shifting from adoration to personal criticism and inside stories. One issue of *Modern Screen* in 1947 headlined Tyrone Power's, Cary Grant's, and Keenan Wynn's divorces; in 1948 another chastised Lana's behavior in London and Ginger Rogers' insistence on playing ingenues.

But the most insidious privacy-shattering institutions of Hollywood were the venerable busybodies Hedda Hopper and Louella Parsons. Louella flattered her way into William Randolph Hearst's heart and confidence in 1924 with the appraisal that he spent too much money promoting Marion Davies' pictures and not enough praising the actress herself. It was a clever ploy, and soon the forty-three-year-old opportunist was writing her now-infamous "Marion Davies never looked lovelier" regularly in Hearst's chain of papers. She was also doing movie reviews, Hearst's Sunday supplement feature, and hosting a successful radio show, *Hollywood Hotel*.

Hedda, a sometimes actress and onetime friend of Louella, became Louella's star rival in 1938, and between them, little was sacred. Studio chiefs and stars alike feared their bitchy pens and venomous tongues. Refusing to give one of these ladies the scoop on a romance, marriage, divorce, or impending birth meant banishment from her column—or what was worse, vindictive, malicious reprisals. And only a handful of celebrities—Garbo, Hepburn, Brando—repeatedly refused to cooperate. For Hedda and Louella wielded their power shamelessly, with little concern about invading a star's privacy, ruining his or her career, or printing erroneous information. Through them the public fed hungrily on Hollywood's dirty laundry. Said Hedda once about her astounding success: "The minute I started to trot out the juicy stuff, my phone started to ring."[2]

Perhaps one of the most brutal victims of both press coverage and public outrage was Ingrid Bergman. Enrapturing fans as the virginal Swedish beauty who, it had been carefully publicized, led a happy, healthy home life as the sturdy wife of a good dentist and mother to their child, Bergman went to Europe in 1949 to make *Stromboli*—and fell in love with her Italian director, Roberto Rossellini. When rumors of a divorce surfaced, this alone sent former fans into a moral frenzy. But when Louella, affectionately known as "Love's Undertaker," broke the news that Ingrid was also expecting Rossellini's child, she not only scooped every other gossipmonger in the nation, but signaled Ingrid's crucifixion. The actress married Rossellini soon afterward, but the damage—in puritan America's eyes—was already done. Banished from Hollywood and from her position as one of the industry's most important (ten top box-office) stars, Bergman—despite being one of the most magnificent screen females in history—did not make an American film again until her Award-winning *Aanastasia* in 1956, and she did not return to Hollywood until 1969 for *Cactus Flower*. It was her first film in the motion-picture capital in twenty years.

An intriguing sidelight: Another top female star also gave birth to an illegitimate child in the mid-1930's, but devised an elaborate series of excuses, being "ill for a year" or "in seclusion for several months" before she glowingly reported the adoption of her daughter from a San Diego orphanage. She saved face and didn't miss a step in developing her first-rate career. The public did not condemn her because it did not know. Yet the simple, sad hypocrisy is that she saved her livelihood by an elaborate ruse while Bergman—painfully honest, futilely courageous—was burned at the stake of public condemnation.

With a great deal of help from the Tinseltown Asps, Hedda and Louella.

It's interesting to note that both columnists were the real-life embodiments of the Evil Women Hollywood had for so long been fleshing out. Like their screen counterparts, Hedda and Louella used ruthlessness to win stories, money, and prestige—all regardless of the consequences to others. Ironically, they achieved legitimacy as "weapons" primarily because the studios sanctioned their ruthlessness. Why? Simple economics. Hedda and Louella wove the myth of movie stars as royalty, movie stars as intimates, and movieland as the American dream. The star publicity and the interest in Hollywood they engendered were priceless.

Hedda and Louella also put their patriotic two cents into the public till in 1947, when the Red Scare hit Hollywood. Amid burgeoning suspicions, the "Unfriendly Ten" appeared before the House Un-American Activities Committee. Subsequently, Hedda—harmless, frivolous dear, what with her ordering 150 hats a year—and Louella—religious dear, what with her ten-foot-high electrically wired Virgin Mary on her lawn—began taking potshots at directors, actors, and writers. Their right-wing patriotism gathered exuberant, dangerous momentum. Hedda especially, counting Joseph McCarthy and J. Edgar Hoover among her good friends, carried on so fiercely and with such a specious lack of knowledge or analytical ability that many conservatives, including John Wayne, urged her to shut up. To no avail.

Fate works its own ironies, however. Hollywood had known its most prosperous year ever in 1946. As the forties came to a close, the industry began corroding—from its very foundation. The Hollywood Purge was draining the industry of some of its best writers (Dalton Trumbo, Ring Lardner, Jr., Abraham Polonski, Carl Foreman); directors such as Edward Dmytryk; and actors (Marsha Hunt, Gale Sondergaard, Betty Garrett, Anne Revere). It was virtually extinguishing fine talent, sapping fresh blood, and discouraging innovative social story treatment. The atmosphere was rank with fear, betrayal, and stagnation.

A creative shot in the arm was desperately needed. But the studios, fighting for their lives, were working on stringent assembly lines; martial rule cramped directors' styles. Taxes soared. First-magnitude stars, warring for freedom from slavish contracts, were (thanks to the efforts of Bette Davis and Olivia de Havilland) finally victorious; they would soon be free-lancing, breaking loose from the paternal studio systems which had been their homes for years.

They would also be pushing the far side of forty. And if Crawford, Davis, Garson, Dietrich, Colbert, and Hepburn were as magnificent as ever, free-lancing did not always solve the needs of an actress who refused to work after 5 P.M. because then her wrinkles began creeping out.

In addition, postwar cultural exchange had rediscovered the European film industry. Foreign movies were threatening to develop their own art-house cults and cut into profits.

And most damaging of all, television was now a reality.

Every Tuesday night Uncle Miltie clowned, mugged, traipsed across tiny home-screen Dumonts or Motorolas in drag, yelling "makeup" for Texaco Star Theater.

And every Tuesday, and sometimes Wednesday through Monday, the nation was glued to the tube. Nobody knew it then, but the moon over Hollywood was waning.

Gasping for breath, the industry would have to pull out all its stops to fill empty picture palaces again. 3-D, CinemaScope, and controversy would be new tricks that the old dogs would parade.

But its ace in the hole was of course a novel kind of woman.

A woman for the fifties. A woman for the Eisenhower reign of peace.

16

THE BIRTH OF THE BOBBY-SOXER

Is there a freedom about an atmosphere conducive to female progress which also encourages other strata of society to break traditional restraints? In the twenties, flaming youth marched alongside the New Woman. And in the forties, Rosie the Riveter and her office counterparts were joined by the teen-ager, or bobby-soxer.

As a unit, teens were the oldest *single* coeducational group left intact by the war. They alone were unburdened by the war effort; in fact, they profited from it. Whereas during the Depression young people often had to take on family responsibilities early, now kids with part-time jobs or baby-sitting assignments while mothers worked split shifts in factories emerged as a rich monetary source for advertisers and merchandisers. (By 1948 the *Saturday Evening Post* would report that baby-sitting had become "a craft dominated by a militant minority of two million high school girls extracting at least $750 million a year.")

Before long, a set of rituals and an accompanying vocabulary were established. Beanies, bobby socks, saddle shoes, pleated skirts and jewel-necked sweaters. Jalopies, the jitterbug, and "jiving." Girls set their hair in rags, wore blue jeans and Dad's old shirts, and in a Purdue University survey, 50 percent of them admitted that their figure was their number one concern. For another third, it was acne.

Ads for pimple creams and face cleansers directly appealed to this new element. "This one complete cream is all I need!" said Deanna Durbin of a famous beauty cream. A major bra manufacturer awarded a "Movie Contract to Perma-Lift Girl" and assured skeptics: "A year ago Greta Christensen was an obscure Chicago high school girl" when she was "discovered" wearing their brassiere. Flame-glo, Stadium Girl, and Chen Yu lipsticks sold for between 10 cents and $1. Manufacturers of junior fashions flourished. And new magazines like *Seventeen*, as well as innovative teen columns in newspapers, offered tips on how to be irresistible.

Modern Screen relayed this advice to its co-ed readers in 1944:

The first step toward not getting stuck begins at home in the privacy of your own room. Dress with real care; apply your party face with skill; be lavish with the mouthwash and non-perspirant. Be convinced, when you greet your fella, that you couldn't possibly look better.

If the dance is being held at school or at the plant, where all the boys know you, beam at them as you come in. Not the glassy-eyed, white-lipped grin of the gal who's positive she's in for a bad night, but a sweet, half-smile that intrigues them. There's nothing wrong with scattering a few come-ons where they'll do the most good, either. . . .

. . . Summing up, it's almost a guarantee that if you can lose that paralyzing, tongue-tying terror of being stuck—you never will be.

Dancing to the rhythms of "Jukebox Saturday Night," "Jersey Bounce," and "Two O'Clock Jump," kids were responsible for the expansion of the jukebox business into an $80,000,000-a-year industry. By 1946 recording companies were selling ten times as many records as they had ten years before. Longer-playing 33 and 45 rpm discs would soon antiquate the standard 78's. And youth culture had crowned its king. "The Voice" was Mr. Frank Sinatra himself, already a living legend at twenty-five, playing to crowds of hysterical, swooning bobby-soxers who converged on him backstage at every performance (10,000 swarmed outside the Paramount Theater during his 1944 engagement).

A bewildered seriocomic Establishment grumbled at these girlish displays of libido. New York City's commissioner of education complained that Sinatra was the reason why high school girls played hooky. Congress, reported the New York *Herald Tribune*, accused that: "The Lone Ranger and Frank Sinatra are the prime instigators of juvenile delinquency in America."[1]

But Hollywood perked up its ears and cheerfully tried to carve itself a slice of the new market's wealth. In *Best Foot Forward*

(1944) "actress" Lucille Ball endured a prep school prom because it would be "good publicity," and teen Virginia Weidler wailed that her acned steady was two-timing her with an older woman. *Janie* (1944) starred Joyce Reynolds as a boy-crazy sixteen-year-old throwing over a neighborhood beau for a soldier; *Mickey* (1948) showed tomboy Lois Butler, the baseball team's star pitcher, blossoming into a delicate beauty. Sophisticated, sweet-sixteen Elizabeth Taylor stole soda jerk Robert Stack from innocent best friend Jane Powell in *A Date with Judy* (1948); at the end, Taylor and Stack plan to marry even though she's barely finished high school. And Judy-Jane must be content to sing "Love Is Where You Find It" into the beardless face of pubescent Oogie Pringle.

Concentrating on the "boy" problems of their virginal protagonists, Hollywood movies exploited adolescent girls as if eager to fill the vacuum of female docility adult women had temporarily escaped. But if movie bobby-soxers revealed no interests or activities other than mindlessly primping and priming for men, statistics left room for doubt. In 1940, *before* the outbreak of war, more girls attended college than ever before, and the ratio of eight females to eleven men on campus would narrow even further after Pearl Harbor. But while women themselves took their education seriously, as early as 1944 static from the usual social channels attempted to belittle their ambition in a manner reminiscent of the thirties' blasts at universities as "spinsters factories." Margaret Barnard Pickel of Columbia University's War Work Information Bureau, wrote in the *New York Times Magazine* that March:

> There is something seriously wrong when so many of our college women think the world is their oyster, when they expect to spend their lives doing work that is always "vital, challenging, executive."
>
> ... A great many of them feel that the B.A. degree in some way entitles them to positions of leadership.
>
> ... This unwillingness to learn, this blindness to the limitations of their training, this feeling that because they have been to college they are capable of doing any sort of executive or administrative work—all these factors seem to me to indicate that something is the matter with the atmosphere in which women are trained at college.

Her lashing out seems proof positive that campus females earnestly tackled their studies, with caps set as firmly on careers as on husbands.

Sucked into endless rounds of slumber parties and malt shop dates and junior proms, screen teen-agers, however, inhabited a world alien to such substantial pursuits. Not even the rash of college movies— flimsy vehicles like *Mother Is a Freshman*, *Father Is a Fullback*, *Here Come the Coeds*, *Good News*, *Too Many Girls*, *Bathing Beauty*, *Apartment for Peggy*, *The Male Animal*, and *Mr. Belvedere Goes to College*—most of which occurred late in the decade and dealt with adults' return to the campus as the GI Bill made education available to all veterans, both male and female, indicated any youthful devotion to books or ideas. College merely provided a fertile hunting ground for husbands. In *Good News* (1947) an effervescent June Allyson is all atwitter because a gold-digging sexpot attempts to steal off with her football hero. In *Mother Is a Freshman* (1949) Loretta Young enrolls in college just to make sure her daughter can take advantage of the family scholarship, but she winds up vying with the girl over Professor Van Johnson. Save for technical facility and extravagant productions, such prevailing attitudes painfully coincided with those primitive notions harbored by the early silent two-reeler series *The Collegians*, which ran from 1926 to 1930 and depicted campus life as an orgy of drinking, petting, and high living for raccoon-clad dilettantes. Nor did it diverge from the image of man-crazy heroines Nancy Carroll and Helen Kane (that boop-boop-a-doop girl) in early college songfests, *Sweetie* and *Honey*. Or from Clara Bow's co-ed in Paramount's first talkie, *The Wild Party* (1929), where girls spent their time slipping into each other's silk lingerie or winking at professors in the lecture hall (Bow managed to get hers, Fredric March).

One rare film attempting to deal seriously with a teen-ager's problems, *Claudia*, unfortunately turned matters into treacle. But then the teen-ager herself was atypical; she happened to be married, removed from the bobby-soxer atmosphere, and her immaturity was reason enough for her difficulties of adjustment. Dorothy McGuire starred as the frazzled and helplessly infantile wife of Robert Young. She naïvely vamps her British neighbor in order to provoke Young's jealousy ("Kissing Gerry made me more in love with you. That's why I asked him to kiss me again, to make sure," she explains). Then she sells their farm (which he loves) to a friend as a surprise because she wants to move back to the city and Mother. Her impossible energy and lack of resources are startling, pathetic. If this movie had been more carefully hewn and focused, it might have presented a sensitive examination of the problems encountered by a girl who marries before she's ready. But two incidents occur which compromise the whole affair: Claudia finds out she's pregnant. And on the same day she discovers her mother is dying. "Claudia has to learn to let go the people she loves, to hold close with open hands," her mother has prescribed earlier. Now accepting the older woman's imminent death marks the girl's successful transition—or at least, so the film says—from adolescence to womanhood.

Claudia enjoyed sufficient popularity for a sequel to be issued three years later. *Claudia and David* (1946) again starred McGuire and Young, this time adjusting to life in the suburbs with a baby. One can assume that *Mickey*, *Janie*, *Judy*, and all the other bobby-soxers would realize similar speedy fulfillment. After all, isn't that what teen-age movie "messages," acne cream, and figure foundations were all about?

Bobby-sox films also prepared an otherwise-distracted youthful audience for the deadly limbo of fifties' woman's films. New personalities, such as Jane Powell, June Allyson, Debbie Reynolds, and, in the early fifties, Doris Day and Janet Leigh, brought a disarming naïveté to the screen—a novel scrubbed kind of heroine, one without pretense, without maturity, and without the womanly stature that had been so distinctive of the greatest stars of the past two decades. These ingenues were the predecessors of the saccharine, candy-brained, starstruck girl-children who would become a staple of fifties' and sixties' movie fiction.

Who would indeed become the buffoons of our age.

FIVE

THE FIFTIES—LOSING GROUND

*In the U.S. at the present time there are,
despite all the women who work in and out of
the home, a greater proportion of aimlessly
idle women than at any previous time or other
place, not excepting imperial Rome.*

—FERDINAND LUNDBERG
& MARYNIA F. FARNHAM, M.D.
Modern Women: The Lost Sex

17

I DO! I DO? . . .

the marrying kind and unmarrying kind

1950: The United States landed in Korea, and Joe McCarthy had a little list—one that trampled constitutional freedoms and opened his unorthodox four-year reign of terror against purported Communists. Two years later we exploded the first hydrogen bomb and afterward dismissed atomic scientist J. Robert Oppenheimer, amid Red smears, for dissenting on the need to stockpile nuclear weapons. And in 1956, with Russia's launching of Sputnik, the space race began.

Still, we chiefly remember the fifties, not for the horror of civil defense drills or witch-hunts, but for kitschy fads like hoola hoops and poodle cuts and crinolines. For Lucy and Miltie and Howdy and Kukla. Something about the signals during the era of Eisenhower passivity disturbingly contradicted each other: There were suburbia/ teen gangs, a spirit of conformity/the Beat generation. The first era of prosperity and "peace" since the twenties rippled with undercurrents of anxiety and alienation and rebellion.

One of the few constants during the decade was the direction women were heading: backward. Not since Grandma starched her bustles had the strains of Mendelssohn been so universally revered, or women so pressured out of the employment market and into conjugal bliss. They married younger than at any previous time during this century, and in 1951 one in three had found a husband by the age of nineteen.

Coincidentally, the 1950 census reported that for the first time women held a numerical majority in the population. If a girl didn't catch her man early, she might never own that vine-covered cottage somewhere between Yalta and my blue heaven.

Why the shift away from the autonomous forties' heroine? Undoubtedly battle fatigue, the emotional strain of wartime separation and denial, accounted for both sexes' eagerly embracing traditional social roles. Then, with 3,000,000 women dumped from the labor force by 1947 (who would *not* be reabsorbed in equivalent numbers until 1955), emphasizing feminine priorities like home and hearth helped ease the job squeeze.

Certain other conditions also placed premiums on early marriage. The GI Bill of Rights entitled veterans to payments for wives and children and to college benefits. With more than 300,000 men taking advantage of the bill, the years they would remain financially dependent were extended sufficiently so that waiting to marry no longer seemed reasonable. Parents began pitching in to help newlyweds, and wives often worked to put their husbands through school.

The surge of available men on campuses meant that the portals of learning also offered fertile territory for husband hunting. Girls whose families could afford it began flocking to colleges and universities. The New York *Times* reported in 1955: "Not so long ago girls were expelled from college for marrying; now girls feel hopeless if they haven't a marriage at least in sight by commencement time." And: "A girl also has strong sexual needs and as strong a wish for secure emotional relationships as her young man. In addition, the well-known statistical fact that males are fewer than females in this country tends to push each girl into desire for early marriage."

Magazines typed the happy home with complacencies like this *Saturday Evening Post* editorial, "That Lost Generation Didn't Get Lost; It Just Settled down and Raised Families." Sociologists warned of spinsterhood. Communities regarded single women over twenty-four —only 30 percent would reach that age solo—suspiciously. And movies, reflecting this insular world where women slipped into masculine shadows and domestic aprons, cleaned house, so to speak. No more were the independent career-minded heroines of the forties; no more the bright and witty women who could carry a picture because their characters astounded us with style and self-importance. The new crop would deal a familiar historical hand, with: WOMEN FIXING TO CATCH THEIR MEN in *Three Coins in the Fountain, Gentlemen Prefer Blondes, Gentlemen Marry Brunettes, How to Marry a Millionaire, How to Be Very, Very Popular, Woman's World, Seven Brides for Seven Brothers, Annie Get Your Gun*; WOMEN PREPARING FOR THE

WEDDING in *Father of the Bride, High Society, The Catered Affair*; SLOVENLY WIVES in *Come Back Little Sheba*; DISCONTENTED WIVES in *Written on the Wind, The Tarnished Angels*, Deborah Kerr in *From Here to Eternity, The Country Girl, No Down Payment, The Big Carnival*; DIVORCING WIVES in *Pfftt* and *The Marrying Kind*; BATTLING WIVES in *Designing Woman* and *Queen Bee*; and ROMANCING WIDOWS in *The Magnificent Obsession, The Blue Veil, The Proud and the Profane, Love Is a Many Splendored Thing*, and Gloria Grahame in *Not as a Stranger*.

Note, too, how few female stars could bear a picture on their shoulders alone anymore. Now it was Deborah Kerr *and* Cary Grant in *An Affair to Remember* (1957). Ava Gardner *and* Clark Gable in *Mogambo* (1953). Audrey Hepburn *and* William Holden *and* Humphrey Bogart in *Sabrina* (1954). Producers often stacked the deck with double or triple-threat names. *Three Coins in the Fountain* (1954) had dewy maidens Jean Peters, Maggie McNamara, and Dorothy McGuire wishing for husbands. *How to Marry a Millionaire* (1953) wasn't enough with a daffy Monroe as the Magooishly myopic husband hunter, but Lauren Bacall and Betty Grable backed her up in Twentieth's second venture into CinemaScope. Television was already so severely cutting into Hollywood's market that the studios—at a time when woman's position was of devalued interest—increased the value of stocking up. If one star was good, two were better, and three was best. (As the studio gross on the above films dramatically demonstrated.)

With the war over, color processing was readily available, and extravagant colorful musicals were yet another attempt to revive box office. Most were unremitting in documenting boy-meets-girl/girl-chases-boy-until-she-gets-him situations. Two of the best, *Annie Get Your Gun* (1950) and *Calamity Jane* (1953), followed the taming and feminizing of buckskin babes who had to dress down their independence and dress up their bodies to get their men. In *Annie*, Betty Hutton vies with Howard Keel as Frank Butler, brags that "Anything You Can Do I Can Do Better," and though she can't get a man with a gun, she can't bring herself to conceal her expertise either. But the wise old Indian Chief fixes Annie's gunsight, and with each target she misses, Butler's pride in himself—and love for her—grows. Perhaps he will be able to forget his dreams of a pink-and-white girl-flower sporting a gardenia and settle for her.

Calamity Jane followed the same formula, but this time Doris Day had her cap set for Keel. Giving a splendid performance, she (like Annie) crackled as the sharpshooter, but when she exchanged her high spirits and numbers like "The Deadwood Stage" for the Oscar-winning "Secret Love," transforming herself from cactus to camelia, the movie weakened considerably.

The most insistently masculine tone of the fifties was set down in another superb musical effort, and *Seven Brides for Seven Brothers* (1954) proves that the heartfelt project has the best chance of succeeding. Directed by Stanley Donen and based on Stephen Vincent Benét's retelling of Plutarch's *Rape of the Sabine Women*, the movie gleefully carries us away with the abduction of six sweet maidens by six strapping brothers, pioneers in the Oregon territory. The seventh bride and brother, playing Mommy and Daddy to the brood, are Jane Powell and—you guessed it!—Howard Keel. They marry an hour or so after Keel strolls into town, meets her, and likes what he sees. "Bless your beautiful hide," he struts like a rooster. But she complies with his proposal, making only one request: "Wait till I do my chores." Naturally his brothers are a surprise to the new wife, and after wailing that he really wanted a maid, she gets down to basics—cleaning them up and educating them. With nightly stories of the Sabine Rapes. Which start them itching.

It is the boys' picture from fade-in to finish. As such, *Seven Brides*, as jovial as it is, so typifies the decade's angsts and attitudes, from Janie Powell's love-at-first-sight acquiescence through the maidens' taming and their wistful ballet (they chorus: "Oh, they say when you marry in June/You're a June bride all your life.") to the final derogatory commonplace: "A girl! A girl? I mighta known Millie had a girl," Keel growls when told his daughter's gender.

What saves the film from completely converting Woman into a passive cipher (all the kidnapped girls are identical in looks) is Janie's spirited self-sufficiency with the unruly brothers and their virginal victims. Also positive are the energetically bawdy allusions of sexual hunger, and when the girls stop squealing, occasionally it's long enough to acknowledge some subtle desire.

But then only the year before, medical "authority" had affirmed the revolutionary premise that females might *indeed* possess sexual feelings. Kinsey, whose *Report on Sexual Behavior in the Human Female* was published in 1953, noted: "We found no basic differences in the anatomy which is involved in the sexual responses of females and males, and we found no differences in the physiologic phenomena which are involved when females and males respond sexually."[1] *Seven Brides*, in one nice, subtle scene, captures the fantasy of one of the girls lounging on her cot in the garret bedroom the brothers relinquished for them. Running her hand over the linen erotically, she speculates dreamily, "I wonder which of the boys sleeps in this bed." That purring gesture clarifies *her* lively desires in a movie where lust and activity and spirit generally belong to the boys—or "the bunch of bull-calves," as Keel calls them.

A sublimely folksy family atmosphere pervaded much of Hollywood's fifties' output. *Little Women, Cheaper by the Dozen, Belles on Their Toes, Life with Father, Stars in My Crown*, and *I Remember Mama* had roots in that postwar pastorale 1947's *The Egg and I*, in which city slicker Claudette Colbert adapts to Fred MacMurray and his chicken farm. In *Father of the Bride* (1950), Spencer Tracy—a middle-class dad the way the Hiltons were in *Since You Went Away*—tears his hair over bills and the fact that no man is good enough for daughter Liz Taylor. But when the marriage is temporarily called off (because her fiancé has planned a honeymoon fishing in Nova Scotia while she begged for someplace "romantic"!), the family almost has a collective coronary. Still, in *Father's Little Dividend* (1951), she makes him a grandpa, so the aggravation is all worth it.

Liz, if her first fifties' films were any indication, might have got stuck, typecast as the bland, doting young wife. At seventeen she was Robert Taylor's bride in *The Conspirator* (1949), and almost always after that she played a wife or lover with no context outside her relationships (*The Last Time I Saw Paris*, 1955; *Rhapsody*, 1954; the *Father* series, *Elephant Walk*, 1954; *Giant*, 1956; *Cat on a Hot Tin Roof*, 1958). Early on, however, her beauty and facility for high-pitched neurotic battles ensured variety within the genre. Stepping in for Vivien Leigh in *Elephant Walk* (1954) when only twenty-two, she competently enacted a dissatisfied wife marooned on her husband's Ceylonese tea plantation, and although he has little time for her, his friend Dana Andrews does. In *Cat on a Hot Tin Roof* (1958), as Maggie the Cat she loves husband Paul Newman but is being destroyed by his sexual indifference to her—and lets him know it. "I want to live," she shrieks. Very healthy. Alone among the young wives, she served as a positive screen model for a loving woman able to vocalize *her* needs and desires. Fans never felt that she could ignore herself for very long, and it was this ego and impatience and self-involvement which sparkled in contrast to all the perfect, selfless martyrs like June Allyson who sobbed and suffered for their men rather than themselves.

The ideal fifties wife, Allyson waited sweetly, nervously, endlessly in *The Stratton Story* (1949), *The Glenn Miller Story* (1954), *Executive Suite* (1954), *Woman's World* (1954), *Strategic Air Command* (1955), and *The McConnell Story* (1956). With so spineless a creature embraced as everybody's dependable and doting wife image, it is both revealing and, more probably, a survival tactic that the most socially ambitious cinematic probes of the decade, the films which will be remembered longest, are totally devoid of females. Films like *The Caine Mutiny*, *The Wild One*, *Time Limit*, *12 Angry Men*, *Mister Roberts*, *The Last Angry Man*, *Moby Dick*, *The Bridge on the River Kwai*, *No Time for Sergeants*, *The Defiant Ones*, *Stalag 17*, *The Young Stranger*. Others virtually exiled women to minor roles: Like Allyson, Teresa Wright in *The Men*, Julie Harris in *East of Eden*, Mildred Dunnock in *Death of a Salesman*, Jean Peters in *Viva Zapata!*, Grace Kelly in *High Noon* and *Rear Window*, Eva Marie Saint in *On the Waterfront*, Anne Francis in *The Blackboard Jungle* can be patient, sniveling, and passively loving appendages supporting their heroes, but if they're not on screen too much, they won't bore the audience to death.

More than ever before, "women's films" divorced themselves from controversial and timely plots and became "how to's" on catching and keeping a man, modern instructionals reworking De Mille's early *Old Wives for New*. In *Les Girls* (1957) show girl Mitzi Gaynor accepts Gene Kelly's proposal of marriage, then invites him up to her apartment for a test. With her hair in curlers, face in cold cream, and feet in a pot of hot water, does he still want her? In *Come Back Little Sheba* (1952) Shirley Booth is a puffy-frump wife whose sloppiness sends her youthful, muscular husband Burt Lancaster to other women. Booth's dowdiness has a similar effect on mate Anthony Quinn in *Hot Spell* (1958); even worse, her age, a constant reminder of his own, is repellent, and he runs off with a girl who could be his daughter.

Reconfirming our investment in veneer—youth and beauty—as a basic aspect of relating and loving, these movies, and especially the Booth portraits of disintegrating marriages, scarcely address themselves to or are aware of the wife's fundamental problems—that immersion in the ennui of daily existence has removed her from the mainstream of living.

Just as the years have robbed her of her looks, so have they ravished her vitality and connection with what's happening. But has she
really any choice?

Not on the screen. The icebox set received raw treatment from the
industry, but those few professional women maintaining vital life-
styles rarely escaped vitriol for single-handedly defying Establishment expectations. So they were assigned characters both pathetic and
neurotic, bitchy and insatiable. Gloria Swanson's fading movie star,
Norma Desmond, in *Sunset Boulevard* (1950) is a despairingly lonely
serpent, empty not merely because her glory has passed, but because
she has not refocused her life on the "real" things—a man and children.
Bette Davis' Margo Channing in *All About Eve* (1950) knows in time
that though her audience approval may be "like waves of love coming
up" each night, it won't keep her warm when the wrinkles set. She
ultimately opts for retirement and the role of wife to her younger
director-boyfriend, but not before she is misunderstood by everyone
she knows (and most likely by the film audience) as a venomous and
jealous *grande dame*. In fact, her suspicions about Eve's true nature
are exactly right; still, as, the star—*ergo*, neurotic—she must feel guilt
and apologize for on-target instincts. "I've been oversensitive to the
fact that she's so young, so feminine, so helpless—all the things I want
to be to Bill," Margo admits. Writer-director Joe Mankiewicz inadvertently points out, however, that the way social and sexual values
are structured, no woman can win. Karen, simply the playwright's wife
(who the author has stated he pities most of all), speaks of "that
helplessness you feel when you have no talent to offer outside of
loving your husband." The third female, Eve, ruthlessly outfoxes
everyone but drama critic De Witt and consequently must enjoy her
stardom with neither friends nor lovers for whom she remotely cares.

Throughout the fifties the female artist-actress consistently chose, or
was forced to reconsider, marriage over theatrical ambitions. Bette
Davis, again as *The Star* (1952), is an on-the-skids Academy Award
winner whose humiliations include a drunken arrest, an embarrassing
screen test for a supporting role where she prances around like a sexy
ingenue, and a hysterical collapse before she learns that she has
neglected "being a woman first."

Paralleling Davis' desperation was Joan Crawford's fierce hysteria.
Virtually stamping that era with her intensity, she once again jumped
on the trendy bandwagon as the penultimate middle-aged widow,

career spinster, or malicious bitch. A playwright in *Sudden Fear* (1952), Crawford plans to extinguish her husband after discovering that he and his girlfriend are plotting to benefit from her generous will; fortunately, the greedy couple kill each other first. In *Torch Song* (1953) she's a Big Musical Star whose humor and humanity, drained by too many years alone in the limelight, blossom at last under the persistent affection of a blind pianist (who conveniently "sees" her as she was in her youth, before he lost his sight). Other Crawford tyrants include the self-centered *Harriet Craig* (a 1950 remake of Dorothy Arzner's *Craig's Wife*) and, the malignant, destructive millowner's wife in *Queen Bee* in 1955. Even the actress' essentially sympathetic roles project a harsh hysteria which somehow converges with the seething emotions of her Evil Women. *Autumn Leaves* (1956), a melodramatic and intermittently touching attempt to deal with the affair of a middle-aged typist and a mentally ill young man, is unsuccessful, partially because her kind of wide-eyed desperation bears a closer relationship to her nasty characterizations than it does to the typist's frustrations and self-doubt. Her pathetic widow involved with a murderous beach boy in *Female on the Beach* (1955) shares this brittleness, suggesting that Crawford's fifties' characters spring not from the tapestries of their individual plot determination, but from the industry's conviction that middle age is a horror chamber and from the studio's willingness to exploit the star's own limitations in appearance and talent. For her lean and hungry fifties' look contrasts astoundingly with the soft and special luminosity of her thirties' and forties' heroines.

Today Joan Crawford is finally acknowledged as one of the screen's great ladies. But few who aren't film buffs realize the roller-coaster turns her career has taken in terms of quality and image and how tenaciously she clung to it when the chips were down. Indeed, they were down almost as often as they were up. After her initial success as the glorious flapper, Crawford glided through the thirties in MGM's sleek society melodramas, enduring mediocre roles and repeated roastings by critics. She begged for the chance to appear in *The Women* and again in *A Woman's Face* (1941). In 1943 she decided to leave MGM:

> Mr. Mayer didn't want me to leave, but he knew how unhappy I was. I left by the back gate. I loved MGM—it was home. But I

longed for challenging parts and I wasn't getting them. There were top executives who thought me all washed up. . . . If you think I made poor films at MGM after *A Woman's Face*, you should have seen the ones I went on suspension *not* to make![2]

Ending a two-year absence from the screen with *Mildred Pierce* (1945) for Warner Brothers, she stayed on at Warner's into the mid-fifties, working in a number of those stark, modern vehicles which marked that studio's style, vehicles like those of Davis and De Havilland, fraught with hysteria and melodrama, but which may have done Crawford as much disservice as the MGM fluff of the previous decades. For these films lacked the humor or lightness Crawford's overpowering presence required as a tempering influence, since she did not exert the same kind of control and technique over her scenes that other Warner's actresses had mastered. Wrote F. Scott Fitzgerald on May 11, 1938:

I'm writing a picture called *Infidelity* [the movie was never made] for Joan Crawford. Writing for her is difficult. She can't change her emotions in the middle of a scene without going through a sort-of Jekyll and Hyde contortion of the face so that when one wants to indicate that she is going from joy to sorrow one must cut away and then cut back. Also, you can never give her such stage direction as "telling a lie" because if you did she would practically give a representation of Benedict Arnold selling West Point to the British.[3]

Emphasizing Crawford's severity was the fifties' style, at least as interpreted by her studio. Without carefully designed MGM clothes and makeup, she was simply delivered up to current fashion without Warner's considering her individual needs. Thus, an unflattering short hairdo, bushy brows, wide mouth, and hard-as-nails makeup cemented the iron image that would underscore her middle-aged screen desperation. A backhanded but significant symptom of the fifties, this physical way of denying Crawford's individuality somehow also coldly highlighted the period's unsympathetic attitude toward the lonely, frantic, and unhappy women she played. Yet our recognition of Crawford's legend is perhaps more a tribute to her persona than her filmography. Except for a brief period in the twenties and again in the forties, she never really stepped in tune with the best films or most inspiring female images Hollywood produced. And after the war, when movies regarded everything short of obliging, weak-willed femininity as a contagious social disease, she was massacred.

The Woman Alone had long served as subject for on-screen exploration; that in the fifties she would become a love-starved pariah seemed a natural counterpoint to the decade's exaltation of matrimony. Consider for a moment the changing treatment of spinsters and career women. Both Davis' *The Old Maid* (1939) and De Havilland's Oscar-winning *To Each His Own* (1946) dealt with retiring, self-sacrificing, masochistic girls who bore illegitimate children after their lovers were killed in the war. Each gave away her baby unwillingly and watched from the wings while the child grew up, unaware of the mother's real identity. Perhaps these women paid for their "sins" by voluntary exile from traditional family life, but they also matured as warm, loving, and independent people. Neither resorted to hysteria; neither declined into withered, jumpy old ladies.

Davis took the Woman Alone out of the realm of moral paraplegia in two other forties' performances, *Now Voyager* (1942) and *Old Acquaintance* (1943). *Now Voyager* concerns the transformation of an ugly duckling, traumatized by her dowager mother, into a cosmopolitan heart-breaker who falls hopelessly for a married man. Choosing to remain single rather than settle for a fortuitous union with another man, she repeats to her lover the line he taught her: "Don't ask for the moon when we have the stars." If the elements of martyrdom are inherent in this comment, somehow the romanticizing of a female who chooses *not* to marry refreshes enough by way of compensation.

Old Acquaintance attempts, somewhat less successfully, a greater nobility. Here Davis is a successful playwright and novelist whose loyalty to her self-centered friend (Miriam Hopkins) prevents her from running off with Hopkins' husband. "There is a certain ecstasy in wanting things you can't have," she has explained to Hopkins enigmatically. Yet while everyone is entitled to dreams, the passivity and—again—martyr's sigh in that remark seems an echo of American puritanism in general and feminine self-denial in particular. By the denouement of *Old Acquaintance*, Davis has missed out on another marriage opportunity, grown ten years older, with ecstasy conspicuously absent. Her character, however, neither bitter nor neurotic, again maintains an opulent, vital and productive life-style.

The fifties would not embellish its Woman Alone so romantically. Heralding the decade's withering-prune approach was William Wyler's *The Heiress* (1949), based on Henry James' turn-of-the-century novel *Washington Square*. But thanks to the sensibilities of both James and Olivia de Havilland as the "entirely mediocre and defenseless creature with not a shred of poise," this dowdy frump—treated like an imbecile by her father—musters both dignity and a sharply cynical awareness of the machinations of the world after being abandoned on the night of her elopement by opportunist Montgomery Clift. A dual set of emotions are at work here, in which De Havilland achieves perhaps her finest screen performance. As much as we, and maybe she, know that Clift wants her for her money alone, we root for the liaison, hoping nothing will go awry. *Better to be second-best* (with Clift) *than a never-finish*, our romantic notions whisper. When he abandons De Havilland to gray spinsterhood, her wrath envelops us. "Yes, I can be very cruel. I have been taught by masters," she retorts years later when he returns.

And her ultimate revenge as she closes him out of her life makes us glad. Her disappointment has forged strength. Yet there is bitterness as well. Vindictive, she has cloaked herself in permanent bleak isolation.

The Woman Alone figured in fifties' movies as a creature so negative and pitiful that one can interpret the vogue as little other than a reinforcement of the decade's belief in marriage-as-salvation. So typically, hellishly American—neurotic, frantic, talky, eccentric, flirting with madness, and alienated from or abusive toward her family—she found a unique champion in Tennessee Williams and his profitable and often poetic wedding with the movies. Having gathered deserved momentum in the late forties with his powerful Broadway plays *The Glass Menagerie* and *Streetcar Named Desire*, Williams nourished the screen with adaptations of his searing, yet tender works—works which, in all fairness, provided mature actresses with deliciously meaty roles. Lingering lovingly, yet unscrupulously on the tragically aging female —once a tempest of passion and dreams, but now souring—Williams artfully destroys the last vision or vestige of her hope, brutally forces the mirror of her reality before her face, and suffocates her in her own neuroses. And her loneliness.

The roster of his pathetic heroines is impressive: Amanda of *The*

Glass Menagerie (Gertrude Lawrence, 1950) dipping into her beaux of the past the way a dipsomaniac dips into the bottle. Blanche of *A Streetcar Named Desire*, made immortal by Vivien Leigh as the hungering, half-crazed moth who "must avoid a strong light," flitting about, feeding on fabrications of her youth and taunting brother-in-law Brando with the urgency of her repressed, even unaware sexuality. Anna Magnani in *The Fugitive Kind* (1958), waltzing on memories of her daddy's wine arbor; wilting, imprisoned by a cancer-ridden husband, but fatally drawn to outsider Val-Snakeskin (Brando). Magnani again in *The Rose Tattoo* as Serafina, the widow who with blind need transplants her lust for her dead husband onto truck-driver buffoon Burt Lancaster. Katharine Hepburn's Mrs. Venable in *Suddenly, Last Summer* (1959), callow and venomous and ultimately alone, clutching and safeguarding the memory of homosexual son Sebastian by attempting to have niece Liz Taylor lobotomized; Geraldine Page in *Summer and Smoke* (1961), the aging, quivering virgin spinster, whose obsessive fantasies about the doctor next door make his ultimate rejection the cause of her breakdown. And finally Page's boozing, doping, fading star, The Princess, in *Sweet Bird of Youth* (1962), who dissipates the past and the future with palliatives, including the fleeting caresses of gigolo Paul Newman.

Never light-handed, Williams suspended reality for the audience by deftly structuring exotic, passionate plots and drawing delicate heroines driven by loneliness and archaic romantic ideals. His poetry cast an ephemeral veil over his neurotics, and somehow repression and obsession were squeezed into a classically heroic mold. Of his concentration on woman's themes, the playwright has mused:

> Maybe that's because the women in my family were much more attractive to me than my father. My mother and my sister and my grandmother were great talkers. They expressed themselves very freely and well. My father would express himself mainly in invectives at me. Now that he's dead, I realize that the poor man was most unhappy and felt that his children were somehow alienated from him, and I think he was deeply hurt by this.

And:
> I feel that so much of contemporary life is a shocking matter, a really shocking matter. And one is obliged to catch the quality

that prevails in contemporary life. If you just read the newspapers in America, you'll see that my plays are far from exaggerations.[4]

Especially if he derived his material from home. For Williams' sister Rose had also suffered from her own particular mental disorders and was the subject of a partially unsuccessful lobotomy in 1936 which must have affected the author overwhelmingly.

Undoubtedly, that he bothered to probe beneath the surface to pathetic paper-fragile feminine souls deserves a certain recognition. On the other hand, these creatures seemed as much victimized by the author's admitted homosexuality and limited knowledge of female resiliency and fortitude as they were by the genteelly repressive society that transformed them into sexual gorgons. Except for the Princess who once enjoyed stardom, and Mrs. Venable who had left her mark on Sebastian, the ladies simply filled the vacuums of their experience by clutching parched memories, wallowing in self-pity, and kindling combustible frustrations—all reasonable turn-of-the-century enterprises for old maids and frustrated widows. But as models for Womankind in the fifties? The sole revelation which caused the conservative author to *seem* radical was that his heroines flailed about so graphically, consuming themselves in their own passions. The intensity of their writhings disguised how antiquated they truly were.

Certainly, had Williams been able to expand his repertoire and search the essence of more modern, complex women, his potency as a working playwright might have been preserved. Still, the negativism of his characters fit in well with fifties' attitudes to woman's place in the social and sexual scheme, and sadly not many stronger prototypes were available by way of contrast.

William Inge's *Picnic*, another Broadway adaptation, did more gently sweep over all aspects of maidenly angst. Drifter William Holden passes through a wilting Midwestern town igniting the anxieties and desires of a cross section of its females—middle-aged schoolteacher Rosalind Russell, teen-aged tomboy Susan Strasberg, and her gorgeous sister Kim Novak. Novak, a dissatisfied beauty with no way out of petty rural stagnation, falls in love under the summer lanterns as they dance to "Moonglow"; Holden awakens her sexually, and her confusion, guilt, and longing produce bewildered tears. Holden does in fact alter these women's lives, tickling the desperation of Russell, who finally prostrates herself before her aging beau and begs him to marry her, and offering Novak his love and salvation from ennui. Only Strasberg can perceive this and advises, "Go with him, Madge. For once in your life, do something bright."

Steaming with sexual tension, the movie—with the exception of overanxious Russell—is kinder than most to its women. And more realistic. If the dramatic Cinderella resolution recalls all the "happily-ever-after" fairy tales we've seen on-screen, our consolation remains in the fact that Inge leaves the real ending in doubt: Holden and Novak may *not* be able to make it together. They may never get to the altar. They may marry and be miserable. What's important is that the drifter helps lift Novak from her lethargy. He is her ticket away from the very limited and stifling choices available. Going with him is her first active step toward controlling her own life, just as Russell's hysterical proposal more extravagantly reorders hers. Her spinsterhood has not, at least, left her a neurotic victim, too passive to seek change.

Subtly, Katharine Hepburn also worked against the atavistic languor of the Woman Alone, although her four spinster movies of the fifties —*The African Queen* (1951), *Summertime* (1955), *The Rainmaker* (1956), and *Desk Set* (1957)—did not really depart from the decade's premise that the middle-aged unmarried female was just half a person. Her spunky TV computer librarian, Bunny Watson, in *Desk Set* is perhaps the most well adjusted and least needy of the group, but the other three females flesh out the brittle, taut stereotypes we've come to expect of nervous maiden aunts. Hepburn, however, brought to this genre her usual intelligence, stoicism, and energy, and if we are to articulate the differences between her spinsters and others, it would be that during the course of the film they are awakened sexually perhaps for the first time in their lives—and it is a positive, not a destructive force. The secretary in *Summertime* allows herself to feel the flush of first passion in a romance which is clearly doomed; Rose, the missionary's sister in *The African Queen*, throws propriety to the wind when she persuades Bogart's Captain Allnut (symbolic name!) to sink the German gunboat—and in loosening up, she sparks love with the swarthy, rough riverboater.

But Lizzie of *The Rainmaker* is perhaps the decade's most provocative and sympathetic portrait of the Woman Alone. The play by N. Richard Nash, directed on screen by Joseph Anthony, succeeds in its stylized lyrical approach to the neurotic, love-starved woman, where Williams, despite his obvious gifts, only dragged her into an abyss of his alienated freaks. Simply it's the tale of a flimflam rain-maker arriving in a drought-ridden Kansas town, promising rain for a small fee, and cajoling the socially backward spinster daughter of a townsman into an awareness of her individuality and sensuality. Totally turned in to female sensibilities, Burt Lancaster's Starbuck frees Hepburn's Lizzie from her conviction that she's "as plain as old shoes." Helplessly ignorant of artifice, the girl has begged her father: "Can a woman take lessons in being a woman? . . . Pop, I'm sick and tired of me. I want to get out of me and be someone else. I'm gonna paint my mouth so it looks like it's always whistling." Echoing the dissatisfaction of millions of women, she'd gladly exchange every-thing about herself for the formula wiles that attract men.

Starbuck, who senses both her fear of his potency and her uncer-tainty about herself, tenderly unleashes her by weaving a mythological dream-woman. Melissande, he calls her. "You're a woman, believe in that," he affirms. "How can I—when nobody else does?" she cries out with that deadly logic based on the tradition that females have drawn definition and self-worth from the value men have placed on them. This time, though, Starbuck is not conning. For once in his life he truly wants to help another—to make her feel her own femininity. Kissing her is not for his pleasure, but so that she will kindle her own. "I'm pretty, I'm pretty," he forces her to chant, and we see her transforma-tion: the surge of passion, the awakening of delight, the power. He, a male, is indeed the source of Lizzie's liberation, but he does not imprison her. Forced to run out of town, he asks her to come with him. "No, I can't go. Melissande is a name for one night—but I gotta be Lizzie my whole life long," she calls. Having been asked, having felt wanted, she is free.

It is at once humorous and sad that in this decade where society decreed that marriage should be the female's supreme goal, where suburban life and all its insulating accouterments (PTA, Girl Scouts, car pools) emphasized Mom's "doing" for the children as part of her *own* familial ecstasy, movies dwelled on the neurotic Woman Alone as if she were a national subversive. Was she the Establishment's allegory warning against deviation from the norm? Or was the fulfilled and happy housewife so unbearably invisible, so dull that she adapted poorly to drama? Often critics laugh off as feminist paranoia accusa-tions that such a profundity of female neurotics in films is biased; they claim that a normal, productive, well-balanced heroine would void conflict and intrigue. In short, she would be a bore. However, most heroes became idols not in terms of their quirks and alienation, but because of their strength of character and courageous deeds. Consider John Wayne's Westerns, Gary Cooper's *Sergeant York*, Bogart's good guys (Philip Marlowe, Sam Spade), Gable's warmhearted hucksters.

It's relevant, too, that a 1951 report in *Variety* cited that the female audience, according to a poll of 3,000 exhibitors, had dropped from 67 percent to 52 percent since 1944. Attendance would keep declining, but the reason was surprising: Television didn't keep the women away as much as the fact that film content didn't interest them. "Not enough handkerchief stuff," was the complaint. Yet this handkerchief stuff was a derogatory synonym for the "women's pictures" which had created heroic, brave, and autonomous female models during the war years. Apparently, women themselves were becoming fed up with the inanity of their middle-aged screen counterparts (as well as with the pronounced rise of Westerns, gangster movies, and male-dominated films to which they could only peripherally relate). As sudsy as Jane Wyman's blind widow was in *The Magnificent Obsession*, she at least evaded the kitchen-and-madness routines and participated in enthralling romance. The picture triumphed, a kitschy conglomerate of noble sacrifice, passion, and pop-culture sentiment.

In all fairness, movies weren't the sole culprits sounding alarms about the desperate situation of the unmarried female. The press also abetted the matrimonial cause. Rufus Jarman, in a 1952 article entitled "It's Tougher Than Ever to Get a Husband" (*Saturday Evening Post*), observed the distinctions between spinster types. The "marginal girl" was defined as one not very attractive and with limited opportunity for meeting men; she was the least likely to marry. (Think of Betsy Blair in *Marty*.) Then there was the "office wife" (Nina Foch in *Executive Suite*) wedded to her employer's career, deriving economic and emotional satisfaction as his handmaiden at the expense of her own personal life. And third, the career girl (all the principals in *Three Coins in the Fountain*, *The Best of Everything*), about whom Jarman commented: ". . . most of the university professors interviewed in connection with this article are of the opinion that most of the girls who are doing post-graduate work for various high-flown careers would drop their studies and get married in a minute if the right man came along." And finally, he quotes one Dr. Emily Mudd's observation that American girls' lack of homemaking experience is a primary reason why 113,000 GI's brought war brides home from the Pacific and Europe.

Flashfire admonitions like the above could not, however, protect the stifling social status quo—which promised Prince Charming and delivered diapers—from the inevitable. A funny thing happened on the way to the sixties. The familial bubble burst. The fireside comfort of neat little suburban lives collapsed. And the divorce rate sky-rocketed. Or, more accurately, it peaked and leveled off right after the war in 1946, then during the mid-fifties rose to new heights. The statistics—that the divorce rate was one-fourth to one-third that of the total number marriages, that (by 1956) 2,000,000 married people were separated, and one-fifth to one-sixth of the couples living together claimed they were unhappy—curdled experts' expectations. Their prescription for a marital utopia was failing dramatically. And everyone wanted to know why.

Social conditions exasperating this trend included earlier marriages where both parties had had no real-life experience beforehand. Often, if the wife *had* worked to put her husband through school and then after a considerable number of years they removed themselves from the campus womb, divorce followed. They had "outgrown" each other. Then, too, with deurbanization and relative economic prosperity, the quest for status and social position became not just an upper-class game, but a suburban preoccupation straining couples' pocketbooks and values. A lower birthrate and an emphasis on peer group independence split open and rendered ineffective the family structure. But most significant of all, the "Hollywood-bred" generations had come of age.

The first phalanx of a society raised on thirties' and forties' movies had married with storybook ideals and movie-star appreciations intact. Modern courtship patterns placed premiums on superficial qualities—appearance, athletic prowess, sex appeal. If every man wanted his hometown Hayworth and every girl her imitation Gable or Ladd, he or she grabbed the next best thing. Rather than shared interests, goals, and needs, the Technicolor concept of rainbows and happy endings prevailed. Few young couples understood that marriage required work, that situations weren't always "for the best," and that being a wife did not, after all, fulfill vague, vast dreams of marital delight. Hollywood had inundated the public with romantic notions, and in the clear light of experiential living, they proved blindingly inadequate.

As the divorce rate continued to soar, women reconsidered their roles as wives, mothers, and housekeepers. And more of them, divorcées especially, found it advantageous to return to work. Business offered a challenging new world, and in the mid-fifties, for the first time in history, the majority of workingwomen did not come from the lower classes (who had been ousted from their blue-collar jobs after the war). Older women from middle- and upper-income groups grabbed the chance to work as secretaries, bookkeepers, administrators. In addition, not only did those who had attended college during the war years set a precedent for the future education of women, but many earned professional degrees. By 1950 the ranks of female physicians and surgeons had risen significantly (the increase from 7,700 to 11,800 was the largest single jump in *any* decade in twentieth-century history). Also, the numbers of social scientists, social and welfare workers, religious workers, teachers and librarians were steadily increasing. The first truly significant number of women were employed as editors and reporters, as natural scientists, college presidents, professors, and instructors (20,000). Engineering appeared to be a newly open, if limited, field. And almost 57,000 females had infiltrated a previously masculine territory, that of accounting and auditing.

Fortunately, despite setbacks eliminating women from the labor force after the war, females with professional and technical training clung tenaciously to their trades. Wrote Cynthia Fuchs Epstein in her book, *Woman's Place*:

> During World War II, for instance, when the young men were off at war, dating did not consume the time of the college co-ed and she redirected her energies to study. . . . Work became an alternative even for those who did marry. Once engaged in an occupation, many had so firm a foothold they were loath to give it up.[5]

How did the movies treat the late fifties' divorce explosion and subsequent renewed interest in the workingwoman? Gems like *The Blackwell Story* (1957), a very straightforward dramatization of the life of America's first female doctor and the prejudice she encountered in her ultimately successful struggle to be admitted to medical school, went unnoticed, while the more common attitude was purveyed by nurse Olivia de Havilland in *Not as a Stranger* (1955). When physician-husband Robert Mitchum, praising her competence in surgery, suggests she's wasting her talents by retiring to wifedom, what does Livvie do? Burst into tears! She equates love with a house and kiddies; his cool appraisal of her abilities becomes a statement of (already-established) indifference to their marriage.

The most typical films about unhappy couples zeroed in on sexual frustration or female infidelity. In *Written on the Wind* (1956), Lauren Bacall retreats from her alcoholic, suspicious husband, Robert Stack, into his best friend Rock Hudson's arms. Dorothy Malone in *The Tarnished Angels* (1957) flees disinterested daredevil husband Robert Stack into reporter Hudson's (again) arms. More sympathetic, but equally superficial, is Deborah Kerr's frustrated wife in *From Here to Eternity* (1953), seeking release with Burt Lancaster on the beach. *Wild Is the Wind* (1957) displays Anna Magnani magnificently enacting a lonely immigrant married to sheepfarmer Anthony Quinn; a helpless captive of a new culture and a language barrier, she's driven by his inattention into an affair with hired hand Anthony Franciosa. Since women have so little else to rely on for distraction or comfort or identification, sex—say the movies—provides instant panacea.

Hollywood may have unwittingly captured growing feminine dissatisfaction with the implacable fifties' mold in two of its soapiest— and most popular—efforts: *Peyton Place* (1957) and *The Best of Everything* (1959). *Peyton Place*, from Grace Metalious' best seller, disrupted the New England puritan pastorale as every variety of sexual skeleton tumbled out of the townfolks' chintz-and-maple closets. And how the women suffered! Lana Turner was the mother of illegitimate daughter Diane Varsi. Hope Lange was raped by her stepfather. Terry Moore was the town tramp. Boredom cultivated lust and petty chatter, little else, and these bitter ladies were helpless to escape their small-town upbringing. In brilliant romantic color, no better argument has come out of Hollywood for the liberation of women than this condemnation of suburban fifties' Americana and of the small minds and restless libidos it produced.

Even so, *The Best of Everything*, from Rona Jaffe's novel, might have provided a good argument for the *Peyton Place* mamas to return their daughters to the sizzling autumnal hearthfires, for in its story of the horrors greeting eager-beaver career girls in a big-city publishing firm, the worst of everything and everyone besets them. Diane Baker becomes pregnant. Aspiring actress Suzy Parker gives herself to Broadway stage director Louis Jourdan, becomes insanely possessive, and one day while spying on him from a fire escape falls to her death. Ambitious secretary Hope Lange is promoted to Joan Crawford's editorial position when the dour *grande dame* decides to try marriage after all. But Crawford can't make a go of it, having been permanently ruined by her career, and when she returns, Lange is booted downstairs; she will soon leave the perilous business world for marriage.

If these trials and tribulations were meant to warn girls not to leave home for careers—they didn't work. Women were sufficiently disillusioned with the kind of romance offered by plain-old-marriage to find the business world exotically attractive. And besides, Hollywood outdid itself with glossy color photography, beautiful people, smart clothing, and designer offices. While the moral whispered, "Stay in the kitchen!" lush city locales promised urban electricity. It was almost like a travelogue for the single life. And a preview of things to come.

Like the Pill. Sexual freedom. And equal opportunity in the business world.

They were just around the corner.

Or almost. First, a parallel fifties' phenomenon, that of the Breasted Blonde, would leave indelible scars.

Margaret Mead observed in 1957: "When we stopped short of treating women as people after providing them with all the paraphernalia of education and rights, we set up a condition whereby men also became less than full human beings and more narrowly domestic."[6]

It is no accident that in this era limiting female participation to the pantry, the inheritors of the Rita Hayworth-Jane Russell physicality were elevated to goddesses by society's obsessive mammary madness. Wasn't this Fantasy Woman more ornamental and peripheral even than Everywife? After all, Everywife discharged daily tasks— tending the children, preparing the meals, shopping and cleaning. But

Everywoman luxuriated in her own uselessness. Her body was ample. Her clothes were form-fitting and uncomfortable. But who noticed? She wasn't required to *do* anything!

Except make her man comfortable.

And you can't get more domestic than that.

18

MAMMARY MADNESS—
heaven-sent and earthbound

"Women are restless and dissatisfied because they cannot or will not accept their physical destiny,"[1] cautioned psychiatrist Dr. Ralph S. Banay in 1947, the year after Howard Hughes invited the public to tussle with Russell.

The Bureau of Labor Statistics estimated that 20,000,000 women, almost one-half the adult female population, were essentially idle during the early postwar years. That is, they were not working, did not have children under eighteen, did not toil on farms, were not aged or infirm.

What then did they do? They played canasta, arranged barbecues and cocktail parties, chauffeured their kids to school, and had plenty of time to ponder that destiny, whatever it was.

Pitching in to help them define themselves, businesses launched a number of the most successful ad campaigns in history. By 1952 the cosmetics industry was selling over $1 billion worth of beauty products yearly. Beauty parlors between 1954 and 1958 expanded their number by a staggering 38 percent to accommodate frequent trimmings for the new pixie and poodle cuts. And corsets became a foundation for milady's wardrobe.

In 1948 4,500,000 "breast pads" or falsies were sold as a result of the Hollywood "sweater girl" trend launched by Lana Turner and other pinups. By 1950 85 percent of women over fifteen wore bras, girdles, or both, with the New York workingwoman up front in the statistics race, her yearly purchase averaging out to four bras and two girdles. Corsets had become a $500,000,000 annual business.

Manufacturers complacently informed the public with comments sounding suspiciously like locker-room gossip—that New York women have bigger busts, Dallas women are taller, Southern women "let themselves sag because of a little extra humidity."[2]

Observed manufacturer Sam Yaffe: "You take those Bali girls [who never wear bras], when they're past 18 they're the sloppiest women in the world."[3]

Fletcher Dodge, executive vice-president of the Corset and Brassiere Association, eulogized: "It's sad but true that seventeen million females over fifteen just don't care how they look. Sometimes it makes a man wonder."[4]

Actually, more women than ever before cared about their appearance. Not only did they have the time to care, but the emphasis on femininity—hourglass shapes harshly defined by cinch belts, peasant skirts, strapless gowns, bulky crinolines, or sheath dresses ensuring that young ladies would sit with their legs together—deliberately abandoned functionalism for style. And sex appeal. All that idleness and dissatisfaction, had created a group particularly susceptible to the media.

Whereas in periods of turbulent integration and feminist progress like the twenties and forties, females—however tentatively—set the vogue in popular culture, silently commanding the media to reflect *their* interests and life-styles, during the stagnant years of the thirties and fifties the reverse occurred. Social and economic pressures sent them scurrying back to the homes, and their own needs for escapism and assurance created a climate of need in which the media dominated *them*, and rechiseled their priorities and notions of beauty. These were damaging dangerous times.

One of the most dangerous aspects of fifties' movies explicitly relates to the kind of heroine the studios glorified as sexy. A panoply of Biblical sagas, like De Mille's earliest epics, allowed plenty of room for sex without censure and splendidly displayed some of Hollywood's most beautiful women in colorful and elaborately draped form-fitting togas. Jean Simmons in *The Robe* (1953), Hedy Lamarr in *Samson and Delilah* (1949), Susan Hayward in *Demetrius and the Gladiators* (1954), Anne Baxter and Debra Paget in *The Ten Commandments* (1956), Gina Lollobrigida in *Solomon and Sheba* (1959) —all frolicked in Biblical and Roman courtyards while scantily clad handmaidens drew their baths and anointed their bodies. But theirs was practically a subliminal message compared with what *would* happen. For as box-office receipts plummeted during the decade, movies earnestly went about standardizing the desirable female. Enter the sex goddess.

How many girls in the past half century have learned to kiss by studying the love scenes of their favorite heroine? Her gait? Her flashing eyes or swift turn of the head? Now, in the fifties, they would study enormous white breasts peering from daring décolletage, breathy little-girl voices, and vacant stares. But because so many women filled up vapid days with beauty worries, because competition for men and essential early marriage was keener than ever and rising divorce rates put women on the marriage market not once but two or three times, sex appeal as sold by the movies caught on with revolutionary and brutal rapidity.

The foremost fifties' manipulator was Darryl F. Zanuck. Marilyn Monroe, the woman who spawned a generation of imitators and parodists and helped revive an industry, rose to stardom in the bosom of Twentieth Century-Fox, which had also nurtured Alice Faye and Betty Grable. Just as MGM bore the stamp of Mayer, so did Twentieth definitely reflect the preoccupations of its chief, Zanuck. For as the legend goes, he liked the ladies. Not their brains, especially, but their bodies. In *Don't Say Yes Until I Finish Talking*, a biography of the tycoon, author Mel Gussow makes these pertinent comments:

> He can sit next to a lady at dinner, and if he is not interested in her, sexually, he is oblivious to her to the point of hostility. If he is interested, then the courtship begins.[5]
>
> A statement like "Sex is very important to Darryl Zanuck, isn't it?" is always greeted by loud laughter.[6]
>
> One director sees sex as the symbol, the chief motivating force, of Zanuck. "He's an emotion. He lives in a frenzy," And he adds, with utmost seriousness, "The single most important thing in Darry Zanuck's life—bigger than movies or success—is sex."[7]

The studio chief's personal life supports this last observation. His longtime marriage broke up over Polish actress Bella Darvi, whom he had imported to groom for stardom. For Zanuck, it wasn't just an affair, and he dropped both his wife *and* studio power to hotfoot it back to Europe in her pursuit. When their relationship ended, he attempted in vain to bestow stardom on three other girlfriends; Juliette Greco (*The Roots of Heaven*), Irina Demich (*The Longest Day*), and his present paramour Genevieve Gilles, a Frenchwoman forty-four years younger than he. He and Gilles have been together for ten years, with seventy-one-year-old Zanuck trying to elevate her celebrity, first through a lavish but tasteless $48,000 short subject, *The World of Fashion*, a monument to Genevieve's lithe body and clothes sense. Her feature debut, the 1970 comedy *Hello–Goodbye*, also flopped. Genevieve, Zanuck's companion and center of his personal life, unwittingly shed revealing light on his consistent and juvenile attitude to women:

> He is so intelligent, but he is like a child. He is in his car with a chauffeur and we'll pass a girl and he will say—"Look at that!" Onassis is like that, too. Darryl has a book with all the girls' names in it, and if he likes one, he puts stars next to her name. Four stars! Five stars![8]

Zanuck's influence on the kind of sex Twentieth brought to the screen—an exploitative and grotesque parody of woman's body as isolated from her mind, emotions, soul, and all other functions that would make her truly human and desirable—is dramatically obvious. Although Twentieth, under his direction, had produced some fine films (including Joe Mankiewicz' *A Letter to Three Wives* and *All About Eve*; John Ford's *The Grapes of Wrath*, *Tobacco Road*, and *How Green Was My Valley*; Elia Kazan's *Gentlemen's Agreement* and *A Tree Grows in Brooklyn*) the studio in the fifties desperately needed this gimmick to renew box-office interest. The movie industry was in trouble.

Eight million TV sets had been sold in 1950 alone. In addition, the five major film companies—Paramount, RKO, Twentieth Century-Fox, Warner Brothers, and Loew's Inc (MGM)—had until 1952 to comply with a Supreme Court decision requiring them to sever their theater operations; no longer would each have its own exhibiting chain to ensure showcases. Finally, the McCarthy purge was still a grim reality. As youthful Senator Richard M. Nixon observed: "The demonstrated activity of Communists within the motion picture industry is a matter of concern to the members of Congress and loyal Americans everywhere."[9]

To lure movie patrons, the industry first tried 3-D, but the optical process required viewers to wear glasses which ultimately broke off, got smeared with popcorn, or were generally ineffective; after a few dreadful attempts, the process was abandoned. So larger screens were employed—Cinerama and, in 1953, CinemaScope. But the biggest business boon was no man-made achievement. It was a natural wonder—Marilyn Monroe.

Much has been written about Marilyn's career. Suffice it to say that her pre-stardom films, prime-stardom films, and independent justification-of-seriousness films (*The Prince and the Showgirl*, 1957; *The Misfits*, 1961) varied no more than the heart scan of a thrombosis victim. Almost entirely she played the delicious dumb blonde with both heart and head as soft as a cotton boll. When variations did occur, these were not found in her work for Twentieth, which seeing the grosses of her first major Cinemascope musical, *Gentlemen Prefer Blondes* in 1953 ($5,000,000, among the top ten box-office pictures of 1954), re-created and re-created the formula. Dizzy, dazzling Marilyn would sing a few whispery songs, mince about in skintight outfits, and bat her eyes naïvely at salty comments—comments like Donald O'Connor's crack about her singing aspirations in *There's No Business Like Show Business* (1954): "Tell me, what's a girl with such pear-shaped tones doing taking singing lessons?" Sometimes, as the butt of all fantasies, her character was cut from little more than cardboard (Marilyn's fallen "angel," Cherie in *Bus Stop*, 1956); more often, a good deal less (her Pola in *How to Marry a Millionaire* in 1953, nearsighted in the best Dorothy Parker jingle tradition, bumps into objects, warmly greets strangers, and boards wrong planes).

Although Marilyn was learning her craft, the schism between her ambitions to play such roles as Grushenka in *The Brothers Karamazov*, and Twentieth's—to have her ring up more dollars through tired rehashes like *How to Be Very Very Popular*—engendered her walkout. In one sense Marilyn won. *How to Be Very Very Popular* (1955) was very, very unpopular, and going down with it was Sheree North, the gal the studio hoped would click as her replacement. Marilyn fled to New York to study with Lee Strasberg, and did not return to Twentieth until it was ready to begin *Bus Stop* under a new co-production deal with her and Milton Greene.

But in another more affecting sense she lost.

For Marilyn did not have the confidence and stamina to juggle major stardom with the public's leering adulation and her own consuming new ambitions. It is interesting that many of her least exploitative, most varied, and totally natural acting assignments were those smaller movies like *Love Happy* and *The Asphalt Jungle* in 1950, and *Monkey Business* and *Clash by Night* in 1952 which she undertook while still a minor contract actress. Even in *Niagara* (1953), the movie that assured Marilyn's celebrity, she was able to make the double-dealing wife, Rose Loomis, very human and sympathetic, though the studio was definitely steering her toward sexploitation with trashy tight dresses and low-cut gowns.

One paradox about her is that as fragile and needy as she eventually proved to be, Marilyn seemed to thrive and draw strength from the early battles, as if simply having that goal—"stardom"—provided some kind of substitute identity. She survived the horrors of her well-known childhood—illegitimacy, foster homes, orphanages. She endured a lousy marriage, worked in a war plant, and had the moxie to storm Twentieth Century-Fox in 1946, charming studio executive and ex-silent comedian Ben Lyon sufficiently to walk out with her first contract. She dusted herself off after Twentieth (the first time round) failed to renew her option, then after Columbia did the same. And she persevered until she was singled out for praise in minor roles which, played by anyone else, might have gone unnoticed.

Stardom came, and with it crowds. Fans accepted her explanation for posing nude—"I was hungry." But the image she and her dramatic coaches, Natasha Lytees, Michael Chekhov (for a short period), and the Strasbergs, mapped out for her included great dramatic roles. At the same time these people, practically crippling her with dependence on them, were not removing any of the definite, stereotyping sexual suggestions in her manner. Or finding scripts worthy of her new aspirations. *Or* appeasing her increasing uncertainties about her talent. In fact, Marilyn's confidence eroded proportionately as her fame mushroomed, and she found herself unable to recite an exclamation or simple three-word sentence without suffering memory lapses or slipping into paroxysms of self-doubt. This was one manifestation of her constant manic drive to prove conclusively she was an actress, not a sexpot, a drive for identity which would finally consume her.

Mark Harris, eulogizing Monroe, suggested insightfully:

At the time of her marriage to Joe DiMaggio in 1954 she must herself have capitulated to a public image of herself which had overwhelmed her private conviction. His life was his body, his power was his power. It must have seemed to her a proper wedding because a proper definition of herself. Within a year it ended. Mrs. Joe DiMaggio she wasn't. That she knew. Nor The Girl upstairs. Nor a pin-up. At this time of her life, said a friend, she was engaged in "an absolute desperate attempt to find out what she was and what she wanted."[10]

She wanted, it seems, to deny her physicalness, that very attribute which had brought her the celebrity she had craved. And which, after fame was won, was the sole identity left her. She tried to reject it. She studied her craft in earnest, married playwright Arthur Miller, read books, converted to Judaism, and tried to have his babies. But self-doubt plagued her. Shortly after their wedding, while making *The Prince and the Showgirl* she shocked her husband with her unprofessionalism and tantrums; he later wrote of his feelings in a diary Marilyn inadvertently read. Thereafter she considered that he had in some sense betrayed her.

Without the combat intensity of the haul to stardom to preoccupy her, Marilyn may have substituted this new struggle, recognition as a serious actress, as a source of identity; fastening on this more serious aspect of her career would be, happily, a long-term struggle. But in view of her obsession, *The Prince and the Showgirl* sent her off in less than splendid style. Marilyn wore elegant, more concealing outfits, but her character scarcely varied from her other slow-witted, naïve studio roles. Even so, her genuine flair for comedy and her extraordinary beauty elevated this picture, as it did others before it, to a work of grace.

She would only make three more films—all tributes to her comic skills and special gift of molding unlikely characters into studies of human fragility. Still, each part, no more demanding than her previous one, inflamed her sense of increasing incompetence. Although her Sugar Kane in *Some Like It Hot* (1959) razzle-dazzled with a spirit not even director Billy Wilder had hoped for, the set was in a continual incendiary state because of Marilyn's lateness, lack of preparation, and inability to remember lines. Absent from the screen for almost two years between *Prince* and *Some Like It Hot*, she had lost a baby, increased her dependence on sleeping pills, and almost died from an overdose. She could not be happy with her man or have his child, two things that might have reconfirmed her self-value. So she threw herself into another second-rate vehicle, *Let's Make Love* (1960), and threw herself at costar Yves Montand. Critics lambasted the film, and Montand returned to his wife.

By the time *The Misfits* went into production, Marilyn and Miller, who had been surrogate father since their marriage, were barely talking. Her dependence on alcohol and pills caused director John Huston to shut down the set while she dried out in a sanitarium.

That Marilyn could, through her drug-dimmed haze, give such an open and touching performance as Roslyn in *The Misfits* is an impressive achievement. It is a tenderly written, but uneven role; however, Miller tailored it for her, and Roslyn obviously represented his noblest and most delicate comprehensions about Marilyn. She eased smoothly into the character's style. She exuded dramatic tension and quiet desperation as the neurotic but sensitive divorcée who guides wrangler Clark Gable away from senseless slaughter of wild mustangs to a deeper appreciation of the value of life. It was her last completed performance, the single one where her character made a positive and serious statement of human sensibilities and where she, a woman, had the inner strength to redirect others.

Marilyn has, in death, been immortalized by those who see her as a symbol of total masculine and industrial exploitation. This is true. And false. It's oversimplification and blatant inaccuracy to accuse the studio system of doing her in. Twentieth may have created and perpetuated a destructive female myth, but Marilyn was twenty-seven in 1953, the year *Gentlemen Prefer Blondes* brought her worldwide fame. She was an adult with enough raw knowledge of the world behind her to understand fully what lay ahead. Marilyn's slow and terrible demise was related more to very personal female insecurities which led her to insist that everyone around her embrace a paternalistic role. The studio, because of its bureaucratic structure, did so least of all, catering to her impersonally as an invaluable, sometimes demanding asset. Marilyn's helplessness required, however, that everyone in her life—from masseur/actor Ralph Roberts to the Strasbergs and Milton and Amy Greene and Miller—make her decisions, keep her distracted, rescue her from overdoses. She trusted her friends too much and felt betrayed too soon; setting up her inordinate demands made their ultimate failure inevitable.

Directors have compared her luminosity and magical communion with the camera as an inexplicable phenomenon akin only to Garbo's. How much of Garbo's essentially appealing void, that quality of which she spoke in *As You Desire Me* ("There is nothing in me, nothing of me; take me, take me and make me as you desire me") was also Marilyn's? In spite of her robust lovely appearance and vulnerable sensitivity, her spirit denied presence; that provocative emptiness longed to be filled, inviting us to violate it with our fantasies—fantasies which created a legend. Everywoman: beautiful, vulnerable, available. And vacuous enough so that on-screen we, and off-screen her men, would read the enigma to suit our egos.

Whatever being a serious actress really meant to her, no matter how much she wanted it to be a primary mission, Marilyn's inability to throw herself into work in times of trouble suggests that despite herself, she had deep in her heart bought the traditional notions of feminine value. Love, or at least desirability, restored her. For when she was in trouble, unsure of herself, she would return to the comfort of the image she obsessively wanted to wipe out. Marilyn, for a theater date, would dress in a low-cut flame-colored dress, not exactly the attire to deflect unwanted stares. In *There's No Business Like Show Business* she insisted on being sewn into a skintight gown, and sang her "Heat Wave" number as suggestively as possible. She refused to wear panties, considering them an encumbrance. George Cukor recalls, "Though she was rather modest, in a curious way, she could also have that total exhibitionist thing. I remember she insisted on using one dress for a number, just one layer of chiffon with a very sketchy pair of drawers. We had to keep strong lights on her to take out the detail."[11] And finally, at thirty-six, shortly before her death, she posed nude for a *Playboy* layout as if to reassure herself during infrequent moments of consciousness that she was still attractive, that her career wasn't slipping, that she was desirable—*ergo*, alive.

The parallels between Monroe and Judy Garland are compelling. Judy, who also relied on pills and died of an apparently accidental overdose, radiated a similar helplessness. Many have overlooked her as a film actress, preferring to recognize Judy at the Palace, wrenching hearts with that tear in her voice; but she was a natural talent for whom not one line of dialogue, piece of timing, or gesture ever seemed false. Her vulnerability in some ways outdistanced Marilyn's simply because her limited traditional beauty denied any sexual connections; thus, it was the vulnerability of a soul, of the girl next door who had somehow strayed into unprotected territory but would take risks anyway. If she didn't have that inexplicable mystique with the camera that Garbo and Monroe had, perhaps Garland's quality was preferable—a zest for living, an adaptability. A willingness to reveal her emotions. And somehow—whether playing the ingenue in *Ziegfeld Girl* (1941) who makes it to the *Follies* on her talent, not her proportions; the farm girl in *Summer Stock* (1950) whose last-minute performance saves the show and wins her Gene Kelly; or singer Vicky Lester in *A Star Is Born* (1954), ready to give up her career for her alcoholic husband, pulling herself together after his suicide to pay him tribute ("This is *Mrs. Norman Maine*," she emphasizes to her first postfuneral audience)—this adaptability created a springboard of resilience ensuring survival.

That same resilience was lacking off the screen. And in this case the studio was specifically to blame. Louis B. Mayer who originally signed her as a consolation prize after having lost Deanna Durbin to Universal, imposed an inhuman diet and work regime on his young star, plying her with appetite depressants by day and sleeping pills by night. Needless to say, Judy's weight battle and alcohol-pill problem stem from habits imposed during her formative teen years in MGM's "paternal" bosom.

More than coincidence, however, is the fact that both she and Marilyn were in the midst of floundering careers and early middle age, Garland forty-seven and Marilyn thirty-six, when they overdosed. For them, fragility had meant not only the key to screen success but to the barbiturates which, in diluting self-doubts and burned-out dreams, also wiped them out.

What Garland and Monroe were about, in life and in their early deaths, was defined deftly by the great French director Jean Renoir, who recently spoke of the importance of an actress' persona in creating her impact. "The camera is a little bit like the knife of a surgeon," the director of *Grand Illusion* observed. "It opens the meat and you find the heart."

And sometimes, along the way, the pain sears too horribly to bear.

Marilyn Monroe's originality and tenderness paved the way for a surge of imitators who lacked the essential humanity that had set her apart from her material. Gradually the genre ballooned to include Sheree North, Barbara Nichols, Mamie Van Doren, Diana Dors, Monique Van Vooren, and those extraordinary self-parodies, Anita Ekberg and Jayne Mansfield. Ekberg's classical facial beauty went unnoticed above her mammoth chest, and only in the totally decadent *La Dolce Vita*, in which she existed in a milieu of freaks, did she not appear grotesque and humorous. The perfect stooge for Bob Hope's obsequious sex jokes in *Paris Holiday* (1957), she actually made few American films despite her enormous publicity.

Jayne Mansfield attempted an all-out campaign to steal the Monroe crown, and not only did she jump at every opportunity to display her vast proportions, but she embraced a life-style rivaling Mae West's. Publicists delighted in her pink Hollywood house, pink heart-shaped pool, pink poodle, and her renegade West muscleman, Hungarian-born Mickey Hargitay. She also threw in her own J.M. hot-water bottles and the entirely insubstantiated fact that she had a phenomenal IQ approaching 158. Mansfield appeared in a few successful fifties' movies whose comic premises lay in the undercurrent of giggles about her figure and sexuality. In *The Girl Can't Help It* (1957), the audience is treated to pointed symbolism like Mansfield joggling down the street while the milkman's ice melts and his milk bubbles. Then Jayne holds the milk bottles to her bosom. "I just want to be a wife, have kids," says our heroine. "But everyone figures me for a sexpot. No one thinks I'm equipped for motherhood."

Recently, in her book *The Descent of Woman*, Elaine Morgan made this same observation, explaining that men like to think that women's physical equipment was designed for their pleasure alone. This would be especially true of the Mammary Woman in whom functionalism is completely abandoned. "The immaturity of the American Male—this breast fetish," director Frank Tashlin (responsible for Mansfield's 1956 *The Girl Can't Help It* and her 1957 *Will Success Spoil Rock Hunter?*) told Peter Bogdanovich. "You can't sell tires without breasts. Imagine a statue with breasts like Mansfield's! Imagine *that* in marble. We don't like big feet or big ears, but we make an idol of a woman because she's deformed in the breasts. There's nothin' more hysterical to me than big-breasted women—like walking leaning towers."[12]

Mansfield in *Will Success Spoil Rock Hunter?* parodies herself, playing Rita Marlowe, the Big Movie Star who saves poor soul Tony Randall's ad campaign by giving her endorsement as "the girl with the oh-so-kissable lips." Intermittently erupting in that high-pitched Mansfield squeal, she languishes in a bubble bath and ribs Marilyn by announcing her next picture as "a Russian drama about two Russian brothers." But mostly the movie is about how her Minervan proportions and sexual clout elevates Randall into a powerhouse simply by association. While he is properly reticent, Mansfield is unfortunate, squirming and squeaking her way through the movie with an embarrassing lack of inhibitions, hardly seeming to mind that we are laughing at her most of all.

In reassessment of the fifties' murderously antifemale approach to mammary madness, only one contender seemed to connect viably to any realistic or vaguely human female image. Kim Novak's nova was born out of Harry Cohn's pique. His Love Goddess Hayworth had married her way out of the public eye, and her comeback films (*Salome, Miss Sadie Thompson, Pal Joey*) didn't have that old kick. Also Cohn was upset that he had let Monroe slip away from Columbia. So he determined to create another box-office bonanza. Kim, who had come to Hollywood as Miss Deep-Freeze, was the gal he chose —a decision he later regretted for the sole reason that the girl had a will of her own. And a fierce sense of independence. Nobody, least of all a commodity, was going to give him sass.

The mogul and his star survived many confrontations. Right from the start he wanted to change her name from Marilyn Novak to Kit Marlowe. Kim, strong-willed, won a compromise on that one. But Cohn, referring to her behind her back as "that fat Polack" (just as Judy Holliday was "that fat Jewish broad"), carefully watched over Kim's life, insisting she diet before he concluded her contract, that she wear a bra, that she live in the YWCA Studio Club.

This kind of meddling was common among studio chiefs, as was drastic wielding of power. After Kim went on suspension rather than accept a salary incompatible with her status, Cohn gave a spiteful interview with *Time* magazine, claiming that *he*, and the films he chose, had made her a star. "If you wanna bring me your wife or your aunt, we'll do the same for them. . . ."[13] Hardly a generous summation.

And middling in accuracy. For Kim fulfilled an important position in toning down fifties' sexuality. In addition to a healthy but not embarrassingly enormous body, she bore a classical profile resembling Garbo's and was peculiarly reticent and emotionless in both facial and vocal expression. The overall effect nicely balanced the cartoonlike vulgarizations of her overripe counterparts. Kim went even further by imprinting her own anesthetized, updated version of the thirties' enigma on her roles, some of the best dramatic parts and most popular films of the era: the sexually tense Madge in *Picnic* (1956); the secretary involved with her aging garment center boss (Fredric March) in *Middle of the Night* (1959); Jimmy Stewart's mysterious, duplicitous lover in *Vertigo* (1958); and the practical but sympathetic Molly in *The Man with the Golden Arm* (1956) were as challenging as her *Pal Joey* (1957), *The Eddie Duchin Story* (1956), and *Jeanne Eagels* (1957) were glamorous.

Granted, Kim could never be accused of overacting; granted, her emotional range was narrow. But there was a provocative quality investing her small-town girls with an existential restlessness. One wonders what a Bergman or Antonioni would have done with her or how subtitles might contribute to her work, and it's not difficult to comprehend why Otto Preminger paid $100,000 to borrow her for *The Man with the Golden Arm* or why Hitchcock chose her for *Vertigo*. Indeed, Kim may have been publicized as a sex symbol, she may have looked like one, but it's a tribute to Cohn's unaccountable good taste at the time (and lack of other hot box-office females) that he cast her most imaginatively and not just as scenery for gawkers.

During the premiere years of her stardom, Kim cooperated with studios and fan magazines, becoming known as the girl with the lavender-tinted hair and lavender-cushioned home. But the oppressive obedience required by the studios ruffled her. There's a good chance that the reticence emanating from her on-screen relates to a distaste for and discomfort with the violation of privacy necessary in movie acting. Occasionally even, her physicalness embarrassed *her*, and in her worst vehicles like *Kiss Me Stupid*, *Jeanne Eagels*, and *The Legend of Lylah Clare* she self-consciously went about being "sexy" with little conviction or joy, as if aware of the sideshow quality of her roles. Today she lives in semiretirement in Big Sur, having had the strength of will to take from Hollywood the most it could give her and then vanish with her personal freedom and sanity intact. Outliving both Marilyn and Mansfield, Kim was able to fuse the role of goddess with that of the confused, modern neurotic and the classically impassive woman. Was that withdrawn image simply a tool of her own survival? Or was the idea of a "deadened" sleepwalker somehow provocative to men in the same way that necrophilia is?

While Novak's embalmed look was in some ways a natural protective reaction to Mansfield and Monroe, the movies imported a discovery who shocked audiences into new delight and indignation. Brigitte Bardot, her name was. The twenty-two-year-old blonde, with the figure as petulant and petitely plumped out as her underlip, unwrapped her sheet to reveal her divine form in husband Roger Vadim's *And God Created Woman* (1957). Eyes popped, so did tempers, as clergymen and citizens' groups denounced the whole business as "obscene," "lewd," and "disgraceful." Nevertheless, this French film grossed $4,000,000 in its initial run here, and many considered Bardot's "sex kitten" the best thing to come out of France since *foie gras*.

What separated Bardot from her predecessors, however, was not simply the Atlantic Ocean or the layers of clothing she so willingly peeled off. She combined two very unique attributes: The first was her youth. Monroe, Mansfield, Ekberg, and Novak retained a staidness unrelated to their chronological age. Brigitte, on the other hand, though no older than Novak at her debut, suggested childish arrogance in her behavior, her style of dress, her lithe movements. That blond baby pout—the successor of Williams' taunting *Baby Doll* (1956) and predecessor of Nabokov's *Lolita* (1962)—commingled with a knowing sexuality. Her style foreshadowed Courrèges, Mary Quant, and the "youth explosion" and tapped the fantasy tradition of the succulent child-woman.

Second, Bardot always seemed to be repressing an uncontrollable anger. Anger against society in general—and men in particular. Perhaps it was her facial set or the teasing lines of her body, but this explosive sullenness (which Jane Fonda, another Vadim ex, later formidably adapted into mocking self-deprecation), this contained rage ordained for Bardot the position as precocious aggressor. How else ensure constant control? It was as if, even then, she understood the dynamics of exploitation. Using her body to taunt, punish, and reward at *her* whim was the only viable statement of her independence she might make in 1957.

Today Bardot, at thirty-eight, seems a peculiar candidate for a misanthrope, but not long ago she told the French magazine *L'Express*, "I hate humanity—I am allergic to it. . . . I see no one. I don't go out. I am disgusted with everything. Men are beasts, and even beasts don't behave as they do." The Women's Movement, as she perceives it, fails as an alternative: "To be fulfilled, women must stay women. And there are no more true women, nor true men. These days you see a mutation of one sex into the other." Toying with the idea of leaving films in a year or so, Bardot compared this voluntary retirement with breaking up an affair: "I leave before being left. I decide,"[14] she said flatly, and with the same abrasive honesty which has sharpened her feline appeal. If Bardot was calculating and a heartless tease, the image she conveyed seemed a good deal healthier than that of all the other goddesses, for she alone knew exactly who she was, what she was doing, and why. In view of this, her anger is refreshing.

Young women identified and wanted to emulate her enough to copy her leonine blond mane and pouty lips; in 1958 the cosmetics industry was revolutionized by the introduction of white and pale lipsticks to achieve a similarly distended, puffy mouth. More important, new interest was kindled in foreign movie imports. Between 1956 and 1960, the American release of films such as Bergman's *The Seventh Seal*, Fellini's *La Strada*, Kurosawa's *Rashomon*, and Truffaut's *The Four Hundred Blows* drew patrons to consider cinema as "art." Audiences responded to the visual-technical creativity and unusually vivid and original ways these pictures explored the human condition. And very slowly a different kind of woman would be introduced to the American public. She would be a woman who could incorporate sexuality with intelligence, sensuality with experience. She would be different from Bardot, or from other voluptuous imports like Claudia Cardinale and Sophia Loren, who in the fifties was still the soaking-wet ornament on the ship's prow in *Boy on a Dolphin*. With Simone Signoret came America's first glimpse of her. Signoret's older woman, who loses Laurence Harvey to a wealthy virginal girl in England's *Room at the Top* (1959), emanated beauty, warmth, and feeling as she poignantly opened the interiors of that forgotten human, the middle-aged woman. But it would not be an immediate or explosive love affair between Europe's mature heroines and the American moviegoing audience.

Hollywood as early as 1950 was thinking young. The Mammary Woman, influencing audiences toward a new ideal of cheap, sensational beauty, had lifted box-office receipts satisfactorily, but movies' survival could not depend on sex alone. A faithful audience required cultivation.

If anything could save the industry, it would be the nation's youth, the generation of war babies who in the fifties were approaching their teen years. They had to be weaned away from their television sets and back to the theaters.

And since women had always composed the major part of audiences, by logical application indoctrinating the preteen and teen-aged female would best perpetuate the habit.

So the movies intrepidly went to work on America's daughters.

19

POPCORN VENUS
allure for the kiddie crowd

"The young must be introduced to and encouraged in the movie habit," announced Robert M. Weitman, managing director of the Paramount Theater in New York, in 1950.[1] Kids bought tickets to the slapstick insanity of Dean Martin and Jerry Lewis and to the gimmick of Donald O'Connor's *Francis (the Talking Mule)* with its five sequels, but the industry's money was really behind the bubbling teen-age Cinderella, a new genre of heroine who bounced from the high school prom into the conjugal bed as fast as she could wrap her bridal veil around Tony Curtis, Tab Hunter, Rock Hudson, Robert Wagner, or, later, Troy Donahue.

Daddy's little girl would merge with Everyman's ideal, and precocious teen Debbie Reynolds, clowning around in Dick Powell's over-sized pajamas in *Susan Slept Here* (1954), froze the frame on the archetypical teen of the decade. Debbie led a gaggle of girls next door. A freckle-faced Doris Day; Pier Angeli, fragile and classically lovely waif-child; Terry Moore, robust heart throb; Janet Leigh, leading youthful modernity to *Prince Valiant* (1954) and other costume epics; and pixie-cut Natalie Wood, perhaps the most exquisite plastic miniature of them all, perpetuated the bland sweet silhouette Jane Powell and June Allyson had cut in the late forties. These snub-nosed beauties, almost indistinguishable from one another and from the lesser teen luminaries (Piper Laurie, Lori Nelson, Venetia Stevenson, Mona Freeman, Mala Powers, and, later, Tuesday Weld), perfectly reflected the faceless, powerless role of women in postwar society. Pretty, amusing, and childish, they enjoyed marvelous popularity among teen fans who could relate to them as they never had to the

283

extraordinary and haughty sophistication of Crawford, Davis, or Lana Turner.

But readers of *Photoplay* and *Modern Screen*, magazines enjoying circulations of more than 1,000,000 apiece, knew that Debbie and Terry and Natalie were just folks. The proof was in the pages— perhaps a layout of Debbie in blue jeans climbing her backyard tree. Or Natalie in a striped boat-neck shirt and white ducks feeding the porpoises at Marineland with Nick Adams. Kids knew that Terry Moore, though sexy, was a devout Mormon and a good girl and that Janet and Tony, wed in 1951, shared the happiest marriage in Holly- wood. Keeping abreast of Liz Taylor's marriages and divorces, they sympathized that her special beauty indeed handicapped her, and only when the merry widow waltzed into the happy Fisher home, leaving Debbie with grief on her face and wet diapers in her hands, did her coast-to-coast admiration society sour. Not that Hedda Hopper helped the situation along by waspishly quoting Liz's defense: "What do you expect me to do? Sleep alone?" Her marriage to Eddie, at once relegating him to position of cuckold and Debbie to wronged wife, would be forgiven only when Liz hovered near death from pneumonia.

Such tidbits delighted girlish escapist readers the way the scandal sheet *Confidential*—a runaway seller—sated adults. In the fifties teen fans didn't even *have* to go to the movies to search out and emulate their favorites; they merely had to read the magazines. But those who did attend were caught up in a rainbow vision of ebullient schoolgirls, orphans, and brides, all naïve, all virtuous, and all so vacuous that the perimeters of their lives were defined solely by their men. Often the stars themselves, and the movies, appealed with energy and grace. Who could dislike the vivacious and exceptionally talented Debbie- virago of *Hit the Deck*, *Singin' in the Rain*, and *Athena*? Who could resist the charms of Audrey Hepburn's fawnlike elegance in *Roman Holiday* and *Sabrina*? Or Leslie Caron's pouting mademoiselle in *An American in Paris*, her waifs in *Lili* and *Daddy Longlegs*, her girl- women in *Gigi* and *Fanny*? Yet the tomboy and the delicate urchin seemed two sides of a dangerous coin minted in the postwar era, one on which the new woman—youthful, helpless—was exactly antitheti- cal to Rosie the Riveter. Even this heroine's physical stature was small.

Consider, too, how the urchin, with her tiny face, dark, luminous eyes, and close-cropped hair differed in physical appearance from the parallel sexual ideal, the Mammary Woman. Subtle moral distinctions existed, too. The blond buxom fantasy creature was greeted with faint contempt and, like the traditional floozy, seemed a succulent conquest—but no man's notion of a mother to his children. A dirty-joke ideal, she reflected the double standard which dichotomized sexual and marital expectations. The paperthin wisp of a gamine—all that was wholesome, clean, and domestic incarnate—existed, however, as the goddess' polar opposite.

Ironically, however, the waif, as portrayed by Audrey Hepburn, provided one of the decade's most intriguing and individualistic heroines. Hepburn simply outdazzled by the sheer force of her piquant *joie de vivre* and the apposite way she was put together. Perhaps it was the unusual combination of a narrow, bony body which she carried like a queen and an elfin face whose doe eyes contradicted by the strength of intelligence in the look, the irregular nose and wide mouth whose smile was at once sensuous, mischievous and absolutely sincere. Then there was her vocal quality, a softened British cadence. Hepburn's presence could elevate the most mundane role because everything about her worked toward a female dignity. Intense and curious, she could span life-styles, leap across different worlds like one truly hungry to experience life. In *Roman Holiday* (1953) she's the princess who runs off, cuts her hair on whim, and winds up a ragamuffin curled in newspaperman Gregory Peck's bed. Their idyll is shattered when she must resume her royal responsibilities. In *Sabrina* (1954), as the chauffeur's daughter with a schoolgirl crush on her employer's playboy son, she learns how to boil an egg and how to be chic at Le Cordon Bleu; on returning home, both the playboy and his brother fall in love with her. In *Funny Face* (1956) the bohemian bookseller is "discovered" and transformed into the fashion industry's highest-paid model. Cinderella stories, of course. Romantic, definitely. But Hepburn, even when embroiled in a simple interlude like *Love in the Afternoon* (1956), managed, with waiflike directness, to obtain the upper hand. In this last, didn't *she* seek out Gary Cooper, having secretly read press clippings of his amorous entanglements? Didn't she set *her* cap for William Holden in *Sabrina*? And willfully embark on her adventure in *Roman Holiday*? It was definitely in fifties' terms, but Hepburn experimented with life *for herself*—often situations were impermanent, but she "grew," and her own delight was contagious. She was least successful as Rima, the ethereal Bird Girl, in *Green Mansions* (1958) and Eliza Doolittle in *My Fair Lady* (1964), parts superficially perfect; but her special civilized elegance and responsive intelligence could not be muted by jungle burlap or a sooty face and cockney drawl. A constantly surprising and modern screen personality, she offered women a positive alternative with her waiflike child-creature, bringing her a chameleonlike adaptability and strength beyond that of Leslie Caron's *Lili* (1953) who meshed tired pathos and need in her love for a puppeteer. Or Reynolds' bumptious tomboy who grew up and calmed down with love.

Playing out this saccharine approach to teen-age females, film encapsulated and alienated them from the mainstream of events. Kinsey in 1953 reported the astonishing fact that one-half of all married young women had premarital sexual experiences; since girls were marrying at eighteen and nineteen, his statistics—if reliable—included many teens. (The invention of penicillin and its civilian application in 1943 diminished the hazards of venereal disease, a fact which surely influenced this new experimentation.) But movies, and mores, found realism a hot potato. *Not Wanted* (1949), an intelligent study of an unwed mother, played tenderly by Sally Forrest and directed by Ida Lupino with equal compassion, was generally disregarded by kids and won a modest following among adults, who preferred the tidy, conforming lives of slick, sweet entertainment.

Yet the bland surface was deceiving; a great deal of subtle ferment prepared the generation for the "youth explosion" of the sixties. Just as a linear look at "Eisenhower prosperity" blots out both the scourge of McCarthyism and its reaction, similarly preaching about teen-agers' frivolous lives avoids dealing with their restlessness. For in the early fifties youth voiced the single dissenting, if inarticulate, wail against the corruption of a politically trembling, morally anesthetized postwar society. Shattering complacency were the Hell's Angels, the urban teen gangs, and the Beat Generation. Desiring only to drift, to experience and sate their sense of adventure, bohemians dropped out long before the acid culture came along, and Allen Ginsberg's *Howl* and Jack Kerouac's *On the Road* popularized the movement as more than a metaphysical search for mystical Beatitude. But mostly, these groups condemned the snoozers blotting up the fat of the land. Even the snoozers' sons were embodied in Holden Caulfield, the confused prep school antihero of J. D. Salinger's 1946 novel *The Catcher in the Rye*, who immediately became a prototype for disillusionment with intellectual pretensions and parental authority.

On-screen motorcyclist Brando stunned us with *The Wild One* and later preppie James MacArthur with *The Young Stranger*. But the visual language and the soul of the fifties' rebel belonged consummately to James Dean. Dean who had completed only three films, *East of Eden, Rebel Without a Cause*, and *Giant*, when he fatally crashed his Porsche in 1955, was, like Montgomery Clift and Brando, sensitive and introspective; but more than either of them, he evoked instant response from youth. Boys saw him as a champion of their restlessness, a surprisingly emotional champion releasing the tears and anger and confusion they were forced to repress, but ultimately a figure as frustrated and ineffectual as they were. Girls wanted to mother and run away with him. At once timid and gentle yet smoldering with bewilderment, good intentions, and self-destructiveness, Dean surpassed Holden Caulfield, the Beats, the Angels, as the sullen, mute center of the anti-authoritarian youth subculture.

And where, you may wonder, did woman fit in while all this rebellion was taking place? She made a very poor showing. She was so thoroughly imprisoned by the marriage myth that even the angry female joining the beatnik or rebel on his antisocial journey did so for that conventional reason: love. Twelve-year-old Frankie (Julie Harris) in Carson McCullers' *The Member of the Wedding* forlornly perceives the identity crisis of all females when she creates a fantasy idyll about her brother and sister-in-law: "They are the we of me," she explains. Never "I"—always the outward search for sustenance through others. Thus, teen-aged girls irretrievably bound their identities and hopes up with those of their men.

The role of women in James Dean's first two films is revealing. Set in Monterey in 1917, *East of Eden* (1954) is the story of a son's embittered attempt to win the love of his rigid Bible-quoting father. Dean is Cal—moody, restless, misunderstood, and reminding the old man of his wife. Because she ran off to become a madam, the boy, her ghost, is "bad," while Aaron, the obedient son, is "good," as is his girlfriend Abra (Julie Harris). Abra's is a safe, maternal position; she has no commitment or existence apart from being (initially) Aaron's fiancée and (later) Cal's succor-confidante. When the old man suffers a stroke because Cal has revealed Mommy's identity and whereabouts to his brother, Abra placates both sides. "It's awful not to be loved. It's the worst thing in the world," she says, begging the paralyzed father to "give Cal some sign that you love him." Here, as the intermediary, the angel of brotherly love—mother, sister, lover, and friend —she will go with Cal and temper his rebelliousness. No needs of her own are stronger than his, and the archetypical comfort she provides differs little from the more mature waiting wife lovers of other fifties' fictions—like patient, stoical Grace Kelly in *The Country Wife* or Eva Marie Saint in *A Hatful of Rain*. The vocabulary of action belongs to the male; the female, his satellite, his bag of peacemaking tricks with the world, must find satisfaction in assuaging *his* anguish or sharing pieces of *his* victories.

Natalie Wood in *Rebel Without a Cause* (1955) captured the popular teen-age idiom more aggressively, and on the surface she launched an independent, saucy female malcontent with her own set of needs and troubles. Still, her relationship to Dean didn't really vary too much from the typical. Her suffering, however, *did* limit the comfort she could give him; it was less maternal and more demanding, and their kindred communion of exiled, misunderstood souls was bound up with the salvation *she* sought (in him) from her father's shallow harping.

Wood's heroine may react violently against her parents, but her anger, callowness of feelings, and dependence on her men are binding. If Dean—or anyone else—"frees" her, he will only regenerate her role as his mother, lover, and daughter—with no independent possibilities, or even moral struggles, of her own.

Sluggishness like this, echoing the way teen-age girls conducted their lives in the fifties, cut across class and race boundaries and applied whether the male turf was a high school football field, a surburban chicken run, or a city gutter rumble. Masculine physical strength and willingness to gamble with violence measured leadership and comradeship, whereas a chick's elegibility for acceptance or "popularity" depended on whether she was somebody's old lady, anybody's old lay, or everybody's cheerleader.

Very few movie genres allowed young women a real lead line on their aggressions. Predictably, the science-fiction horror thrillers, inspired perhaps by our anxieties surrounding Sputnik and the subsequent space race, conjured up all sorts of female demons. Some, as in

Above, Jean Arthur in *Mr. Smith Goes to [Wash]ington* (1939). *Courtesy of Columbia [Pictur]es*

[Belo]w, Rosalind Russell in *His Girl Friday* [(1940]). *Courtesy of Columbia Pictures*

Above, Bette Davis.
Courtesy of Warner Brothers/United Artists

Below, Joan Crawford in *Humoresque* (1946). *Courtesy of Warner Brothers/United Artists*

THE SENSUALISTS

Ingrid Bergman and Humphrey
Bogart in *Casablanca* (1943).
*Courtesy of Warner Brothers/United
Artists*

Lauren Bacall *Courtesy of Warner
Brothers/United Artists*

Ann Sheridan in *Nora Prenti
(1947). Courtesy of Warner Bro
United Artists*
Jennifer Jones and Joseph Co
Duel in the Sun (1947). Cou
MOMA

THE SPINSTERS

Olivia de Havilland in *The Heiress* (1949). *Courtesy of Universal Pictures*

Katharine Hepburn in *The Rainmaker* (1956). *Courtesy of Paramount Pictures*

Clark Gable and Marilyn Monroe in *The Misfits* (1961). *Courtesy of United Artists*

THE GODDESS . . .

Marilyn Monroe in *The Misfits* (1961).
Courtesy of United Artists

Jayne Mansfield
in *The Girl Can't Help It* (1957).
© 1956, Courtesy of 20th Century

. . . AND HER ACOLYTES

Top left, Kim Novak in *Picnic* (1955).
Courtesy of Columbia Pictures
Top right, Brigitte Bardot in *And God Created Woman* (1956).
Left, Anita Ekberg in *La Dolce Vita* (1961).
Bottom Left, Sophia Loren
Bottom right, Jeanne Moreau in *Viva Maria* (1968). *Courtesy of United Artists*

POPCORN VENUS...

Debbie Reynolds

Natalie Wood *Courtesy of Warner Brothers/ United Artists*

Audrey Hepburn in *Sabrina* (1954). *Courtesy of Paramount Pictures*

Shirley MacLaine *Courtesy of United A.*

Sandra Dee as *Gidget* (1959). *Courtesy Columbia Pictures*

Doris Day *Courtesy of Universal Picture*

. . GROWS UP

e Fonda as *Barbarella* (1967).
urtesy of Paramount Pictures

Ann-Margret in *Bye Bye Birdie*
(1962). *Courtesy of Columbia Pictures*

Genevieve Waite as *Joanna* (1968).
© 1968, *Courtesy of 20th Century-Fox*

Raquel Welch as *Hannie Caulder*
(1971). *Courtesy of Paramount Pictures*

Lois Weber, director. *Courtesy of MOMA*

BEHIND THE SCENES

Frances Marion, Oscar-winning scenarist. *Courtesy of MOMA*

Anita Loos, scenarist and satir *Courtesy of MOMA*

Dorothy Arzner, director. *Cou Dorothy Arzner*

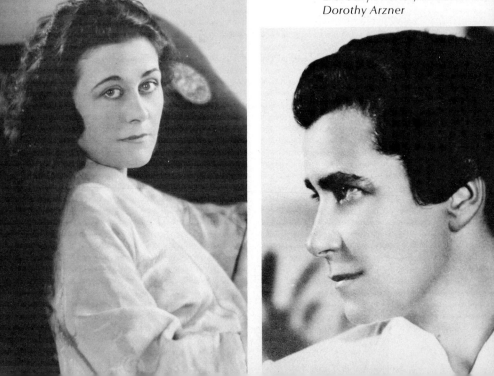

Wasp Woman (1959) and *Leech Woman* (1960), were transformed by cosmetics or youth-giving formulas into monsters. Female fiends from the future horrified the world in *Astounding She Monster* (1958) and *Terror from the Year* 5000 (1958). Promiscuous girls were transformed, judgmentally, into monsters in *Frankenstein's Daughter* (1958) and later *Frankenstein Created Woman* (1966). Other sci-fi pictures dealt with the mutilation of women into carnival freaks (*She-Freak*, 1967) or just into disfigured creatures (*Hypnotic Eye*, 1960). And of course a grotesque gaggle of standard monster women appeared in *The Serpent* (1966), *She Creature* (1956), *Cult of the Cobra* (1956), *Cat Girl* (1957), and *She Devil* (1957). Many of these allegories, like free-association male nightmares on the inherent fear inspired by beautiful or aggressive females, almost embarrass today with their blunt, childishly Freudian images.

But she-demons notwithstanding, the prevailing mood of the fifties was repressive. Conventional expectations precluded exploration of life, squelched fantasies, and inhibited sexuality. Kinsey in 1953 pointed out not only that "unrealistic moral codes" forbidding pre-marital sex hindered couples' psychological adjustments during the first few years of marriage so that by the time the wife developed her appetites, the husband had lost his, but also that 28 percent of the women in the country *became* frigid as a result of early teachings. Harsh laws, too, dealt with alleged sex offenses. For instance, he noted, in most states girls of sixteen to nineteen could be sent to institutions for petting. In Michigan boys could be sentenced to life imprisonment for the same activity if they were over sixteen (and the girl, younger).

Paradoxically, however, parents and schools encouraged early socializing. Girls wore lipstick and nylons at twelve, when co-ed parties and kissing games became *de rigueur*. Junior high schools held dances and proms, and mothers enrolled their children in ballroom classes before they even reached puberty.

Teen-agers' restlessness and confusion, however, soon found an acceptable outlet. Rock and roll. Its aggressive, sexy beat and simple relevant lyrics spoke to teen-agers of their own heartaches and prob-lems and abandoned the mushy romantic promises of Patti Page, Kay Starr, and Rosemary Clooney for a sometimes-cryptic exuber-ance. "Sh-Boom" by the Crew Cuts started it all in 1954. The follow-ing year the top tune was "Rock Around the Clock" by Bill Haley and the Comets. Elvis Presley's "Don't Be Cruel" topped the 1956 national charts, and groups like the Platters ("Great Pretender," "My Prayer"), the Diamonds ("Little Darlin'"), The Everly Brothers ("Bye Bye Love"), and adolescent personalities like Santo and Johnny, Fabian, Frankie Avalon, Bobby Darin, and Johnny Mathis were sending teen-agers in droves to the local record shop. By 1958 teen-age girls controlled 70 percent of all record sales.

Cleverly, the youthful medium of television picked up on this new trend. In 1957 the American Broadcasting Company aired for the nation a Philadelphia-based teen show, and before long 40,000,000 viewers were tuning in daily to *American Bandstand*.

Once again a phenomenon of popular culture threatened to cut back movie audiences, as music-crazy American girls ignored Hollywood. A 1957 *Saturday Evening Post* survey found that 26 percent of young people between ten and nineteen, and 10.7 percent between twenty and thirty-four did *not* attend motion pictures. It hardly required genius to figure out that Elvis Presley, whose hip-swiveling gyrations "in concert" were unleashing the aggressive sexuality which James Dean had promised but not delivered, would be a minor messiah. He would bring the youthful flock back into the fold. Sure enough, when *Love Me Tender* arrived on neighborhood screens late in 1956, it became one of the year's top moneymakers. Elvis immediately soared into the elite of the ten top-grossing stars in 1957. After interruption for military service between 1958 and 1960, he returned to movies and remained in the top ten between 1961 and 1966. Because of the overwhelming impact he had on his youthful female fans, it is certain that the type of costar who captivated Elvis in *Loving You, Jailhouse Rock, Kid Galahad, Girls! Girls! Girls!, King Creole,* and the other Presley showcases became important models for female audiences to emulate. So Ann-Margret, Jill St. John, Debra Paget, Donna Douglass (later of *The Beverly Hillbillies*), Nancy Sinatra, Dolores Hart, Judy Tyler, and other flossy, plastic, heavily made-up, man-crazy females served as ideals, living handbooks on how to win such a special, sexy heart as Elvis'. Those lucky heroines—confusingly alike in appearance—were pretty, peppy, good dancers, brave motorcycle back-seaters and hot-rod maidens. Like diminutive sex goddesses, they wore tight capri pants and long hair, displaying their marvelous bodies seductively. Like the tomboy, they gave the hero a little sass, but were mostly loving and pliable. What wasn't on the surface wasn't important.

1957 was a landmark year for bringing back the youth audiences. On the top ten list Pat Boone (third) beat out even Presley (fourth), having just debuted in *Bernardine*, one of those simpering comedies about crew-cutted, yearning high school boys who concoct the dream of an ideal woman and tag her Bernardine. Two years later Boone's advice to the acned lovelorn, *'Twixt Twelve and Twenty*, would become the top nonfiction book in the nation, and this clean-living gentleman (and father of four girls) would also cause a minor publicity volcano during the filming of *April Love* (1958) by refusing his first screen kiss—to be planted on a peaches-and-cream Shirley Jones, fresh from her own triumphs as America's sweetheart of *Oklahoma!* and *Carousel*. Declining, however, for religious and personal reasons, Pat explained, "I've always been taught that when you get married you forget about kissing other women." And "I'm just not going to do anything in the movies that I wouldn't do in private life."[2] Finally, however, he discussed the matter with his wife, Shirley, who consented "although she would prefer to keep that part of our lives solely to ourselves." At the time of this tempest, Pat was twenty-five.

1957 also brought Debbie Reynolds overwhelming popularity as *Tammy*, a resourceful, pigtailed bayou waif whose innocence wins a society magnate away from his sophisticated girlfriend (Mala Powers). Not only did it provide Debbie with the number one song across the country that year ("Tammy"), but it gave movies a smash worthy of sequels. So in 1961 Sandra Dee replaced Debbie (now twenty-nine) as Pollyanna-of-the-swamps, and in *Tammy Tell Me True* she lands schoolteacher John Gavin. Then as a nurse's aide in *Tammy and the Doctor* (1963) Sandra cures lonely hearts by arranging marriages for everyone—and heart throb Peter Fonda for herself. (Does this smack of what Shirley Temple was doing at eight? Jane Withers at eleven?) All on the up and up, with no sex, please—but much burgeoning wistfulness and the kind of saccharine patience bestowed only on professional virgins.

Of these, Debbie trouped the longest and loudest. Detouring briefly into adult comedy with *It Started with a Kiss* (1958) and *The Rat Race* (1960), she returned to her old sunshiny tricks with *The Pleasure of His Company* in 1961. Here, she plays a dewy bride-to-be enamored of her *bon vivant* father (Fred Astaire). Daddy, a literal stranger arriving allegedly to give his daughter away, but really to whisk her off as a companion in his meanderings, provides geriatric temptation, and Debbie winsomely moons over him, much to the distress of jealous fiancé Tab Hunter. Compounding the unpalatable script even further was the same naïveté she'd been selling on screen for eleven years, made ludicrous now by the fact that Debbie was twenty-nine, and that in the early sixties teen-agers were a good deal more sexually aware than those whose vintage was *Singin' in the Rain* (1952). During the post-Kennedy years the Reynolds superstar would dim as she attempted to run an even keel between virginal spunk (*The Singing Nun*, 1966) and marital urbanity (*Divorce American Style*, 1967). In *The Unsinkable Molly Brown* (1964), she even reinvigorated her tomboy cutup, but despite a sizable talent as a light comedienne, such choices—and her adamant unwillingness to adapt to the times—essentially effected her own exile.

The Reynolds neo-Victorian swan song peevishly sidesteps any connection to modern realities. For certainly the Liz Taylor strumpet of *Butterfield 8*—aware, cynical, and mature enough to fight for what she wants (a man and respectability) in a tough and difficult world—presents a more realistic image of life's ambivalence than the innocent merriment of a winsome swamp girl. Than a foolish socialite bride who has not a passion, pain or thought to call her own—who grabs a man and leans hard, for as the vortex of her life, he must round out its meaning, shield her from herself, and make sense of her own physical presence on earth.

The danger of such distorted "entertainment" philosophies didn't concern Debbie—or Hollywood. During January, 1958, the New York *Times* published the first comprehensive nationwide survey conducted by the Opinion Research Corporation for the Motion Picture Association of America. The industry's campaign had succeeded. Of the thousands of men, women, and children polled the previous summer, statistics indicated that 52 percent of the moviegoing audience was under twenty, 75 percent under thirty, and this time the decline in attendance was definitely blamed on television, with one out of three people claiming that otherwise they would have gone to the movies at least once the preceding month. The colorful mindless fun that was Elvis and Pat and Debbie was, however, revitalizing the industry.

On the eve of the sixties, Debbie Reynolds' brand of femininity would be usurped by a younger, more sympathetic and believable heroine. Sandra Dee did not possess the zany Reynolds clownsmanship or agility, but she fused a good many fifties' notions about little girls. While she presented the most passive, fluttery pink-and-white-ribbons perfection, her ample mouth recalled the petulance of an adolescent Bardot. By scaling down this image of feline sexuality for the nubile high school set, Dee wove the transition between the fifties' naïveté and the sixties' nymphet, exhibiting a provocative self-awareness, almost a fear of her own sexuality, which in view of the decade's moral expectations, was sensible. And this is why she enjoyed a swift and sweeping success, giving new dimensions to such a traditional virgin role as *The Reluctant Debutante* (1958), in which the sweet young thing is tempted away from stuffy British suitors by a dashing young American drummer. Then in *Imitation of Life* (1959), as Lana Turner's earnest daughter, she's left alone by Mommy so often that she falls in love with Mommy's lover. And with the attractively mounted *A Summer Place* and *Gidget* in 1959, the seventeen-year-old actress ascended into the top ten box-office circle, where she remained through 1963.

Both *Gidget* and *A Summer Place* pandered to the female teen market more directly, and with more surface romantic gloss, than any other fifties' film save *Rebel Without a Cause*. The first is the summer odyssey of a teen-age tomboy adopted as a mascot by a bunch of surfers during the crucial months between babyhood and young womanhood. The boys dub her "Gidget"—a combination of girl and midget—and Dee after some pleasant childish anguish emerges with a boyfriend, an ability to surf, a new femininity, and the knowledge that she helped redirect the life-style of a perennial bum. At its best the picture catalogs youthful feminine priorities. A friend bemoans Gidget's social failures with "Poor Francie, I don't know how she's going to face going back to senior year!" And Dee tries every allure from bust exercises to paying an escort to make her "crush" jealous, from bribing the guys in order to attend their end-of-summer bash, to running off with their leader Cahuna (Cliff Robertson) for "one of your little private parties." It all works because Sandra Dee with her blond pigtails and skinny legs seems so young and vulnerable; her attempts are funny, not desperate, and audiences *know* that she's a good girl who would blanch at impropriety. As aggressive as she is, overt fifties' attitudes still hang heavy over little *Gidget's* life. Her mother explains the family slogan: "To be a real woman is to bring out the best in a man." When Cahuna quits surfing and picks up his former profession as a pilot, she realizes she is, indeed, just that for having returned him to the fold of conventional responsibilities.

Moviegoers greeted *Gidget* so enthusiastically that a 1961 sequel (and more recently a TV special) was made. *Gidget Goes Hawaiian* starred not Dee, who had grown too old to play a Popcorn Venus at the kiddie matinee, but Deborah Walley, properly cute, yet without the original's sweetness. Also, since her passage from childhood had been taken care of in the first film, *Hawaiian* simply settled into the bikini-beach-party syndrome of date bait and teen jealousies that would proliferate in the early sixties.

A Summer Place, however, returned Dee to the beaches—trauma in the Maine sand dunes—this time with only Troy Donahue and a monstrous set of mismatched parents. In this modern "problem" melodrama exploiting the teen market, Troy gets Sandra "in trouble." The movie as late as 1959 entirely avoided the issue of abortion as an alternative. (The atmosphere had changed little since 1951 and the audaciously raw *Detective Story*. In that film policeman Kirk Douglas reacted to news that wife Eleanor Parker had patronized the local abortionist with a violence and disgust akin to the husband in Lois Weber's conservative 1916 *Where Are My Children?*). In fact, *A Summer Place*, perhaps even more insidious, while indulging tears, repentence, and evading issues, presented a new terrifically romantic atmosphere. *Gidget*'s beach was sterile, but here Sandra Dee was almost all grown up. Even youthful motherhood and a shotgun wedding couldn't diminish the fact of teen-age eroticism which had never been explored so directly.

And kids responded to it. The movie, opening on October 23, 1959, had by January 6, 1960, already grossed more than $1,900,000; the heroine's pregnancy was almost immaterial, for the picture was tied up in such an attractively passionate package that nobody cared. Troy and Sandra were milky-blond and beautiful. The settings were lush. The theme song, "A Summer Place," was sexy and became a hit. Who could condemn such an invitation to indiscretion? And the movie, relevant in other ways, abandoned the usual tomboys next door, mumbling misfits, and street-urchin Cinderellas. Ripe, driven, on the threshold of adulthood, these kids' excruciating adolescent yearning was a very real problem. *A Summer Place* communicated with teen audiences in the same way rock music did. And whether good citizens of the community and moral guardians in the industry liked it or not, the glorious Technicolor, sexy mood and music, and breathtaking plastic prettiness of its people breathed an iconoclastic spirit, sowing the seeds of doom for the old morality.

Marjorie Morningstar, a watery but nonetheless attractive adaptation of Herman Wouk's best seller, had the year before benefited from a similar subtle seduction. As the Jewish Princess detoured by adventurous dreams from the princess pattern of middle-class marriages and babies, Natalie Wood projected proper loveliness, but could muster neither sufficient intensity nor the connection with a *gemütlich* family tradition to make Marjorie as interesting or headstrong as she should have been. Thus, her intoxication with the bohemian world of theater and her "daring" affair with cynical Noel Airman (Gene Kelly) fell flat, and her eventual return to the Hebraic bosom— marriage to a nice Jewish playwright—didn't carry the sting of compromise, pain, and relief it should have. Still, the dynamics of romantic modern locales, exotic backstage camaraderie, and gorgeous people affecting girls with *A Summer Place* impressed here, too. Out of the staid fifties' abyss these glossy pictures were offering a secret alliance, presenting glamorous alternatives and striking imaginative chords.

As the emotional and plot content of fifties' movies dwindled, Hollywood being afraid to bankroll anything too innovative or controversial, relied on surface to create the major impact. Most movies were being shot in color now with fantastic sets and costumes. Because pictures in the last years of the decade were counterpointing a society paralyzed by stringently old-fashioned social and moral codes, these production values floated the magic carpet of escape, and teenage girls hopped on for the ride.

One disadvantage of a popular medium is that one buys not only the good, but also the bad. For adolescents, especially vulnerable, movies structured behavior and standardized values. Girls who learned the rules of flirtation and sexual conduct from Sandra Dee and her golden counterparts, Yvette Mimieux, Carol Lynley, and Tuesday Weld, also took their beauty cues from them. Rhinoplasty, or nose surgery, became an obsession with middle-class teen-agers; discouraged from the individuality which had separated the great screen ladies from the ranks, they demanded Elizabeth Taylor noses, or Sandra Dee noses, or Kim Novak noses. They could have a cleft in their chin like Carroll Baker or their breasts enlarged like Monroe. One top plastic surgeon recently estimated that since the fifties more than 120,000 breast-implant operations have been performed—and the source of this fetish is of course the fifties' ideal set forth by the Mammary Woman.

Appearance was everything. Grace Kelly's perfection had won her a prince. One-hundred-thousand-dollar-a-year cover girl Suzy Parker knew, too, the importance of veneer. "I thank God for high cheekbones every time I look in the mirror in the morning,"[3] she admitted exuberantly.

Hollywood, hawker of plastic vapidity, spawned a sameness, a blandness in its leading ladies. The cool blond beauty of Kelly, Tippi Hedren, Martha Hyer. The serene sincerity of Dana Wynter, Barbara Rush, and Deborah Kerr. Occasionally an original like Audrey Hepburn or Judy Holliday or Joanne Woodward surfaced, but interesting actresses were cubbyholed and misused. Susan Kohner, a dark, brooding girl with a uniquely irregular face, might have given *Marjorie Morningstar* the ethnic and emotional boost it needed to click. But she was typecast in secondary leads—as Juanita Moore's tempestuous black daughter who passes for white in *Imitation of Life* (1959); as George Hamilton's smirky, whiny rich-bitch sister who complicates sister-in-law Natalie Wood's extracurricular marital activities by marrying Robert Wagner in *All the Fine Young Cannibals* (1960)—because she didn't conform to the prevalent notion of stardom and beauty.

More mature actresses whose talents were poorly utilized, both Gloria Grahame and Jan Sterling were stereotyped as trashy broads, leftovers from the thirties' kitchen. Grahame especially, with a wry sense of humor and a persona as soft and motherly as it was cynical and sexy, deserved more than the blowsy-gangster's moll in *The Big Heat* (1953); more, too, than the cameo of a lusty, amoral widow stalking good doctor Robert Mitchum in *Not as a Stranger* (1955). Given varied roles, cast against type as she was—successfully—in *Oklahoma!* (1955) and *The Greatest Show on Earth* (1952), she might have added flexibility and sparked some intelligence in the flaccid array of fifties' screen heroines.

However, Grahame was not singled out for a raw deal. The decade was, if not merciless, then indifferent to its outstanding stars, Crawford, Davis, De Havilland, Fontaine. Only one glamor perennial survived the period. And although Lana Turner brought nostalgic senti-

ment and old-fashioned g-l-a-m-o-r to such melodramatic claptrap as
Peyton Place (1957), *Imitation of Life* (1959), *Portrait in Black*
(1960), *Madame X* (1966), part of the reason she succeeded where
others failed is that her image was founded on a beauty ideal rather
than on any strength of character. According to Adela Rogers St.
John, "The real Lana Turner is the Lana Turner everyone knows
about. She always wanted to be a Movie Star, and loved being one.
Her personal life and her Movie Star life are one."[4]

Change, however, was hovering at the edge of the sixties. Hollywood had gone through the relevant and significantly womanless
"problem" films of the period and through the mammary comedies. It
had cultivated the youth audience like a garden of seedlings, yet even
with the flux of under-thirty viewers, it could not reverse the down-
ward trend in profits. By 1959 the studio output was less than half
that of 1950 (from 383 to 187 productions per annum). Imports,
however, had surpassed the all-American product, increasing in that
same period from 239 to 252 a year. The industry would never be
the same.

And neither, surprisingly, would woman. The postwar college influx
had set a new precedent. By the close of the decade intelligent middle-class girls were expected to attend college. And while a good
percentage were only hunting for husbands, others picked up degrees
and career ambitions. Soon bright, determined females seeking jobs
and mates would swarm to urban centers. Never had credentials and
education meant so little to so many.

It was a bull market. The males called the shots and spelled them
youth and beauty. Just like in the movies. And grateful for the scraps
of participation, woman in 1960 didn't care. She thought she was
home free.

But then didn't everyone? We would even have a movie-star President and a ravishing First Lady. How handsomely they realized the
same kind of wholesome values that six decades of brass bands and
Max Steiner crescendos and Pickford Pollyannas had instilled in us.

It did seem perfect then, didn't it?

SIX

SIXTIES INTO SEVENTIES— REVOLUTION AND RENAISSANCE

Women on certain jobs are every bit as
good as men. We wouldn't think of having
a man sell brassieres.
—Drummond Bell
Vice-president of Montgomery Ward

20

SING A SONG OF SINGLE SCENES
straddling the moral fence

"I am the man who accompanied Jacqueline Kennedy to Paris," the President proudly recounted amid global ardor.

The First Lady at thirty-one—with two small children, tastes made exquisite by cultivation and education, and a whispery hush of a voice —exuded classical elegance and feminine poise, refining our notions of youth and beauty for an affluent society, reassuring us of those values carefully culled in the fifties. Her little inaugural pillbox hat, bouffant coiffures, delicate long white evening gloves form a collage to the times. Her princess dresses and carefully accessorized Chanel suits were mass-produced, reinvigorating the American ready-to-wear industry. Movie stars, cover girls, beauty contestants suddenly all resembled Jackie. She wholesaled chic for American womanhood.

It was a joyous love affair, with our Utopian Matron reflecting the nation's moral tone, a conservative cosmopolitanism. For all was not that free in 1960. Witness the public vitriol poured on Elizabeth Taylor and Richard Burton, who fell in love while filming *Cleopatra*. In May, 1962, Georgia Congresswoman Iris Blitch prepared a statement for the House and the *Congressional Record* formalizing her hope that Attorney General Robert F. Kennedy might "take the measures necessary to determine whether or not the two are ineligible for reentry into this country on grounds of undesirability."[1]

The courts refused a pregnant Mrs. Sherrye Finkbine the right to an abortion although it had been proven that thalidomide produced malformed babies.

Sarah Gibson Blanding, president of Vassar, warned students in

1962 that those wishing to indulge in premarital sex or excesses of alcohol must withdraw.

In 1963 a student couple at the University of Connecticut were threatened with punitive measures for their "uncontrolled public displays of affection."[2] And in 1964 a Cleveland woman was arrested for issuing birth control information to her teen-age daughter.

Out of this climate resistant to change struggled a new breed of woman. She may have emulated Jackie's chic, thought abortions were the ultimate defilement, and pitied Eddie Fisher; but she possessed another set of problems altogether: She was single. Having waved good-bye to peak marriage age—eighteen (even in 1963!), armed with a college education and searching for a husband and interim job, the sixties' gal was too young and vital to be considered a spinster, too old to be a teen. Menial employment for which she was over-educated and the weight of her own chastity conflicted with reality. The inequities of the double standard chafed more painfully.

Being single, a state legitimized when Grossinger's Hotel held the first singles weekend on record in 1962, was aptly, if taciturnly, captured by movies which reduced the "problem" to the question of: *Will she or won't she?* Love stories focused on this central dilemma to the exclusion of most other plot or character conflicts. It was, in a sense, a cinematic first; imagine a Bette Davis-Paul Henreid scenario, a Tracy-Hepburn or Turner-Gable love story revolving around whether she'll give him a tumble, when, and if he'll stick around for more! But in *Come September* (1961), Rock Hudson advises Sandra Dee, a college girl vacationing at his Italian villa with boyfriend Bobby Darin, to remain virginal for her husband; this with his curvaceous mistress Gina Lollobrigida currently installed in the villa. In *Splendor in the Grass* (1961) Natalie Wood is so torn by repressing natural urges that she suffers a breakdown, and sweetheart Warren Beatty, after relieving his energies with the town's loose women, marries someone else. *Sunday in New York* (1964) finds Jane Fonda fighting to protect herself from amorous Rod Taylor, whom she met while alighting from a bus when her jacket flower caught on his suit button; she wins both the battle and Taylor.

The Carry Nation of Hollywood's chastity crusade, however, was Doris Day. Straddling the moral fence with a sophistication and enthusiasm which could simultaneously titillate, evoke laughter, and maintain the status quo, she combined style, wit, and fiercely defended virtue in movies like *Pillow Talk, Lover Come Back*, and *That Touch of Mink*. In all fairness to Day, these comedies attest as dramatically to her flexible talent as do her fine early portrayals of *Calamity Jane*, of tormented chanteuse Ruth Etting (victimized by insanely possessive gangster James Cagney) in *Love Me or Leave Me* (1955), and of the frantic but level-headed wife in Hitchcock's *The Man Who Knew Too Much* (1956). And when she first slipped into the sex-comedy posture, Day's material was witty and her character strong and snappy.

Pillow Talk (1959) displayed her as a stylish interior decorator battling, sight unseen, party-line Don Juan Rock Hudson who ties up their phone whispering sweet nothings to a string of girls. The plot, revolving around their romance after a chance meeting (where Hudson willfully withholds his identity), derives sneers and giggles from the evolution of Day's anticipation that he might be "fresh" into worry that he might be "impotent" into fury that he's her phonemate. Most irritating is the caveman ending where—carried by Hudson unwillingly through the streets to his apartment—she capitulates to marriage. Yet many other facets of her character were admirable. A rare heroine who was single (and not a teen-ager), capable (and not masculine), established (but not desperate), she fends off rich bachelor Tony Randall, but expresses her anger succinctly toward Hudson when he accuses her of having bedroom problems. With a certain precise perspective she retorts: "At least mine can be solved in one bedroom. Yours couldn't be solved in a thousand."

Day's folly was not *Pillow Talk*, but that she patterned a number of similar movies almost exactly on it in the eight years that followed. Her next two, *Lover Come Back* and *That Touch of Mink*, retained a certain lightness and novelty in their flirtation with the risqué. They also earned millions. And Day clung tenaciously to this guaranteed box-office formula. *Move Over Darling* (1963, adapted from the uncompleted Monroe vehicle *Something's Gotta Give*), *Send Me No Flowers* (1964), and *Do Not Disturb* (1965) replayed the stalled seduction situation, with slight accommodations for age, marital status, and plot variations. But by the end of her cycle it was all most embarrassing, almost obscenely so.

For between *Pillow Talk* and *The Glass Bottom Boat* (1967), Day was running against the tide of graphic and sophisticated screen sex. Never had she been more antiseptic, virginal, and all-American, not even opposite Danny Thomas in *I'll See You in My Dreams* (1952). Yet now she was forty-three and had miraculously wrung dry every drop of her purity, causing audiences to question whether prolonging it was virtue or idiocy.

A few fitful attempts at family entertainment pictures followed before Doris Day switched to television. There she has enjoyed high ratings doing what she does naturally—playing the bland, aging female Huck Finn. Wrote Dwight Macdonald astutely in his book *On Movies*:

> Doris Day has become Betty Grable's successor as a sex symbol that offends no one and so does well at the box office. She is as wholesome as a bowl of cornflakes and at least as sexy. She has the standard American figure: long-legged, tallish (everything is on the -ish side) with highish smallish breasts and no hips or buttocks to speak of. And the standard American (female) face, speaking in terms of aspirations rather than of realities: Nordic blonde, features regular, nose shortish and straightish, lips thinnish, Good Bone Structure. . . . She has the healthy, antiseptic Good Looks and the Good Sport personality that the American middle class—that is, practically everybody—admires as a matter of duty. Especially the females. No competition.[3]

Macdonald, however, dismisses Doris' popularity with the female audience too easily. "No competition" is too pat and uncharitable. More precisely, Doris managed to combine a quite modern ability to express her anger at men and a certain élan in taking care of herself with a comfortingly old-fashioned attitude toward love and marriage. Those older audiences who disapproved of the disturbing changes in morality found her a pleasant ally in their bewilderment, pleasant enough, indeed, to keep her reigning in the top ten between 1959 (*Pillow Talk*) and 1966.

But as early as 1961 women had begun to articulate in strong terms their search for alternate, if temporary, life-styles. That February, Joan Didion wrote "New York: The Great Reprieve" for *Mademoiselle* magazine:

> Girls who come to New York are, above all, uncommitted. They seem to be girls who want to prolong the period when they

can experiment, mess around, make mistakes. In New York there is no gentle pressure for them to marry, to go two by two, to take any indelible step; no need, as one girl put it, "to parry silky questions about what everyone at home refers to delicately as my *plans*." New York is full of people on this kind of leave of absence, of people with a feeling for the tangential adventure, the risk adventure, the interlude that's not likely to end in any double-ring ceremony.

The following year Gloria Steinem further unsettled the status quo with "The Moral Disarmament of Betty Coed" (*Esquire*, September, 1962): "Writers in or out of Hollywood should be warned that they can no longer build plots on loss of virginity or fainting pregnant heroines and expect to be believed."

But it was Helen Gurley Brown's "how to" book *Sex and the Single Girl* that exploded onto the best-seller list signaling revolution. With refreshing brio Mrs. Brown advised unmarried women on the dynamics of romance for its own sake (live alone, dress more expensively than you can afford, surround yourself with sensual fabrics, serve up ambrosial recipes):

> You may marry or you may not. In today's world that is no longer the big question for women. Those who glom on to men so that they can collapse with relief, spend the rest of their days shining up their status symbol and figure they never have to reach, stretch, learn, grow, face dragons or make a living again are the ones to be pitied. They, in my opinion, are the unfulfilled ones.[4]

All very heady stuff for 1962. But Mrs. Brown, herself having married "the man I wanted" for the first time at thirty-seven, knew whereof she spoke; she was a messiah whose time had come. Taking over the editorship of *Cosmopolitan*, she doubled the magazine's ad revenue in just three years. Today feminists reject *Cosmo*'s teasing as sexual objectification on a par with *Playboy*'s and categorize Helen Gurley Brown too easily as a lace 'n' lingerie stepinfetchit. Yet a year before Betty Friedan's brilliantly documented and angry *The Feminine Mystique* scrutinized the ennui and disillusion of the suburban housewife, Mrs. Brown spoke directly, happily to thousands of single women, sanctioning an audacious life-style, removing the stigma from being single and the guilt from being sexual. She freed women's minds from worry as surely as the Pill was liberating their bodies.

Physicians first began prescribing birth control pills commercially around 1960. The original doses were arbitrarily massive—Enovid was cut from ten to five milligrams of strength simply for the expedience of reducing the price of each monthly supply for reasonable purchase ($4.00 to $3.50). Since this was a 99 percent foolproof and rarely messy method of contraception, and few were aware of potential health complications, married women from the beginning preferred it to other standard methods. For singles, however, the Pill at first presented a moral dilemma since it presupposed calculated preparations for sexual encounters. On the other hand, abortions were illegal, difficult to obtain, unsafe, and expensive. Understandably, women went cautiously.

So did movies. The industry had loosened its codes since 1953, when *The Moon Is Blue* was refused a seal of approval because the word "virgin" had been spoken. But now a strangely inconsistent and uneasy application of propriety harnessed the virtue of serious and attractive heroines but loosened the reigns on the lighter ones, rather in the way Pickford characters or buffoon ladies once got away with certain attitudes. For example, in 1958's *Auntie Mame*, frumpy secretary Agnes Gooch could emit a strangled "Live! Live! Live!" and ten minutes later audiences laugh when she reappears, quite pregnant. But to admit in 1961's *Breakfast at Tiffany's* the tatty truth that Holly Golightly received powder room money for her favors and not for the attendant was another story. Such an acknowledgment might have glamorized the trade and also tarnished the elegant image of leading lady Audrey Hepburn.

Suitably and unwittingly, the task of clearing the air and loosening public inhibitions fell to Shirley MacLaine. In *The Apartment* (1960) and *Two for the SeeSaw* (1962), she made kookiness sad, not elegant; promiscuity human, not trashy. In *The Apartment* she's a plain little elevator operator who swallows sleeping pills because married lover Fred MacMurray is indifferent to her. Clearly this affair is no fun, and when Jack Lemmon, at whose place their trysts have occurred, brings her back to consciousness, she sighs, "I think I'm going to give it all up. Why do people have to love people anyway?" Lemmon's clumsy kindness, we know, will deliver her from the misery of her affair and restore her faith.

Exemplifying the ambiguities of both Hollywood's and the country's attitudes toward illicit sex, *The Apartment* was in the most overt sense a breakthrough. MacLaine's Fran Kubelek in her ordinariness approaches the kind of sweet, defenseless girl of that era who gets detoured into a hurting sexual relationship when in fact she really wants marriage. Not particularly freer than her chaste compatriots, she is more stupid—a victim of loneliness and naïveté. Doubtlessly, director Billy Wilder was able to capture the frankness of the situation, the warm exchanges between her and Lemmon without censorship because the movie was ostensibly a comedy.

MacLaine's persona—elfin, soulful innocence—additionally shielded her from outrage. Neither the public nor censors carped. *Two for the Seesaw* in 1962 dared to go even further, no doubt influenced by imported successes such as *La Dolce Vita* (1961) and *Never on Sunday* (1960), which had proved that films geared specifically for "adult" as opposed to "family" audiences could reap large profits. While MacLaine as Gittel Mosca, a nice beatnik dancer from the Bronx, is perhaps too rural-American to interpret the soul of this Italian-Jewish city girl, again it is precisely her freckled impishness which makes the girl's avant-garde morality digestible. For Gittel has an affair with a married lawyer, Robert Mitchum (it's not her first), gets pregnant by him, stoically endures an abortion, and ultimately rejects marriage because she realizes he still loves his wife. Again, also the catch to her freedom is her good and downtrodden heart, a traditionally feminine virtue balancing her unconventionality. The beatnik dancer in leotards is far removed from the Kennedy Dream Woman. Nevertheless, she maintains a fierce pride we must admire —and which sets her apart from most of her screen counterparts, girls who went through with pregnancies out of desperation, confusion, or lack of choice. Among these were Natalie Wood in *All the Fine Young Cannibals* (1960) and *Love with the Proper Stranger* (1963), Rita Tushingham in *A Taste of Honey* (1961), Leslie Caron in *The L-Shaped Room* (1962), Connie Stevens in *Parrish* (1961), Sandra Dee in *A Summer Place* (1959), and Catherine Deneuve in 1964's *The Umbrellas of Cherbourg*. All single, and all suffering the consequences of the industry's *reductio ad absurdum* equation: *Will she or won't she?*

Hollywood's tentative and superficial exploration of such timely subject matter in the early sixties was, unsurprisingly, as much a question of money as it was a response to the needs of women. American movies were floundering. Great showmen and moguls like Louis B. Mayer, Harry Cohn, Cecil B. De Mille were gone, their studios torn by artistic and administrative chaos. The few consistently big box-office stars now free-lanced at astronomical salaries. Location shooting in Europe saved money on rising labor costs, yet production facilities lying fallow at home ate up additional expenses. Fear of failure and the misshapen but indigenous adage that "bigger is better" shifted focus to multimillion-dollar extravaganzas—*Spartacus* (1960), *Ben Hur* (1959), *West Side Story* (1961), *Lawrence of Arabia* (1962) and finally *Cleopatra* (1962). (*Cleopatra*, reputed to have cost $30,000,-000, caused rebellion and near-bankruptcy at Twentieth Century-Fox, where both executive and creative heads rolled.) Like Cinerama, these epics ballyhooed the prospective return of the confirmed TV viewer to the theaters. The introduction of controversial themes on sex, prostitution (the musical *Irma La Douce*, also starring MacLaine; the drama *Walk on the Wild Side* with Barbara Stanwyck as a bordello's lesbian madam), and abortion was to have accomplished the same. One small matter, however, evaded Hollywood's attention: its own quality of perception.

Sinking so much money into extravaganzas and *safe* pictures, movie-makers hesitated to handle controversial subjects *except* in the gaudiest, flimsiest way. Europe, England in particular, was, however, reveling in a new frankness. Writers like John Osborne and John Braine were among the "angry young men" who peeled away society's veneer to give us brutally honest dramas of working-class life like *Look Back in Anger* (1959), *Room at the Top* (1959), and *Saturday Night and Sunday Morning* (1960). From England, too, came Shelagh Delaney's *A Taste of Honey*, (1961) a fragile tale of friendship between two outcasts—a pregnant waif and a homosexual who set up house together while he nurses her through the birth of her child. In 1965 *The Leather Boys*, a harbinger of the youth (and gay) films to come, was a powerful, if flawed, attempt to capture the seedy pathos of the British Rockers, those tough leather-jacketed motorcyclists, and East End Teddy Boys.

Most absorbing about *The Leather Boys*, though, is its horrific portrait of a teen-age marriage. The girl, Rita Tushingham, immature and stupid, fills her days with beauty parlor appointments and movies; at night she reads comics and distributes cracker crumbs all over the sheets. The boy finds her disgusting and won't make love. They separate, and he, unaware, takes in a homosexual roommate while she engineers ruses to win him back (a fake pregnancy, a new hairdo). The film's power is derived chiefly from the tragedy of their immaturity, which prevents communication on the most basic level, and calls into question that society which guides kids toward relationships without the foggiest notions of sharing—or of responsibility.

With varying degrees of success and sensitivity, English movies were tuning in to the problems and life-styles of young people—and of women in particular. Two highly influential pictures, *Darling* (1965) and *Georgy Girl* (1966), examined in lively and appealing terms revolutionary changes both in morality and women's status, changes our movies at home were reluctant to handle. *Darling* glamorously exposed the shallow existence of a "modern" beauty. Charging through a marriage, lovers, an abortion, orgies, she finally attains the storybook ideal or at least its trappings—marriage to an Italian prince —but finds life at the top entirely empty and lonely. It is interesting that audiences, responding more to the savvy and style of *Darling*'s leading lady Julie Christie, lost the thread of what might otherwise have been a tale of moral condemnation. Yet the ambiguity of tone, her splendid selfishness touched by discontent, beguiled us as a sketch of our own emerging, impatient society, one in which immediate gratification and surface sheen were quickly replacing traditional values in importance.

"If I could just feel complete," Darling moans. *So what!* we say; she's Gorgeous, she's having FUN. And here are other contradictions: She may be decadent and miserably unhappy, but she's manipulative and canny enough to survive when she finds out what or who will "complete" her. But as dangerously sensual as she may seem, she even admits that sex itself is not particularly gratifying ("We could do without sex. I don't really like it that much," she begs a homosexual companion for a relationship).

Darling's flaw is that she's an opportunist lacking direction. Neither sinner nor heroine, she's a strong and curiously amoral woman whose existence is filled with vanities, meaningless moments, and a kind of healthy decadence, as though *La Dolce Vita* had been hit by a clean-up campaign; but in some childish, backhanded way she is also a woman saying, "My role in this world is not enough." The Cinderella stories do not fill her up. Nor does life.

Georgy Girl in 1966 brought us another novel heroine and living situation wrought from the decade's social and sexual rebellion. The story is of an eternal triangle gone obtuse. Georgy, huge, awkward, a female Brontosaurus (Lynn Redgrave), shares a flat with Charlotte Rampling (a flighty and cynical playgirl-musician) and Charlotte's boyfriend, Alan Bates, a cigar-chomping cartoon of a fellow. When Charlotte becomes pregnant, she and Bates marry, but the living situation remains the same. Except that the expectant mother, increasingly despondent, withdraws from her mates' company—and Georgy and Bates fall in love. The baby born, Charlotte takes off, and Georgy mothers it. She mothers it so well that Bates, neglected, also takes off. Happily, wealthy widower James Mason who once offered Georgy a "contract" for an affair, marries her, allowing the mothering to go on uninterrupted.

This charming, yet uneven movie is surprisingly old-fashioned, for if one looks closely, it negates both of its female characters as crippled, desperately incomplete in one way or another. Charlotte Rampling as a new breed of woman (very much like *Darling*, but traveling in tackier social circles) is an irritable and brazen bitch, unhampered by commitments to her husband or newborn child. For both *Georgy Girl*'s director Silvio Narizzano and *Darling*'s John Schlesinger, sexual liberation has brought this modern female a glacial aloofness and frightening isolation broken only by moments of fitful promiscuity, moments of instant now sensation—as if sex, the liberator amortizing other emotional aspects of fulfillment, ironically provided brief comfort.

However, Georgy, that galumphingly large child of freaky genes and bad luck, finds that sex isn't enough. In fact, it isn't anything. Instant motherhood channels her smother love, and when Bates—who truly loved her—leaves, he complains, "That's where you're a freak, George—not being big and ugly. It's that—to save people."

Mawkish and stoical, Georgy may cushion us against the selfishness of now women like Rampling and Christie, but she is the kind of old-fashioned self-sacrificing "Mom" who withdraws simply to avoid dealing as an equal with adults. To avoid hurt and failure. Superior to her ward, she effects a sublime, total escape, imprisoning herself in the substance of old-world values.

Paradoxically, one important reason for the film's popularity was our pleasure that this hippopotamic and unassuming innocent *could* manage a semblance of assimilation into the "new society." That she *could* be taken as she was, even loved by Bates without drastic makeovers, plastic surgery, or artifice. The ugly duckling here *never* emerges swan, but she *becomes* lovely and lovable to those who know her. In an age of stringent and increasingly narrow standards of youthful attractiveness, Georgy reassured. She didn't, like Katharine Hepburn's Lizzie in *The Rainmaker*, need a man to release her softness; that was there already (though, ironically, no man could ignite her sexuality). Other homely heroines would follow—Rita Tushingham in *The Knack* and Barbra Streisand's *Funny Girl*. (Yet Tushingham's eyes could melt icebergs, and Streisand would seduce with her silvery voice and sensual, if irregular, features.) Georgy, to an American audience reared on the compact attractiveness of Natalie Wood, Debbie Reynolds, and Doris Day, was an oddity. And a relief.

It's interesting, too, that the two female characters are the broadly drawn halves of an emotional circle, while the men (Bates and Mason) hold fast to individual idiosyncratic behavior patterns but nevertheless interact more evenly toward their environment and needs. Generous with their emotions, both expect a certain responsiveness in return. Lecherous Mason may be Georgy's aging patron saint, but we know that he has sexual fantasies about her and will finally realize these dreams. Bates leaves her only after *she* has excluded him from her routine, her sex life. Maybe he's a bit of a cad—after all, it's his child—but his decision to split is one of self-preservation.

Was it a relief that both *Georgy* and *Darling* were in the end ambivalent about sex? Does that mean that with a permissive morality, disillusion clouds romance? That women basically don't care about lovemaking? Or is this view somehow safe and comforting to men and traditionalists? Did power of suggestion, rather than imminence of action, once heighten the physicality of Hayworth, Monroe, or Gardner? It is significant that these most modern sixties' heroines permitted to be adult in their sexual behavior are nevertheless denied the essence of enjoyment which such behavior should trigger. They know it. And announce it.

We can only assume that the movie world was uncomfortable with this unique and complex figure, because she would be relegated to increasingly trivial roles as the decade wore on. And this despite her more equal participation in life and love relationships. For example,

Michelangelo Antonioni's *Blow-Up* (1966), perhaps the glossiest and most influential artistic treatment of pop culture, virtually excised women from the center of activity, although up to this point Antonioni's most interesting protagonists had been female. In following a London photographer, David Hemmings, through his pop world of fashion and photojournalism into the illusory core of a mystery, revealed in blow-ups of a roll of film, the director uses females for show. For confusion. For titters. They are Hemmings' objects: First, the blank posturing mannequins toward whom the hero is paternalistic, commanding, and condescending. Then the magnificent Amazonian model Veruschka, to be seduced by Hemmings' Nikon—the mechanization of the modern obligatory bedroom scene. Also, the two teenyboppers, groping him in an infantile ménage of skinny legs, budding breasts, self-conscious shrieks, and torn sheets of colored paper. And finally enigmatic Vanessa Redgrave, the woman photographed, the only one who has something he wants—the answers to the mystery. Unwilling to unravel it, she is abstract, noncommittal, the pop remnant of Antonioni's classically alienated existential queen, Monica Vitti (in *L'Avventura*, 1959; *La Notte*, 1960; *L'Eclisse*, 1962; and *Red Desert*, 1964). But Hemmings is openly contemptuous of Redgrave's exoticism because her reality exists outside his dominion (adoring models with no secrets, no private worlds). To obtain control, he humiliates, seduces, deceives (returning the wrong roll of film to her). When she vanishes, he shrugs; those interiors, her realm, make little difference. For the film finally belongs to *him*. *Blow-Up* is the glamor and self-possession and cool assurance of his world.

Is this indication of importance indeed what happened when single women appropriated the privilege of sexual choice? Did they—the girls who took the Pill, moved into the singles apartment complexes that sprouted on the West Coast around 1965, vacationed in co-ed summer houses on Fire Island and the Hamptons, trooped off to singles weekends in the Catskills, and filled out cards for computer dating services—play out their trump card unwittingly? Was sex a club, a weapon, to be withheld in exchange for recognition, for "relationships" and love?

In a 1965 article entitled "The Pill and Morality" in the *New York Times Magazine*, Andrew M. Hacker observed, "Whether national character will be weakened is a question that simply cannot be answered."

That Antonioni's mid-sixties' London had simplified woman, formerly an intriguing and willful enigma to the director, into just another impudence of op abstraction is significant. And that these gangling teen-age "birds" who in providing casual physical pleasure rendered other "adult" females useless is also significant. For what one manufacturer aptly labeled a "youthquake" was upon us.

21

FLOWER CHILDREN
nodding off in camelot's rubble

Somewhere between Dallas and Liverpool, the optimism of the New Frontier vanished. In the wake of the President's murder followed a generation of revolution, reevaluation, and overhaul, a generation in which flower children and blacks, chicanos and women demanded "now" gratification, tangible change, a decade during which bombardment of events—Oswald's shooting, ghetto riots, Vietnam, campus unrest, the Martin Luther King-Medgar Evers-RFK assassinations— assaulted us regularly in our living rooms.

Like Pied Pipers delivering our children from bleak reality, four boys who would be catalysts of urgent frivolity crossed the Atlantic. It was 1964, and Beatlemania seized the music business, fashion, the imaginations of the young. Overnight we became a nation of Anglophiles. All the world listened to British rock groups; women wore Mary Quant clothes and Sassoon geometric haircuts, and tried to look like Twiggy and Jean Shrimpton. The vocabulary and style became "mod." Girls were "birds." Hemlines ascended. But soon even clothing styles for men and women would assume a sameness, as distinctions between the sexes blurred. Age was the line of demarcation dividing the under-twenty-five's and untrustworthy over-thirties. Those for peace, free love, and long hair; others, against. Good guys and bad.

But the kids of America had to be ready for this. Without preparation, how indeed could one swap Annette Funicello for Janis Joplin? Nancy Sinatra for Grace Slick? Sandra Dee for Twiggy? To simply attribute the cultural revolution to the Beatles is like saying Valentino invented the tango (not so, he just spread the step). And for our pampered teen society, satiated with, yet increasingly wary of, affluence and complacency, the seeds of change were already there. Suburban parents had unwittingly been priming their offspring since the mid-fifties. In 1960 there were 18,000,000 teen-agers who, like their parents, were keeping up with the Joneses. The purchase of records, automobiles, clothes, and college educations for them no longer seemed a privilege, but a universal birthright. High school girls spent almost $74,000,000 on "back-to-school" clothes in 1960, and Grace and Fred Hechinger, in their astonishing book *Teen-Age Tyranny*, noted at the time: "The fifteen to nineteen group is reported to have spent twenty million on lipstick, twenty-five million on deodorants and nine million dollars on home permanents in a typical year."[1]

Teen idols reinforce the cult of conspicuous consumption. Frankie Avalon, Bobby Darin, and Elvis, all wealthy, bought homes for and supported their parents, drove ornate cars, and were models of sartorial splendor. Precocious Tuesday Weld bragged to reporters: "I can change my clothes as much as fifteen or twenty times a day." And: "I had six cars last year. The one I liked most was a Mercedes. After that I had a Lincoln Continental because I thought that was very elegant."[2]

Movie magazines carried descriptions of Natalie Wood's and Bob Wagner's elaborate honeymoon house, bought for $75,000, then transformed with an estimated additional $200,000 into an elaborate Grecian Revival home.

Teen-agers, affected by the values of their heroines, were also marked by the media; on the influence of television advertising, David Riesman wrote in *The Lonely Crowd*: "One must listen to quite young children discussing television models, automobile styling, or the merits of various streamliners to see how gifted they are as consumers long before they have a decisive say themselves. . . ."[3]

But then, suddenly, pampered kids were supposed to be adults. And responsible. When would this metamorphosis occur? After high school? College? Grad school? Who indeed wanted to leave the womb and forfeit the treasures of youth because of some arbitrary dictate?

The social-sexual situation was equally confusing. "Dating" and "going steady" offered status in school. But sex, despite the tease of constant contact, advertising, and movies, was *naughty*. During the early sixties, 40 percent of all brides were teen-agers, and 50 percent of all young women were married by the time they reached twenty.

Saturation advertising in teen magazines drew parallels between romance and purchasing power (hope chests, china, bridal gowns, wedding presents, lavish receptions). Yet considerably more realistic was a statewide Iowa study indicating that thirty-nine percent of all girls who'd married in high school had been pregnant first. And the number of illegitimate births had almost doubled between 1950 and 1960 (from 141,600 to 224,300).

"It is through the mass media that the images and desires of teen-agers are at once standardized and distorted,"[4] observed the Hechingers. Early-sixties pre-Beatles youth movies betrayed just how alarming this standardization and distortion could be. The genre was the beach party picture. Its witless parade of teen paradises was no doubt influenced by the success of *Where the Boys Are* (and *Gidget* before it). This 1961 musical jamboree was different from the Presley or Boone pictures or the Sandra Dee soap operas in that it followed the odyssey of four (allegedly) college girls, Dolores Hart, Yvette Mimieux, Paula Prentiss, and Connie Francis, heading for a Fort Lauderdale Easter holiday of boys, beer, and parties. To point out the novel freedom that these females could be so mobile as to actually go "where the boys are" hardly compensates for the movie's frenetic emptiness, with the coeds attempting to live it up without trading in their virtue. Presley and Boone at least concentrated on individual relationships; here and in the films to follow, the group ethic prevails —and a gluttonous pleasure in boy-girl carousing, very much like "jock" fraternity parties but more impersonal.

It took the sharp commercial instincts of James H. Nicholson and Samuel Z. Arkoff to pare the complexities of teen existence down to rock bottom. These foresighted businessmen who propagated the beach formula and founded American International Pictures threw out plot and personality and put together a series of semiparodying, semislapstick stupidities. Ghosts or apes (*Bikini Beach*, 1964) crawled out of woodworks, and bumbling motorcycle gangs took pratfalls; bad guys were "dum-dum" adults (Keenan Wynn in *Bikini Beach*, 1964; Robert Cummings in *Beach Party*, 1963; Don Rickles in *Muscle Beach Party*, 1964). And the dramatic climax was always that moment when former Mouseketeer Annette Funicello cried that beau Frankie Avalon must "wait" until they were married. No one thought about school. About yesterday or tomorrow. Oddly, however, the atmosphere on the beach was the most antiseptic and asexual possible.

Yet the genre survived through 1967 with variations like *Beach Blanket Bingo* and *How to Stuff a Wild Bikini*, which New York *Times* critic Howard Thompson dubbed in 1967 "the answer to a moron's prayer."

At a glance these precious beach-party innocents seemed worlds apart from the hip, aggressive teenyboppers or alienated swingers who would people pop movies. Actually, the difference would be in degrees of impatience as unformulated questions were tested: *How immediately can we be gratified? How soon is "now"?*

By the time Beatlemania had displaced the beach bunny, "now" was yesterday. And the quest for acquisition had intensified. Mod paraphernalia—Courrèges dresses, boots, and miniskirts—was becoming *de rigueur*, and soon the fashion industry adopted this badge of youth's self-indulgent defiance. On April 25, 1966, *Newsweek* reported that, "In five years, pop has grown like The Blob, from a label for what appeared to be a minor phase of art history to a mass psyche." A psyche which flitted about, swallowing up cultchur-passions from *Batman* to Baby Jane Holzer to Warhol's soup cans, before coming home to roost once more at the feet of youth.

1967 was the year of *Sergeant Pepper's Lonely Hearts Club Band*. That album catapulted the Beatles into "legitimacy," and the nation into the "know." Suddenly, kids from Eureka, South Dakota, to Chattahoochee, Florida, had discovered not just marijuana, but marmalade skies and LSD.

Drugs. Introductions into the highest circles on the best authority. The plastic asexuality of Hollywood's Goody-Two-Shoes like Natalie and Doris and Debbie, the inability of movies to absorb what was happening and reproduce it for public consumption, had created a vacuum. Creeping into it was a novel phenomenon: the Superstar— the rock hero as mythic figure. Only Elvis and James Dean had ever approached the cult worship that John, Paul, George, and Ringo, Mick Jagger, Janis Joplin, and Jimi Hendrix were inspiring. And they deified drugs in their music. The Beatles' "Yellow Submarine." The Jefferson Airplane's "White Rabbit." The Stones' "She's a Rainbow." Ex-Harvard Professor Dr. Timothy Leary proselytized "turning on, tuning in, dropping out," and conducted acid-and-meditation retreats in Millbrook, New York. The Beatles admitted to taking drugs, then went off to the Himalayas for a mystical experience with Maharishi

Mahesh Yogi. Other rock stars (even the Beach Boys) joined them, as did actress Mia Farrow.

Kids who couldn't afford gurus ran off to communal pads in the Haight-Ashbury and the East Village. Sex, drugs, rapping, a passion for total independence to "do their thing" forced renunciation of traditional values—the pop artifice of clothing, purchasing power, education, employment. Looking "natural," they created costumes out of odds and ends and nodded off in the name of peace and love. They were flower children.

Why drugs? Common sense suggests a correlation with youthful promiscuity, especially among females. After decades of repression, to expect fifteen- and sixteen-year-old girls to adapt to a radically casual morality without severe anxieties and guilt, without the need for a numbing crutch, is insensitive at best.

Why drugs? To dull the sense of helplessness lost with the Kennedys' idealism? To erase the facts of violence in our cities, at Berkeley and Chicago and Columbia, at Kent State, in Vietnam? A schism as wide as the "credibility gap" was separating the law-and-order Establishment from the youth of America.

Why drugs? Was there really an alternative? How organically they seem to have grown out of those indulgences (and contradictory expectations) showered on the postwar young by Depression parents, out of that materialistic conditioning by mass media and easy acquisition! Kids, accustomed to "now" gratification, quite naturally gravitated toward drugs. Nothing could be more immediate or internalized than a euphoric high.

The most astonishing aspect of Hollywood in the mid-sixties was its total inability to reflect the tapestry of the youth culture—and perhaps, also, its *unwillingness* to do so. During these years of turmoil, the industry opted out of making meaningful contributions in interpreting the role of the new young woman, choosing instead the safe, sweet, familiar way of *Mary Poppins* (1964), *The Sound of Music* (1965), and *My Fair Lady* (1964). Taking modern risks meant filming gossipy, bitchy soap operas like *The Group* (1966) or *Valley of the Dolls* (1967).

By default, then, most films depicting pop culture were English imports—and often very stupid ones at that—picking up on the "groovy" and amoral girl-women who had become our new heroines. Judy Geeson, looking like Sandra Dee, starred in *To Sir with Love* and *Here We Go Round the Mulberry Bush* in 1967, and the excruciatingly distasteful *Prudence and the Pill* (1968). In *Alfie* (1966) Michael Caine loved and left a slew of gals, including Jane Asher and Shelley Winters. Lynn Redgrave and Rita Tushingham played two awkward friends letting loose in swinging London for a *Smashing Time* (1967). Tushingham again enacted a playful virgin and the target for seduction by inept Michael Crawford in *The Knack* (1965). Other films glorifying swinging London and, no doubt generating tourist business for the British Isles, included *The Jokers*, *Kaleidoscope*, *Casino Royale*, *I'll Never Forget Whatshisname*, *Bedazzled*, *The Strange Affair*, *Otley*, *Thirty Is a Dangerous Age*, *Cynthia*.

With all these wildly clever, freewheeling carryings-on, the fact that these heroines at their best were no more able to get a grip on their lives than their slightly more mature counterparts *Darling* and *Georgy* is significant, impressing us with certain truths and attitudes about the market value of woman in a drug- and sex-sated culture. To the world at large, youth was an amorphous group of kids, defined not by sex, but by age. Yet could the female really assimilate into the counterculture on an equal footing with men? More equal than she had ever been before, yes—but *totally?* In communes, who cooked and cleaned? At rock concerts, who were the "groupies"—eager and nubile, waiting patiently for the privilege of a night with a superstar? Who in the radical student movement worked mimeographing machines and perked the coffee? Women. When Charles Manson and his "family" were arrested for the gruesome California mass slayings of Sharon Tate and others, it emerged that he and the other "family" men spent their days relaxing and making love; the girls "in his power" were the slaves—they cooked, cleaned, scavenged food, made love (at the men's whim). At Charlie's whim, they also murdered. (How anachronistic that sexual freedom would enslave women all over again! More subtly. And deceptively.)

Joanna (1968), although in fact a dandified and pretentious movie, deals with the loose edges of the quintessential youth heroine. This time she's a sweet-stupid London dolly who, at seventeen, is already burned out. As in *Darling*, life holds little pleasure, robbed of its richness by too much unimportant sex and too many shallow relationships. But Joanna, guided by a dying lord, Donald Sutherland, to find meaning and love, decides to have the baby she is carrying by a black lover. This instant Pop Solution to feminine ennui and alienation (think of *Georgy*, *Poor Cow*, and others) would be humorous if it weren't such a subtle sermon against woman's self-determination, sending her back to the bonds of *Kinder* and *Küche* she has only recently slipped.

But director Michael Sarne, responsible also for *Myra Breckinridge*, likes to have his cake and eat it. Tiny teen Joanna is to be his earth mother; she is also his sex object to exploit seminude, from bed to bed, boutique to boutique, to hang clothes, men, or existential platitudes upon—a modern showpiece.

Played by Genevieve Waite, a baby-faced, reed-slender blonde who strongly resembles Twiggy, Joanna indeed embodies the decade's renovated sex kitten. Her emotional lineage might be *Darling*'s, but physically her family tree reveals a bit of Hayley Mills' childish faun, a good deal more of Carroll Baker's *Baby Doll* and Sue Lyons' *Lolita* —less abrasive and smug perhaps, but the kind of nymphet who radiates the assurance of pubescent irresistibility. Yet most unique is the elevation to an ideal of this gamine helplessness and little-boy body—an almost violent reaction to the breast-and-buttocks fetishes of the Monroe period. Joanna is the sixties' sex symbol. Waite's heroine, as nonthreatening and pure as a nine-year-old, signified a futuristic trend: woman as androgyne—the abrogation of woman-as-she-is-loved-and-known.

Hollywood tried it here, tentatively, with Mia Farrow, the fragile flower child who lopped off her feminine locks one day while furious at boyfriend Frank Sinatra. She caused sufficient sensation to become the momentary favorite of newspapers and magazines and the momentary wife of Francis Albert. Yet Mia provoked more interest as Allison on television's original *Peyton Place* than in the variety of roles she developed for the screen. *Rosemary's Baby* had a built-in success because of the interest in Ira Levin's best seller, but her performance was sedate, even stilted. Other parts—her strange, psychopath in *Secret Ceremony*, her bland youthful love interest in *A Dandy in Aspic*, her curiously dated blind girl victimized in *See No Evil*— hardly registered. Should Mia, in the mid-sixties, have been cast *according* to type, perhaps Hollywood might have contributed something valuable to the youth genre.

As it was, moviegoers had to make do with the rotten "satirical"

Candy (1968), yet another nymphet stumbling naïvely from one dirty old man to another. And with the too-late flower child, Leigh Taylor-Young, whose butterfly tattoo placed strategically on her thigh in *I Love You Alice B. Toklas* (1968) gets Peter Sellers even higher than marijuana brownies. When Hollywood finally related to the sixties' girl, it was with embarrassing limitations. Woman, as in *Candy* or *Toklas*, might be a sex object, but in the industry's puritanical view, she could not really be free. And hardly human.

We even had our variation on *Joanna. Sweet November* (1968). The plot: Sandy Dennis, afflicted with an unnamed incurable disease, devotes each of her last months to liberating a different man from his psychological problems. By living with each one, loving him, having sex with him—*voilà!*—she releases his potential with an ease that deserves the studious attention of psychiatrists, mistresses, and wives, then sends him on his way. Sandy Dennis can't be blamed for acting in this, but director Robert Miller is either incurably romantic, celibate, or love-hungry to assume that carefully nurtured sex opens magic doors to human fulfillment. Clearly he missed the point of the sexual revolution (that women might enjoy sex *themselves*), but willingly cashed in on it; as if omnicure and omnipleasure weren't enough, sex became an act even more charitable and Christian—a doomed girl's sacrifice for another's happiness.

Hollywood's general insensitivity to both women and youth hurt the industry more than it affected its audiences. For movies, no longer relating to their needs, lost patrons. During the thirties more than 90,000,000 moviegoers attended films regularly each week. In the mid-sixties that figure had been halved. Also, business conglomerates began engulfing studio complexes. By 1966 United Artists had merged with Transamerica, a holding company. Paramount was part of Gulf & Western. Warner's would ally itself with Seven Arts and then Kinney Communications, Columbia with Screen Gems, a television subsidiary. Twentieth Century-Fox, riddled by infighting, turned its major attentions to producing television series, as did Universal, and MGM, after declaring bankruptcy, would be taken over by former CBS president James Aubrey. In seats of authority once guarded proudly by shrewd moguls who knew and loved the business, calculating executives now sat. The process of making a film is lengthy at best—at least a year—but their temerity about exploring youth movies, their lack of contact with the pulse of our culture may have delayed the genre too long for it to be anything other than gratuitous.

When, finally, did these new Hollywood magnates wake up to its profit potential? The critical and box-office sweep of Joseph E. Levine and Mike Nichols' *The Graduate* (1967) opened more than a few eyes. In 1968 enthusiasm for the Leacock-Pennebaker documentary *Monterey Pop* and for movies like the animated version of the Beatles' *Yellow Submarine* awakened others. But with the emergence of the student populace during the 1968 Democratic Convention as a sizable and violent force of political protest, the industry sensed that the counterculture had come of age.

At least when it came to profits.

1969: The year of *Easy Rider*, Dennis Hopper's angry anti-Establishment drug picture. The year of *Midnight Cowboy* and *Alice's Restaurant* and *Medium Cool*. It had all been a long time coming.

1970: The protest films at last. *Getting Straight. The Strawberry Statement. The Magic Garden of Stanley Sweetheart* and a plethora of American International Pictures (in their post-beach-party phase) like *Wild in the Streets, Angel, Angel, Down We Go,* and *Three in the Attic*. The cynical and virulent black humor of Robert Altman's *M.A.S.H.*

But where was woman? In most of these movies, female roles were negligible—nonexistent, purely sexual, or purely for laughs. Candy Bergen in *Getting Straight*, an absurd exploitation of campus brutality, warms Elliott Gould's bed, but her connection with either her own sexuality or the student siege is tenuous. In *Midnight Cowboy* Brenda Vaccaro gives pickup Jon Voigt a late-night tumble. Dennis Hopper and Peter Fonda in *Easy Rider* resort to women for sexual release only when they're tripping on acid. Altman litters *M.A.S.H.* with nurses Sally Kellerman and Jo Ann Pflug straight out of *New Yorker* cartoons, one the stereotyped sweet-piece-of-Nightingale who makes up the covers and throws herself between them; the other the obsessive, crotchety young-old-maid who needs a good lay and, when she gets it, becomes the butt of the platoon.

This genre, as it turned out, really reinforced masculine dominions. It was as if females, once their sexual freedom had become commonplace, no longer concerned anybody as people. Political involvement, the drug scene, the whole counterculture had evolved into a "relevancy" trip so that even that traditional female stronghold, the love story, was obsolete. And the allegedly "equal" women, counterparts of our antiheroes—our Fondas and Hoffmans, Goulds and Voigts and Redfords—had been driven from the screen.

Only *Alice's Restaurant* gave us a warm portrait of a mature female, one who was so incredibly real and human that she virtually held the otherwise-just-cute movie together. Pat Quinn as Alice, famed restaurant proprietor of reality and song, may simply embody our ideal Mother Earth, grown-up Wendy watching over her army of lost boys. But her gift is that, while being Everyone's Surrogate Mommy, she still maintains her dignity and self-awareness, a sense of humor and of privacy. Whether doting on Arlo and other hippies she shelters in a converted church or interacting with her husband Ray—fighting, loving, laughing, angry, exhausted—Quinn gives Alice a robust charm and explosive honesty, forces us to see the complexity of her feelings for her husband and how the dual role of Mother Earth and Wife finally drains the relationship.

In the drought blighting female heroism, Pat Quinn stood head and shoulders above most others, and especially nice was her attitude —as young and alive as the kids'. Her image betrayed a smaller generation gap than did the roles of many more contemporary actresses. Like Ali MacGraw.

If ever a star seemed manufactured to meet the exigencies of an industry desperate to unify its two major profit sources—the conservative Middle American Establishment and youth—it was Ali. There's a soft really girlish quality about her, like the Girl Scout you used to buy cookies from or the nice kid you knew at camp who grew up to be tall and eclectically chic and pretty. But the paradox is that when she adds dialogue to her look, the meaning of her celluloid persona changes. Disturbingly. The role is irrelevant: Whether she's snotty-rich Brenda Patimkin in *Goodbye, Columbus* (1969), dying Jennifer in *Love Story* (1970), or Steve McQueen's iron-nerved wife in *The Getaway* (1972), she emerges the same wry, smirking finishing-school graduate.

Yet it is symptomatic of the malaise of Hollywood, of its limited notions of the depth or range of the modern young woman, that after her movie debut, carefully packaged by Paramount and her then-husband-to-be, Robert Evans, Ali achieved major stardom. It is also ironic that while her on-screen image is so unfinished, she packaged a certain look copied by millions of American girls—long dark hair parted in the center, natural brows and makeup, crocheted beanies. Not since women removed their Liz Taylor-Cleopatra makeup to emulate Jackie and then Twiggy has a screen personality wielded such fashion clout. So obviously she fulfilled certain female needs. Was it simply her pleasing physical appearance? The fact that, after all those alienated, winsome pop "objects," here was a girl who in her smugness maintained control and independence? Or going even further, that while she enjoyed men, she verbalized a certain calculated hostility toward them? Perhaps it was that Ali's heroines, always alert, involved themselves, whether with a man or a bank robbery; they carefully avoided the I'm-used-up-and-searching-for-meaning syndrome that may have accurately reflected certain female sentiments, but was hardly optimistic or entertaining.

Her wholesome and glowing all-American surefootedness reassured. Ali MacGraw served as conductor out of the teenybopper phase toward a more conservative restoration of familiar values. The self-involved new girl next door. Not innocent and ingenuous like Debbie or Dee. Not sensuous and empty like Julie Christie, gawky like Lynn Redgrave or budding like Genevieve Waite. Yet signifying that America's affair with the swinging "pop" object had ended.

With reason. The climate had changed. Peace, love, and music at Woodstock in 1969 became tragedy and murder at Altamont four months later (*Gimme Shelter*). The Beatles had split up. Jimi Hendrix was dead. . . . Joplin also. Brian Jones of the Stones, Jim Morrison of the Doors.

Substantial numbers of kids, burned out from too many highs, sought direction from religion—Hare Krishna and Buddhism, mysticism, the Jesus Movement. Others simply renewed themselves by romanticizing nature and staging a return to the earth through ecology, health foods, or communal farm life.

Progress has been made, though—and by women especially. They had won their sexual freedom, thanks to the truculent spirit of maverick flower children. And also a sense of unity. Abortion—an issue in a sexually free society—was a *woman's* problem. So, surprisingly, was the youth movement, which hid a built-in inevitability of discrimination: Whoever heard of a thirty-five-year-old groupie? No woman wanted to be considered over the hill at thirty or even fifty. Why should society worship thirty-year-old rock idols and sixty-year-old movie heroes, yet judge a "bird's" desirability by her youth? As the media, with great amusement, devoted coverage to Women's Movement activities after 1968, women began asking questions. Examining their status.

22

CLINICIANS OF DECADENCE:
unnecessary objects, hermaphrodeities, & yawnporn

Once upon a time sex was romance. . . . Paul Henreid lighting two cigarettes between his lips, then meaningfully handing one to Bette Davis. Bergman whispering to Bogart, "Kiss me, kiss me as if it were the last time." Leigh and Gable embracing while Atlanta burned.

Today, however, to be clinical is to be in. In the last decade the primacy of permissiveness has transformed sex into an act, behavior, a problem so "relevant" that moviemakers have, poker-faced, appointed themselves pop culture's lab specialists with an earnestness akin to that of Masters and Johnson. With sagging profits and vacant theaters urging them on, they have detailed, dissected, magnified the sex act. And in so doing, intimacy has been isolated; romance demystified.

It seems incredible that not long ago ingenuous movies "glorifying" prostitutes—*Irma La Douce, Never on Sunday, Breakfast at Tiffany's* —posed censorship problems. George Cukor's 1962 *The Chapman Report* was snipped to pieces by scared studio officials *before* it even reached the censors, simply because this study of the sexual psyches of three wives included frigidity and nymphomania, not necessarily in graphic deed, but in theme.

How amusing that once moviegoers went to watch James Bond not just for the comic-book violence and sci-fi gadgetry of the genre, but also because Ursula Andress, rising from the water in a skimpy bikini, made *Dr. No* very sexy. Because the beautifully butch Pussy Galore(!) (Honor Blackman), the leader of Amazonian spies in *Goldfinger*, surrenders to Bond in a haystack like one immovable object giving way to another. We were sure—just as we were sure of Dean Martin's Matt Helm series and Michael Caine's Harry Palmers

—that a plethora of beauties in microskirts would fall in and out of bed with them. The accompanying leers and ogles were a part of what movies *then*, in the early sixties, called "sex." And even if these ladies had "liberated jobs" as spies and double agents, their "governments" must have known as well as the movie's producers that Mata Hari (or even *Modesty Blaise*) performed ultimately and most efficiently in bed. For then, when the decade was young and we had not yet separated the "freedom" of the burgeoning sexual revolution from the double standard, women at their best were merely objects—to be loved and seduced by males who cared, if not for their minds, then at least for the conquest.

And in those days Hollywood objectified a young actress who had sprung her star quality on the industry one Academy Award night. It was 1962, and Ann-Margret sang "Bachelor in Paradise"; you didn't need to be a genius, not even a mogul, to see that she was hot, obviously talented, blooming with youth. Yet what Hollywood did with her is a precise and pathetic example of how a nation and an industry can mishandle an actress and misunderstand changing values and behavior patterns in women. Even as the all-American teen of Sweet Apple, Ohio, in *Bye, Bye Birdie* (1962), they decked Ann-Margret in slinky toreador pants, gave her hip-swiveling musical numbers, and let her hair tumble like Bardot's. And *that* was when she was supposed to be wholesome. Giving Hollywood the benefit of the doubt— since it was only 1962 and studios were searching frantically for an heiress to the Monroe throne—is fine, but how, then, does one explain the elaboration of Ann-Margret's teen tigress into a vulgar and antiquated "piece" over the next four years? With *Bus Riley's Back in Town, Kitten with a Whip* (which A-M herself parodies in her nightclub act), *Viva Las Vegas, The Cincinnati Kid*, and *Stagecoach*, her image was caste like bronze for puerile masturbatory fantasies; she was the local drive-in queen, aping those juvenile delinquents on probation in awful fifties' prison movies. The only difference was that her voice was soft, and her energy was redirected from rioting to dashing about on motorcycles or leaping into a throbbing dance whenever the script permitted.

Between 1962 and 1966, however little Ann-Margret's or Hollywood's definition of a delicious trick changed, the nation's values did. In the first years of the decade, the smutty side of sex titillated— with newspaper headlines that thirteen-year-old Long Island teen-agers were operating a call-girl service, that surburban matrons, even schoolteachers, had joined a prostitution ring. But the Pill was becoming a *fait accompli* for single women; having sex didn't mean being a tramp. Yet if Ann-Margret was chronologically in tune with the swinging new youth society, her soul was bound up with black lace garters. Who in the audience actually connected with her? Grade school kids? Delinquent girls? Malt-shop rejects? Dirty old men? Ann-Margaret had allowed Hollywood to install her just two steps away from the grindhouse flicks where kittens really were j-d's and did carry whips (*Angelique in Black Leather*). Wrote Pauline Kael:

> . . . Ann-Margret comes through dirty no matter what she plays. She does most of her acting inside her mouth. Julie Andrews could play a promiscuous girl in *The Americanization of Emily* and shine with virtue. Ann-Margret gleams with built-in innuendo. She's like Natalie Wood with sex, a lewd mechanical doll. Men seem to have direct-action responses to Ann-Margret: they want to give her what she seems to be asking for.[1]

When Mike Nichols signed her to play Bobby in *Carnal Knowledge*, eyebrows were raised. It was 1969, and people thought of Ann-Margret as hopelessly old-fashioned, unsalvageable. Under duress from her husband-manager Roger Smith, she had obediently taken off her clothes in *C.C. and Company*, but neither her nudity nor costar Joe Namath's presence made the effort worthwhile. Nichols, however, was perhaps the only filmmaker who could see the fragility and range behind the cardboard front. Playing a thirtyish single girl desperate to marry, have a home and family, not just because age is narrowing her eligibility, but because her life is dull and meaningless, her work menial, Ann-Margret lent great poignancy to the picture. Nichols cleverly skimmed the surface of her former roles; Bobby is simply kitten-with-a-whip grown older, panicking. And in showing us her soft, frightened interiors, he finally managed to utilize her very human warmth and gave the screen one of its most thoughtful and disturbing portraits of a female caught up in and devastated by the decade's double standards.

Ann-Margret has done nothing of similar merit since. And it is possible that her own romantic notion of femininity and her reliance on men to shape her career have contributed to her financially profitable but desultory image. She and husband Smith enjoy drawing a parallel between her and Monroe, and she sweetly explains her old-fashioned proclivities this way: "It's Roger's opinion, not mine that counts. He has complete autonomy over me. After all, I enjoy being a girl, having someone to take care of me, being told where to go and what to do. . . ."[2]

Fickle town that it is, Hollywood clutched Ann-Margret to its bosom after *Carnal Knowledge*, ballyhooing her as movies' last link with opulence and glamor until it became evident that she would not indeed replace Monroe. And conveniently, another beauty—more bosomy, more aloof, and calculatingly artificial—was waiting to take her turn. *One Million Years B.C.* (1966) is forgotten by now, but Raquel Welch in her loincloth bikini—and the most magnificent body imaginable—cut an unforgettable figure. She also assured the safe passage, or evolution, of the sex object into the laboratory. Ann-Margret may have been "dirty," but compared to Raquel, she projected very human qualities, a certain warmth, a real, if cheap, eroticism, humor, vitality. But Welch, sculpted out of the same don't-touch-me marble as Ursula Andress, called up even more sadistic muses than the leather-clad kitten. Think how she's been poured into rubber diving suits (*Fantastic Voyage*), cowboy suede and leather (*Hannie Caulder*; *100 Rifles*), how she's been thrown into roller derby rinks to kick, push, and shove other women (*Kansas City Bomber*). And most fitting of all? *Myra Breckinridge* (1970).

Here Raquel, literally the artificial female by virtue of a sex change eventually—*what irony!* we are supposed to feel—becomes a lesbian. It was both ill advised and distasteful for her to bulldoze her way through this one, more Hercules than Sappho, while as a grotesque counterpoint Mae West minced in and out, making the impact due a seventy-seven-year-old drag queen. Once in a while Mae even suggested that spiffy comedy and swell innuendo of thirty years ago. But this onetime mistress of entendre—who insisted her character's name be changed from LeTITia to LeTICia—had lost touch; her presence remained one ghastly female embarrassment out of many. For *Myra Breckinridge*, rather than being the irreverent satire on homosexuality and sex-role reversals that author Gore Vidal had intended, emerged, with West, Welch, and director Michael Sarne at the core of the grotesqueries, as a savage bludgeon, a multimillion-dollar ode to and by woman haters. While the movie flatters no one, the females—genderless really, yet with voracious and perverse appetities—are parodied most cruelly.

How snugly, too, this movie plugged into what Raquel's screen image had hinted at for some time. The sensual, yet detached face is taut, immobile, and hints at cruelty. The old-fashioned sex object is modernized, not by aloofness (Dietrich and Garbo had *that*), but toughness. Welch, you feel, could get along without men, without sex. Somewhere in America audiences must be responding to her stunning control, disregarding the veiled indifference of her persona and still idolizing her as a sex symbol. Their response endorses having sex with a statue. After all, despite her twenty-odd movies, do we know Raquel Welch any more intimately than a *Playboy* centerfold?

Are men attracted to her brand of emotionlessness because it protects them from the myth of female sexuality as a bottomless, draining well? Now that "liberated" women are pressuring men to connect sex with affection, are men disinterested? Despite all the loving sex partners around, psychiatrists chart a rise in male impotence. The increasing importance of the prostitute in urban society and hard-core pornography in movies (at $5 a throw) attests to a masculine preference for the alienated sex experience. Are "free" women also threatening? Sexually judgmental? Do peep shows and massage parlors provide thrills because they're "dirty," "illicit"? Did Victorianism and also religion teach chastity as a way, not unlike a peekaboo fan dance, to keep masculine blood boiling?

The willingness of well-known actresses such as Liz Taylor (*The Sandpiper*), Julie Andrews (*Darling Lili*), Susannah York (*The Killing of Sister George*), Jane Fonda (*Barbarella*), Cybill Shepherd (*The Last Picture Show*), Vanessa Redgrave (*Isadora*), Ann-Margret, Maria Schneider (*Last Tango in Paris*) to appear on screen nude is—like trends toward porno and prostitution—symptomatic of a new intimacy. Or, rather, a shattering of the old intimacy, redefining it in its most clinical and external terms. In today's open society where men prefer to free themselves from sexual attachments by paying prostitutes, where encounter groups direct participants to "be intimate" in a few hours or a weekend either by touch therapy or confessionally throwing up their Freudian pasts, where people strip bare for each other one night and pass unspeaking the next, what could be more natural than to transfer the meaning of intimacy to assuage alienation?

Intimacy once also meant selective sharing of privacy. Now there is none. The sexual revolution affected the media, too, so that personalities openly defying convention immediately invited the public into their secret lives: Mia Farrow, Vanessa Redgrave, Catherine Deneuve, Barbara Hershey Seagull, Joanna Pettit, Patty Duke all became mothers without rushing to the clergyman. Famous ladies clamor to parade their bodies in *Playboy*. Burt Reynolds, naked, discreetly places his hand in *Cosmopolitan*'s centerfold. John Lennon and Yoko Ono pose, fully, frontally nude, and hold press conferences in bed. *Motion Picture* magazine runs a smear in which a former Twentieth Century-Fox press agent details her days and nights with Paul Newman. Writer Merle Miller sparks a fad when in the New York *Times* he poignantly comes out of the closet; soon personalities are discreetly allying themselves with respect to gender. Bette Davis announces on a national talk show that she'd been a virgin on her first bridal night—and advises against it.

In 1966 we criticized Robert Rimmer's novel about communal marriage, *The Harrad Experiment*, as wildly fantastic; today the film version seems dated. Nonfiction bestsellers like *Open Marriage* discuss, even suggest, it as an alternate life-style. And people live it.

Movies, at one time "how tos" on attracting a partner—how to flirt, kiss, be desirable—now accept desirability or ignore it completely to concentrate on the clinical aspects of sex or show the infinite possibilities of combinations. Once it was *A Man and a Woman*. Then, *Bob and Carol and Ted and Alice*. Or *All the Loving Couples*. Or *Therese and Isabelle*. Now it's *Deep Throat*, *Sugar Cookies*, and *The Devil in Miss Jones*.

David Riesman in *The Lonely Crowd* called sex the "last frontier" of privacy. Today porno movies diminish that distinction, zooming in in glorious color on genitalia in casual combinations. In a movie like *Deep Throat*, the "star" Linda Lovelace works her head off under the guise of pleasuring herself. Yet what has Lovelace guarded for her own privacy? Her technique. In a recent interview she confessed that she practiced controlling her gag reflexes for her role, but refused to reveal her secret, which resulted in her splendid performance of fellatio!

Deep Throat's overwhelming success—the movie reportedly cost only $25,000 to produce and has earned well over $3,000,000—lies not merely with its star's expertise, not even with the alienated nonchalance of another female actress who enjoys cunnilingus while smoking a cigarette, but with the masculine fantasies it stimulates, realizes. There is something about Miss Lovelace's shaved pubis which seems borrowed from a Harold Robbins novel; on one hand, it is verification of cleanliness, of sex without mess. Also, it's illicit, whorey. And finally, it is a symbolic denial of her womanhood, returning the adult to the state of a pure, not yet developed girl-child. Which is probably as close as porno and *Lolita* have moved so far.

But the prime convenience of *Deep Throat*, of course, is that the movie's gimmick—the fact that Miss Lovelace's clitoris is located in her throat—creates an ultimate fantasy which neatly does away with the female genitalia. Her vagina is desensitized, unimportant; the only juices of hers that flow are saliva. Fellatio can now satisfy both her partner, and by some lazy, generous masculine imagination of relocation, her, too!

Is life reflecting "art" (syn. popular culture)? Or "art" life? Feeding each other, inextricably intertwined, our mores are changing so rapidly that we can hardly fix where one begins and the other leaves off.

More open portrayals of homosexuality coincide, for instance, with the momentum gained by recent organized movements such as Gay Activists Alliance, Mattachine Society, lesbian liberation's Redstockings, S.C.U.M., Daughters of Bilitis, and private individuals who have campaigned and risked censure to legitimize those sexual preferences once termed sick or criminal or destructive to society. Not long ago an extremely delicate and explosive theme to be touched on gently (*e.g.*, the "strange" boys of *Rope* and *Compulsion*), today handling of homosexuality varies from implicit (*Lawrence of Arabia*, *The Best Man*, *Reflections in a Golden Eye*, *If . . .*, *Child's Play*, *The Servant*, *Midnight Cowboy*) to explicit (*Fellini Satyricon*, Schlesinger's *Sunday Bloody Sunday*, Pasolini's *Teorema*, *The Gay Deceivers*, William Friedkin's *The Boys in the Band*).

In fact, because of this new permissiveness, a number of filmmakers who have created the body of their work in climates of restrain are now overindulging personal fantasies or obsessions never before allowed to surface undisguised. For instance, Luchino Visconti's last three films, *The Damned*, *Death in Venice*, and *Ludwig*, have embodied the director's own descent into a world of fanatic masculine narcissism and passion.

Lesbianism has also been treated with corresponding frankness in recent years, but with considerably less compassion, at least by English-speaking movie makers. At one point, however, the reverse was suggested, and although the dyke warden in 1951's *Caged* was certainly an instantly recognizable "lezzy," Von Sternberg early played on the eroticism of a masculine female when he put Dietrich in top hat in *The Blue Angel* and then directed her to kiss a woman nightclub patron during *Morocco*. Mamoulian played on the masculine-feminine nature of Garbo with *Queen Christina*, and George Cukor slyly directed a shockingly boyish Katharine Hepburn to pass as a male in *Sylvia Scarlett*. Both versions of Lillian Hellman's play *The Children's Hour* (the 1936 attempt, entitled *These Three*, and 1962) were circumventive, but sympathetic to the definitive latency of their schoolteacher protagonists. And from Europe have come intelligent and tender films like Leontine Sagan's 1931 *Maedchen in Uniform*, Jacqueline Audry's *The Pit of Loneliness* (1951), and the recent sensational *Therese and Isabelle* (1968), from a memoir by novelist Violette Leduc. As shocking as *Therese and Isabelle* was, including a scene in which one schoolgirl kissed the other's belly (and many in the audience walked out), it also attempted to idealize a youthful love idyll. Today the tendency is instead to play up eroticism, destruction, or both—and always as part of a disgruntled menage.

The Killing of Sister George (1968) portrays a triad of clawing neurotic women—the mannish radio star Beryl Reid, hostile and irritable because she's about to lose her longtime job; her ultra-fem mistress, Susannah York, feebly pathetic, playing with dolls and submitting to the humiliation of drinking Reid's dirty bath water to prove her love; and Coral Browne, a strong, manipulative intruder luring York away. *Sister George* is an ugly film, deriving sustenance from the sensationalism with which a thin story is blown up. Little is credible; the women, as might be expected, are properly vulturelike. And totally extraneous is the scene in which Beryl Reid suckles Susannah York's breast; this seems an afterthought to exploit the lesbian-nudity box-office lure.

If movies have salvaged any kind of sexual privacy, it is masculine. The rape scene in *Deliverance* (1972) horrifies as a private violation of the male victim, but also as a violation of audience sensibilities; women raped on the screen merely evoke yawns. Similar familiar principles apply within the commercial homosexual genre: Gay men rarely strip or involve themselves in passionate interactions on screen; homosexual women are constantly depicted in sensual and suggestive acts. This inequity bolsters the suspicion that lesbian movies are the yellow journalism of the screen, yet in the name of "modernity" and "relevance" we accept them.

Hollywood appears most comfortable with movies like *The Fox* and *X, Y, and Zee* in which the lesbian relationships are offset by a man's presence; inevitably male and female vie with each other for the prize. In the case of *The Fox* (1968, vaguely based on D. H. Lawrence's story), the male, Keir Dullea, intrudes on two women living on an isolated farm. He and strong, handsome Anne Heywood develop an attraction, which threatens her whining friend, Sandy Dennis. However, Dennis' convenient death beneath a falling tree and the sensationalism of her meek, cautious affection toward Heywood pale beside the (unnecessary) sequence of Heywood masturbating.

For flamboyance, however, nothing and no one upstage Elizabeth Taylor. In *X, Y, and Zee* (1972) she plays a miserable, screeching bitch of a wife (again) who seduces Susannah York (again) not out of any true homosexual feelings, but in order to bring hubby Michael Caine home. Caine, thinking the grass greener in York's sedate, shy arms, walks in one day and finds that Liz has got there first. Her sexual activities, very much like Sandy Dennis' in *Sweet November*, are colored not by need or desire, but by some external "value": Dennis was freeing men to be themselves, and so is of the highest seraphic order, but Liz, we understand, has merely engaged her own sexuality as a passionless tactical defense.

Still, by the sheer presence of her celebrity she lured the curious as surely as York's suckled breast and Heywood's masturbatory trance did. Jumping on the bisexual bandwagon, Liz—the chief working remnant of Hollywood's glory—by sheer presence also anointed the genre with respectability. It's like casting Carol Burnett in a Warhol picture. The story, however, has little else to speak for it besides the flimsy lurid camp of her "liberated" performance.

And that flimsiness perhaps is the most negative truth about the current lesbian honesty in movies. Pauline Kael in reviewing an early (1966) threesome, *10:30 P.M. Summer* (starring Melina Mercouri, Romy Schneider, and Peter Finch), wrote: "Movies always seem to be both behind and ahead of the culture. Though the sexual revolution has scarcely found its way onto the screen, and movies rarely deal with the simplest kind of heterosexual life in our time, they're already treating bisexuality—like the kids who are on pot and discussing the merits of LSD before they've had their first beer."[3]

One of the most influential figures in turning screen sexuality inside out in recent years, pop artist and filmmaker Andy Warhol has opened the underground closet and confronted with total irreverence all our convictions and sanctimonies. His world is one of misfits—of sexless creatures, homosexuals, ambisexuals, and grotesque female predators. For them, deviation is the norm, and they smile out of great Satyricon-like faces with blank bleeding eyes. *Trash* (1970) gives us a searing look at a drug-addicted male hustler (Joe Dallesandro) whose habit interferes with his sex life. A variety of women attempt to arouse him through a variety of sex offerings and in various states of undress. Only Holly Woodlawn, a transvestite with a sweet humility and self-deprecating humor, reaches out and affects Joe. Opening our eyes to that fringe world of nether creatures, her humanity dissipates our prejudices and disgust, and Holly easily steals the film.

Yet whatever sympathy she elicits in *Trash* evaporates in *Women in Revolt* (1972). This time the Warhol-Morrissey team bids us to endure her and two other transvestites, Jackie Curtiss and Candy Darling, as they spoof women's lib and play out their love/hate female fantasies. But when the bizarre flash of their free and bawdy improvisation settles, it is their hate and contempt which agonize its way up from the screen. No longer is this homosexual milieu "camp." For clearly, though the "girls" have borrowed their notions of feminity, their gestures and styles from old Joan Crawford, Ginger Rogers, and Lana Turner movies, the benignity of dandyism has vanished; their femaleness, fully and desperately indulged here, is tainted with bitchiness, self-consciousness, and anger. Beautiful, blond Candy (playing the rich Monroe-type gal who wants to be a movie star), Jackie (a wry and witty bohemian who has a baby to prove her "liberation"), and Holly (a bisexual nymphomaniac) inflate female weaknesses into coy grotesqueries. Too self-conscious of their own shock value and full of self-hate to be able to afford empathy toward women, their humor—a consciousness-raising group which turns into an orgy; a casting-couch seduction; endless "girl talk" and liberation chatter foaming with shrieks and swishes—is no more insightful than the most vicious *Harvard Lampoon* parody. The fact is that as rewarding a theatrical ritual it might be for Candy, Holly, and Jackie to costume themselves as females, their predilections, interests, and problems are of the male homosexual world; because the female role, with all its passivity and artifice, is alluring enough to be in some way responsible for their own gender confusion (so that they are not heterosexuals or homosexuals either), woman-hating-through-imitating is an understandable and safely distant expression of anger.

Warhol's *Heat* (1972) reflects this searing contempt—again. And again it is disarming in its kinky vulgarity, but the laughs begin to pale as antifeminine grotesqueries hit out more hideously. Director Morrissey fills his snide takeoff on *Sunset Boulevard* with handsome, ambivalent male characters and shrewish monster-women: Sylvia Miles, a fading movie star; Andrea Feldman (in her final role before her suicide), with two red circles of rouged cheeks, as her lesbian daughter, shacking up in a cheap motel with an infant child and a girlfriend given to burning Feldman's body with lit cigarettes; and Pat Ast, the enormous mountain of a motel proprietor, are all waiting to devour gorgeous hustler and sometime-actor Dallesandro. Both Miles and Feldman, of the canyon school of acting, bellow their way through fights and flirtations. They are the dumb, whorey, and desperately cruel caricatures that give men reason to turn homosexual or impotent. The only stunner is the impenetrable Dallesandro, serving each female for what he can get from her, then moving on. And who can blame him?

There is also another kind of screen cruelty—the literal kind—which in the past few years has been irretrievably bound up with female sexuality. So fused are these two elements that we cannot avoid speculating on their relationship to woman's latest bid for sexual and social freedom. Reminiscent of the forties' *films noirs* (which also occurred at a time of relative female autonomy), this genre is, however, not nearly as well crafted, subtle, or suggestive. Also, motivations are more explicitly sex-related, where once greed, unrequited love, and simple, unsophisticated psychosis provided sufficient reasons to plunge us, and the characters, into terror. Now we have psychotic mass lady killers such as transvestite Rod Steiger in *No Way to Treat a Lady*; Richard Attenborough in *10 Rillington Place*; Rock Hudson in Roger Vadim's *Pretty Maids All in a Row*. (When Vadim, the man who brought Bardot, Deneuve, and Fonda under his wing, stoops to high school stranglings in which leggy co-eds are dropping right and left, you *know* it must be a trend.) In Alfred Hitchcock's *Frenzy*, a perverse, orange-haired necktie strangler stalks women who hardly put up a fight before their breath fails them. (Who would have dreamed how avant-garde Chaplin's 1947 *Monsieur Verdoux* would seem two decades later?)

Most revealing, though, is the facility with which moviemakers have equated female sexuality with psychopathy: Catherine Deneuve hacking away in Polanski's *Repulsion* (1965); the bunch of seething, hungry seminary girls in *The Beguiled* (1971), repaying the fickle attentions of wounded Clint Eastwood by cutting him up in tiny pieces; Jessica Walter, rejected by Clint Eastwood in *Play Misty for Me* (1972), maniacally attempting to stab him and girlfriend Donna Mills. Even in *Last Tango in Paris* (1973), "normal" Maria Schneider puts a bullet through Marlon Brando, although we are never sure why. Is it because he is finally making marital and emotional demands on her? Because the demands come too late? Because their insulated fantasy world is stifling, tempting, and, most of all, threatening? Or does she see him as a loser, one whose presence and life-force impinges on her rationality? Panicked, the girl survives the lure by killing the bait.

These films, equally pretentious, make swift, faulty connections, but because they are so glib and superficial, they don't disturb us as deeply as Robert Altman's *Images* (1972). For this is a serious and sophisticated effort documenting the interiors of a woman undergoing a breakdown. The visual elements are beautiful, all tinkling chimes and blue-green skies and landscapes, with elaborate, confusing cutting so that we don't know what heroine Susannah York is dreaming and what is true; but this is a false suspense maker, all sound and fury, camouflaging the defects. In her insanity she ultimately kills her husband (and perhaps her lover). Why? Altman alludes to sexual guilt over an affair. A possible regretted abortion. Sorrow over inability to have childen. These are the only glimmers of motivations he allows. Since the woman writes children's books, we expect her to be semi-intelligent; surely something other than sex should help define her collapse. But that never happens. York is consumed with sexual fantasies and a tortured conscience. Her insanity—and sanity—have apparently been limited by Altman's own naïveté (remember *M.A.S.H.*), which here seems touchingly sophomoric: Trying to pin the most pathological kind of breakdown on infidelity is like weighing down an ass with a lunar module. Does Altman understand the female psyche so poorly? Or is he parading the masculine ego in a self-congratulatory strut? *Images* is a pretty but empty shell, a monument to the kind of virtuoso falsehoods that filled our neighborhood screens years ago. It is a man's romantic misinterpretation.

Less romantic perhaps, but of the same genus, is the chestnut which flowered in the mid-sixties—the last gasp of the aging maniac. For this woman, sex has faded, and dementia has set in. The causes range from unrequited love to loneliness to obsession with Daddy and sibling rivalry. They hardly mattered, however, for the show *really* consisted of seeing great ladies in various horrific states: Joan Crawford in *Straight Jacket*; Bette Davis and Joan Crawford in *Whatever Happened to Baby Jane?*; Davis and De Havilland in *Hush, Hush, Sweet Charlotte*; Davis as *The Nanny*; Zsa Zsa Gabor in *Picture Mommy Dead*; and Tallullah Bankhead in *Die! Die! My Darling* all terrorized us in full shrew regalia because those were the best roles available.

Violence is not just a sex-linked need either. Modern movies have woven it into the pattern of their erotica. The exuberant bullet-blistering sadism of, say, *Bonnie and Clyde* (1967) takes on an erotic dimension, and the artificial excitement of killing replaces Clyde Barrow's impotence (his actual homosexuality is glossed over) as a bond deepening his relationship with Bonnie Parker. In a similar way violence is brought into erotic focus in *A Clockwork Orange* (1971), but because it is an across-the-boards social mutation—with middle-aged men getting beaten up and paralyzed, old men getting whacked on their heads, young men on their cups, and women being either crushed with phallic sculptures or gangbanged to Beethoven—the abusive malevolence seems democratic, with gender simply defining the form of abuse. Also, the film's extreme stylization distances us so that it isn't nearly as "real" or as disturbingly pointed as the sadistic pleasure of more realistic films.

Sam Peckinpah in *Straw Dogs*, for instance, dourly clings to the philosophy of man's primal instinct for cruelty, and his *The Wild Bunch* illustrates it by showing tiny children who rip the wings off insects. But in *Straw Dogs* (1971) the elaboration is sexual. The director gravitates toward the dizzy little blonde who with bee-stung lips, large bosom, and sluttish sensibilities is turned on by brutality.

Susan George is central to such action here. As the wife of Dustin Hoffman, a priggish mathematics student, she has no apparent interest except to wander idly about the small Welsh town where they live while he works on his equations. Boredom charges her libido. Her skimpy outfits charge the town ruffians, among them a rejected suitor already jealous of squarish, bookish alien Hoffman.

Peckinpah doesn't bother to tell us what Susan George and Hoffman, so absurdly opposite, have in common, nor does he sympathize with the girl's isolation as Hoffman commits himself totally to his work. Eventually her old boyfriend rapes her, but the telling gesture in the scene is her submission and ultimate pleasure in his brutality. Finally, she is gangbanged, and her husband, having sheltered his instincts and anger by ignoring the atmosphere of repressed hostility, must now set aside his civilized cloak. He and his wife survive what her sexiness has wrought by resorting to mass murder.

Yet the director manipulates the story so that neither the sex nor the killings grow organically from events. Everything hinges on the trashiness of George, on the preoccupation of Hoffman, on the mismatch of their marriage. The town boys are rowdy, women are scarce, the atmosphere is as primitive as Appalachia—yet she struts about in shorts as if she were in Miami. So many similar contrivances and suspensions of credibility build to the rape scene that it seems to be Peckinpah's sweet baby—perverse and wicked and illogical in its psychological assumptions.

Are moviegoers so deadened to tenderness that brutality is the most satisfying way to charge their libidos? If not, why have sex and violence become so inextricably bound, coursing through Hollywood's most popular movies? Can this phenomenon be divorced from the sexual revolution, although it seems so clear that the appearance of brute strength on screen has paralleled the growth of female autonomy off? Look at the New Heroes, the law-and-order breed: Gene Hackman in *The French Connection*; Hackman and Lee Marvin in *Prime Cut*; Marvin in *Point Blank*; Paul Newman's *The Life and Times of Judge Roy Bean*; Clint Eastwood's spaghetti Westerns, plus *Dirty Harry*, *Joe Kidd*, *High Plains Drifter*; Steve McQueen as *Junior Bonner*, *Bullitt*, and in *The Getaway*; George C. Scott's *The New Centurions* and *Patton*; Al Pacino and James Caan in *The Godfather*: One can detect in these modern heroes who carry films *without* a significant female love interest an aura of eroticism springing directly from their stance. Might as right. Law and order. Strong, silent. The gun as penis.

These are not merely the most popular males on screen; they are the most popular (and sexy) *stars*. The biggest moneymakers of 1972, in this order, were Clint Eastwood, George C. Scott, Gene Hackman, John Wayne, Barbra Streisand, Marlon Brando, Paul Newman, Steve McQueen, Dustin Hoffman, and Goldie Hawn. Only two women. The idea of sexuality—despite today's permissiveness—seems to be less and less related to women. Perhaps men are replacing them as sex objects. Think of the Mark Spitz beefcake poster which is one of the fastest-selling ever. Or those James Dean, Brando, or Bogart posters. Or, even, our adulation for rock singers.

The exorcism of women from major movies has been particularly true since 1960. Recall *Butch Cassidy and the Sundance Kid*, *Lawrence of Arabia*, *Patton*, *Dr. Strangelove*, *The Longest Day*, *Mutiny on the Bounty*, *The Dirty Dozen*, *The Great Escape*, *Grand Prix*, *Becket*, *The Green Berets*, *The Cowboys*, *2001: A Space Odyssey*, *Catch 22*, *The Candidate*, *Tell Them Willie Boy Is Here*, *Marooned*, *Ice Station Zebra*, *Jeremiah Johnson*, *Downhill Racer*, to name a few others. The sixties' woman may have seized on a more productive life-style than ever before, but the industry has turned its back on reflecting it in any constructive or analytical way. How perversely appropriate that violence and sexuality should have converged. For on-screen females are not even necessary; heroes—and apparently the audience—can wax orgasmic without them. It is the cinema of auto-eroticism.

The short-haired conservative idols of Hollywood's golden days have traveled toward self-sufficiency in a womanless celluloid world. The strong silent hero may look all-male, but exercising his virility in violent heroics leaves him no time or patience for the opposite sex. In his self-satisfied Homeric world, as lethal and clinical in its violence as yawning pornography is in recording "sex," how far is he indeed from the homosexual? The sexless? Both and neither, all and none. Saturation. Immediate gratification. No gratification. Unisex. Androgyny.

Who would have dreamed the New Hero would find commonality with our androgynous superstar? That John Wayne would approach Mick Jagger?

Pop culture's calling card seems to be the decadence of a new

generation of grotesques. The music business is thriving on hermaph-
roditic images—Jagger, David Bowie, Alice Cooper, The Dolls, The
Cockettes, and Lou Reed, all funky rock heroes of either unisexual or
effeminate stance.

"One of the prime functions of popular favorites," commented
sociologist Orrin Klapp in Alvin Toffler's book *Future Shock*, "is to
make types visible, which in turn make new life styles and new tastes
visible."[5] Thus, today's culture absorbs yesterday's prophecy. But to
blame the trend on the counterculture alone, when Hollywood's biggest movie heroes are propagandizing us similarly, if more subtly, is
unfair.

Performance (1970), a disturbing movie, brings the androgynous
counterculture and the violence-oriented mainstream into unique and
thoughtful focus. As Chas, a British gangland thug, rough-up man for
an extortion and porno empire, James Fox is the epitome of the small-
time Establishment. While his Mafia-like boss enjoys sitting in bed and
reading nudie-boy magazines, Fox himself displays so great a penchant for sadism (sexual and otherwise) that he must flee, and disguised, he rents a room from retired rock star Mick Jagger.
Ensconced in a bizarre ménage, Jagger, sexy Anita Pallenberg, and
little French Michele Breton who just happens to resemble a boy with
her short hairstyle and breastless body, happily make love, bathe, and
nibble on hallucinogenic mushrooms. But when Fox is seduced by
the magic food into their sybaritic routine, relationships become more
complex. Jagger and Pallenberg get caught up in the steel-and-lead
excitement of his pistol, and he and Jagger get caught up in each
other's lives.

They are high, but the rondelet is not just sexual; it's a narcissistic
charade, with Fox being transformed into the hippie, and Jagger into
the fifties-style leather boy. Finally, male and female slip in and out of
each other's roles, threatening Fox's conditioning. "Did you ever have
a female feeling," Pallenberg asks, and he insists, like a man running
from the temptation of a double seduction, "No, I'm a *man*. I feel like
a man all the time." "*He's* a man," she explains of Jagger, "a male
and female man." When Fox beds down, the love scene startles—it
looks like Jagger but is boyish Michele. Is she his sublimated desire for
the singer? The confusion increases as identities absorb each other.
At the end Fox is deceived, and when the gang arrives, he puts a
bullet through Jagger's head. Has Jagger informed on him? Is Fox

prompted by the singer's attraction, his willingness to "go away" with him? Does Fox kill that feminine part of himself or simply the person forcing him to confront it? Experiencing with Breton a novel tenderness, he—uncannily resembling Jagger now—exits, and on our last flash of him, inside the racketeers' car, it is literally Jagger. Or is it? The gangster and hippie, the violent and erotic, Establishment and counterculture, macho and androgynous are at last one.

Is *Performance* a portent of things to come? A few years ago *Harper's Bazaar* pulled a picture they were planning to run; it showed two women kissing full on the mouth. Last year two high-fashioned Italian slick magazines, *Linea Italiana* and *Italian Vogue*, included lengthy fashion spreads. In one, men dressed as females modeled haute couture apparel; in the other, mannish mannequins draped in elegant gowns carried whips and devastatingly entombed expressions. Today American kids paint their nails black and emulate Alice Cooper. Orgies and wife swapping, nude therapy and touch therapy alleviate middle-class boredom. Why not androgyny? No sex. Omnisex.

In 1967 Roger Vadim gave us *Barbarella*, a pop satire based on the futuristic Italian comic strip. Jane Fonda's space-age heroine, when forced to make love "the old-fashioned way," by coupling, explained that earthlings, finding it too distracting, had developed scientific sexuality: Partners swallow a pill and hold hands until their exaltations are in perfect complement. A few jolts, curling hair, and smoke—"the essence of man"—make the event very neat, programmed, and passionless. But any more passionless than *Dirty Harry* or *Deep Throat*?

Any more clinical?

If the sexual cornucopia released in the sixties has truly contributed to our alienation and impotence, if our emotions live in vacuums and our libidos can only be resuscitated through violence, pornography, or freaky sex, what's left?

Is there any hope for intimacy in movies? In life?

23

CHANGING—
breakthrough or backlash?

"We're being made to look like Lolitas and lion tamers,"[1] wailed historian Barbara Tuchman in the mid-sixties. The truth below the surface of that remark was that while society emphatically changed its orientation toward single women, youth, and sex roles, nobody cared about America's wives and mothers or females over thirty. Too many dizzying and sensational trends were shaping the times for attention to be paid; how nice to think that in the midst of upheaval, the family unit would remain stable.

But "stable" did not mean "happy." And "unhappy" homemakers got to thinking. Everybody was "doing his own thing." The press was full of suggestions for "getting it together." But what? Certainly that didn't refer to the little lady who cut up green apples for pie or stuck a daisy in the toilet tank. She was *already* doing her thing.

And although the divorce rates kept rising and the number of females seeking psychiatric treatment and institutional help dwarfed that of men (whereas in 1943 the balance was different, with 68,549 men and 49,853 women admitted to institutions), the nation was too caught up in flamboyance to worry that the harping discontent of drab Mrs. America meant "her thing" was not enough.

And movies? Hollywood's female audiences had defected to the TV habit and were now tuning in and out of the droning humdrum homilies of the afternoon soaps. Little on-screen related to them, and if *Auntie Mame*, *Pillow Talk*, and *Imitation of Life* lured over-forty America back to the theater, it was for pure escapism. Nice, wasn't it, to see Rosalind Russell, middle-aged and down on her luck, fortuitously finding a genteel Southerner to lift her from the ranks of Macy's saleswomen? Doris, verging on middle age also, but chipper and flirtatious? Or Lana, a veritable institution, being romanced by a man youthful enough to attract her teen-age daughter?

But the dearth of movies for mature women was also related, no doubt, to the growing disdain we were nursing for Mom and marriage. Momism, the monkey Philip Wylie had attached to the well-coiffed, idle female's nape with his 1942 novel *Generation of Vipers*—a well-timed but persistent comic myth of speciousness, stupidity, and bossiness—was viciously regenerating: In movies she was embodied by the malevolent, controlling, fascistic mother and wife, Angela Lansbury, in *The Manchurian Candidate* (1962). Selfish and irritable Shelley Winters, responsible for causing daughter Elizabeth Hartman's blindness in *A Patch of Blue* (1965); Shelley, again a whining windbag in *Wild in the Streets* (1970). Ruth Gordon protecting sonny boy from Tuesday Weld in *Lord Love a Duck* (1966), grandiosely observing, "In our family we don't divorce our men—we bury them." Bette Davis as Mum in *The Anniversary* (1968) verbally dueling with her cheeky son's fiancée for the boy's obedience, trying to hammer him into a docile robot like his two brothers—one a married clod, the other a perverse retard who fondles ladies' underwear stolen from neighboring clotheslines. Philip Roth's archetypal Mrs. Portnoy was not the first, you see; *she* simply bore the most active son.

Smother love, the most common interpretation of Momism, may, however, have been a natural consequence for women with time on their hands, smaller families, and no life of their own. But in the sixties with kids assuming independence so much earlier, the needs of young and old clashed. Household gadgetry, in addition, endowed women with large expanses of free time. But what to do with it? Something was wrong. Yet to question the foundation of one's own past, a life already lived, was painful.

Fortunately, if subtly, the groundwork for augmenting feminine options and life-styles was being set down. In December, 1961, President Kennedy signed an executive order establishing the President's Commission on the Status of Women. For the first time in history, the economic and social position of American woman would be formally studied, with recommendations made toward alleviating those prejudices, customs, and habits acting "as barriers to the full realization of women's basic rights."

Coinciding with the publication of the commission's findings was the arrival of Betty Friedan's incendiary and brilliant *The Feminine Mystique*, which so eloquently explored the dissatisfactions of American women. Wrote Friedan in 1963: "We can no longer ignore that voice within women that says: 'I want something more than my husband and my children and my home.' "² For, ideally, "in the end, a woman, as a man, has the power to choose and to make her own heaven or hell."³

Rather than explore beneath the surface of confusion, movies skimmed along the sleek edges of the problem. Feminine discontent was absorbed as marital morass. And that, even, was through no keen Hollywood observation, but a product of the never-fail studio barometer, the box office, provoked by the overwhelming success of a wickedly uproarious Italian satire, Pietro Germi's *Divorce Italian Style* (1962). Here the only way unhappy husband Marcello Mastroianni can honorably extricate himself from marriage is to find his (mustachioed) wife in a love nest and kill her—a crime of passion for which he's acquitted. The movie's devilishness, more cynically definitive but less pointed in exposition than Columbia's early-fifties comedies starring Judy Holliday (*Pffft*, *The Marrying Kind*), rang a bell in America and spurred a number of tepid divorce romps. *Marriage on the Rocks* (1965) starred Deborah Kerr as an overlooked wife who wins a Mexican divorce and ex-husband Frank Sinatra's best friend; once their wedding nears, Frank's indifference vanishes, and he determines to win back his prize. With slight variations, that was the benign formula for *Mary, Mary* (1963) and *Divorce American Style* (1967), both starring Debbie Reynolds in rare "adult" ventures, and even for those Walter-Mitty let's-have-an-affair films like *The Secret Life of an American Wife* (1968) and *A Guide for the Married Man* (1967). While indicating that people were mulling over the concept of fidelity, these movies all safely returned the distracted mates to their spouses after suitable interludes.

How properly ironic that it fell to Elizabeth Taylor—viewed unjustly as the Circe of the sixties—to tackle those needy-wife roles in modern marital exercises. For all the melodrama and gaudy hypertension into which Liz's career has deteriorated, she almost singlehandedly gave us a body of films in which her characters—beneath the glittering layers of Hollywoodiana and occasionally incoherent scripts—questioned their relationships and externalized their emptiness. *The VIPs* (1963), for example, verbalizes how ephemeral and unsatisfactory are the *whys* of love, how needy couples are, and how insensitive to each other. The plot is simple: Elizabeth Taylor is deserting her disinterested millionaire husband, Richard Burton, for penniless charmer Louis Jourdan, but fog has delayed their plane overnight—long enough for Burton, roused from his lethargy, to make a final bid for reconciliation. But it is the trio's declarations of attitudes which tell the most. Jourdan reveals to Burton why Liz is leaving him ("She'd rather have had the odd toy duck from Woolworth's providing she knew you'd chosen it yourself"), but he too is limited in his appreciation of her: "I love you because you're the most beautiful and desirable woman I've ever met in my life," he whispers, "because you have eyes like diamonds . . . I love you as you look, as you look now at this moment." Considerably chilled, she perceives that Jourdan regards her as a bauble, just as her husband has. "I'm not yours just as I'm not his. Love me, *need* me, but as a person, not as a possession," she cries. Since Burton needs her more, she returns to him.

Smacking of old-fashioned neurotic sentiment, this is an excellent equation of early-sixties' notions: Sacrifice = Happiness. Love = Need. The heroine's real tragedy is in the sorry little *she* asks of her men—not sharing, not laughing together, not caring—while at a point of great personal pain and reevaluation herself. "Need" nevertheless satisfies all concerned, and although a private-duty nurse might have remedied the situation with equal aplomb, it appears to be the movies' definition of a workable relationship.

Who's Afraid of Virginia Woolf? (1966) deals with a more specific kind of need, the twisted saprophytic kind that welds Liz's Martha and Burton's George—he a college professor and she the president's daughter—together from the first clawing humiliation and devastating insult to the last. The way *Woolf*'s author Edward Albee tells it, it is the woman's need to devour and her man's to be gobbled up. And Liz, wielding savageries as if they were blades, is not alone in her manipulation; Sandy Dennis, the pallid, pregnant "guest," gets mileage from a different pose—this helpless "bunny" whines, cries, feigns sickness, feigns pregnancy and frailty. Her husband, George Segal, like Burton, is allegedly the victim. But is one victimized if he *consciously* forfeits control? Control inherent in his knowledge of his wife's "tricks," her own vulnerability, and the truth of their relationship?

Says Liz, after polishing off her mate (verbally) and then guest

Segal (sexually): "I am the earth mother and you are all flops . . . you know, there's always been only one man in my life who can make me happy—George—who can keep learning the games as quick as I can make them up . . . who has made the hideously hurting insulting mistake of loving me. I must be punished for it." Albee opens up raw territory here, examining the idea of self-loathing and contempt as the source of Liz-Martha's grotesqueness. Yet so busy is he pouring vitriol all over his bogeywomen that he doesn't probe deeper into the real human dilemma. He is not genuinely concerned with these females: Why did they marry their mates? What were their backgrounds? Since women are prime movers of torture and dissonance, we can only wonder about their exuberant, unharnessed energies—and observe how sad it is that these should be expended in frustration alone.

While *Virginia Woolf* slammed its females the hardest, its intent was more general. Martha and George fight boredom with games; they fight emptiness by inventing a child to love; they communicate only with knifelike parries, drawing from self-hatred the blood of humiliation—and, finally, a drop of tenderness. Albee held this distorted mirror up to audiences who responded—outraged, shocked, yet touched by the anguish and desperation no Debbie Reynolds or Deborah Kerr divorce farce could evoke. The desperation neither Hollywood nor many of us wanted to examine.

Usually the success of one film sparks several imitations, and perhaps the industry might have continued its probe into the heart of relationships had not the youth film genre begun to prove so lucrative. Liz, too, got sidetracked. She became Mrs. Burton during the filming of *Virginia Woolf* and repeatedly proclaimed that making movies was secondary to family life. Judging by her output, she was a woman of her word, and interesting performances in *The Taming of the Shrew* and *Reflections in a Golden Eye* have been overshadowed by such weak vehicles as *Secret Ceremony, Boom!, The Only Game in Town, Hammersmith Is Out,* and *X, Y, and Zee.* Before filing divorce papers in the summer of 1973, Liz admitted that she knowingly rejected good scripts that would separate her and her husband for long periods of time. She also priced herself out of more adventurous independent projects; for some reason, her most recent movies resemble leftovers from the old MGM script department.

What's worse is the persistent impression of antiquation. Those *grande dame*-gestures, highly volatile emotions, and outmoded styles, recalling the obvious embarrassment of Jennifer Jones' Pearl in *Duel in the Sun*, suggest that directors and clothing designers are too intimidated by her legend to offer restraints. But who will curb her heavy style, the flounces and ponchos and golden caftans, the gobs of ornate jewelry? Today urban audiences cluck at the unwitting camp she has become, sensing Liz has lost herself to her *Cleopatra* eyes and *Virginia Woolf* fury. Obviously choosing the comfortable role and costume, she has voluntarily exiled herself from the relevancies of modern life.

Culture shock, caused by the mid-sixties' affinity for youth, hastened the virtual retirements of Doris Day, Debbie Reynolds, Audrey Hepburn, Sandra Dee, and Natalie Wood; one star, however, thrived on it —Julie Andrews. During those first turbulent years of change, 1965 through 1968, Andrews carried on a love affair with conservative America, as if to assure moviegoers that virtue and happy endings still existed, that the hills were indeed alive with the sound of music —not rock music, either. She was the screen's reigning female star then and in 1966 and 1967 the top box-office draw of the year, thanks especially to *Mary Poppins*, *The Sound of Music*, and *Thoroughly Modern Millie*, whose receipts proved that the public longed for magic and traditional "entertainment." In those days the audiences paid for distraction—colorful comedies and James Bond thrillers—as if "relevant" movies might overload and sabotage their digestive processes.

But a steady diet of sweets sickens. By 1968 disenchantment was pushing delight aside, and with *Star!*, a soggy musical biography of Gertrude Lawrence, Twentieth Century-Fox had a gigantic bomb on its hands. Andrews was trying to "modernize" without giving up that surefire bigpic musical formula. As Gertie, she was hardly "sweet," in fact most of her performance was quite good, but here was Hollywood's lark all grown-up and crotchety and dramatic, yet so weighed down by the lugubrious structure of the movie that her impact was lost. *Star*'s run was diastrous, and it was later released, briefly, under another title to try to recoup losses.

Still, Julie Andrews was not able to renounce the kind of movie that had won her fame. *Darling Lili* (1969), about a World War I Mata-Hari-type in love with the officer from whom she is extracting information, was related more in ambiance to *Chitty Chitty Bang Bang* than to any similarly plotted Garbo or Dietrich vehicle. Some of

Darling Lili amused tremendously, but it suffered from frosted-confection glitter, as if Mary Poppins had been parachuted over the Meuse-Argonne. Again the pace was snail-slow, the costumes and sets were artificial, with a few musical numbers thrown in to show off the bell-pure Andrews voice. And for the sake of modernity, in a year when *Easy Rider, I Am Curious (Yellow)*, and *The Damned* arrived on-screen, there was a slapstick bedroom scene followed by that wonderful moment when Rock Hudson, barging in on Andrews in the shower, accuses her of being a virgin. Insulted, she slugs him—and we know that times have *really* changed!

As an actress, though, Andrews is much more complicated than her typical vehicles suggest. That Victorian cleanliness which makes her appear wooden in already-wooden roles (*Poppins, Lili*), is but a hairbreadth away from a certain unique character strength. For in *The Americanization of Emily* and especially in the early music-hall sequences of *Star!* we are allowed to peek beneath the proper British nanny exterior to a salty, raucous, and independent dame who—cast against type—might be interesting in the sophisticated, subtle roles which Vanessa Redgrave and Glenda Jackson are monopolizing right now.

Although Barbra Streisand replaced Andrews as movies' Spectacular Nightingale (*Funny Girl, Hello, Dolly!* and *On a Clear Day You Can See Forever*), the increasing importance of European actresses in the sixties—not just Englishwomen Redgrave, Jackson, and Christie, but also others like Catherine Deneuve, Jeanne Moreau, Liv Ullmann, Bibi Andersson, and Anna Karina—corresponded with the general obsolescence of the American star system. While Hollywood was producing extravagant epics, reluctant to gamble on fresh talent or ideas, foreign directors such as Fellini, Antonioni, Godard, Truffaut, Bergman were sending us movies both visually and thematically innovative. Working with modest budgets and outside bureaucratic hierarchies, these men explored political and personal relationships and re-created the private fantasies and philosophies most fascinating to them. In 1962 European films satisfied the market that Hollywood with its penchant for multimillion-dollar musicals was abdicating. Out of 798 pictures licensed by New York that year, 582 were from abroad. Europe's vision of woman was therefore bound to affect America's.

For instance, before Simone Signoret in *Room at the Top*, what

American studio chief would have imagined that a woman could be middle-aged, plump, and also sexy? Before Jeanne Moreau, the idea of a sex symbol with small bosom and the experience of years written into her irregular features was unique. Think, too, of the striking individuality of Anouk Aimée, Monica Vitti, Giulietta Masina. Hardly "star types," yet womanly in their luminous and unique personalities.

Why, generally, do European actresses present multiple-dimensioned personalities while our American stars flatten out like uncorrugated cardboard? Isn't American society more flexible in allowing women alternates to traditional role playing and life-styles? How does one account for discrepancies in cultural associations, myths, and movie images? Americans don't polarize their women as either madonnas or whores as, one suspects, some Latin cultures do. We do worse: In our exuberant lack of introspection, we caricature screen heroines. With the exception of Teresa Wright, Joanne Woodward, Anne Bancroft, and a few other actresses of magnificent nuance, we categorize. We overplay. Overdress. A floozy dress or tight pants tell the whole story. Or a platinum wig. Or spectacles, or cleavage. Our women slide into easy character niches (tomboy Debbie, volatile Liz, kooky Liza).

But European moviemakers don't give us such easy signals—and in analyzing their films, current jargon like "aggressive" or "fulfilled" or "object" or "possession" or "bitch" is less useful, because in the course of the films their women often reveal themselves as rich, complex human beings, combining all those elements unpredictably. Catherine Deneuve in Buñuel's *Belle de Jour* is not *just* an impassive bourgeois housewife, looking like Madonna incarnate; she's a woman burning with a shameless willingness to act out her lewdest fantasies. Audiences see a range of emotions, not histrionics; they are party to her fantasies and fears and desires. Nothing stagnates, and no one is readable at a glance. Yet movies such as these compel us by expanding and sharing their females' complex identities, rather than limiting them.

A prime example of the difference between American and European attitudes toward leading ladies is Sopia Loren's career. Loren, had she not returned to Italy for de Sica's adaptation of the Alberto Moravia novel *Two Women* in 1961, might still be wandering about in the tattered peasant blouses that were her blazon in *Boy on a Dolphin* (1957), *Desire Under the Elms* (1958), and *El Cid* (1961). Even after winning both American and British Academy Awards for *Two Women*, her portrayal of a mother who finds refuge with her daughter in a small town and is raped by marauding Moroccan soldiers, she worked in some atrocious English-language movies—like *The Condemned of Altona*, *The Fall of the Roman Empire*, *Operation Crossbow*, *Judith*, *Lady L*, and *A Countess from Hong Kong*. Yet the full range of her talent was to reveal itself in European-made *Boccaccio 70*, *Yesterday, Today and Tomorrow*, *Marriage Italian Style*, *Sunflower*, *The Priest's Wife*, and recently *White Sister*, all of which display not just her tempestuous surface, but her polish and warmth as a comedienne.

It is interesting that only in Italy, a devoutly Catholic country where a sea of piety traditionally divides women into the chaste and the soiled did Sophia find directors who could work successfully *against* such stereotypes. It is interesting that such a narrow and repressive atmosphere could also produce an iconoclast of mischief and humor who would so sweepingly shock the cinema and American audiences out of their tight little moral preoccupations—and *that* without really elevating his own feminine ideals beyond the madonna/whore schism. Federico Fellini.

Of his impact, director George Cukor noted: ". . . after seeing Fellini's *Satyricon*, there's only one way I can think of ancient Rome. . . . So all these things accumulate and other people's visions become a part of you."[4] Similarly, Fellini's women have stamped their presence on us, whether we have been audiences at first-run movie houses or seen *La Dolce Vita* or *La Strada* in their repeated television showings and despite the fact that his world is one of male supremacy. For his females are as extreme as his visions. Fellini's alternative to purity is decadence. He may sympathetically linger over the innocent Gelsomina in *La Strada* (1954), but she, like the poor little matchgirl, is a storybook creature who cowers idiotically in the face of Anthony Quinn's brute strength; as an adult, her etherealism is more freakish than decadent. What hope is there either for the smiling, open teen-age girl in *La Dolce Vita* (1959) when the women in the film—Anita Ekberg reeling around the fountain, Nadia Grey stripping (though others at the orgy, disinterested, barely notice)—devour their men like hungry jackals? Marcello in *8½* (1963) can't even recall his own sexual initiation without conjuring up the obese and greasy prostitute Serafina to dirty the memory.

With *Juliet of the Spirits* (1965) Fellini, however, turned his full attention to his female character (then afterward in *Satyricon*, 1970; *Clowns*, 1971; and *Roma*, 1972, he significantly exorcised her from his celluloid vision). Here the artifice of his dreamworld becomes the artifice of magic, of disguise, by which his females survive. "Put on a little makeup, at least wear some lipstick," her husband tells plain timid heroine Giulietta (Giulietta Masina, Fellini's off-screen wife). Her maid chimes in, "For me, when a man says something is so, then it's got to be so." Even her therapist accuses her of wanting to lose her already-unfaithful husband, of being afraid of happiness. Though fascinated by the wigs she sets and the fanciful sexual female creatures she befriends, she's reluctant to relinquish the slim thread of her own identity; she, the lone "natural" woman, in contemplating suicide communicates with the wind. Is that the only fresh breeze in a suffocating world of garish man-eating females? Does death alone safeguard innocence?

For Fellini, the middle ground between fleshy excess and ascetic, spiritual denial is barren. So extravagantly does he dichotomize that his women wear badly, like last year's tinsel. Still, as Cukor pointed out, such vivid impressions stay with us as recurring nightmares long after the movies themselves have left the circuits. Also Fellini almost single-handedly made "orgy" a household word among moviemakers; sexual decadence and the obligatory bacchanalia (replacing the obligatory bedroom scene) are to this day popping up with new combinations and vigor (from the lusty dinner-table seduction in *Tom Jones* to *Darling, Accident, Blow-Up, The Damned*). Because of him, decadent promiscuity is chic, mainly because his females, for all their limitations, were so unabashedly, vulgarly extreme that they freed our sex-oriented industry from an almost-prurient sterility.

Fortunately, other directors working out their personal statements gave us females who were unique to our own image of ourselves and not quite as carnal. One of the most attractive aspects of the European heroine was that she was a woman, not a little girl. She could be desirable *and* intelligent, mysterious *and* direct. In these respects, Jeanne Moreau was one of the happiest things to happen to the American woman in the sixties. And François Truffaut's *Jules et Jim* (1962) was the exquisite melding of director, movie, star, and persona.

Essentially the story of *Jules et Jim* is simple: Two bohemian friends in pre-World War I Paris meet Catherine (Moreau), the haunting Everywoman of their dreams who gives their lives new vitality and magic. She marries Jules, the more placid of the two but, restless, bored, and unchallenged, soon turns to Jim. Possessing Jim is difficult, though. Willful, unable to control him, she inflicts her will one last time and drives off a bridge, killing them both.

If this recalls Bette Davis' *In This Our Life* (1942) or dozens of other Hollywood movies, so it was meant. Truffaut, like Godard and other French "New Wave" directors, studied and borrowed from Hollywood of the thirties and forties, from gangster movies and the works of Hitchcock. And if Moreau brings to mind the Garbo-Dietrich Everywoman, so, too, was this intended. Just as buffs have idealized Garbo as the Sphinx or Dietrich as the Mona Lisa, Truffaut introduces Catherine first as a primitive stone head, a piece of statuary. "It was a woman's face with a haunting smile," and both Jules and Jim are obsessed in their search for a real-life counterpart. Catherine "surpassed their hopes. They were struck dumb." But Truffaut will not surrender to the obvious clichés. He fills out his characters and narrative with unsentimental tenderness—and plays subtly against the passive enigma of Everywoman. Catherine is the genesis of the twentieth-century liberated woman, fiercely competitive, yet impish—she dons knickers and paints on a mustache so that as Thomas she can "have a good time" with Jules and Jim. Typically, in the rush of the freedom on which she insists, she limits and misuses it. Her irresistibility guarantees a certain power of choice; she can seesaw between husband Jules and friend Jim simply because Jules fears that in being possessive he will lose her. Yet Catherine has not cultivated the depth with which to absorb and be pleasured by experience. Nor can she accept the solid, steady joys of a husband and child. With time, her restlessness deteriorates into fierce, crazy impatience and insane ego.

Here too, Moreau's Catherine resembles the egocentric Bette Davis neurotic of the thirties, but it is again only a skeletal correspondence. For Truffaut is compassionate and romantic toward his heroine. She is a positive life-force, misused; a ravishing mystery who in revealing herself to us unravels herself, who in opening up for her men cuts herself off from caring. Davis, in similar roles, never changed pitch. Her insanity was one-dimensional, demanding and strident rather than exquisite, malignant rather than desperate, opaque rather than opalescent.

The range Moreau can suggest in a single performance and the humanity with which she informs even the most uninspired parts (the German prostitute in *The Victors*, 1963; the Western whore in *Monte Walsh*, 1970—both Hollywood "assessments" of what to do with a sensual older woman) has given moviegoers a substantial alternative to the vacant, nubile heroines decorating American pictures during the early and mid-sixties. For many, Moreau will always be Truffaut's Everywoman—and by far the most sophisticated and intriguing of his heroines.

There is a lyricism about Truffaut which reaches a perfect balance with *Jules et Jim*, but which in his later movies, like *Stolen Kisses* (1968), *Bed and Board* (1971), and *Two English Girls* (1972), occasionally deteriorates into soft, grand gesture. The romantic and spiritual rather than sexual nature of his preoccupations emerges refreshingly in most of his movies (one great exception: the bawdy, vicious *Such a Gorgeous Kid Like Me*, 1972), and even in his choice of heroines like Claude Jade and Catherine Deneuve. These are girls more reticent, innocent, and classically perfect-looking than Moreau girls, however, whom he can shower with easy tenderness because they are tender-looking in the first place. Perhaps that is why he and Moreau worked together in more harmonious and mutually expansive combination.

The heroines of Ingmar Bergman are even more thoroughly laid out for us as lab species. Rather than being compassionate the way Truffaut is, Bergman's lens objectively exposes his women—their passions, insanity, ruinous secrets, and worst fears. It is as though, as he unveils them layer by layer with each new film, their humanity astonishes him anew. And it is through his own fascination that this gloomy and thorough scientist somehow draws beauty from the utter fragility of each woman's basic isolation.

Bergman is not an easy director, and his most recent movies, especially, are "fun" in the way that undergoing surgery without anesthesia might be. Television audiences are now able to view his *Sawdust and Tinsel*, *The Seventh Seal*, *The Magician*, *Wild Strawberries*, *The Virgin Spring*, and other early works whose allegorical pageantry and medieval ritual enriched their visual and dramatic elements. But films like *Persona* and *Cries and Whispers* pare down externals and refocus on the human viscera, probing the dynamics of women's relationships with each other as no other director has seemed interested in doing.

Persona (1965), for example, studies two women, one an actress (Liv Ullmann) who has inexplicably gone mute, refusing to utter a word for more than three months; the other, a young nurse, Alma (Bibi Andersson), who takes care of her in the country. Filling up the silences with her own chatter, the nurse careens about nervously, confessionally, adoringly. It is an almost-erotic intimacy in which she suggests that they might exchange places, looking as alike as they do. The actress, at first receptive, is then mocking, manipulative. Those shared silences disintegrate, for she appears afraid of "the hopeless dread of 'being'—not seeming, but being . . . to be seen through; perhaps wiped out." The nurse, under pressure and humiliated by her patient, cracks and seems to be taking on the other's persona—madness.

Cries and Whispers (1972) explores a similar theme. This time the director confines four women in a nineteenth-century manor house; two sisters and a servantwoman wait as the third sister dies an excruciatingly slow death. The death and their confinement act as catalysts to exposing unresolved family entanglements and forcing self-revelations: that the dying spinster has found both sexual and maternal comfort in the servant (Cari Sylwan), who has more love to give than either blood sibling. That the repressed older sister Karin (Ingrid Thulin) sufficiently loathes her husband and sex to slash her genitals with broken glass, punishing him—and herself. That she also loathes her voluptuous, sly younger sister Maria (Liv Ullmann) precisely because the girl is sexual, sexual even toward her. Yet Maria merely baits Karin with "false promises and wet smiles" just as she baits everyone else. For Karin, incestuous intimacy, held in abeyance, frightens most because she desires it most. "You touched me, don't you remember?" she pleads to an indifferent Maria as they, with their husbands, leave the empty house.

Bergman, again with objectivity rather than compassion, is drawing a maze of relationships. Between the dying Harriet Andersson and a memory of a neglectful mother, between sisters, between wives and husbands. Closeness seems impossible; even among kin, rivalry and sex impede truth. The servant and the dying woman, we feel, have shared more than the other two can ever hope for. As in *Persona*, electricity charges any attempt at spiritual closeness. The actress in

Persona and Maria in *Cries and Whispers* (both played by Ullmann) exist as the same type of manipulative, teasing woman—begging for another to open up (the actress through silence, Maria vocally), and later—after evoking a confession, realization, or emotions from the other—withdrawing. When the parties separate into their own worlds, it will be the Almas and the Karins who are permanently scarred by the confrontation, but are the Marias of the world affected at all?

Is Bergman, by heightening the eroticism of his all-women films, forcing us to confront a condition of human closeness which we refuse to acknowledge—that one must accept physical intimacy before one can hope for true spiritual communion? Maybe desire is simply an easy, distracting way to fill the voids of ourselves, to make us *feel* as if we're close without actually *being* so. Or is his preoccupation less philosophical and more human; as with other men, does the imposition of such "Sapphic" conditions simply supply titillation in otherwise-stark pictures? Bergman's terrain is almost-virgin territory, for few have tried to get so close to women before; not even women have thought until recently to evaluate or cherish female friendships. Bergman may or may not reveal us to ourselves, but at least he invites us to think.

Even the director's repertoire of actresses is unique to movies. Ingrid Thulin, Harriet Andersson, Bibi Andersson, Liv Ullmann are an austere and solid group, without cajolery or coquettishness, rather like the women who pioneered in the American West. Their perceptions, conversations, and gestures indicate an intelligence with which Hollywood has always been impatient. For introspection, without snappy wit or glibness, leans heavily on our concepts of "entertainment" and also of femininity. It's an anti-box-office intellect, and these are anti-box-office women. They care nothing for St. Laurent clothes or wood-paneled dishwashers but take themselves and the quality of their lives seriously.

And American audiences respond enough to their intensity for the industry to import stars of the caliber of Liv Ullmann or Jeanne Moreau. But then, ambivalently, Hollywood imprisons them in sleazy formula pictures such as *40 Carats* or *Monte Walsh*, hoping like hell that the Bergman or Truffaut personae will leak a bit of class into common efforts.

Yet if Hollywood has scarcely thought to take its heroines seriously in the past, consider that until recently women did not take *them-*

selves seriously either. Since the formation of the National Organization for Women (NOW) in 1966, however, women not only are learning, but insisting that others learn too. Unfortunately, pressuring the Supreme Court to legalize abortions was probably far simpler than convincing moviemakers to risk the profits violent Clint Eastwood Westerns like *High Plains Drifter* can assure them.

But women may take comfort, for every dozen or two womanless or woman-humiliating movies, there are one or two deserving portraits. How many "blaxploitation" pictures came and went before two noteworthy films—Diana Ross' lovely and agonizing portrait of Billie Holiday in *Lady Sings the Blues* (1972) and Cicely Tyson's watchful, proud, and loving mother in *Sounder* (1972)—finally gave women, black women in particular, lyrical and sensitive roles? Women may have to endure more Eastwood macho and Goldie Hawn giggles and old-timers' nostalgia (like Maggie Smith's "eccentricity" in 1969's *The Prime of Miss Jean Brodie* and her even more mannered artificiality in 1972's *Travels with My Aunt*) before anything of consequence turns up.

And women may have to survive more well-meaning failures like *T. R. Baskin* (1971), which documented the loneliness of a single girl in Chicago, but failed because Candy Bergen's heroine was too pretty for us to believe in her man troubles, too vapid for us to care about her alienation, and also because the scriptwriters wrote as if they'd never encountered, let alone talked to, an unmarried woman.

Or *Up the Sandbox* (1973), in which Barbra Streisand is sometimes quite funny and real as a harried New York City mother with radical fantasies and lots of timely complaints about diapers and stifled potential. But she does an uncharacteristic about-face in the final minute of the movie and decides abruptly, joyously, to tie herself down with a third baby. Why? Who knows? Even so, the actress herself has never been more interesting, suggesting that she and modern "small" roles were made for each other.

Diary of a Mad Housewife (1970), based on the successful Sue Kauffman novel and with a marvelously broad script by Eleanor Perry, one of the few women and finest screenwriters in the industry today, approach a similar situation from another angle. This time the heroine could bring herself to have an affair but not to leave her whining boor of an Ivy League husband. *Diary of a Mad Housewife* might be criticized, justly, as too caricaturish. Yet those images—as with Fellini's—are unforgettable. Who can miss the recognition of husband Richard Benjamin's clumsy romanceless seduction: "How's about a little ole roll in da hay?" Or the horror as he, propped up in his sickbed, wheezes: "Tee-een! Where's my lemonade!" Still, Frank Perry's genial direction belies the anger and frustration written into the script.

Movies like these create a tension of awareness, but they need not be patronizing toward men in order to depict heroines worth watching. Or learning from. In *Rachel, Rachel* (1968) Joanne Woodward compassionately depicted the lonely and aching interiors of a prim spinster teacher who, at thirty-five, experiences sex for the first time. Shirley MacLaine, now a novice politician and an author, has in three recent films portrayed widely different characters, yet none of them were weak or stupid. In the Western *Two Mules for Sister Sara* (1969) she's a prostitute who, disguised as a nun, saves loner Clint Eastwood's life. In *The Bliss of Mrs. Blossom* (1968) she nicely juggles, yes, manipulates, a stuffy, well-providing husband and a lover who settles in her attic for four years, romancing her by day; ultimately Mr. B discovers the situation, and when he does, the two men exchange places. Finally in *Desperate Characters* (1971), the most severe and uncompromising of the three films, she enacts a wife so anesthetized by her routine marriage that she cannot even respond to a lover or bring herself to break away. Like *Housewife*, *Desperate Characters* is deadly in its anger, but flawed in that its aimless neorealism bored audiences, as well as her.

Yet movies needn't be tedious either to give us women either aware in their joy of life or struggling to reconcile or divest themselves of pain. It is the truth of their position and the degree of their intelligence that is most affecting. Think of *Klute* (1971), specifically successful because of Jane Fonda's gritty and needy call girl, Bree, who through analysis and a tentative, yet touching relationship with a cop develops the strength to begin a straight life. In Peter Bogdanovich's *The Last Picture Show*, (1971), Ellen Burstyn is attractive as a cynical mother dispelling her daughter's romantic notions with bitter, realistic advice that the girl sleep around rather than marry a boy with no future. Astonishingly sympathetic to its females, *The Last Picture Show* also confronts with Cloris Leachman a situation few films have cared to deal with so sensitively—that of a closed-up middle-aged wife, old before her time, who seduces a high school boy. Clutching at their pathetic romance, she blooms and then, humiliated when he turns to a girl his age, grasps fruitlessly, childishly, like a wronged debutante.

Perhaps the most gloriously intelligent film of the past few years, *Sunday Bloody Sunday* (1971)—with a finely crafted script by Penelope Gilliatt and direction by John Schlesinger—articulates in stark unsentimental terms the dilemma of the New Woman. Here she's Glenda Jackson, strong and introspective, solid and brooding in the way that Bergman's heroines are. Not the nubile teenybopper flying from bed to bed. Not the receptionist with a "glamor" job in a "blue chip company" as the ads tell us. And not young and unused and optimistic. Jackson's heroine has a solid, responsible but dull job in an employment firm; she lives alone in an untidy flat and has annoying, ghastly parents. She's also in love and sharing a younger bisexual artist with a conservative middle-aged doctor. But the relationship, while assuaging her emptiness, is painful and abysmally compromising. After careful thought, Jackson breaks it off. "I used to believe that anything was better than nothing," she tells him sadly. "Now I know that sometimes nothing is better." Even if it means more loneliness, perhaps permanent loneliness, Jackson is embodying not a mythic vision of courage, but the kind of small but hurting bravery today's divorced, widowed, or single women must face in day-to-day living. Their choices, like hers, are not romantic, for sustained romance implies artifice. They are instead practical, ensuring integrity and, more important, survival.

Does this sound like a bleak future? Have women, in fighting for liberation—that is, equality, choice, and opportunity—brought about their own isolation? Or is the isolation a result of adjusting endless years of movie sunsets and promised kisses to the uncertainties and alienation of existence? *Sunday Bloody Sunday* probes modern life; it does not present it as an ideal. Movies have not as yet been able to construct an ideal which is possible and which assimilates the realities of *today's* world. Even now, after exhausting changes in society—and a few in films—to predict that sexism is on its way out seems fanciful. To state unequivocally that the Women's Movement has implanted itself in the soul of America is wishful.

Will there ever be a day when Hollywood cannot even conjure up the image of a *Soylent Green* (1973) with its futuristic fantasy—apartments with built-in girls as furniture? The unevenness of the infrequent films dealing with mature women reflects the industry's ambivalence about female freedom, but even more, one suspects, it reflects ignorance. What the hell is a liberated, fulfilled human being? It's easy to construct her in parts, to say what she isn't. To feel embarrassment that Goldie Hawn, a pleasant, big-eyed bit of fluff, is on the top ten box-office list while actresses like Faye Dunaway, Dyan Cannon, Brenda Vaccaro, and Joan Hackett are either too long absent from the screen or mismanaged and stereotyped. While Glenda Jackson wins an Academy Award one year and then returns to second-rate costume epics such as *Lord Nelson* the next. How can movies, sometimes our "art," always our most potent popular culture inspiration, help us find the answers?

If we boycott films and turn to television, we lose. Television, the easy anesthetizer, has long held captive onetime movie fans. Today only 18,000,000 to 20,000,000 people attend the movies each week, whereas talk shows create overnight celebrities; the slang of an Archie Bunker or Maude revolutionizes patterns of speech and modes of viewing the world. But "family audiences," sponsors, and programming "in the public interest" limit material. More important television lacks larger-than-life size, heightened colors, and unbroken concentration—all seductive properties of movies' special transporting power. Of their sheer impact.

What about the studios? Paramount, Columbia, Warner's, United Artists, and Twentieth are no deafer now than they were in their heyday, but the sound of gold in the cash drawers perks up ears faster than reams and years of proselytizing or any burning sense of responsibility. Is it a dream to presume that women could be delivered from the lethargy of television back to movies? Perhaps. But the pictures must exist, and women must know about them—which means a comfortable advertising budget and a neighborhood run lasting longer than two blinks of an eye.

The directors? One might hope that the new breed might be sensitive to the times. But biggies like William Friedkin (whose virtuoso promise with *The Night They Raided Minsky's*, *The Birthday Party* and *The Boys in the Band* has been set aside for such flash pieces as *The French Connection*) and Don (*Dirty Harry*) Siegal are too busy turning violence into money. Francis Ford Coppola admitted that "I think in the best sense I try to have a female sensibility, a gentleness," and spoke recently of his desire to make an erotic film *for* women, utilizing sensual sound stimuli. His provocative 1969 study of a fed-up runaway wife, *The Rain People*, and his soft tread in extracting sentiment from Mafia matters in *The Godfather* (1972) indicates that he might well succeed; but Coppola is now directing his attentions to *The Godfather*'s sequel. Peter Bogdanovich, when asked whether he had consciously fashioned his complicated and moving females in *The Last Picture Show* out of any awareness of feminist issues, replied with the yawn of a man who had indeed spoken intimately with Welles and Ford, "The whole subject bores me." One might assume from this that *Picture Show* was his finest hour, but in 1973 *Paper Moon*'s unabashed affection for nine-year-old heroine Addie (Tatum O'Neal) suggests that Bogdanovitch is either more thoughtful than he lets on or just lucky.

Do women wait for a floundering industry to come around to them, or can they find salvation with female directors? More precisely, can they find female directors at all? Yes, but most are working in television documentaries because financing women is considered a high risk situation. Barbara Loden's *Wanda*, about a pathetic simpleton of a wife who runs off with a petty criminal, was an excellent first effort which received fine reviews and a decent New York run. Still, Loden had difficulty backing her next project. Similar obstacles have hindered the work of Mary Ellen Bute (*Passages from Finnegans Wake*), and Shirley Clarke (*The Cool World*, *The Connection*) has simply given up the hassle and redirected herself, despite brilliant and innovative talent, to the expediencies of videotape.

In fact, Elaine May is the only female director working on a regular basis today, but judging by *A New Leaf* (1970) and *The Heartbreak Kid* (1972), she is like an Uncle Tom whose feminine sensibilities are demonstrably nil. May enjoys broad caricatures, especially of her women characters, and there's something self-serving and snide about them. Their menacing "satire" recalls *The Women*, but Clare Boothe Luce's play, for better or worse, was written forty years ago; May works in the present. In *A New Leaf*, she directs herself as the classic drippy spinster, a weirdo rich botanist named Henrietta transformed into awkward loveliness by a money-hungry dilettante. *The Heartbreak Kid* is even more discomforting, exhuming fifties' stereotypes: the sloppy lower-class bride (Jeannie Berlin, May's real-life daughter); the shrewd loudmouthed groom (Charles Grodin), who is marrying about half a notch down, and the Sunshine WASP (Cybill Shepherd). Groom meets WASP on his honeymoon while he is being sufficiently soured by lower-class virgin's lovemaking (What did she *do* that was so bad?), by the sight of egg salad running out of her mouth, and finally by her blistering sun poisoning. After a piercing scene in which he tells her that not only the honeymoon but the marriage is over, he runs off to win the WASP. And we are supposed to feel, *How funny! How sad!* It's a tricky movie, because a lot of it *is* funny, the scenes are quick, and it's all treated casually. But May stands aside and chuckles at her misfit women (even as, in *A New Leaf*, she herself portrays one). The bride in *The Heartbreak Kid* gets special buffoon treatment, which reflects on the director's *idea* of characterization rather than the character herself. So what is essentially a grotesque story anyway becomes weighted, for the sake of comedy, against the girl. Everyone else is smooth America; she's a leftover from the Yiddish stage or Ellis Island.

There is, in all fairness, a possibility that May has simply not toned down her straight-faced self-parody which in the early sixties made her and Mike Nichols a unique comedy team. In that case it is a stylistic rather than attitudinal handicap. On the other hand, when Nichols and May broke up, he emerged as Broadway's and then Hollywood's Golden Boy while she, a woman, found fewer opportunities as a director. How much of her toughness stems from bitterness, from denying her femaleness? But why not compassion instead? *She's been there*, as they say; she knows what's at stake.

As it happens, one fine and witty movie has emerged from and about the political mainstream of the Women's Movement. *The Year of the Woman* (1973), a first directorial attempt by poetess Sandra Hochman, a documentary on female participation in the 1972 Democratic Convention, is a visual collage of events, personalities, and pointed sexism put together with splendid whimsy and cunning, and Hochman herself does much of the interviewing of politicians (such as Charles Evers) with wry humor. It's all unabashed propaganda—with lawyer Florynce Kennedy crying "Jockocracy" as a band of feminists pounce on newsmen for biased convention reporting; with stripper Liz Renay slithering onto the floor as male delegates monopolize her, unconcerned about what she does or doesn't have to say; with women parading about in masks and singing "Mine eyes have seen the glory of the flame of women's rage." The one flaw: So much of the material, a year later, is already old-hat. Still, the director-star, who does a terrific tap dance straight out of a Gene Kelly musical and gently banters with humorist Art Buchwald, feeds the audience rhetoric with a spoon so sugar-coated that you needn't be female or feminist to have fun.

In other words, Hochman, in making her point, uses the same tools with which Hollywood, since its earliest days, has seduced audiences. *Fun. Laughter. Entertainment. Fantasy. Distraction.* Until recently, whoever thought to look beneath the surface, to question the images and values of all those marvelously enjoyable films?

As long as movies exist, so does the danger that we will surrender ourselves unquestionably to their instant makeovers and portable ideals. Hollywood's sound stages may now be producing television series, and fan magazines sell only with lurid lines about Jackie Onassis or Liz Taylor. Rona Barret, try as she might, will not replace the clawing legends that were Hedda and Louella, because celebrities hardly keep any secrets and because without a contract system columnists have little star-making or -breaking power. But those are mere technicalities. Flickering images which fascinated seventy years ago mesmerize even today. Movies are escape. And we anoint the actresses embodying our fantasies as deities, our Popcorn Venuses.

Their magnetism will draw us while power is attractive, or while we need the security of being beautiful or desirable. (If we look like Joanne, do we get Paul? If we resemble Liz, is Richard ours?) Girls, unprompted, rush out and chop off their hair like Liza, knit caps and crush daisies into books like Ali, tattoo tiny Leigh Taylor-Young butterflies on their thighs. How many women of elevated consciousness still want noses like Liz or breasts like Brigitte? The New York *Times* reported that more than 500,000 cosmetic surgery operations were performed in 1969, that female customers for them outnumbered males twenty to one, and that the majority age was between forty-five and sixty. On the screen no one grows old. Why should we?

"Nowadays, Hollywood has an incredibility problem," the New York *Times* suggested not long ago. "There isn't a young romantic star unreal enough to thrill us, just a rotating stock of earthbound boys and girls who are no longer required to have their noses bobbed, their teeth fixed, or lifts put in their shoes."[5]

This elegy to the past falls into the fantasy trap carefully cultivated during the heyday of Mayer and Warner and Cohn. It also misses the point. If we can't stop going to films the way we thumb through *Harper's Bazaar* or *Vogue*, if movies unconsciously or consciously define and reflect us, shouldn't we, once aware, look for substance as well as chimera?

It is time to start utilizing feminine resources. And reinterpreting the American Dream.

EPILOGUE

FEMINIST FOOTHOLDS IN FILMMAKING

"Women, far more than men, it is reasonable to suppose, have suffered hasty eclipse for want of adequate mention in the permanent records,"[1] wrote Anna Garlin Spencer in 1912. As if to support her statement, film histories barely mention female participation behind the scenes. However, feminine resources were not always anathema in Hollywood. In its youth, especially, and before it became a powerful elitist operation, the industry's hunger for material and moviemakers left little room for sexual prejudice. By the end of World War I the roster of women who had made significant contributions to the American cinema was a good deal more substantial than it is today.

Both Frances Marion and Anita Loos were leading scriptwriters, and their ranks were rapidly to expand and include Jeanie MacPherson, a Griffith actress whom De Mille hired as his script assistant in 1915. She wrote—alone or in collaboration—almost all his screenplays until her death in 1946. June Mathis, specializing in tailor-made vehicles for her prodigy Valentino, scripted, among others, *Eye for an Eye* and *The Red Lantern* and oversaw the editing of Von Stroheim's lengthy and complex masterpiece *Greed*. Bess Meredyth came to the moving-picture world in 1917 and by 1919 had already written ninety features. Dorothy Parker got her first break penning titles for Lillian Gish's *Remodeling Her Husband* in 1920. By the early twenties Sonya Levien and Lenore Coffee had also achieved prominence.

Among the handful of female film editors, Rose Smith earned distinction as a chief cutter on *Intolerance* (1916). And Annie Bauchens, who came to De Mille as a secretary, edited every one of his pictures beginning with *We Can't Have Everything* in 1918. Said De Mille shortly before his death in 1959, "In every contract I sign to produce a

367

picture, one essential clause is that Anne Bauchens will be its editor. That is not sentimental. She is still the best film editor I know."[2]

This ambitious and creative group appeared on the scene in the years when filmmaking was casual and without prestige, when directors were often hired from the ranks of actors to help "grind out another sausage," as D. W. Griffith put it. Producers and directors admired imagination, regardless of gender, and whoever could suggest plots or business for the one-, two-, and four-reelers was welcome. Indeed, Mary Pickford often wrote her own screenplays; occasionally actors in rehearsals would improvise a scene or bit of action so beguiling that it would become the plot for a future movie. Sometimes a director would be attracted by ideas or story lines and, without scripts at all, would dramatize them in visual language. But most often the scenarist was called on to supply plot material.

Anita Loos stands out not only for her prolific contributions, but because she was a teen-ager when she began sending scripts to Biograph. Quickly she assumed the stance of a child prodigy, and with a brilliant, witty mind which could conceive one slapstick situation after another, she turned out 105 script ideas between 1912 and 1915, all but 4 of which were made into films. *The New York Hat* (1912), one of her first ventures and the last film Mary Pickford did for Biograph, was a naïve but charming story in which the village gossip concocts a romance between a minister and little Mary. *A Girl Like Mother* had a determined heroine who tries to remodel herself after her beau's mother in order to land him; unfortunately, she identifies the wrong woman as "mother" and mimes not an apple-pie sweetheart, but a female of questionable virtue. And *Saved by the Soup* concerned a female spy in our Secret Service who overhears at a dinner party news which could destroy the United States. By spelling out "call the cops" in her first-course alphabet soup, she and the butler effect a solution and can entertain a leisurely dessert.

Loos' fertile imagination was not the only attribute working in her favor. Her petite beauty made her as much a public personality as the youthful stars of the period. She recalls:

I had begun to get publicity of the soapy type generally inspired by film actresses. Very soon after I entered the films, *Photoplay* magazine had sprung into enormous general popularity, and when its publisher and his editor first visited Hollywood from the main office in Chicago they chose to "discover" me. The fact that movies were actually written instead of being ad-libbed on the set, and that one of the authors was young, and for a writer, rather toothsome, made me seem a sort of West Coast Aspasia. Articles about me began to decorate *Photoplay*, together with photographs. One effusion, headed "The Soubrette of Satire," read, "Next to Mary Pickford, Edna Purviance, and Neysa McMein's cuties, Anita Loos ranks right along as a leading cause of heart disease."[3]

Unfortunately, too, she ranked right along as a leading purveyor of nonsensical whimsy which generally reinforced traditional stereotypes. Loos, the *enfant terrible* of the silent screen, credits herself with a most Victorian adaptation of Voltaire which Griffith included among his *Intolerance* subtitles: "When women cease to attract men, they often turn to reform as a second choice." This attitude in 1916 was, if not passé, then still steeped in *fin de siècle* clichés which labeled suffragettes as spinsters.

Loos' own youth and her predilection for relationships with dominant, controlling men appears to have taken precedence over her fine mind in dealing with female characterizations. Commenting on her relationship with writer-director John Emerson, she has admitted: "When, after our marriage, he first heard himself addressed as Mr. *Loos*, it hit his egotism with a bang that reverberated as long as he lived. Had I been a femme fatale, I couldn't have destroyed him more thoroughly."[4] Nevertheless, Emerson was flirtatious, unfaithful, and often insisted on credit (his name first) for coauthoring her scripts when in fact he had nothing to do with them. Loos, however, adored him. Once, in clarifying her distant feelings for a more ardent and faithful admirer, she explained, "Today the reasons why I couldn't fall in love with Rayne have become obvious; he gave me full devotion and required nothing in return, while John treated me in an offhand manner, appropriated my earnings, and demanded from me all the services of a hired maid. How could a girl like I resist him?"[5]

And how could a girl like Loos fail to write, in the more than 200 screenplays of her career, material that would reflect this preference for subservience to her men? Her gift for creating plots that appealed primarily because they *were* so attuned to the life around her was abetted by her own notions of virile men, lovingly passive women, and traditionally happy endings. If she is to be considered in any way avant-garde, it would be for the piquant and mischievous humor that enlivened (or inspired) her work and reached a pinnacle with *Gentlemen Prefer Blondes* (and its gold-digging heroine, Lorelei), which, according to H. L. Mencken, "made fun of sex, which has never before been done in this grand and glorious nation of ours."[6] Written originally as a novel in 1926, *Gentlemen* was not to be captured on film until 1928 and then as a musical in 1953.

What is striking about Loos is that although her age (and consequently her experiences) limited the scope of her early material tremendously, it may also have accounted for her success. For it is unlikely that in any other era the thoughts of a teen-aged girl— granted, an exceptional one—could have so directly corresponded to the dreams of millions of women who were just beginning to take their moviegoing seriously.

Frances Marion, on the other hand, ultimately developed her strength in writing dramatic films. Marion, whom writer Adela Rogers St. John recently called "the greatest scriptwriter who ever lived," as a young girl subscribed to the advice of close family friend, author Jack London, who had suggested that if she wanted to write, she should accumulate fascinating "life" experiences. She tasted the boredom of working at a telephone switchboard, the bohemia of an artist's colony, and the exhaustion of clerking in a small shop before her natural flare for the dramatic led her to movies. With the encouragement of Pickford and director Lois Weber, Marion went from extra to heavy to scenario writer and then scenario editor. By 1918 she was earning $30,000 a year, and her success lasted for decades, including *Zander the Great* (1927), *The Cossacks* (1920), *The Scarlet Letter* (1926), and *The Wind* (1928). These last two, both written for Lillian Gish, exemplify the writer's finely disciplined mature style.

Marion continued to win acclaim as a writer of talkies, and among her credits are *Min and Bill* (1930), *The Big House* (1930), *The Secret Six* (1931), *Hell Divers* (1932), and *Clear All Wires* (1933). All these, except *Min and Bill*, were action dramas, glib and fast-paced, with gangsters and gun battles. *The Secret Six*, set among the Chicago stockyards and speakeasies, attacked bootlegging and organized crime, racketeers and corruption. *The Big House* depicted in harsh, unsentimental terms the horrors of penitentiary life. Marion's films were without romance and alarmingly naturalistic, exactly the antithesis of Loos and the archetypical "women's pictures."

As one of the powers behind the Mary Pickford throne in the pre-Jazz Age years, Marion not only wrote for her, but exerted so great an influence on the star that in 1921 Pickford entrusted to her the task of directing two of her films: *Just Around the Corner* and *The Love Light*. The last is noteworthy as one of the few early movies in which Mary (then twenty-eight) played an adult role—that of a girl whose husband, unknown to her, is a German spy. Perhaps both writer and star suspected even then that within a few years Mary would romp her way out of a career, but this adult film as a Pickford vehicle was coolly received by the public.

Marion was an exception as a female director in commercial cinema, but she was not successful or unique. At the time limitations on females were perhaps more intense in life than in the industry where those who could, did. Among those were Alice Guy-Blaché, Dorothy Davenport, Elizabeth Picket, Louise Long, and Nazimova (though without screen credit). When Griffith turned over the direction of the Dorothy Gish comedy, *Remodeling Her Husband* to her sister, Lillian, in 1920, he confidently assured Lillian that because she was a woman, she'd be in a better position to deal with financial and production hassles than he was.

Lillian Gish was also, by virtue of her long experience in films and her close relationship with her sister, able to elicit a delightful performance from her. Given completely free reign, the girls chose a whimsical farce which had originally intrigued Dorothy as a magazine cartoon: A husband accuses his wife of being too dowdy. Furious, she orders him to follow her down the street as she makes faces, sometimes seductive, sometimes funny, winks, and generally entices the stares of every man who passes by.

No more than an amusingly expanded one-liner, in the hands of female director and star this film evolved, however, into a novel approach to handling masculine dissatisfaction and feminine pliability. For Dorothy, the "dowdy" wife, did not become less so in order to satisfy her husband's ideal; by liking herself enough and by leading her man to believe that others found her captivating, she was able to change *his* opinion of her. How many male directors would have permitted—or utilized—a story which, though light, mocked men and their eccentric notions of beauty?

It's to Griffith's credit that he let the Gish girls go ahead with the movie, though his confidence was justified when Lillian brought it in for only $50,000. It later netted more than $460,000 and proved the second biggest moneymaker of all Dorothy's comedies. But Lillian, who would often work with her directors in the cutting room, never again attempted to direct. Although she proved herself enormously competent at the helm of *Remodeling Her Husband*, the grueling administrative tasks of the director did not appeal to her.

Perhaps the first major female director was Lois Weber (1882–1939), whom *Photoplay* in 1918 referred to as director, author, musician, and "anesthetist to the suffering world." Weber, a brilliant woman who had been a child prodigy, gave up her career as a pianist at the age of seventeen when during a concert the black keys fell off the piano; the demands of live public appearances were too nerve-racking, she later explained. In 1905 she married Phillips Smalley, and together they directed early ventures such as *The Jew's Christmas* (1913), *The Merchant of Venice* (1914), and *The Dumb Girl of Portici* (1916), with dancer Anna Pavlova.

But Weber's most interesting directorial efforts were her controversial films, *The Hypocrites* (1914), *Where Are My Children?* (1916), and *The Hand That Rocks the Cradle* (1917). The strongest in the series, *Where Are My Children?*, melodramatically emphasized the nobility of motherhood, yet while its conservatism corresponded to popular sentiment, the film boldly, even audaciously acknowledged abortion as an alternative. The story concerns rich women who prefer not to bear children and consult an abortionist without their husbands' knowledge. When the doctor is caught and sentenced to fifteen years of hard labor, he tells the prosecuting attorney to "see to your own household." The lawyer returns home, and on finding his wife with her childless friends, tells them: "I have just learned why so many of you have no children. I should bring you to trial for manslaughter, but I shall content myself with asking you to leave my house." After they leave, he turns to his wife and cries, distraught, "Where are my children?" Through the years, she, his "murderess," tries to change, but we are told that "having perverted nature so often, she found herself physically unable to wear the diadem of motherhood." Everywhere she goes, she gazes longingly at tots playing. The titles warn us that she will always "ask the silent question, *Where are my children?*" In the final scene, the couple are seated unhappily in their parlor, and Weber superimposes tiny youngsters crawling all over them, as in a dream.

Weber's sentimental support of motherhood could have been expected of any director of that period, yet by bringing the alternative to the surface, also by utilizing sophisticated, attractive female characters and an abortionist who was neither swarthy nor sinister-looking, she mitigated the "horrors" of a taboo subject and—wittingly or otherwise—educated female moviegoers to an awareness of this possible novel option.

By 1918 and the release of *Idle Wives*, Weber was earning more than $5,000 a week and was known, according to *Photoplay* columnist Cal York, as "the highest paid director in the world." Even if exaggerated, surely this indicates how highly esteemed she was, yet only today are her contributions to moviemaking being acknowledged.

Paradoxically, the 1918 peak of fame curbed Weber's initiative and willingness to handle controversial subjects. Perhaps a desire to maintain success or fear of failure led her to concentrate on traditional stories treated with a more compromising tone. In 1919—the year Congress ratified the bill to grant women suffrage—she turned out *A Midnight Romance*, a gumdrop about the son of a millionaire whose social status prevents him from marrying a chambermaid.

Weber's best received and possibly least interesting films were *The Sensation Seekers* (1926) and *The Marriage Clause* (1926). In the latter she is much more in the twenties' spirit with a modern romance about an actress and her lover who are deterred from wedded bliss first by a clause in her contract stipulating she must not marry, then by a renegotiating of contracts in which the lover is fired and forced to seek work elsewhere. Starring Francis X. Bushman and Billie Dove, it knew a modest success, but came nowhere near fulfilling the potential the director had shown between 1914 and 1918.

Deeply interested in psychology in those early years before Freud became a household word, Weber was unique, too, in her fascination with reincarnation. She strongly felt that human impulses and talent were gifts from other lives; how else, she argued, would she have been able to play the piano so well as a child? Looking back, one wonders why she never attempted to explore these avenues in films.

Did the Roaring Twenties and the rising sun of bedroom farces (like De Mille's and Von Stroheim's) diminish her power as one of Hollywood's leading directors? Or did the growth of big studios limit not only the material she was permitted to work with, but also her own usefulness? Unfortunately Weber's decline resists analysis because of the scanty documentation of her career—a loss both in terms of understanding woman's role in society and of having a more complete history of the cinema.

"The whole course of evolution in industry," observed Anna Garlin Spencer, "and in achievements of higher education and exceptional talent, has shown man's invariable tendency to shut women out when their activities have reached a highly specialized period of growth."[7] By 1920 motion pictures were the nation's fourth largest industry. By 1928 and the arrival of talkies, capital investment in Hollywood was $500,000,000. Already women were on their way out. It was an excision which would occur with startling rapidity.

Whereas in 1928, out of 239 scenarists, 52 were female, by 1935 the total number had risen to 583; only 88 women, however, were working. In 1940 out of 608 screenplay writers, a mere 64 were women. As for directors, only one female managed to secure a steady position once the golden years of the thirties had arrived: Dorothy Arzner.

Arzner directed seventeen features and many of the screen's prominent leading ladies between 1927 (*Fashions for Women*, her debut) and 1943: Clara Bow (*Get Your Man*, 1927; *The Wild Party*, 1929); Ruth Chatterton (*Sarah and Son*, 1930; *Anybody's Woman*, 1930); Claudette Colbert (*Honor Among Lovers*, 1931); Katharine Hepburn (*Christopher Strong*, 1933); Rosalind Russell (*Craig's Wife*, 1936); Joan Crawford (*The Bride Wore Red*, 1937); and Merle Oberon (*First Comes Courage*, 1943). A former medical student, Arzner apprenticed as an editor on epic silents such as *Blood and Sand* and *The Covered Wagon* before writing the shooting script for *Old Ironsides*. Next came the chance to direct. "I seemed to know I was going to be a director," she admits today. "I loved every piece of work I was given to do, which I think was partly responsible for my advances." She also learned the technical aspects of her craft inside out. "Besides, in the silent days Hollywood and Paramount were growing. They needed young directors."[8]

During the late twenties Arzner played down the fact that she was a woman, even refusing to allow her directorial credit to appear alone on the screen. "I wanted my pictures to stand up on their own." Still, the press treated her as an oddity, with interviewers dwelling on her appearance and clothing styles or making comments like this one in the *World-Telegram* on July 24, 1936:

> Her silence and deadly earnestness are communicated to performers and technical crews, and the work goes forward in an atmosphere almost funereal.
>
> All this may make for efficiency, but the effect of morale is debatable. A woman whose name I wouldn't like to mention told me she'd give a day's salary if the director would only cuss a bit, or give somebody the old hot-foot, or otherwise relieve the tension.

It would be fascinating to know if any female director ever brought a picture in over budget. Arzner, the total professional, perhaps rarely went out on an innovative limb, but she never botched a film, lost her temper with colleagues, and could always be counted on for a clever and sleekly competent package. "I don't believe I ever asked for a job. Of course, some men did not like to work with a woman director —Darryl Zanuck was one—but Paramount, RKO, Harry Cohn of Columbia, MGM, Sam Goldwyn all sought my services. I was not particularly ambitious. However, I did seem to make the grade, and as I remember, the polls chose me as one of the Ten Best Directors in Hollywood," she points out. Harry Cohn once even followed her home and begged her to work with him. Arzner agreed, only on the condition that she be exempted from mandatory story conferences aboard his yacht. Cohn relented.

If the body of Arzner's work reveals little of an avant-garde or elevated consciousness that might have helped divest the screen's female mythology of its potency, perhaps it is because she was a product of American society and was also required to conform within the studio system. Little today can be said in support of Clara Bow's obsessively stalking Fredric March in *The Wild Party*, of Katharine Hepburn's honorable (but pregnant) suicide in *Christopher Strong*, or of Crawford's Cinderella charade in *The Bride Wore Red*. Yet now, almost as if to expiate herself, Arzner explains:

> The only problem was to tap my own creative center enough to hope to make a box-office success with each picture. I knew if

I failed in that, I would not have the kind of fraternity men had one for another to support me. No one was handing me wonderful stories to make. I was usually having actors' first starring roles, and naturally they were only concerned with their own lives.

Within the framework of run-of-the-mill stories, however, the director, by refusing to "tolerate interference in the way I handled anything," utilized her authority to effect subtle, mitigating nuances, nuances open to interpretation as "feminine sensibilities":

There was a touching scene in *Sarah and Son* where Philippe de Lacy, the young boy, broke down and cried in his pillow after being quite a little man. He was upset because his foster mother wouldn't let him do any of the boyish things he wanted to. Ben Schulberg, the top Paramount producer, said I should retake the scene, that the boy was a sissy to cry. When we shot it originally, Philippe did it so well that all the tough electricians and grips applauded his performance. My response to Ben Schulberg was, "You'll have to get another director if you want to retake that scene. But I'll make a bargain with you. If the audience doesn't applaud that scene, I'll retake it." When we previewed the picture, the audience burst into applause. Ben Schulberg, who was sitting behind me, leaned forward and whispered, "That's no proof it couldn't have been better."
The scene stayed untouched.

Arzner also gives instances illustrating what in her experience has been the difference between masculine and feminine points of view:

In *Craig's Wife* there was a crucial moment when Rosalind Russell was left alone with *her house*. The audience hated her up to that point, and I only had one close-up left with which to turn their emotion to sympathy. Russell did it so perfectly that in movie theaters handkerchiefs began coming out, and many women cried as they moved up the aisle. I even received two pictures from unknown people who'd photographed that moment in the theater with their Leica cameras. So you know it must have meant something to people. It was the regeneration of Mrs. Craig.
But in talking to George Kelly who wrote the play, I told him I was following it as faithfully as possible in making the movie, but that I believed Mr. Craig should be down on his knees to

Mrs. Craig because she'd made a man of him. I believe he'd been dominated by his mother who, before she died, had told his aunt to stand by him because she didn't approve of Mrs. Craig. So the aunt is in the house throughout the play. George Kelly rose to his six-foot height and said, "That's not my play. Harriet Craig is an SOB and Craig is a sweet guy."

So there you are—a woman's point of view vs. a man's.

Kelly even had Harriet Craig tell how her mother had slaved for her father and how he had gone off with another woman and left her penniless. So we know what made Harriet Craig what she was. But it made a man of Craig, and she received enlightenment: "A woman who loves her home more than her husband is generally left alone."

Dorothy Arzner retired from commercial moviemaking in 1943 after completing *First Comes Courage*, a war film too violent for her liking. During World War II, she directed the Women's Army Training Films and has since then set up a professional studio moviemaking program at UCLA and a Motion Picture Department at the Pasadena Playhouse. She also hosted a radio program, *You Were Meant to Be a Star*, and not long ago she filmed fifty Pepsi-Cola commercials in three weeks at the request of Joan Crawford.

"I was led by the grace of God to the movies," Arzner now comments. "I would like the industry to be more aware of what they're doing to influence people for good and for bad. There's no doubt that we're affected by our environment."

Like the American women before her, Dorothy Arzner concerned herself little with technical innovations and less with radical feminist statements. Although she improvised the first moving microphone by insisting that sound technicians at Paramount attach a mike to a fishing pole balanced on a ladder and thus follow Clara Bow about the sound stages in *The Wild Party*, Arzner admits that back then her prime objective was "making entertainment. Stories were light and theatrical. We did not know the word *social significance*." In addition, the safe way may have been the *only way* to survive in a competitive business where box office alone counted and where women in authority were suspect.

It is interesting to note that in Europe where the filmmaking situation was less rigid, female directors were more willing and able to experiment: German-born Lotte Reiniger pioneered the first animated silhouettes with the 1924 short film *The Flying Coffer*. *The Adventures of Prince Achmed* (1926), which took three years to complete, was the first full-length animation, and like the other fairy tales she would depict, it evoked a dark, lyrical, and delicate fantasyland, exploring with similar mechanical tools the make-believe out of which Disney's empire would one day evolve.

At the same time Frenchwoman Germaine Dulac was enjoying a prosperous directorial career. By 1925 she had made sixteen well-received movies, including *La Souriante Madame Beudet*, about an unhappy wife hampered by a sulking, oppressive husband and distracted by daydreams of handsome lovers. Dulac's sympathetic attitude to the woman is enhanced by her technique—soft focus for her fantasies; hard focus and a distorted lens for her mate—and it's not surprising that in later years the director co-published a feminist newspaper, *La Fronde*. As a filmmaker she soon progressed to free-form experiments in cinematic images, psychological associations inspired by poems or music, and lyrical visions. And finally in 1927's *La Coquille et le Clergyman* (*The Seashell and the Clergyman*), she presented a boldly surrealistic anticlerical diatribe which—two years prior to the masterful Buñuel-Dali collaboration *Le Chien Andalou*, in which a razor blade gouges across an eye—she used trick photography to split a hateful general's head down the middle and audaciously showed a tormented priest masturbating under his cassock. That both Antonin Artaud, père to the Theater of the Absurd, and the prestigious Cinematheque Français credited Dulac as the mother of surrealism is fitting in view of her brilliant originality.

If Dulac and Reiniger thrived in an atmosphere conducive to experimentation, Arzner and the few other Hollywood-based women were not allowed, nor would they probably have wanted, such freedom. The risks were too great, and their numbers too small. Indeed, it would be six years between Arzner's departure from feature filmmaking and Ida Lupino's emergence as the next "token" female director.

Appropriately Lupino didn't decide to direct; the task simply fell to her when the director of a film she'd co-written and produced became ill. "We were much too poor to hire a director," she says today. Consequently, the actress, who had grown up in a show business family (her father, Stanley Lupino, was a superb vaudeville comedian) and had been appearing in films for eighteen years, took over. The movie, *Not Wanted* (1949), sympathetically documented the anguish and trauma of an unwed mother forced to sign away her child for adoption. It also proved a modest success. In directorial efforts that followed, Lupino explored other "women's situations"— *The Young Lovers* (1950) dealt with how a girl, paralyzed by polio, confronts her fears of sexual inadequacy and her fiancé's pity. *Outrage* (1950) was concerned with the effects of rape on a woman's psyche. And *Hard, Fast and Beautiful* (1951) depicted a tennis player prodded by her social-climbing mother into the ruthless world of competitive athletics. Though solutions were usually upbeat and pat (unwed mother finds loving man; polio victim recovers), Lupino, if only superficially, tackled subject matter especially daring, considering that these films were made in the repressive early fifties.

And as with Arzner, nuance often was Lupino's most effective tool or asset. *The Bigamist* (1953), for instance, is a trite story of a salesman so cowed by his self-sufficient businesswoman-wife that he sets up a household and helpmeet elsewhere. But unique characterizations expand the rudiments: The bigamist (Edmond O'Brien) is ineffectual and pathetic, not malicious; his wife (Joan Fontaine) is distracted, a bit haughty, but loving; and the "other woman" (Lupino) is simply a lonely, unprepossessing waitress, not a chippy or vamp. Such treatment, working against stereotypes, imbued the threesome with unexpected humanity and pathos.

Today, however, Lupino brusquely rejects the notion that her films reveal a special feminine sensibility: "They were not *only* about women's problems, they were definitely about men's, too. I certainly wasn't about to crash the man's world because I had no idea of wanting to be a director. I *had* to take over my first picture; with the second, we couldn't afford anybody else. I think men are the greatest thing since coffee, Seven Up, tea! Nobody can get me to say anything about our opposite sex."⁹

Interestingly, Lupino does not regard her successful directing career as gratifying and insists that it has all been simple economic necessity. If one includes the numerous television features she has directed, the total is sufficiently large so that "I've lost count," but she explains: "I would like to be quietly, happily married and be able to stay home and write."

Directing, for Lupino, is still a tense experience. " '*Am I going to do a good job and bring it in on time?*' you think. And believe me, *Bring it in on time* is such a major factor in television that I'd sometimes get absolutely sick to my stomach days beforehand. But when the crew would ask, 'What's the first setup?' I made sure I was perfectly calm and prepared when I replied. Then I'd be so nervous that I'd get home at night and not be able to eat. So any ladies who want to take over men's jobs—if that's what they really want—had better have strong stomachs."

It is ironic that Lupino's comprehension of woman's social-economic role corresponds with Hollywood's most traditional, conservative attitudes. "If a woman is capable of running a trucking outfit and has to go out and work, she should be allowed to do that and be paid exactly as a man," she says. "But if she's simply bored because she doesn't want to stay home and look after the house, I have no sympathy with her whatsoever. If my husband [actor Howard Duff] were rich, bless his heart, and I could stay home and take care of the house and write screenplays and lyrics, I'd do it. But I direct simply because it's a livelihood; I have no alternative."

Arzner and Lupino, the sole women who during the past forty years had substantial careers as Hollywood directors, both were inordinately competent, disciplined, and efficient. To their cast and crews they revealed low profiles devoid of hysterics. One wonders, in the light of Lupino's remark that she "couldn't afford" anyone else, whether their services were also less expensive than those of their male colleagues. As token women they worked well within the system, and although it is an intriguing fact that those few females directing outside Hollywood (Shirley Clarke, Maya Deren, Mary Ellen Bute, and most recently Barbara Loden) have produced controversial or experimental films of excellent and inspirational quality, it also seems that despite acquiescence to industry dictates, even despite themselves, both Arzner and Lupino managed to imbue their *oeuvres* with many tender perceptions and thoughtfully unusual characterizations.

Indeed, just as Marion, Loos, and Weber here (and Reiniger and Dulac abroad) were instrumental in breathing life and form and style into motion pictures when they were an impressionable young art form, so did Arzner and Lupino prove that women could hold on when the big moneymen moved in. They were our female pioneers. Yet for too long all their contributions have gathered dust, suffering from "hasty eclipse" and lack of recognition.

And denying us a heritage, a cornerstone on which to build.

REFERENCES

PREFACE
[1] David Robinson, *Hollywood in the Twenties* (New York, Paperback Library, 1970), p. 176.

ONE: EMERGING FROM VICTORIANISM
1. A Victorian Primer
[1] Emily James Putnam, "The Lady," in *Feminism: The Essential Historical Writings*, Miriam Schneir, ed. (New York, Random House, 1972), p. 251.
[2] Elizabeth Meredith, "Creating Fashions in Dress," *Cosmopolitan* (1905), p. 45.
[3] Charlotte Perkins Gilmore, "Women and Economics," in *Feminism*, op. cit., p. 242.
[4] Harry Benjamin and R. E. L. Masters, *Prostitution and Morality* (New York, Julian Press, 1964), p. 96.
[5] Emma Goldman, "The Traffic in Women," in *Feminism, op. cit.*, p. 310.
[6] Theodore Dreiser, *Sister Carrie* (New York, Bantam Books, 1950), p. 1.

2. The Moving Pitcha Show Begins
[1] Mark Sullivan, *Pre-War America*, Vol. 3, *Our Times* (New York, Scribner's, 1930), p. 532.
[2] Lewis Jacobs, *The Rise of the American Film: A Critical History* (New York, Teacher's College Press, Columbia University, 1967), p. 62.
[3] Goldman, *op. cit.*, p. 317.
[4] *Moving Picture World* (November 7, 1914), p. 764.

3. Mary's Curls, Griffith's Girls
[1] Alexander Walker, *The Celluloid Sacrifice* (London, Joseph, 1966), p. 45.
[2] Athene Farnsworth, "How Mary Pickford Stays Young," *Everybody's Magazine* (May, 1926), p. 37.

381

3 Walker, *op. cit.*, p. 54.

4 Aljean Harmetz, "America's Sweetheart Lives," New York *Times* (March 28, 1971).

5 Frederick James Smith, "The Moral and the Immoral Photoplay," *Shadowland* VI, Vol. III, No. 1 (September, 1920).

6 Harmetz, *op. cit.*

7 *Ibid.*

8 Anita Loos, *A Girl Like I* (New York, Viking Press, 1966), pp. 101–2.

9 Robert M. Henderson, *D. W. Griffith: His Life and Work* (New York, Oxford University Press, 1972), pp. 190–91.

10 "A Doll's House" in *Ibsen: Four Major Plays*, trans. by Rolf Fjelde. A Signet Classic (New York, New American Library, 1965), p. 108.

11 De Witt Bodeen, "Blanche Sweet," *Films in Review* (November, 1965), p. 552.

12 *Vladimir Nabokov The Annotated Lolita*, edited, with preface, introduction and notes by Alfred Appel, Jr. (New York, McGraw-Hill, 1970), p. 20.

13 *Ibid.*, p. 22.

14 *Ibid.*, p. 19.

15 Iris Barry, *D. W. Griffith: American Film Master* (New York, Museum of Modern Art, 1965), p. 52.

16 Bernard Rosenberg and Harry Silverstein, *The Real Tinsel* (New York, Macmillan, 1970), p. 403.

17 David Robinson, *op. cit.*, p. 170.

18 Robert M. Henderson, *op. cit.*, p. 118.

19 Anita Loos, *op. cit.*, p. 91.

20 *Ibid.*, p. 94.

21 John Dorr, "The Movies, Mr. Griffith & Carol Dempster," *Cinema Magazine* (Fall, 1971), p. 24.

22 Edward Wageknecht, *The Movies in the Age of Innocence* (New York, Ballantine Books, 1971), p. 117.

23 Dorr, *op. cit.*, p. 24.

24 Wageknecht, *op. cit.*, p. 70.

25 1928 Radio Speech in possession of the Paul Killiam Collection, the Museum of Modern Art Film Library (MOMA).

4. Old Mores for New

1 Mark Sullivan, *Over Here*, Vol. 5, *Our Times* (New York, Scribner's, 1933), p. 634.

2 *The Autobiography of Cecil B. DeMille* (New York, Prentice-Hall, 1959), p. 209.

3 *Ibid.*, p. 214.

4 *Ibid.*, p. 209.

5 Phil Koury, *Yes, Mr. DeMille* (New York, Putnam's, 1959), p. 180.

6 *Ibid.*, p. 197.

7 *Ibid.*, p. 202.

8 Robinson, *op. cit.*, p. 103.

9 *The Autobiography of Cecil B. DeMille*, *op. cit.*, p. 41.

10 Robinson, *op. cit.*, p. 107.

11 *Photoplay* (March, 1922).

¹² Bob Thomas, *Thalberg Life and Legend* (New York, Doubleday, 1969), pp. 82–83.
¹³ Andrew Sarris, "Erich Von Stroheim," *Interviews with Film Directors* (New York, Avon Books, 1967), p. 501.

TWO: THE TWENTIES
5. Delineating the Flapper
¹ Angela Taylor, "This Flapper's Altered Fashion's Course," New York *Times* (October 26, 1971).
² New York *Times* (November 26, 1923), p. 15.
³ Angela Taylor, *op. cit.*
⁴ *Ibid.*
⁵ Agnes Rogers, *Women Are Here to Stay* (New York, Harper and Brothers, 1946), p. 131.
⁶ Dorothy Arzner's letters to the author, June, 1972.
⁷ H. L. Mencken, "In Defense of Woman," *A Mencken Chrestomathy* (New York, Alfred Knopf, 1956), p. 39.
⁸ Rogers, *op. cit.*, p. 191.

6. Revamping the Vamp
¹ *Variety* (May 6, 1921).
² Henry James Forman, *Our Movie Made Children* (New York, Macmillan Company, 1935), p. 164.
³ *Ibid.*
⁴ *Ibid.*, p. 216.
⁵ *Ibid.*, p. 134.
⁶ Herbert Blumer and Philip M. Hauser, *Movies, Delinquency and Crime* (New York, Macmillan Company, 1933), p. 222.
⁷ *Ibid.*, p. 232.
⁸ *Film Daily Yearbook*, 1922–1923.
⁹ Norman Zierold, *The Moguls* (New York, Avon, 1972), p. 284.
¹⁰ Pola Negri, *Memoirs of a Star* (Garden City, Doubleday & Company, 1970), pp. 202–3.
¹¹ *Ibid.*, pp. 227–28.
¹² Frances Marion, *Off with Their Heads!* (New York, Macmillan Company, 1972), p. 89.
¹³ Judy Klemesrud, "Name, Nose, Teeth, Bosom, Hair, Kidneys—Everything But Eyelashes Is Real," New York *Times* (October 10, 1971).

7. The Love Parade Limps Along
¹ Anthony Dawson, *Elinor Glyn* (Garden City, Doubleday & Co., 1955), p. 279.
² Stanley Frank, "Grandma Gloria Swanson Comes Back," *Saturday Evening Post* (July 29, 1950).
³ *Ibid.*
⁴ Herman G. Weinberg, *The Lubitsch Touch* (New York, E. P. Dutton & Company, 1968), p. 41.

[5] *Ibid.*, p. 58.

[6] Mae West, *Goodness Had Nothing to Do with It* (Englewood Cliffs, N.J., Prentice-Hall, 1959), p. 98.

[7] Weinberg, *op. cit.*, p. 57.

[8] *Ibid.*, p. xxi.

[9] *Ibid.*

[10] John Keats, *You Might As Well Live: The Life and Times of Dorothy Parker* (New York, Simon and Schuster, 1970), p. 218.

[11] Zelda Fitzgerald, "Eulogy on the Flapper," *Metropolitan Magazine* (June, 1922).

THREE: THE THIRTIES

8. The Whole Town's Talking . . . But Why Are They Lying to Me?

[1] *U.S. Women's Bureau Bulletin*, No. 155, 1937.

[2] Bosley Crowther, *Hollywood Rajah: The Life and Times of Louis B. Mayer* (New York, Dell Paperback, 1960), pp. 175–76.

[3] Bob Thomas, *op. cit.*, p. 115.

[4] *Ibid.*, p. 281.

9. Gentlemen Prefer Blondes—and Ladies Become 'Em

[1] Simone de Beauvoir, *The Second Sex*, trans. and ed. by H. M. Parshley (New York, Bantam Paperback, 1961), p. 147.

10. Ah, Sweet Mystery of Womanhood Goes Sour

[1] De Beauvoir, *op. cit.*, p. 153.

[2] Josef von Sternberg, *Fun in a Chinese Laundry* (New York, Macmillan Company, 1965), p. 120.

11. The Landscape of Social Fantasy

[1] Elsa Maxwell: "I Married the World," *This Fabulous Century: 1930–1940* (New York, Time-Life Books, 1969), p. 154.

[2] G. Graham, "Women, Are They Human?" *Canadian Forum* (December, 1936), pp. 21–23.

FOUR: THE FORTIES

12. The Rise and Fall of Rosie the Riveter

[1] "When Women Wear the Overalls," *Nation's Business* (June, 1942).

[2] Paul Gallico, "The Texas Babe," in *The Thirties: A Time to Remember*, Don Congdon, ed. (New York, Simon & Schuster, 1962), p. 73.

[3] Rowland Shepard, "Why a Women's Bar Association?," *Woman Lawyer's Journal* (March, 1946).

13. Pin the Tail on the Pinup

[1] Bob Thomas, *King Cohn: The Life and Times of Harry Cohn* (New York, G. P. Putnam's Sons, 1967), p. 279.

[2] Murray Schumach, *The Face on the Cutting Room Floor* (New York, William Morrow and Company, 1964), p. 55.

[3] *Ibid.*, p. 59.
[4] *Ibid.*, p. 55.

15. Fantastic On-Screen Is Fanatic Off
[1] Rex Reed, "Bette Davis," *Conversations in the Raw*, Signet Edition (New York, New American Library, 1969), p. 17.
[2] George Eells, *Hedda & Louella* (New York, G. P. Putnam's Sons) p. 173.

16. The Birth of the Bobby-soxer
[1] *This Fabulous Century: 1940–50* (New York, Time-Life Books, 1969), p. 48.

FIVE: THE FIFTIES
17. I Do! I Do?
[1] Bill Davidson, "Kinsey: On the Difference Between Men and Women," *Collier's* (September 4, 1953).
[2] Lawrence J. Quirk, *The Films of Joan Crawford* (New York, Citadel Press, 1971), p. 20.
[3] "May 11, 1938," *The Letters of F. Scott Fitzgerald*, Andrew Turnbull, ed. (New York, Dell-Laurel Edition, 1966), p. 446.
[4] Gordon Gow, *Hollywood in the Fifties* (New York, Praeger, 1971), pp. 52–53.
[5] Cynthia Fuchs Epstein, *Woman's Place* (Berkeley, University of California Press, 1971), p. 77.
[6] "American Man in A Woman's World," Margaret Mead, *New York Times Magazine* (February 10, 1957), p. 23.

18. Mammary Madness
[1] "American Woman's Dilemma," *Life* (June 16, 1947), p. 114.
[2] Peter Martin, "Her Half Billion Dollar Shape," *Saturday Evening Post* (October 15, 1949), p. 28.
[3] *Ibid.*
[4] *Ibid.*
[5] Mel Gussow, *Don't Say Yes Until I Finish Talking: A Biography of Darryl F. Zanuck* (Garden City, Doubleday & Company, 1971), p. 174.
[6] *Ibid.*, p. 173.
[7] *Ibid.*, p. 175.
[8] *Ibid.*, p. 274.
[9] Martin Quigley, Jr., and Richard Gertner, *Films in America: 1929–1969* (New York, Golden Press, 1970), p. 205.
[10] Michael Conway and Mark Ricci, *The Films of Marilyn Monroe* (New York, Citadel Press, 1964), p. 13.
[11] Gavin Lambert, *On Cukor* (New York, G. P. Putnam's Sons, 1972), p. 180.
[12] Ian and Elisabeth Cameron, *Dames* (New York, Praeger, 1969), p. 76.
[13] Thomas, *King Cohn, op. cit.*, p. 330.
[14] *Newsweek* (March 5, 1973), p. 45.

19. Popcorn Venus
   [1] Quigley and Gertner, *op. cit.*, p. 187.
   [2] New York *World-Telegram* (January 11, 1958).
   [3] *This Fabulous Century: 1950–60* (New York, Time-Life Books, 1970), p. 47.
   [4] "Lana Turner Filmography," *Films in Review* (June-July, 1958), p. 476.

SIX: SIXTIES INTO SEVENTIES
20. Sing a Song of Single Scenes
   [1] "Georgia Legislator Scores Miss Taylor and Burton," New York *Times* (May 23, 1962), p. 38.
   [2] Grace and Fred M. Hechinger, "College Morals Mirror Our Society," *New York Times Magazine* (April 14, 1963), p. 120.
   [3] Dwight Macdonald, *On Movies* (New York, Berkley-Medallion Edition, 1971), p. 137.
   [4] Helen Gurley Brown, *Sex and the Single Girl* (New York, Pocket Books, 1963), p. 246.

21. Flower Children in Camelot's Rubble
   [1] Grace and Fred M. Hechinger, *Teen-Age Tyranny* (New York, Crest Books, 1963), p. 131.
   [2] *Ibid.*, p. 111.
   [3] David Riesman, *The Lonely Crowd* (New Haven, Yale University Press, 1964), p. 75.
   [4] Hechinger, *op. cit.*, p. 86.

22. Clinicians of Decadence
   [1] Pauline Kael, *Kiss Kiss Bang Bang* (Boston, Atlantic-Little, Brown & Company, 1965), p. 41.
   [2] Henry Erlich, "Ann-Margaret: The Prude and the Passion," *Look* (June 15, 1971), p. 55.
   [3] Kael, *op. cit.*, p. 167.
   [4] Alvin Toffler, *Future Shock* (New York, Bantam Books, 1971), p. 308.

23. Changings—Breakthrough or Backlash?
   [1] Marylin Bender, *The Beautiful People* (New York, Dell Paperback, 1968), p. 25.
   [2] Betty Friedan, *The Feminine Mystique* (New York, Dell Paperback, 1973), p. 27.
   [3] *Ibid.*, p. 10.
   [4] Lambert, *op. cit.*, p. 160.
   [5] Jane Scovell Appleton, "Where Have All the Garbos Gone?" in New York *Times* Arts & Leisure section (April 15, 1973), p. 13.

EPILOGUE: FEMINIST FOOTHOLDS IN FILMMAKING
   [1] Anna Garlin Spencer, "Woman's Share in Social Culture," in *Feminism*, *op. cit.*, p. 277.
   [2] *The Autobiography of Cecil B. De Mille*, *op. cit.*, p. 120.
   [3] Loos, *op. cit.*, pp. 132–33.

[4] *Ibid.*, p. 181.
[5] *Ibid.*, p. 183.
[6] *Ibid.*, p. 267.
[7] Spencer, *op. cit.*, p. 277.
[8] All Dorothy Arzner quotes, unless otherwise specified, are reprinted from private correspondence with the author between June and September, 1972.
[9] All Lupino quotes are reprinted from a conversation with the author in June, 1973.

BIBLIOGRAPHY

"A New Headache." *Business Week* (October 17, 1942).

ADAMS, CLIFFORD R., "The Lonely Girl in the Big City." *Ladies' Home Journal* (May, 1962).

ADAMS, ELSIE, AND BRISCOE, MARY LOUISE, *Up Against the Wall, Mother* .... Beverly Hills, Glencoe Press, 1971.

AGEE, JAMES, *Agee on Film: Reviews and Comments.* Boston, Beacon Press, 1964.

"Air Markers: Women Pilots Help Make Private Flying Safe." *Newsweek* (August 22, 1936).

ALBERT, DORA, *Mae West:* "I've Been in Who's Who and I Know What's What." *Pageant* (May, 1970).

"Amazons in the Arsenal." *Nation's Business* (July, 1943).

American Film Institute Catalogue. The Twenties.

"American Woman's Dilemma." *Life* (June 16, 1947).

ANGER, KENNETH, *Hollywood Babylon.* Phoenix, Arizona, Associated Professional Services, Inc., 1965.

APPEL, ALFRED, JR., ed., *Vladimir Nabokov The Annotated Lolita.* New York, McGraw-Hill, 1970.

APPLETON, JANE SCOVELL, "Where Have All the Garbos Gone?" New York *Times* (April 15, 1973).

ARDMORE, JANE, *The Self-Enchanted: A Biography of Mae Murray.* New York, McGraw-Hill, 1959.

ASTOR, MARY, *A Life on Film.* New York, Delacorte Press, 1967.

ATHERTON, GERTRUDE, "The Woman in Love." *Harper's Bazaar* (May, 1910).

BAINBRIDGE, JOHN, "Garbo Is 65." *Look* (September 8, 1970).

BALLINGER, WILLIS J., "Why I Would Not Send a Daughter to College." *Forum & Century* (May, 1932).

BARRY, IRIS, *D. W. Griffith: American Film Master.* New York, Museum of Modern Art, 1965.

389

BART, PETER, "Hollywood: New Riches, New Doubts." New York *Times* (December 12, 1966).

BAXTER, JOHN, *Hollywood in the Thirties*. New York, Paperback Library, 1970.

BEHMER, RUDY, *Memo form David O. Selznick*. New York, The Viking Press, 1972.

BENDER, MARYLIN, *The Beautiful People*. New York, Dell Paperback, 1968.

BENGIS, INGRID, *Combat in the Erogenous Zone*. New York, Alfred A. Knopf, 1972.

BENJAMIN, HARRY, AND MASTERS, R. E. L., *Prostitution and Morality*. New York, Julian Press, 1964.

BERGMAN, ANDREW, *We're in the Money: Depression America and Its Films*. New York, New York University Press, 1971.

BILQUIST, FRITIOF, *Garbo*. New York, G. P. Putnam's Sons, 1960.

BLUMER, HERBERT, AND HAUSER, PHILIP M., *Movies, Delinquency and Crime*. New York, Macmillan Company, 1933.

BOECKEL, RICHARD M., ed., "Beauty Business." *Editorial Research Reports* (affiliated with *Congressional Quarterly*), Vol. II (1960).

BOLL, ELEANOR STOKER, "Should Parents or Cupid Arrange Marriages?" *New York Times Magazine* (December 13, 1959).

BOSSARD, JAMES H. S., "Eight Reasons Why Marriages Go Wrong." New York *Times* (June 24, 1956).

BOW, CLARA, "Evoking Emotions Is No Child's Play." *Theatre Magazine* (November, 1927).

Box-office moneymakers: New York *Times* (January 11, 1970, section III, and February 24, 1971).

BRECHER, EDWARD M., *The Sex Researchers*. Boston, Little, Brown & Company, 1969.

BRITTON, NAN, *Honesty or Politics?* New York, Elizabeth Ann Guild, 1932.

——, *The President's Daughter*. New York, Elizabeth Ann Guild, 1927.

BROOKS, LOUISE, "Gish and Garbo: The Executive War on Stars." *Sight and Sound* (Winter, 1958/59).

BROWN, HELEN GURLEY, *Sex and the Single Girl*, Giant Cardinal Edition. New York, Pocket Books, 1963.

CAMERON, IAN AND ELISABETH, *Dames*. New York, Praeger, 1969.

CAPRA, FRANK, *The Name Above the Title*. New York, Macmillan Company, 1972.

CARVER, GERTRUDE, "The Prerogatives of a Lady." *Harper's Bazaar* (November, 1930).

CHRISTY, GEORGE, "Mae West Raps." *Cosmopolitan* (May, 1970).

CHURCHILL, LADY RANDOLPH, "Extravagance." *Harper's Bazaar* (May, 1915).

"Clara Bow, the 'It' Girl, Is Dead," New York *Herald Tribune* (September 28, 1965).

"Clean Pictures Up to the Public." *Literary Digest* (January 31, 1925).

"Closeup: Young Executive in a Hurry." *Life* (January 13, 1958).

CONGDON, DON, ed., *The Thirties: A Time to Remember.* New York, Simon and Schuster, 1962.

Contraception and Enovid. *Time* (February 17, 1961).

CONWAY, MICHAEL, AND RICCI, MARK, *The Films of Jean Harlow.* New York, Citadel Press, 1965.

——, *The Films of Marilyn Monroe.* New York, Citadel Press, 1964.

COTTRELL, JOHN, *Julie Andrews.* New York, Dell Publishing Company, 1968.

COWLEY, MALCOLM, "The Vice Squad Carries On, Part I." *New Republic* (June 25, 1930).

CRAVEN, THOMAS, "Salome and the Cinema." *The New Republic* (January 24, 1923).

"Credit Expert Analyzes Movie Queens' Morals." *Literary Digest* (August 29, 1925).

CROWTHER, BOSLEY, *Hollywood Rajah: The Life and Times of Louis B. Mayer.* New York, Dell Paperback, 1960.

DALLAIRE, VICTOR, "The American Woman? Not for This G.I." *New York Times Magazine* (March 10, 1946).

DAVIDSON, BILL, "Kinsey: On the Difference Between Men and Women." *Collier's* (September 4, 1953).

DAVIS, KINGSLEY, "The American Family—What It Is and Isn't." *New York Times Magazine* (September 30, 1951).

DAWSON, ANTHONY, *Elinor Glyn.* Garden City, Doubleday & Company, 1955.

DE BEAUVOIR, SIMONE, *The Second Sex,* translated and edited by H. M. Parshley. New York, Bantam Books, 1961.

DEER, IRVING AND HARRIET, eds., *Languages of the Mass Media: Readings in Analysis.* Boston, D. C. Heath and Company, 1965.

DE MILLE, CECIL B., *The Autobiography of Cecil B. De Mille,* Donald Hayne, ed. New York, Prentice-Hall, 1959.

DICKENS, HOMER, *The Films of Marlene Dietrich.* New York, Citadel Press, 1971.

DICKSON, GENE, "Housewife-War Worker." *The New Republic* (October 18, 1943).

DIDION, JOAN, "The Great Reprieve." *Mademoiselle* (February, 1961).

Dorothy Arzner: an interview. *New York World-Telegram* (July 24, 1936).

"Dorothy Arzner: Distaff Director." New York *World-Telegram* (November 21, 1936).

DORR, JOHN, "The Movies, Mr. Griffith & Carol Dempster." *Cinema Magazine* (Fall, 1971).

DREISER, THEODORE, *Sister Carrie*. New York: Bantam Books, 1958.

"Earlier Marriage—Why?" *U.S. News* (June 20, 1952).

EELLS, GEORGE, *Hedda and Louella*. New York, G. P. Putnam's Sons, 1972.

EFRON, EDITH, "Television Should Be Censored." *TV Guide* (August 22, 1970).

ELLMANN, MARY, *Thinking About Women*. A Harvest Book. New York, Harcourt, Brace, Jovanovich, 1968.

"Employment: Woman's Work." *Newsweek* (February 12, 1973).

EPSTEIN, CYNTHIA FUCHS, AND GOODE, WILLIAM J., *The Other Half*. California Press, 1971.

EPSTEIN, CYNTHIA FUCHS, *Woman's Place*, Berkeley, University of California Press, 1971.

ERLICH, HENRY, "Ann-Margaret: The Prude and the Passion." *Look* (June 15, 1971), p. 55.

"Fade-Out of the Women." *Time* (September 4, 1944).

FARNSWORTH, ATHENE, "How Mary Pickford Stays Young." *Everybody's* (May, 1926), p. 37.

"Females in Factories." *Time* (July 17, 1944).

FIGES, EVA, *Patriarchal Attitudes: The Case for Women in Revolt*. Greenwich, Conn., Fawcett Publications, 1970.

FITZGERALD, ZELDA, "Eulogy on the Flapper." *Metropolitan Magazine* (June, 1922).

FLEXNER, ELEANOR, *Century of Struggle*. Cambridge, Mass., Belknap Press, 1959.

FORD, CHARLES, *Femmes Cinéastes (ou le triomphe de la volonté)*. Paris, Editions Denoël, 1972.

FORMAN, HENRY JAMES, *Our Movie Made Children*. New York, Macmillan Company, 1935.

FRANK, STANLEY, "Grandma Gloria Swanson Comes Back." *Saturday Evening Post* (July 29, 1950).

FREWIN, LESLIE, *Dietrich: The Story of a Star*. New York, Avon Books, 1967.

FRIEDAN, BETTY, *The Feminine Mystique*. New York, Dell Paperback, 1973.

———, "Up from the Kitchen Floor." *New York Times Magazine* (March 4, 1973).

"Georgia Legislator Scores Miss Taylor and Burton." *New York Times* (May 23, 1962).

GEROULD, KATHERINE FULLERTON, "Hollywood: An American State of Mind." *Harper's Magazine* (May, 1923).

"Getting Rid of the Women." *Atlantic* (June, 1945).

GIBBONS, CARDINAL, "Pure Womanhood." *Cosmopolitan* (May–October, 1905).

GISH, LILLIAN, with Ann Pinchot, *The Movies, Mr. Griffith & Me*. New York, Avon Books, 1970.

GLYN, ELINOR, "Letter to Caroline." *Harper's Bazaar* (September, 1913).

GOLENPAUL, DAN, ed., *Information Please Almanac, Atlas and Yearbook: 1972*, 26th ed. New York, Simon and Schuster, 1971.

GORDON, RUTH, *Myself Among Others*. New York, Atheneum, 1971.

GORDON, RUTH, AND KANIN, GARSON, *Adam's Rib*. The MGM Library of Film Scripts. New York, Viking Press, 1972.

GORNICK, VIVIAN, AND MORAN, BARBARA K., eds., *Woman in Sexist Society: Studies in Power and Powerlessness*. New York, Signet Paperback, New American Library, 1972.

GOW, GORDON, *Hollywood in the Fifties*. New York and London, Praeger, 1971.

GRAHAM, G., "Women, Are They Human?" *Canadian Forum* (December, 1936).

GREER, GERMAINE, *The Female Eunuch*. New York, McGraw-Hill, 1971.

GRIFFITH, D. W., 1928 Radio Speech. From the Paul Killiam Collection at the Museum of Modern Art Film Library.

GRIFFITH, LINDA ARVIDSON, *When the Movies Were Young*. New York, E. P. Dutton Company, 1925.

GRIFFITH, RICHARD, AND MAYER, ARTHUR, *The Movies*. New York, Simon and Schuster, 1970.

GRUENBERG, SIDONIE M., "Why They Are Marrying Younger." *New York Times Magazine* (January 30, 1955).

GUILES, FRED LAWRENCE, *Norma Jean*. New York, McGraw-Hill, 1969.

GUSSOW, MEL, *Don't Say Yes Until I Finish Talking: A Biography of Darryl F. Zanuck*. Garden City, Doubleday & Company, 1971.

HACKER, ANDREW M., "The Pill and Morality." *New York Times Magazine* (November 21, 1965).

HARMETZ, ALJEAN, "America's Sweetheart Lives." New York *Times* (March 28, 1971).

———, "She Wanted to Be a Mooovie Star." New York *Times* (November 12, 1972).

HARPER, IDA HUSTED, "The Plea for Women's Suffrage." *Harper's Bazaar* (April, 1910).

Harper's Bazaar, bound volumes, 1910–15, 1920–31.

HAWES, ELIZABETH, *Why Women Cry—or Wenches with Wrenches*. New York, Reynal & Hitchcock, Inc., 1943.

HECHINGER, GRACE AND FRED M., "College Morals Mirror Our Society." *New York Times Magazine* (April 14, 1963).

———, *Teen-Age Tyranny*. New York, Crest Books, 1963.

HELLMAN, LILLIAN, *An Unfinished Woman*. Boston, Little, Brown & Company, 1969.

HENDERSON, ROBERT M., *D. W. Griffith, His Life and Work*. New York, Oxford University Press, 1972.

———, D. W. Griffith, The Years at Biograph. New York, Farrar, Straus & Giroux, 1970.

HERRICK, ELINORE M., "What About Women After the War?" New York Times Magazine (September 5, 1943).

HICKS, NANCY, "Women on College Faculties Are Pressing for Equal Pay and Better Positions in Academic Hierarchy." New York Times (November 21, 1971).

HIGHAM, CHARLES, AND GREENBERG, JOEL, Hollywood in the Forties. New York, Paperback Library, 1970.

"Hommage à Germaine Dulac." Cinemathèque Française program notes, 1956.

HOLE, JUDITH, AND LEVINE, ELLEN, Rebirth of Feminism. New York, Quadrangle Books, 1971.

HOPPER, HEDDA (and James Brough), The Whole Truth and Nothing But. New York, Pyramid Books, 1963.

HOWE, HUBERT, "What Kind of Women Attract Men Most?" Photoplay (February, 1924).

IBSEN, HENRIK, A Doll's House, Ibsen: Four Major Plays, trans. by Rolf Fjelde. A Signet Classic. New York, New American Library, 1965.

JACOBS, LEWIS, The Rise of the American Film: A Critical History, rev. ed. New York, Teachers College Press, 1967.

JACOBSON, PAUL H., American Marriage and Divorce. New York, Rinehart & Company, 1959.

JARMAN, RUFUS, "It's Tougher Than Ever to Get a Husband." Saturday Evening Post (February 23, 1952).

"Professional Activity and Specialty of Women Physicians in the United States and Possessions: December 31, 1970 (a graph)," Journal of American Medical Women's Association (October, 1972).

KAEL, PAULINE, Going Steady. New York, Bantam Books, 1971.

———, I Lost It at the Movies. New York, Bantam Books, 1966.

———, Kiss Kiss Bang Bang. Boston, Atlantic-Little, Brown & Company, 1965.

KANIN, GARSON, Tracy and Hepburn: An Intimate Memoir. New York, Viking Press, 1970.

KAUFFMAN, STANLEY, A World on Film. New York, Delta Books, 1967.

KEATS, JOHN, You Might As Well Live: The Life & Times of Dorothy Parker. New York, Simon and Schuster, 1970.

KEMPTON, MURRAY, Part of Our Time: Some Monuments & Ruins of the Thirties. New York, Delta Paperback, 1967.

KLEMESRUD, JUDY, "Name, Nose, Teeth, Bosom, Hair, Kidneys— Everything But Eyelashes—Is Real." New York Times (October 10, 1971).

KOENIGIL, MARK, Movies in Society (Sex, Crime & Censorship). New York, Robert Spekker & Sons, 1962.

KOURY, PHIL, Yes, Mr. De Mille. New York, G. P. Putnam's Sons, 1959.

Ladies' Home Journal, bound volumes, 1904, 1905.

LAMBERT, GAVIN, *On Cukor*. New York, G. P. Putnam's Sons, 1972.

"Lana Turner Filmography." *Films in Review* (June–July, 1958).

LEIGHTON, ANN, "The American Matron and the Lilies." *Harper's* (December, 1946).

LEWIS, ARTHUR H., *The Day They Shook the Plum Tree*. New York, Harcourt, Brace & World, 1963.

LIFTON, ROBERT JAY, ed., *The Woman in America*. Boston, Beacon Press, 1965.

LOOS, ANITA, *A Girl Like I*. New York, Viking Press, 1966.

MACDONALD, DWIGHT, *On Movies*. New York, Berkeley-Medallion Edition, 1971.

MACLAINE, SHIRLEY, *Don't Fall Off the Mountain*. New York, W. W. Norton & Company, 1970.

MACPHERSON, VIRGINIA, "Interview with Virginia Van Upp." *P.M. New York* (December 31, 1944).

"Mae West." *Current Biography* (November, 1967).

"Man's World or Woman's?" *New York Times Magazine* (August 10, 1947).

MANDEVILLE, E. W., "When Cash Talks Virtue." *Outlook* (December 10, 1924).

MARION, FRANCES, *Off with Theirs Heads!* New York, Macmillan Company, 1972.

MARSHALL, M., "Besides the Point: Ads of Girdles, Brassieres, et al." *Nation* (October, 1950).

MARTIN, PETER, "Her Half Billion Dollar Shape." *Saturday Evening Post* (October 15, 1949).

MASTERS, R. E. L., *Forbidden Sexual Behavior & Morality*. New York, Lancer Books, 1962.

McQUADE, JAMES S., "Your Girl and Mine." *Moving Picture World* (November 7, 1914).

MEAD, MARGARET, "American Man in a Woman's World." *New York Times Magazine* (February 10, 1957).

——, "Modern Marriage—The Danger Point." *Nation* (October 31, 1953).

——, "What Women Want." *Fortune* (December, 1946).

MENCKEN, H. L., *A Mencken Chrestomathy*. New York, Alfred A. Knopf, 1956.

MEREDITH, ELISABETH, "Creating Fashions in Dress." *Cosmopolitan* (1905).

MEZERICK, A. G., "The Factory Manager Learns the Facts of Life." *Harper's* (September, 1943).

MILFORD, NANCY, *Zelda*. New York, Avon Books, 1971.

MILLER, FRIEDA S., "What's Become of Rosie the Riveter?" *New York Times Magazine* (May 5, 1946).

MILLETT, KATE, *Sexual Politics*. New York, Avon Books, 1971.

Modern Screen, 1945–49.

MOORE, COLLEEN, *Silent Star*. Garden City, Doubleday & Company, 1968.

MORGAN, ROBIN, ed., *Sisterhood Is Powerful: An Anthology of Writings from the Women's Liberation Movement*. New York, Vintage Books, 1970.

Motion Picture Almanac, bound annual volumes, 1930–72.

Motion Picture Association Survey, conducted by the Opinion Research Corporation, New York *Times* (January 17, 1958).

Motion Picture Magazine, January through December, 1920.

MOWRY, GEORGE E., *The Twenties: Fords, Flappers & Fanatics*. Englewood Cliffs, N.J., Prentice-Hall, 1963.

Mrs. America, the debut of. New York *Times* (November 18, 1946) and *Time* (November 25, 1946).

NEGRI, POLA, *Memoirs of a Star*. Garden City, Doubleday & Company, 1970.

NEILSON, W. A., "Should Women Be Educated Like Men?" *Forum* (February, 1929).

"Newsmakers—Brigitte Bardot." *Newsweek* (March 5, 1973).

New York *Times* film reviews, 1914–1973. New York, Arno Press, 1969–1971.

NOBLE, PETER, *Bette Davis*. London, Skelton Robinson, 1948.

NOLAN, WILLIAM F., *John Huston: King Rebel*. Los Angeles, Sherbourne Press, 1965.

O'NEILL, JOSEPH JEFFERSON, "Love Gets the Fadeout but Faith Wins the Crowd." *Collier's* (February 7, 1925).

PACE, ERIC, "Lovely and Wise Heroine Summoned to Help the Feminine Cause." New York *Times* (October 19, 1972).

Pat Boone's *April Love* kiss: New York *World-Telegram* (July 26, 1957 and January 11, 1958), Newark *Evening News* (July 7, 1959), New York *Herald Tribune* (March 25, 1960).

PERCY, WALKER, *The Moviegoer*. New York, Popular Library, 1962.

PERKINS, F., "Women in Industry." *Independent Woman* (May, 1937).

Photoplay Magazine, 1912–1930.

PICKEL, MARGARET BARNARD, "A Challenge to the College Woman." *New York Times Magazine* (March 5, 1944).

——, "There's Still a Lot for Women to Learn." *New York Times Magazine* (November 11, 1945).

PICKFORD, MARY with CAMERON SHIPP, *Sunshine and Shadow*. New York, Doubleday & Company, 1955.

PIDGEON, M. E., "Difference in Earnings of Women and Men." *U.S. Women's Bureau Bulletin*, No. 152. U.S. Department of Labor, 1938.

——, "Employment Fluctuations and Unemployment of Women." *U.S. Women's Bureau Bulletin*, No. 113. U.S. Department of Labor, 1933.

———, "Women in the Economy of the U.S.A.—A Summary." *U.S. Women's Bureau Bulletin*, No. 155. U.S. Department of Labor, 1937.

Plastic surgery: *Newsweek* (May 31, 1971) and New York *Times* (September 27, 1971).

PRESTON, ALICE, "The Things of Girls." *Ladies' Home Journal* (March, 1904).

"The Profit Curve." *Time* (September 18, 1950).

QUIGLEY, MARTIN, JR., AND GERTNER, RICHARD, *Films in America: 1929–1969*. New York, Golden Press, 1970.

QUIRK, JAMES R., "Are the Stars Doomed?" *Photoplay* (March, 1928).

———, "Are Women's Colleges Old Maid Factories?" *Photoplay* (November, 1921).

———, "The Chief Essentials of Beauty." *Photoplay* (March, 1922).

QUIRK, LAWRENCE J., *The Films of Joan Crawford*. New York, Citadel Press, 1971.

RAMSAYE, TERRY, *A Million and One Nights*. New York, Simon and Schuster, 1926.

RAUSCHENBUSH, WINIFRED, "Fashion Goes American." *Harper's* (December, 1941).

"Recommendations on Separation of Women from Wartime Jobs." *Monthly Labor Review* (September, 1945).

REED, REX, *Conversations in the Raw*. Signet Edition. New York, New American Library, 1969.

REINIGER, LOTTE, "The Adventures of Prince Achmed." *The Silent Picture* (Autumn, 1970).

"Remolding Entire Lives by Surgery." *Literary Digest* (May 9, 1936).

"Repairing Accident-Damaged Faces." *Literary Digest* (February 13, 1937).

"Report on the decline in film audiences." *Variety* (January 10, 1951).

RIESMAN, DAVID, *The Lonely Crowd*. New Haven, Yale University Press, 1964.

RINGGOLD, GENE, *The Films of Bette Davis*. New York, Citadel Press, 1970.

ROBINSON, DAVID, *Hollywood in the Twenties*. New York, Paperback Library, 1970.

ROE, CONSTANCE, "Can the Girls Hold Their Jobs in Peacetime?" *Saturday Evening Post* (March 4, 1944).

ROGERS, AGNES, *Women Are Here to Stay*. New York, Harper & Brothers, 1946.

ROSENBERG, BERNARD AND SILVERSTEIN, HARRY, *The Real Tinsel*. New York, Macmillan, 1970.

ROSENBERG, BERNARD, AND WHITE, DAVID MANNING, eds., *Mass Culture: The Popular Arts in America*. Glencoe, Ill., Free Press, 1957.

ROSENTHAL, JACK, "For Women, A Decade of Widening Horizons." New York *Times* (April 18, 1971).

———, "Two-Thirds of Job Gains in '60s Made by Women." New York *Times* (February 12, 1973).

ROSSI, ALICE S., "Equality Between the Sexes: An Immodest Proposal." *Daedalus*, V. 93, No. 2 (Spring, 1964).

ROTHA, PAUL, with an additional section by Richard Griffith, *The Films Till Now: A Survey of World Cinema.* Spring Books. Feltham-Middlesex, The Hamlyn Publishing Group Ltd., 1967.

SANGER, MARGARET, "The War Against Birth Control." *The American Mercury* (June, 1924).

SANN, PAUL, *Fads, Follies and Delusions of the American People.* New York, Crown, 1967.

SARRIS, ANDREW, *Interviews with Film Directors.* New York, Avon Books, New York, 1969.

SCHICKEL, RICHARD, "Growing Up in the Forties." *New York Times Magazine* (February 20, 1972).

SCHNEIR, MIRIAM, ed., *Feminism: The Essential Historical Writings.* New York, Random House, 1972.

SCHUMACH, MURRAY, *The Face on the Cutting Room Floor.* New York, William Morrow and Company, 1964.

"The Second Sexual Revolution." *Time* (January 24, 1964).

"Sex in the Factory." *Time* (September 14, 1942).

SHENKER, ISRAEL, "Catching Up with Anita Loos, or, How Times Have Changed." New York *Times* (April 26, 1973).

SHEPARD, ROWLAND, "Why a Woman's Bar Association?" *Woman Lawyer's Journal* (March, 1946).

SHULMAN, IRVING, *Harlow: An Intimate Biography.* New York, Dell Paperback, 1964.

SMITH, AGNES, "The Real Sirens of the Screen." *Photoplay* (September, 1926).

SMITH, FREDERICK JAMES, "Does Decency Help or Hinder?" *Photoplay* (November, 1924).

———, "Foolish Censors." *Photoplay* (October, 1922).

———, "The Moral and the Immoral Photoplay." *Shadowland VI*, Vol. III, No. 1 (September, 1920).

———, "The Secret Moral Code of the Screen." *Photoplay* (October, 1926).

SMITH, HELENA HUNTINGTON, "Profiles: Gloria Swanson." *The New Yorker* (May 18, 1930).

SOLOMON, JOAN, "Roles People Learn." *The Sciences* (March, 1973).

SPENSLEY, DOROTHY, "What Is 'It'?" *Photoplay* (February, 1926).

ST. JOHN, ADELA ROGERS, "The Loves of Charlie Chaplin." *Photoplay* (February, 1923).

STEINEM, GLORIA, "A Bunny's Tale." *Show* (May, 1963).

———, "The Moral Disarmament of Betty Coed." *Esquire* (September, 1962).

Statistical Abstracts of the United States, Bureau of Census, 1941, 1942, 1972.

SULLIVAN, MARK, *Over Here*, Vol. 5, *Our Times*. New York, Charles Scribner's Sons, 1933.

———, *Pre-War America*, Vol. 3, *Our Times*. New York, Charles Scribner's Sons, 1930.

A Survey of the Legal Status of Women (in the 48 states). Cleveland, Ohio, National League of Women Voters, Acorn Printing Company, 1924.

SUTTON, MAY G., "Women and Dress." *Harper's Bazaar* (May, 1910).

TAYLOR, ANGELA, "Pola Negri's Memoirs: Best Roles Were Played in Real Life." New York *Times* (April 24, 1970).

———, "Colleen Moore: This Flapper's Altered Fashion's Course." New York *Times* (October 26, 1971).

"That Lost Generation Didn't Get Lost; It Just Settled Down and Raised Families." *Saturday Evening Post* (July 18, 1953).

This Fabulous Century: 1920–30, 1930–40, 1940–50, 1950–60, 1960–70. New York, Time-Life Books, 1969–71.

THOMAS, BOB, *King Cohn: The Life and Times of Harry Cohn*. New York, G. P. Putnam's Sons, 1967.

———, *Thalberg Life and Legend*. Garden City, Doubleday & Company, 1969.

TOFFLER, ALVIN, *Future Shock*. New York, Bantam Books, 1971.

"Trends in Educational Attainment of Women," Wage and Labor Standards Administration, U.S. Women's Bureau, Department of Labor, October, 1969.

TURNBULL, ANDREW, ed., *The Letters of F. Scott Fitzgerald*. New York, Dell-Laurel Edition, 1966.

TYLER, PARKER, *The Hollywood Hallucination*, rev. ed. New York, Simon & Schuster, 1970.

———, *Screening the Sexes*. New York, Holt, Rinehart & Winston, 1972.

"U.S. Filmmakers De-Emphasizing Sex." New York *Times* (April 20, 1971).

U.S. Women's Bureau Bulletins, No. 27, 1922; No. 30, 1927; No. 91, 1931. Department of Labor, Washington, D.C.

Valentino, Rudolph, "Woman and Love." *Photoplay* (March, 1922).

VAN UPP, VIRGINIA, Obituary. *Variety* (April 15, 1970).

Variety (bound volumes and on microfilm), 1905–21.

VIDOR, KING, *A Tree Is a Tree*. New York, Harcourt, Brace & Company, 1953.

VON STERNBERG, JOSEF, *Fun in a Chinese Laundry*. New York, Macmillan Company, 1965.

WAGEKNECHT, EDWARD, *The Movies in the Age of Innocence*. New York, Ballantine Books, 1971.

WAGER, WALTER, ed., *The Playwrights Speak*. New York, Delta Books, 1968.

WALKER, ALEXANDER, *The Celluloid Sacrifice*. London, Joseph, 1966.

WEINBERG, HERMAN G., *The Lubitsch Touch*. New York, E. P. Dutton & Company, 1968.

WEINBERG, L., "Motion Pictures as a Social Force." *Current History* (April, 1925).

WEST, MAE, *Goodness Had Nothing to Do with It* (Englewood Cliffs, N.J., Prentice-Hall, 1959).

"When Women Wear the Overalls." *Nation's Business* (June, 1942).

"Why Vicious Movies Pay Best." *Literary Digest* (November 20, 1924).

"Why Women Quit." *Business Week* (October 16, 1943).

"Women and Public Opinion." *Harper's Bazaar* (April, 1910).

Woman's Home Companion, August, 1900.

"Women in Business I." *Fortune* (July, 1935).

"Women in Business II." *Fortune* (August, 1935).

Women in business. *Newsweek* (February 27, 1956).

"Women in the Labor Force." *Business Week* (December 29, 1945).

"Women on Women." *The American Scholar* (Autumn, 1972).

"Women's Chance." *Art Digest* (May 15, 1932).

"Woman's Place." *Business Week* (May 16, 1942).

WOLFE, W. BERAN, "Why Educate Women?" *Forum* (March, 1929).

WOOLF, VIRGINIA, "Women and Fiction." *Forum* (March, 1929).

WRIGHT, DOROTHY M., "Junior College Students View Women's Roles." *Journal of National Association of Women Deans and Counselors*, V. 30, No. 2 (Winter, 1967).

ZIEROLD, NORMAN, "Garbo and Her Court." *McCall's* (August, 1969).

———, *The Moguls*. New York, Avon Books, 1972.

INDEX